Measuring
the User Experience

Measuring
the User Experience

Collecting, Analyzing, and Presenting UX Metrics

Third Edition

William (Bill) Albert
Thomas S. (Tom) Tullis

British Library Cataloguing-in-Publication Data
A catalogue record for this book is available from the British Library.

Library of Congress Cataloging-in-Publication Data
A catalog record for this book is available from the Library of Congress.

ISBN: 978-0-12-818080-8

For Information on all Morgan Kaufmann publications visit our website at https://www.elsevier.com/books-and-journals

Publisher: Katey Birtcher
Senior Acquisitions Editor: Stephen R. Merken
Editorial Project Manager: Alice Grant
Production Project Manager: Umarani Natarajan
Cover Designer: Greg Harris

Typeset by MPS Limited, Chennai, India

Printed in India
Last digit is the print number: 9 8 7 6 5 4 3 2

Working together to grow libraries in developing countries

www.elsevier.com • www.bookaid.org

This book is dedicated to my mentor, co-author, and dear friend—Tom Tullis.
May your memory be a blessing.

Contents

Welcome to the third edition of *Measuring the User Experience*! We are so excited to share the latest and greatest tools and technologies for measuring the user experience. Since the first edition was published in 2008, we have seen remarkable changes in the user experience profession. In the early 2000s, UX teams were considered a novelty or luxury within many large organizations, and usually nonexistent within smaller organizations. Now, nearly every type of organization, big and small, has some type of UX team, including dedicated UX researchers and designers. Organizations now see UX as a key differentiator in their product and business strategy, and rely on user research to drive design and innovation.

When Tom and I first conceived of this book in 2006, UX research was almost strictly qualitative, focused largely on usability testing. UX metrics were very limited in number and scope, with very little consistency in data collection, analysis, and presentation. Since this time, there has been tremendous interest and use of UX metrics. UX researchers are now seeking more quantitative analysis skills to complement their qualitative research experience. There are many new reliable UX metrics, measuring all aspects of the experience. The tools and technologies have also taken a giant leap forward in the past decade, allowing us to capture and analyze nearly every aspect of the end-user experience, across products, platforms, and environments. The UX field is rapidly maturing, and metrics are a key part of this evolution.

In this book, we take a very holistic approach to user experience. We believe that UX covers all aspects of someone's interaction with a product, application, or service. Many people seem to think of the user experience as some nebulous quality that can't be measured or quantified. We think it can be. And the tools for measuring it are metrics like the following:

- Can users use their phone to set up a telehealth visit with their doctor?
- How long does it take employees to submit their monthly expense report?
- How many errors do users make in trying to reset a password?
- What is the frustration level when assembling a new piece of furniture?
- What do people first notice when they approach a shelf display at a grocery store?
- How many users get into a new "destination-based" elevator without first choosing their desired floor, only to discover there are no floor buttons inside the elevator?

- What specific features are most important in a robotic vacuum cleaner?
- What emotions are most relevant when using a college cost calculator?
- How much experience is required to be proficient in using a call center application?

These are all examples of behaviors, attitudes, and feelings that can be measured. Some may be easier to measure than others, but they can all be measured. Success rates; times; number of mouse clicks, taps, or keystrokes; self-reported ratings of frustration or delight; facial expressions; and even the number of visual fixations are all examples of UX metrics. And these metrics can give you invaluable insight into the user experience.

Why would you want to measure the user experience? The answer is simple: to help you improve it. With most consumer products, apps, websites, and services these days, if you're not improving, you're falling behind. UX metrics can help you determine where you stand relative to your competition and help you pinpoint where you should focus your improvement efforts—the areas that users find the most confusing, inefficient, or frustrating.

This book is a how-to guide, not a theoretical treatise. We provide practical advice about what metrics to collect in what situations, how to collect them, how to make sense of the data using various analysis techniques, and how to present the results in the clearest and most compelling way. We're sharing practical lessons we've learned from our 50-plus combined years of experience in this field.

This book is intended for anyone interested in improving the user experience for any type of product or service, whether it's a consumer product, computer system, application, website, service, or something else entirely. If it's something people use or interact with, then you can measure the user experience associated with it. Those who are interested in improving the user experience and who could benefit from this book come from many different perspectives and disciplines, including usability and UX professionals, interaction designers, information architects, service designers, product designers, web designers and developers, software developers, graphic designers, and marketing and market-research professionals, as well as project and product managers.

So, what's new in this third edition of the book? Here are some of the highlights:

- A new chapter focused on measuring emotional engagement, including facial expression analysis, and the iMotions platform.
- Many new metrics are covered, such as AttrakDiff, Kano Method, Google's HEART framework, the new Bentley Experience Scorecard, and many more.
- Five new case studies highlighting creative ways that different UX teams are measuring the user experience (Chapter 11, Case Studies, is entirely new.) and using UX metrics to drive change within their organization.

- New tools for collecting and analyzing UX data, such as GuessTheTest, youXemotions, and PremoTool.
- Many new examples throughout the book to walk you through the process of collecting, analyzing, and presenting UX metrics.

We hope that you will find this book helpful in your quest to improve the user experience for your products and services. We'd like to hear about your successes (and failures!). We really value the feedback and suggestions that many readers have given us about the second edition. Much of that feedback helped shape the changes and additions we made in this edition.

First and foremost, I would like to acknowledge my co-author, Tom Tullis. Tom passed away in April 2020 due to complications from COVID-19. Working with Tom on this book has truly been one of the highlights of my professional career. I have learned so much from him over the years, and I cannot begin to express my gratitude for what he has done to make me a better researcher, writer, and educator. Tom was a teacher in every sense, and this book exemplifies how much he cared about educating the next generation of UX professionals. Tom always put his heart into the book, constantly discovering new UX metrics, the latest tools and technologies, and little "tips" to make everyone's job a little easier, and of course sharing the history of famous researchers like Rensis Likert (pronounced LICK-ert). His spirit will live on in this book, and his impact will be felt throughout the UX community for many years to come.

I also want to acknowledge Cheryl Tullis, Tom's daughter. After Tom passed away, Cheryl was incredibly helpful in making sure that I had everything I needed to complete the book. I could not have done it without you, Cheryl!

I would like to thank Alice Grant at Elsevier for shepherding us through the publication process. I was so grateful that you and the rest of the Elsevier team allowed me to take all the time I needed after Tom's passing. Thank you so much for your understanding and patience. It meant a lot to me.

I would also like to thank the reviewers: Brian Traynor, Mike Duncan, and Victor Manuel González. Your feedback was very helpful in giving us suggestions for the third edition, especially making sure the content is relevant for both students and practitioners.

A special thanks to all of our case study contributors: Zach Schendel at Netflix; Sandra Teare, Linda Borghesani, and Stuart Martinez at Constant Contact; JD Buckley at JD Usability; Kuldeep Kalkar at UserZoom; and Eric Benoit, Sharon Lee, and Juhan Sonin at GoInvo. Your case studies help bring UX metrics to life and highlight all the creative ways to measure the user experience.

In addition to our case studies, we were very fortunate to have special contributions from Karl Madsen at Optimal Workshop, Bryn Farnsworth at iMotions, Sarah Garcia at UE Group, Deborah O'Malley at GuessTheTest, Keith Karn at Human Factors in Context, Pieter Desmet at PremoTool, and Andrew Schall at Modernizing Medicine. Your contributions to the book are invaluable by illustrating some of the latest tools and technologies in user experience research.

I want to acknowledge all my wonderful colleagues at the Bentley University User Experience Center, particularly Jessica Marriott for her work on the iMotions virtual dressing room case study, and Marissa Thompson and Heather Wright Karlson for their invaluable contributions to the development of the Bentley Experience Scorecard. Also, a very special thanks to Ali-Jon Kret who provided exceptional research support on emotion-based UX metrics.

I would like to thank Darek Bittner from Ginko Bioworks for his contribution to the cover design.

Last but of course not least, I would like to thank my wife, Monika Mitra, for all of her love and support throughout the process; my son, Arjun Albert, for his never-ending supply of wonderful questions and creative solutions; and my daughter, Devika Albert, for her work on the references, and for being an inspiration for hard work, focus, and determination.

My father, Tom Tullis (co-author of this book), was renowned for his many passions. His family, photography, genealogy, corny dad jokes … and teaching. Throughout his career he had held a variety of jobs, but he prided himself most on the impact he was able to have as a teacher and writer.

As I was growing up, he taught me to be humble, compassionate, logical, curious, and generous. As I was starting my own career in the field he had helped establish, he taught me how to conduct a heuristic evaluation, the concepts of Fitt's, Hick's, and Jakob's laws, the importance of collecting both quantitative and qualitative data, how to calculate and interpret a SUS score, and the correct pronunciation of "Likert."

Bill Albert is (like my father was) a brilliant man, and has greatly honored my dad in the writing of this edition of *Measuring the User Experience*. You will learn a vast amount of useful information from reading this book. My hope is that in addition to the knowledge that is applicable to the field of user experience, you also will gain a glimpse at the life's work of my father – a man who was always willing not only to teach any individual whatever they sought to learn but also to listen to them and encourage their passions.

William (Bill) Albert is Senior Vice President and Global Head of Customer Development at Mach49, a growth incubator for global businesses. Prior to joining Mach49, Bill was Executive Director of the Bentley University User Experience Center (UXC) for almost 13 years. Also, he was Director of User Experience at Fidelity Investments, Senior User Interface Researcher at Lycos, and Post-Doctoral Researcher at Nissan Cambridge Basic Research. He has more than 20 years of experience in user experience research, design, and strategy. Bill has published and presented his research at more than 50 national and international conferences, and published in many peer-reviewed academic journals within the fields of user experience, usability, and human-computer interaction. In 2010 he co-authored (with Tom Tullis and Donna Tedesco) *Beyond the Usability Lab: Conducting Large-Scale Online User Experience Studies*, published by Elsevier/Morgan Kauffman.

Since 2013, he has been Co-Editor-in-Chief of the *Journal of User Experience* (formerly *Journal of Usability Studies*). Bill has been awarded prestigious fellowships through the University of California Santa Barbara and the Japanese government for his research in human factors and spatial cognition. He received his BA and MA degrees from the University of Washington (Geographic Information Systems) and his PhD from Boston University (Geography-Spatial Cognition). He completed a Post-Doc at Nissan Cambridge Basic Research. Follow Bill as @ UXMetrics.

Thomas S. (Tom) Tullis retired as Vice President of User Experience Research at Fidelity Investments in 2017. Tom was also an Adjunct Professor in Human Factors in Information Design at Bentley University since 2004. He joined Fidelity in 1993 and was instrumental in the development of the company's User Research department, whose facilities include state-of-the-art Usability Labs. Prior to joining Fidelity, he held positions at Canon Information Systems, McDonnell Douglas, Unisys Corporation, and Bell Laboratories. He and Fidelity's usability team have been featured in a number of publications, including *Newsweek*, *Business 2.0*, *Money*, *The Boston Globe*, *The Wall Street Journal*, and *The New York Times*.

Tullis received his BA from Rice University, MA in Experimental Psychology from New Mexico State University, and PhD in Engineering Psychology from Rice University. With more than 35 years of experience in human–computer interface studies, Tullis has published over 50 papers in numerous technical journals and has been an invited speaker at national and international conferences. He also holds eight United States patents. He co-authored (with Bill Albert and Donna Tedesco) *Beyond the Usability Lab: Conducting Large-Scale Online User Experience Studies*, published by Elsevier/Morgan Kauffman in 2010. Tullis was the 2011 recipient of the Lifetime Achievement Award from the User Experience Professionals Association (UXPA) and in 2013 was inducted into the CHI Academy by the ACM Special Interest Group on Computer–Human Interaction (SIGCHI).

CHAPTER 1

Introduction

CONTENTS

User experience, or UX as it's usually abbreviated, is all about a person's total experience with a product or system, including emotional reactions, attitudes, ability to succeed efficiently, and many other aspects. UX metrics are the ways we measure the various aspects of this experience. These metrics include behaviors we can directly observe and measure (e.g., how long it takes someone to set an alarm on their smartphone), attitudes that we must infer by asking users about their experience (e.g., how likely they are to recommend this product to someone else), and even aspects that require specialized equipment to measure (e.g., eye tracking data).

The primary goal of this book is to show how UX metrics can be used in evaluating and improving the design of any product. When some people think about UX metrics, they feel overwhelmed by complicated formulas, contradictory research, and advanced statistical methods. We hope to demystify much of the research and focus on the practical application of UX metrics. We'll walk

Measuring the User Experience. DOI: http://dx.doi.org/10.1016/B978-0-12-818080-8.00001-7

you through a step-by-step approach to collecting, analyzing, and presenting UX metrics. We'll help you choose the right metrics for each situation or application and show you how to use them to produce reliable, actionable results without breaking your budget. We'll give you guidelines and tips for analyzing a wide range of metrics and provide many different examples of how to present UX metrics in simple and effective ways.

Our intention is to make this book a practical, how-to guide about measuring the user experience of any product. We aren't going to give you a lot of formulas; in fact, there are very few. The statistics will be fairly limited, and the calculations can be done easily in Excel or some other common software package or web application. Our intention is to give you the tools you need to evaluate the user experience of nearly any type of product without overwhelming you with unnecessary details.

This book is product-neutral. The UX metrics we describe can be used for practically any type of product. This is one of the great features of UX metrics: They aren't just for websites. For example, task success and satisfaction are equally valid whether you evaluate a website, a smartphone, or a microwave oven.

UX metrics have a longer "shelf life" than any specific design or technology. Despite all the changes in technology, the metrics essentially stay the same. Some metrics may change with the development of new technologies to measure the user experience, but the underlying phenomena being measured don't change. Eye-tracking is a great example. Many researchers wanted a method for determining where exactly someone is looking at any point in time. Now, with the latest advances in eye-tracking technology, measurement has become much easier and far more accurate. The same can be said for measuring emotional engagement. New technologies in affective computing allow us to measure levels of arousal through very unobtrusive skin conductance sensors as well as facial recognition software. This has offered glimpses into the emotional state of users as they interact with different types of products. These new technologies for measurement are no doubt extremely useful; however, the underlying questions we are all trying to answer don't change that much at all.

So why did we write this book? There's certainly no shortage of books on human factors, statistics, experimental design, and user research methods. Some of those books even cover the more common UX metrics. Does a book that focuses entirely on UX metrics even make sense? Obviously, we think so. In our (humble) opinion, this book makes five unique contributions to the realm of user experience research:

- We take a *comprehensive* look at UX metrics. No other books review so many different metrics. We provide details on collecting, analyzing, and presenting a wide range of UX metrics.

- This book takes *a practical approach*. We assume you're interested in applying UX metrics as part of your job. We don't waste your time with unnecessary details. We want you to be able to use these metrics easily every day.
- We provide help in making the *right decisions* about UX metrics. One of the most difficult aspects of a UX professional's job is deciding whether to collect metrics and, if so, which ones. We guide you through the decision process so that you find the right metrics for *your* situation.
- We provide many *examples* of how UX metrics have been applied within different organizations and how they have been used to answer specific research questions. We also provide in-depth case studies to help you determine how best to use the information revealed by the UX metrics.
- We present UX metrics that can be used with *many different products or technologies*. We take a broad view so that these metrics can be helpful throughout your career even as technology evolves and products change.

This book is organized into three main parts. The first part (Chapters 1 to 3) provides the background information needed to get up to speed on UX metrics.

- Chapter 1 provides an *overview* of user experience and metrics. We define user experience, discuss the value of measuring the user experience, share some emerging trends, dispel some of the common myths about UX metrics, and introduce some of the newest concepts in UX measurement.
- Chapter 2 includes *background* information on UX data and some basic statistical concepts. We also provide a guide for performing common statistical procedures related to different UX methods.
- Chapter 3 focuses on *planning* a study involving metrics, including defining participant goals and study goals and choosing the right metrics for a wide variety of situations.

The second part (Chapters 4 to 10) reviews the general types of UX metrics, as well as some special topics that don't fall neatly into any single type. For each metric, we explain what it is, when and how to use it, and when not to use it. We show you how to collect the data and different ways to analyze and present it. We provide examples of how it has been used in real-world UX research.

- Chapter 4 covers various *types of performance metrics*, including task success, time on task, errors, efficiency, and ease of learning. These metrics are grouped under an "umbrella" of performance because they measure different aspects of the user's behavior.
- Chapter 5 focuses on *self-reported metrics*, such as satisfaction, expectations, ease-of-use ratings, confidence, usefulness, and awareness. Self-reported metrics are based on what users share about their experiences, not what the UX professional measures about their actual behaviors.
- Chapter 6 looks at *measuring usability issues*. Usability issues can easily be quantified by measuring the frequency, severity, and type of issue. We also discuss some of the debates about appropriate sample sizes and how to capture usability issues reliably.

- Chapter 7 is devoted to measuring visual attention using eye-tracking technology. This technology has become more accurate and less expensive over the past few years, leading to its greater use. We describe the basics of eye-tracking, what kind of visual attention metrics you can get from it, and how you can use these to improve the user experience by understanding visual attention patterns.
- Chapter 8 is devoted to *measuring emotional engagement*. These metrics include a wide range of techniques for measuring emotional reactions such as joy, engagement, and even stress. All these metrics capture something about how the body, and especially the face, reacts as a result of the experience of interacting with a user interface.
- Chapter 9 discusses *how to combine different types of metrics and derive new metrics*. Sometimes it's helpful to get an overall assessment of the user experience of any product. This global assessment is achieved by combining different types of metrics into a single UX score, summarizing them in a UX scorecard, or comparing them to expert performance.
- Chapter 10 presents *special topics* that we believe are important but that don't fit squarely into one of the five general categories. These include A/B testing on a live website, card-sorting data, accessibility data, and return on investment (ROI).

The third part (Chapters 11 to 12) shows how UX metrics are put into practice. In this part, we highlight how UX metrics are actually used within different types of organizations and how to promote the use of metrics within an organization.

- Chapter 11 presents five unique *case studies* that we have asked other researchers to contribute. Each case study reviews how different types of UX metrics were used, how the data were collected and analyzed, and the results. These case studies were drawn from UX professionals in various types of organizations.
- Chapter 12 provides 10 *steps to help you move forward in using metrics* within your organization. We discuss how UX metrics can fit within different types of organizations, practical tips for making metrics work within your organization, and recipes for success.

1.1 WHAT IS USER EXPERIENCE?

Before we try to measure user experience, we should know what it is and what it isn't. While many UX professionals have their own ideas of what constitutes a "user experience," we believe the user experience includes three main defining characteristics:

- A *user* is involved (broadly defined as a human)
- That user is interacting with a product, system, or anything with an interface
- The user's experience is of interest and observable or measurable

In the absence of a user doing something, we might measure attitudes and preferences, such as in a political poll or survey about your favorite flavor of ice cream. There has to be behavior, or at least potential or anticipated behavior, to be considered user experience. For example, we might show a screenshot of a website and ask the participant where they *would* click if it were interactive.

You might also notice that we haven't limited this discussion to any particular type of product or system. We believe that any system or product can be evaluated from a user experience perspective, as long as there is some type of interface between the system or product and the user. We're hard-pressed to think of any examples of a product that doesn't have some type of human interface. We think that's a good thing, since it means that we can study almost any product or system from a UX perspective.

Some people distinguish between the terms *usability* and *user experience*. *Usability* is usually considered the ability of the user to use the product to carry out a task successfully, whereas *user experience* takes a broader view, looking at the individual's entire interaction with the product, as well as the thoughts, feelings, and perceptions that result from that interaction.

Another term you often hear is customer experience, or CX. Without a doubt, there is some overlap between CX and UX. But the focus of CX tends to be on the customer and their entire *relationship* to a *company* or *brand*. UX, on the other hand, focuses more on a user's entire *interaction* with a *product* or *system*. You will find that some of the same metrics are used in both domains. For example, the Net Promoter Score (Chapter 5) is often used in both CX and UX. Not to complicate matters, there are other "experiences" that are the focus of researchers, such as "patient experience" or the "student experience." For the purpose of this book, we will use the term "user experience" to encapsulate the broader set of experiences for any individual or group related to the actual use of a product or system.

The user experience can sometimes mean the difference between life and death. For example, the health industry is not immune to poor usability. Usability issues abound in medical devices, procedures, and even diagnostic tools. Jakob Nielsen (2005) cites one study that found 22 separate usability issues that contributed to patients receiving the wrong medicine. Even more troubling is that, on average, 98,000 Americans die every year due to medical error (Kohn et al., 2000). While there are no doubt many factors behind this, some speculate that usability and human factors are at least partially to blame.

In some very compelling research, Anthony Andre (2003) looked at the design of automatic external defibrillators or AEDs. An AED is a device used to resuscitate an individual who is experiencing cardiac arrest. AEDs are found in many public spaces such as shopping malls, airports, and sporting venues. An AED is intended to be used by the general public with no background or experience in life-saving techniques such as CPR. The design of an AED is critical, since most individuals who are using an AED are experiencing it for the first time, under a tremendous amount of stress. An AED must have simple and clear instructions and deliver them in a way that is time-sensitive and mitigates user errors. Andre's research compared four different AEDs. He was interested in how each of them performed in terms of users delivering a shock successfully within a specified time limit. He was also interested in identifying specific usability issues that were impacting user performance with each of the machines.

In his 2003 study, Andre assigned 64 participants to one of four different machines. Participants were asked to enter a room and save a victim (a manikin lying on the floor) with the AED they were assigned. The results he found were shocking—no pun intended! While two machines performed as expected (0% errors from a sample of 16 participants for each machine), two other machines did not fare so well. For example, 25% of the participants who used one of the AEDs were not able to successfully deliver a shock to the victim. There were many reasons for this outcome. For example, participants were confused by the instructions on how to remove the packaging for the pads that adhere to the bare chest. Also, the instructions on where to place the electrodes were somewhat confusing. After Andre shared his research findings with his client, they agreed to address these issues as part of a product redesign effort.

Similar situations can arise on a regular basis in the workplace or the home. Just think of the written instructions for such actions as lighting the pilot light on a furnace, installing a new lighting fixture, or trying to figure out a tax form. A misunderstood or misread instruction can easily result in property damage, financial loss, personal injury, or even death personal injury, or even death. User experience plays a much wider role in our lives than most people realize. It's not just about using the latest technology. User experience impacts everyone every day. It cuts across cultures, age, race, gender, and economic class.

Saving lives is, of course, not the only motivation for a good user experience. Championing user experience in a business setting is often geared toward increasing revenue and/or decreasing costs. Stories abound of companies that lost money because of the poor user experience of a new product. Other companies have made ease of use a key differentiator as part of their brand message.

The Bentley University User Experience Center (www.bentley.edu/uxc) had the opportunity to work with a major hospital on the redesign of their charitable giving website. They were concerned that visitors to their website would have difficulty finding and making donations to the hospital's charitable foundation. Specifically, they were interested in increasing the number of recurring donations, as it was an excellent way to build a more continuous relationship with the donor. Our research included a comprehensive usability evaluation with current and potential donors. We learned a great deal about how to not only improve navigation but simplify the donation form and highlight the benefits of recurring donations. Soon after the launch of the new website, we learned that the redesign effort was a success. Overall, donations had increased by 50%, and recurring donations increased from 2 to 19, a 6715% increase! This was a true success story, one that also benefits a great cause.

In recent years, particularly in the U.S., the user experience of voting has garnered much attention, and not in a good way. It perhaps started with the so-called "butterfly ballot" in the year 2000 U.S. presidential election. George W. Bush and Al Gore were the two primary candidates. The election had come down to one state, Florida. Whoever won Florida would win the election. Palm Beach County had used the infamous butterfly ballot, shown in Fig. 1.1. Votes were cast by punching holes in the center column. But the holes were labeled both from the left and right. So, for example, punching the second hole was actually a vote for Pat Buchanan, on the right, rather than a vote for the second candidate on the left, Al Gore. We don't know how many people accidentally voted for Pat Buchanan when they intended to vote for Al Gore. Bush won Florida's electoral votes, and thus the Presidency, by a margin of only 984 votes out of 5.8 million cast. That's only 0.02%.

Some insight into the impact of the butterfly ballot comes from a study done by a group of Canadian researchers (Sinclair et al., 2000) right after the election. They created two mock ballots for the Prime Minister of Canada. One used the butterfly ballot, and the other used a single-column ballot. They conducted the study in a shopping mall. Participants were randomly assigned one of the two ballot designs. After voting, the participants were asked for whom they had voted.

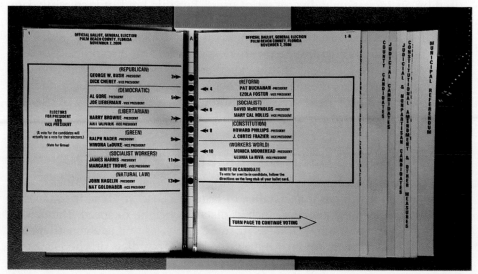

Fig. 1.1 The infamous "Butterfly Ballot" used in Palm Beach County, Florida, in the 2000 U.S. presidential election.

A total of 63 people used the single-column ballot, and they made no errors. A total of 53 people used the butterfly ballot, and they made four errors. So, in this case, the butterfly ballot yielded an error rate of 7.5%. If 7.5% of the voters using the butterfly ballot in Palm Beach made errors, that could easily have resulted in a different outcome to the entire presidential election.

User experience issues continue to plague the voting process. In 2018, again in Florida but this time in Broward County, they used a three-column design for their ballot. The first column was a long set of instructions, in three different languages, about how to cast your vote. One of the most contested elections was for the U.S. Senate, with two candidates running: Rick Scott (Republican) and Bill Nelson (Democrat). But the vote for U.S. Senate was at the bottom of the first column, beneath all the instructions. Broward County is statistically one of the most Democrat-leaning counties in Florida. Oddly, they reported about 25,000 fewer votes in the Senate race than in the Governor's race, which was prominently placed at the top of the second column. It seems likely that some voters simply missed the Senate race at the bottom of the long column of instructions. Scott won the Senate election state-wide by a margin of only 10,000 votes. If even just half of the 25,000 voters in Broward who failed to vote in the Senate race had voted for Nelson, he would have won.

These examples illustrate that even something as apparently simple as a paper ballot for voting can have significant user experience issues. And these issues can impact our governments and even society.

User experience takes on an ever-increasing role in our lives as products become more complex. As technologies evolve and mature, they tend to be used by an increasingly diverse set of users. But this kind of increasing complexity and evolution of technology doesn't necessarily mean that the technologies are becoming easier to use. In fact, just the opposite is likely to happen unless we pay close attention to the user experience. As the complexity of technology grows, we believe that user experience must be given more attention and importance, and UX metrics will become a critical part of the development process to provide complex technology that's efficient, easy to use, and engaging.

1.2 WHAT ARE USER EXPERIENCE METRICS?

A *metric* is a way of measuring or evaluating a particular phenomenon or item. We can say something is longer, taller, or faster because we are able to measure or quantify some attribute of it, such as distance, height, or speed. The process requires agreement on how to measure these things, as well as a consistent and reliable way of doing it. An inch is the same length regardless of who is measuring it, and a second lasts for the same amount of time no matter what the timekeeping device is. Standards for such measures are defined by society as a whole and are based on standard definitions of each measure.

Metrics exist in many areas of our lives. We're familiar with many metrics, such as time, distance, weight, height, speed, temperature, volume, and so on. Every industry, activity, and culture has its own set of metrics. For example, the auto industry is interested in the horsepower of a car, its gas mileage, and the cost of materials. The computer industry is concerned with processor speed, memory size, and power requirements. At home, we're interested in similar measurements: how our weight changes when we step on the bathroom scale, where to set our thermostat in the evening, and how to interpret our electricity bill every month.

The user experience field is no different. We have a set of metrics specific to our profession: task success, user satisfaction, and errors, among others. This book gathers all the UX metrics in one place and explains how to use these metrics to provide maximum benefit to you and your organization.

So what is a UX metric, and how does it compare to other types of metrics? Like all other metrics, UX metrics are based on a reliable system of measurement: Using the same set of measurements each time something is measured should result in comparable outcomes. All UX metrics must be *observable* in some way, either directly or indirectly. This observation might be simply noting that a task was completed successfully or noting the time required to complete the task. All UX metrics must be *quantifiable*—they have to be turned into a number or counted in some way. All UX metrics also require that the thing being measured represent some aspect of the user experience, presented in a numeric format. For example, a UX metric might reveal that 90% of the users are able to complete a set of tasks in less than 1 minute, or 50% of users failed to notice a key element on the interface.

What makes a UX metric different from other metrics? UX metrics reveal something about the user experience—about the personal experience of the human being using a product or system. A UX metric reveals something about the interaction between the user and the product: some aspect of *effectiveness* (being able to complete a task), *efficiency* (the amount of effort required to complete the task), or *satisfaction* (the degree to which the user was happy with their experience while performing the task).

Another difference between UX metrics and other metrics is that they measure something about *people* and their behavior or attitudes. Because people are amazingly diverse and adaptable, we sometimes encounter challenges in our UX metrics. For this reason, we will discuss *confidence intervals* with most UX metrics to reflect the variability in the data. We will also discuss what metrics we consider relevant (and less relevant) in a UX context.

Certain things are not considered UX metrics, such as overall preferences and attitudes not tied to an actual experience of using something. Think of some standard metrics such as the Presidential Approval Ratings, the Consumer Price

Index, or the frequency of purchasing specific products. Although these metrics are all quantifiable and may reflect some type of behavior, they are not based on actually using something in order to reflect the variability in the data.

UX metrics are not an end unto themselves; rather, they are a means to help you reach an informed decision. UX metrics provide answers to your organization's critical questions that can't be answered by other means. For example, UX metrics can answer these critical questions:

- Will the users recommend the product after using it?
- Is this new product more efficient to use than the current product?
- How does the user experience of this product compare to the competition?
- Does the user feel good about the product or themselves after using it?
- What are the most significant usability problems with this product?
- Are improvements being made from one design iteration to the next?

1.3 THE VALUE OF UX METRICS

We think UX metrics are pretty amazing. Otherwise, why would we write this book? Measuring the user experience offers so much more than just simple observation. Metrics add structure to the design and evaluation process, give insight into the findings, and provide information to the decision-makers. Without the insight provided by metrics, important business decisions may be made based on incorrect assumptions, "gut feelings," or hunches. As a result, some of these decisions are not the best ones.

During a typical usability evaluation, it's fairly easy to spot some of the more obvious UX issues. But it's much harder to estimate the size or magnitude of the issues. For example, if all eight participants in a study have the same exact problem, you can be quite certain it is a common problem. But what if only two or three of the eight participants encounter the problem? What does that mean for the larger population of users? UX metrics offer a way to estimate the number of users likely to experience this problem. Knowing the magnitude of the problem could mean the difference between delaying a major product launch and simply adding an additional item to the bug list with a low priority. Without UX metrics, the magnitude of the problem is just a guess.

UX metrics show whether you're actually improving the user experience from one product to the next. An astute manager will want to know as close to certain as possible that the new product will be better than the current product. UX metrics are the only way to really know if the desired improvements have been realized. By measuring and comparing the current with a new, "improved" product and evaluating the potential improvement, you create a win-win situation. There are three possible outcomes:

- The new version tests better than the current product: Everyone can sleep well at night knowing that improvements were made.
- The new version tests worse than the current version: Steps can be taken to address the problem or put remediation plans into place.
- No difference between the current product and the new product is apparent: The impact on the user experience does not affect the success or failure of the new product. However, improvements in other aspects of the product could make up for the lack of improvement in the user experience.

UX metrics are a key ingredient in calculating an ROI. As part of a business plan, you may be asked to determine how much money is saved or how revenue increases as a result of a new product design. Without UX metrics, this task is impossible. With UX metrics, you might determine that a simple change in a data input field on an internal website could reduce data entry errors by 75%, reduce the time required to complete the customer service task, increase the number of transactions processed each day, reduce the backlog in customer orders, cut the delay in customer shipments, and increase both customer satisfaction and customer orders, resulting in an overall rise in revenue for the company.

UX metrics can help reveal patterns that are hard or even impossible to see. Evaluating a product with a very small sample size (without collecting any metrics) usually reveals the most obvious problems. However, there are many more subtle problems that require the power of metrics. For example, sometimes, it's difficult to see small inefficiencies, such as the need to re-enter user data whenever a transaction displays a new screen. Users may be able to complete their tasks—and maybe even say they like it—but many small inefficiencies can eventually build up to impact the user experience and slow down the process. UX metrics help you gain new insights and lead toward a better understanding of user behavior.

1.4 METRICS FOR EVERYONE

We've been teaching a class on UX metrics, in one form or another, for well over a decade. During this time, we've met many UX and non-UX professionals who have little to no background in statistics, and even a few who were terrified of anything that looks like a number. Despite this, we have continually been impressed and inspired by how these folks are able to quickly and easily learn the basics of how to collect, analyze, and present UX metrics. UX metrics are a very powerful tool but also easily accessible to almost anyone. The key is simply to try and learn from your mistakes. The more metrics you collect and analyze, the better you will get! In fact, we even see some individuals who use this book simply as a guide to what types of UX metrics make the most sense for their organization or project and then go off and ask someone else to do the dirty work. So, even if you don't want to get your hands dirty, there isn't an excuse for incorporating UX metrics into your work.

We've written this book to be easy and approachable to the broadest possible audience. In fact, we favor simplification rather than a deep dive into heavy statistical analysis. We feel this will help attract as many UX and non-UX people as possible. Of course, we strongly encourage everyone to go beyond this book by creating new metrics tailored to your organization, product, or research practice.

1.5 NEW TECHNOLOGIES IN USER EXPERIENCE METRICS

Earlier, we stated that UX metrics apply to a vast array of products, designs, and technologies. In fact, even with new technologies emerging every day, UX metrics still remain highly relevant. However, what does change quite rapidly are the technologies themselves that better allow us to collect and analyze UX data. Throughout this book, you will get a sense of some of the newest technologies that might make your job a little easier, and certainly more interesting. We wanted to highlight a few of the technologies that have emerged in the last few years.

There are some exciting new advances in the world of eye-tracking. For decades, eye-tracking was restricted to the lab. This is no longer the case. Goggles are now available that can be used to track eye movements in the field. So, as your participant is walking down the aisle at the supermarket, you can gather data on what they are looking at and for how long. Of course, it is a little tricky when different objects occur in approximately the same location and different depths. But, no doubt they are improving these goggles with each new release. Eye-tracking is even moving beyond hardware. For example, there is new technology that collects eye movement data through the participant's webcam. So no longer are you restricted to using dedicated eye-tracking hardware.

Another exciting new technology is in the area of affective computing. For decades, UX professionals have gained insight into a user's emotional state by listening to and observing the participant, and, of course, asking all the right questions. These qualitative data have been, and will always be, extremely valuable. However, advances in affective computing have added a new dimension to measuring emotional engagement. We are now able to combine data from sensors that measure skin conductance, along with facial recognition software that analyzes different facial expressions and eye movements. Together, these three pieces of data tell the researcher something about the level of arousal, the valence (whether it is a positive or negative emotion), and their visual attention patterns.

There are a host of new unmoderated testing tools that make data collection very easy and affordable. Some tools such as UserZoom and Loop11 are powerful and affordable for collecting a lot of UX data very efficiently. Other tools such as Usabilla and Userlytics do a very nice job of integrating both qualitative and quantitative data for a reasonable price. Other tools such as UsabilityTesting.com allow you to essentially run qualitative-based, self-guided usability studies very easily and quickly. And, of course, there are some very specialized tools that help track clicks or mouse movements. It is very exciting that there are so many new technologies that UX researchers can add to their suite of tools.

Analyzing open-ended responses has always been very laborious and imprecise. It is all too common for researchers to disregard verbatim comments or just randomly select a small sample for quotes. In the last few years, verbatim analysis software has greatly improved to the point that researchers now have the ability to analyze open-ended responses any researchers

1.6 TEN MYTHS ABOUT UX METRICS

There are many common myths about UX metrics. Some of these myths may come from a lack of experience with using metrics. Perhaps these myths arose from a negative experience (such as someone from marketing screaming about your sample size) or even other UX professionals complaining about the hassles and costs associated with using metrics. Ultimately the source of these myths doesn't matter. What matters is to separate fact from fiction. We've listed 10 of the most common myths surrounding UX metrics and a few examples that dispel these myths.

Myth 1: Metrics Take Too Much Time to Collect

At best, UX metrics can speed up the design process and, at worst, should not impact the overall timeline. Metrics are quickly and easily collected as part of a typical iterative design process. Project team members may incorrectly assume that full-blown surveys need to be launched or that you have to be testing in the lab for two straight weeks to collect even basic UX metrics. In fact, there are some fairly simple UX metrics you can collect as part of your everyday testing. Adding a few extra questions at the beginning or end of each usability session will not impact the length of the session. Participants can quickly answer a few key questions as part of either a typical background questionnaire or follow-up activities.

Participants can also rate tasks for ease of use or satisfaction after each task or at the end of all tasks. If you have easy access to a large group of target users or a user panel, you can send out an e-mail blast with a few key questions, perhaps with some screenshots. It's possible to collect data from hundreds of users in just 1 day. Some data can also be quickly collected without even involving the user. For example, you can quickly and easily report the frequency and severity of specific issues with each new design iteration. The time it takes to collect metrics doesn't have to be weeks or even days. Sometimes it's just a few extra hours or even minutes.

Myth 2: UX Metrics Cost Too Much Money

Some people believe that the only way to get reliable UX data is to outsource the study to a market research firm or UX consultancy. Although this may be helpful in some situations, it can also be quite costly. Many reliable metrics don't cost an arm and a leg. Even as part of your everyday testing, you can collect incredibly valuable data on the frequency and severity of different usability issues. You can also collect huge amounts of quantitative data by sending out short e-mail surveys to fellow employees or a panel of targeted users. Also, some of the best analysis tools are actually free on the web. Although money does help in certain situations, it is by no means necessary to get some reliable metrics.

Myth 3: UX Metrics Are Not Useful When Focusing on Small Improvements

Some project team members may question the usefulness of metrics when they are interested in only some fairly small improvements. They may say it's best to focus on a narrow set of improvements and not worry about metrics. They may not have any extra time or budget to collect any UX metrics. They may say that metrics have no place in a rapid-pace iterative design process. Analyzing usability issues is an obvious and incredibly valuable solution. For example, looking at the severity and frequency of usability issues and why they occur is an excellent way to focus resources during the design process. This approach saves the project both money and time. You can easily derive UX metrics based on previous studies that might help you answer key usability questions. UX metrics are useful for large and small projects alike.

Myth 4: UX Metrics Don't Help Us Understand Causes

Some people argue that metrics don't help us understand the root cause of user experience problems. They assume (incorrectly) that metrics serve only to highlight the magnitude of the problem. But if they concentrate on only success rates or completion time data, it's easy to see why some might have this perception. Metrics, however, can tell you much more about the root cause of a poor user experience than you might initially think. You can analyze verbatim comments to reveal the source of the problem and how many users experience it. You can identify where in the system users experience a problem and use metrics to tell where and why some problems occur. Depending on how the data are coded and the methods used, there is a wealth of UX data that can help reveal the root cause of many UX issues.

Myth 5: UX Metrics Are Too Noisy

One big criticism of UX metrics is that the data are too "noisy." Too many variables prevent getting a clear picture of what's going on. The classic example of "noisy" data is measuring task completion time in an automated usability study when the participant goes out for a cup of coffee or, worse, home for the weekend. Although this may happen on occasion, it should not deter you from collecting task time data or any other type of usability data. There are some simple things that can be done to minimize or even remove noise in the data. UX data can be cleaned up so that extreme values are not used in the analysis. Also, specific metrics can be carefully chosen to mitigate noisy data. Well-defined procedures can be used to ensure that appropriate levels of consistency are achieved in evaluating tasks or usability issues. Many standard questionnaires have already been widely validated by many researchers. The bottom line is that with some careful thought and a few simple techniques, a lot of the noise in UX data can be significantly reduced to show a clear picture of user behavior and attitudes.

Myth 6: You Can Just Trust Your Gut

A lot of design decisions are made on a "gut level." There's always someone on the project team who proclaims, "This decision just feels right!" One of the beauties of metrics is that having the data takes a lot of the guesswork out of design decisions. Some design options are truly borderline cases, but they might actually have an impact on a large population. Sometimes the right design solutions are counterintuitive. For example, a design team may ensure that all the information on a web page is above the fold, thereby eliminating the need to scroll. However, UX data (perhaps in the form of task completion times) may reveal longer task completion times because there's not enough white space between the various visual elements. Intuition is certainly important, but data are better.

Myth 7: Metrics Don't Apply to New Products

Some people shy away from metrics when evaluating a new product. They may argue that since there is no point of comparison, metrics don't make sense. We would argue just the opposite. When evaluating a new product, it's critical to establish a set of baseline metrics against which future design iterations can be compared. It's the only way to really know if the design is improving or not. In addition, it's helpful to establish target metrics for new products. Before a product is released, it should meet basic UX metrics around task success, satisfaction, and efficiency.

Myth 8: No Metrics Exist for the Type of Issues We Are Dealing With

Some people believe that there aren't any metrics related to the particular product or project they are working on. Whatever the goal of the project, at least a couple of metrics should tie directly to the business goals of the project. For example, some people say they are only interested in the emotional response of users and not in actual task performance. In this case, several well-established ways of measuring emotional responses are available. In other situations, someone might be concerned only with awareness. Very simple ways to measure awareness also exist, even without investing in eye-tracking technology. Some people say that they are only interested in more subtle reactions of users, such as their level of frustration. There are ways to measure stress levels without actually asking the user. In our years of UX research, we have yet to come across a business or user goal that was not measurable in some way. You may have to be creative in how you collect the data, but it's always possible.

Myth 9: Metrics Are Not Understood or Appreciated by Management

Although some managers view user experience research as providing only qualitative feedback about a design or product, most managers see the value of measurement. It has been our experience that UX metrics are not only understood but very much appreciated by upper-level management. They can relate to metrics. Metrics provide credibility to the team, the product, and the design process. Metrics can be used to calculate ROI. Most managers love metrics, and UX metrics are one type of metric they will quickly embrace. UX metrics can also be real attention-grabbers with senior management. It's one thing to say there's a problem with the online checkout process, but it's an entirely different thing to say that 52% of users are unable to successfully purchase a product online once they've found it.

Myth 10: It's Difficult to Collect Reliable Data With a Small Sample Size

A widely held belief is that a large sample size is required to collect any reliable UX metrics. Many people assume that you need at least 30 participants to even start looking at UX data. Although having a larger sample size certainly helps increase the confidence level, smaller sample sizes of 8 or 10 participants can still be meaningful. We will show you how to calculate a confidence interval that takes into account the sample size when making any conclusion. Also, we will show you how to determine the sample size you need to identify usability issues. Most of the examples in this book are based on fairly small sample sizes (fewer than 20 participants). So not only are metrics possible to analyze with fairly small sample sizes; doing so is quite common!

CHAPTER 2
Background

CONTENTS

In this chapter we will cover background information about data, statistics, and graphs that apply to just about any user experience metrics. Specifically, we will address the following:

- The basic *types of variables and data* in any user experience study, including independent and dependent variables, and nominal, ordinal, interval, and ratio data.

Measuring the User Experience. DOI: http://dx.doi.org/10.1016/B978-0-12-818080-8.00002-9

- Basic *descriptive statistics* such as the mean and median, standard deviation, and the concept of *confidence intervals*, which reflect how accurate your estimates of measures like task times, task success rates, and subjective ratings actually are.
- Simple *statistical tests* for comparing means and analyzing relationships between variables.
- Tips for *presenting your data visually* in the most effective way.

We will use Microsoft Excel for all of the examples in this chapter (and really in most of this book) because it is so popular and widely available. Most of the analyses can also be done with other readily available spreadsheet tools such as Google Docs or OpenOffice. Alternatively, you can use statistical software such as R or SPSS.

EXCEL TIPS

Throughout this book, we will use short tips, like this one, to show how to do certain things in Excel. Note that we have tested these methods using Excel 2016 for Windows. Older versions of Excel, and the Macintosh version, may be somewhat different.

2.1 INDEPENDENT AND DEPENDENT VARIABLES

At the broadest level, there are two types of variables in any user experience study: independent and dependent. Independent variables are the things you manipulate or control for, such as two alternative designs you're testing or the ages of your participants. Dependent variables are the things you measure, such as success rates, number of errors, user satisfaction, completion times, and many more. Most of the metrics we discuss in this book are dependent variables.

When you design a study, you should have a clear idea of what you plan to manipulate (independent variables) and what you plan to measure (dependent variables). The most interesting outcomes of a study are at the intersection of the independent and dependent variables, such as whether one design resulted in a higher task success rate than the other.

2.2 TYPES OF DATA

Both independent and dependent variables can be measured using one of four general types of data: nominal, ordinal, interval, and ratio. Each type of data has its own unique characteristics, and, most importantly, supports specific types of analyses and statistics. When collecting and analyzing user experience data, you should know what type of data you're dealing with and what you can and can't do with each type.

2.2.1 Nominal Data

Nominal (also called categorical) data are simply unordered groups or categories. Without order between the categories, you can say that they are different, not that one is any better than the other. For example, consider apples, oranges, and bananas. They are just different; no one fruit is inherently better than any other. The words are just names—they don't measure "fruitness."

In user experience, nominal data might be characteristics of different types of users, such as Windows versus Mac users, users in different geographic locations, or males versus females. These are typically independent variables that allow you to segment the data by these different groups. If a study included users representing different personas, those personas could be considered nominal data. Nominal data also include some commonly used dependent variables, such as the number of users who clicked on link A instead of link B, or users who chose to use a web site versus a mobile application.

Among the statistics you can use with nominal data are simple descriptive statistics such as counts and frequencies. For example, you could say that 45% of the users are female, or there are 200 users with blue eyes, or 95% clicked on link A.

CODING NOMINAL DATA

One important thing to consider when you work with nominal data is how you represent, or code, it. In analyzing nominal data, it's not uncommon to represent the membership in each group using numbers. For example, you might code males as group "1", females as group "2", and non-binary as group "3." But remember that those figures are not data to be analyzed as numbers: An average of these values would be meaningless. (You could just as easily code them as "F" and "M.") To use another example, you wouldn't add up the numbers on the backs of Red Sox and Yankees players' uniforms and say that the Red Sox are a better team because the sum of their numbers is higher. The software you're using for your analysis can't distinguish between numbers used strictly for coding purposes, like these, and numbers whose values have true meaning.

2.2.2 Ordinal Data

Ordinal data are ordered groups or categories. As the name implies, the data are organized in a certain way. On a nominal scale the values are just labels. They are not measuring anything. But in an ordinal scale the values arrange the data into a meaningful order. You can think of ordinal data as ranked data. For example, the list of the top 100 movies, as rated by the American Film Institute (AFI), shows that their 10th best movie of all time, *Singing in the Rain*, is better than their 20th best movie of all time, *One Flew Over the Cuckoo's Nest*. But these ratings don't say that *Singing in the Rain* is *twice* as good as *One Flew Over the Cuckoo's Nest*. One film is just *better* than the other, at least according to the AFI. Because the distance between the ranks is not meaningful, you cannot say one is twice as good as the other. Ordinal data might be ordered as better or worse, more satisfied or less satisfied, or more severe or less severe. The relative ranking (the order of the rankings) is the only thing that matters.

In user experience studies, the most common examples of ordinal data come from task success and self-reported data. For example, 74% of users might have successfully completed a task while 26% failed it. Or users might have been asked to rate a website as "excellent," "good," "fair," or "poor." These are relative rankings: You can assume that an "excellent" website provides a more positive user experience than a "good" one, but the ratings don't tell us how much more positive it is. Or if you were to ask the participants in a study to rank order four different designs for a web page according to which they prefer, that would also be ordinal data. There's no reason to assume that the distance between the page ranked first by a participant and the page ranked second is the same as the distance between the page ranked second and the one ranked third. It could be that the participant really loved one page and hated all three of the others.

The most common way to analyze ordinal data is by looking at frequencies. For example, you might report that 40% of the users rated the site as excellent, 30% as good, 20% as fair, and 10% as poor.

IS IT OK TO CALCULATE AN AVERAGE RANK?

Let's assume you had 10 participants rank order three designs they interacted with in a usability study and got these results:

Design	P1	P2	P3	P4	P5	P6	P7	P8	P9	P10	Avg	# 1st	# 2nd	# 3rd
A	1	2	1	1	1	2	3	1	2	1	1.5	6	3	1
B	2	1	3	2	2	1	1	3	3	2	2.0	3	4	3
C	3	3	2	3	3	3	2	2	1	3	2.5	1	3	6

Is it OK to calculate the average ranks for those three designs, as shown in the "Avg" column? In other words, can you consider the design that got the lowest average rank as the "winner"? Statistics purists would say no, because you can't assume that the intervals between each of the ranks are equal. Instead, you should count the number of times each design was ranked first, second, or third. We think it's also more compelling (and understandable) to say that 6 out of 10 participants ranked Design A first rather than that its average rank was 1.5.

2.2.3 Interval Data

Interval data are ordered data where the differences between the values are meaningful. An example of interval data familiar to most of us is temperature. The difference between 40°F and 50°F is the same as the difference between 60°F and 70°F. The distances between all of the values are the same. But unlike the final type of data we will discuss shortly, ratio data, interval data do not have a true zero point that signifies the complete absence of the attribute being measured. Defining 0°C or 32°F based on when water freezes is completely arbitrary. The freezing point of water does not mean the absence of heat; it only identifies a meaningful point on the scale of temperatures. Dates are another common example of interval data.

In user experience, the System Usability Scale (SUS) is one example of interval data. SUS (described in detail in Chapter 5) is based on self-reported data from a series of questions about the overall usability of any system. Scores range from 0 to 100, with a higher SUS score indicating better usability. The distance between each point along the scale is meaningful in the sense that it represents an incremental increase or decrease in perceived usability. But note that 0 doesn't really mean the complete absence of usability, so it's not a ratio scale.

Interval data allow you to calculate a wide range of descriptive statistics, including an average and standard deviation. There are also many inferential statistics that can be used to generalize about a larger population. Interval data provide many more possibilities for analysis than either nominal or ordinal data. Much of this chapter will review statistics that can be used with interval data.

One of the debates you can get into with people who collect and analyze subjective ratings is whether you must treat the data as ordinal or if you can treat it as being interval. Consider these two rating scales:

o Poor o Fair o Good o Excellent

Poor o o o o Excellent

At first glance, you might say those two scales are the same, but the difference in presentation makes them different. Putting explicit labels on the items in the first scale makes the data ordinal. Leaving the intervening labels off in the second scale and only labeling the end points make the data more "interval-like." That's the reason that most subjective rating scales only label the ends, or "anchors," and not every data point. Consider a slightly different version of the second scale:

Poor o o o o o o o o o Excellent

Presenting it that way, with 9 points along the scale, makes it even more obvious that the data can be treated as interval data. The reasonable interpretation of this scale by a user is that the distances between all the data points along the scale are equal. A question to ask yourself when deciding whether you can treat data like this as an interval is whether a point halfway between any two of the nine data points makes sense. If it does, then it makes sense to analyze the data as interval data.

2.2.4 Ratio Data

Ratio data are the same as interval data but with the addition of an absolute zero. This means that the zero value is not arbitrary, as with interval data, but has some inherent meaning. With ratio data, the differences between the measurements are interpreted as a ratio. Examples of ratio data are age, height, weight, and temperature on the Kelvin scale. In each example, zero indicates the complete absence of age, height, weight, or heat.

In user experience, the most obvious example of ratio data is time. A task that took 2 minutes to complete took twice as long as a task that took 1 minute. Ratio data let you say something is twice as fast or half as slow as something else. For example, you could say that one user is twice as fast as another user in completing a task.

All of the analyses that you can do with interval data can also be done with ratio data. Although there are a few relatively obscure analyses that you can only do with ratio data (e.g., calculating a geometric mean), there really aren't many differences between interval and ratio data in terms of the available statistics.

2.3 DESCRIPTIVE STATISTICS

Descriptive statistics are essential for any interval or ratio data. Descriptive statistics, as the name implies, describe the data, without saying anything about the larger population. Inferential statistics let you draw some conclusions or infer something about a larger population above and beyond your sample.

The most common types of descriptive statistics are measures of central tendency (such as the mean), measures of variability (such as the standard deviation), and confidence intervals, which pull the other two together. In the following sections, we will use the sample data shown in Table 2.1 to illustrate these statistics. These data represent the time, in seconds, that it took each of 12 participants in a usability study to complete the same task.

2.3.1 Measures of Central Tendency

Measures of central tendency are simply a way of choosing a single number that is in some way representative of a set of numbers. The three most common measures of central tendency are the mean, median, and mode.

The mean is what most people think of as the average: the sum of all the values divided by how many values there are. The mean of most user experience metrics is extremely useful and is probably the most common statistic cited in usability reports. For the data in Table 2.1, the mean is 421/12 = 35.1 seconds.

CALCULATING MEASURES OF CENTRAL TENDENCY

The mean of any set of numbers in Excel can be calculated using the "=AVERAGE" function. The median can be calculated using the "=MEDIAN" function, and the mode can be calculated using the "=MODE" function. If the mode can't be calculated (which happens when each value occurs an equal number of times), Excel returns "#N/A".

The median is the middle number if you put them in order from smallest to largest: Half the values are below the median and half are above the median. If there is no middle number, the median is halfway between the two values on either side of the middle. For the data in Table 2.1, the median is equal to 33.5 seconds (halfway between the middle two numbers, 33 and 34). Half of the users were faster than 33.5 seconds and half were slower. In some cases, the median can be more revealing than the mean. For example, let's assume the task time for P12 had been 150 seconds rather than 50. That would change the mean to 43.4 seconds, but the median would be unchanged at 33.5 seconds. It's up to you to decide which is a more representative number, but this illustrates the reason that the median is sometimes used, especially when larger values (or so-called "outliers") may have too much of an influence on the mean. By the way, the median uses only the ordinal properties of the set of numbers and ignores the intervals between them.

The mode is the most commonly occurring value in the set of numbers. For the data in Table 2.1, the mode is 22 seconds, because two participants completed the task in 22 seconds. It's not common to report the mode in usability test results. When the data are continuous over a broad range, such as the task

Participant	Task Time (Seconds)
P1	34
P2	33
P3	28
P4	44
P5	46
P6	21
P7	22
P8	53
P9	22
P10	29
P11	39
P12	50

Table 2.1 Time to Complete a Task, in Seconds, for Each of 12 Participants in a Usability Study.

NUMBER OF DECIMAL PLACES TO USE WHEN REPORTING DATA

One of the most common mistakes many people make is reporting user experience data (mean times, task completion rates, etc.) with more precision than it really deserves. For example, the mean of the times in Table 2.1 is technically 35.08333333 seconds. Is that the way you should report the mean? Of course not. That many decimal places may be mathematically correct, but it's ridiculous from a practical standpoint. Who cares whether the mean was 35.083 or 35.085 seconds? When you're dealing with tasks that took *about* 35 seconds to complete, a few milliseconds or a few hundredths of a second make no difference whatsoever.

So how many decimal places should you use? There's no universal answer, but some of the factors to consider are the accuracy of the original data, its magnitude, and its variability. The original data in Table 2.1 appear to be accurate to the nearest second. One rule of thumb is that the number of significant digits you should use when reporting a statistic, such as the mean, is no more than one additional significant digit in comparison to the original data. So, in this example, you could report that the mean was 35.1 seconds.

times shown in Table 2.1, the mode is generally less useful. When data have a more limited set of values (such as subjective rating scales), the mode is more useful.

2.3.2 Measures of Variability

Measures of variability reflect how much the data are spread or dispersed across the range of values. For example, these measures help answer the question, "Do most users have similar task completion times or is there a wide range of times?" In user experience studies, some variability is caused by individual differences among your participants. Other variability might be caused by your independent variables, such alternative designs you're testing. There are three common measures of variability: the range, the variance, and the standard deviation.

The range is the distance between the minimum and maximum values. For the data in Table 2.1, the range is 32, with a minimum time of 21 seconds and a maximum time of 53 seconds. The range can vary wildly depending on the metric. For example, in many kinds of rating scales, the range is usually limited to five or seven, depending on the number of values used in the scales. When you study completion times, the range is very useful because it will help identify "outliers" (data points that are at the extreme top and bottom of the range). Looking at the range is also a good check to make sure that the data are coded properly. If the range is supposed to be from one to five, and the data include a seven, you know there is a problem.

EXCEL TIP: CALCULATING THE VARIANCE

The minimum of any set of numbers in Excel can be determined using the "=MIN" function and the maximum using the "=MAX" function. The range can then be determined by MAX-MIN. The variance can be calculated using the "=VAR" function and the standard deviation using the "=STDEV" function.

Variance tells you how spread out the data are relative to the average or mean. The formula for calculating variance measures the difference between each individual data point and the mean, squares that value, sums all of those squares, and then divides the result by the sample size minus 1. For the data in Table 2.1, the variance is 126.4.

Once you know the variance, you can easily calculate the standard deviation, which is the most commonly used measure of variability. The standard deviation is simply the square root of the variance. The standard deviation of the data shown in Table 2.1 is 11.2 seconds. Interpreting the standard deviation is a little easier than interpreting the variance, since the unit of the standard deviation is the same as the original data (seconds, in this example).

EXCEL TIP: DESCRIPTIVE STATISTICS TOOL

An experienced Excel user might be wondering why we didn't just suggest using the "Descriptive Statistics" tool in the Excel Data Analysis ToolPak. (In Excel 2016 for Windows, you can add the Data Analysis ToolPak using "Excel Options" > "Add-Ins".) This tool will calculate the mean, median, range, standard deviation, variance, and other statistics for any set of data you specify. It's a very handy tool. However, it has what we consider a significant limitation: the values it calculates are static. If you go back and update the original data, the statistics don't update. We like to set up our spreadsheets for analyzing the data from a study before we actually collect the data. Then we update the spreadsheet as we're collecting the data. This means we need to use formulas that automatically update, such as MEAN, MEDIAN, STDEV, etc., instead of the "Descriptive Statistics" tool. But it can be a useful tool for calculating a whole batch of these statistics at once. Just be aware that it won't update if you change the data.

2.3.3 Confidence Intervals

A confidence interval is an estimate of a range of values that includes the true population value for a statistic, such as a mean. For example, assume that you wanted to know how accurately the mean time, 35 seconds, for the sample shown in Table 2.1 represents the mean time for all the possible users, or the population mean. You could construct a confidence interval around that mean to show the range of values that you are reasonably certain will include the true population mean. The phrase "reasonably certain" indicates that you will need to choose how certain you want to be, or, put another way, how willing you are to be wrong in your assessment. This is what's called the confidence level that you choose, or conversely, the error, or alpha level, that you're willing to accept. For example, a confidence level of 95%, or an alpha level of 5%, means that you want to be 95% certain, or that you're willing to be wrong 5% of the time.

There are three variables that determine the confidence interval for a mean:

- The sample size, or the number of values in the sample. For the data in Table 2.1, the sample size is 12, since we have data from 12 participants.
- The standard deviation of the sample data. For our example, that is 11.2 seconds.
- The alpha level we want to adopt. The most common alpha levels (primarily by convention) are 5% and 10%. Let's choose an alpha of 5% for this example, which is a 95% confidence interval.

The 95% confidence interval is then calculated using the following formula:

$$\text{Mean} \pm 1.96 \times (\text{Standard Deviation}/\text{sqrt}[\text{Sample Size}])$$

The value "1.96" is a factor that reflects the 95% confidence level. Other confidence levels have other factors. That formula shows that the confidence interval will get smaller as the standard deviation (the variability of the data) decreases, or as the sample size (number of participants) increases.

EXCEL TIP: CALCULATING A CONFIDENCE INTERVAL

You can quickly calculate the confidence interval for any set of data using the CONFIDENCE function in Excel (Fig. 2.1). The formula is easy to construct:

$$= \text{CONFIDENCE(alpha, standard deviation, sample size)}$$

Alpha is your significance level, which is typically 5% (.05) or 10% (.10). The standard deviation can be calculated using the STDEV function. The sample size is simply the number of cases or data points you are examining, which can be calculated using the COUNT function. Fig. 2.1 shows an example. For the data in Table 2.1, the result of this calculation is 6.4 seconds. Since the mean is 35.1 seconds, the 95% confidence interval for that mean is 35.1 ± 6.4, or 28.7–41.5 seconds. So you can be 95% certain that the true population mean for this task time is between 28.7 and 41.5 seconds.

Confidence intervals are incredibly useful. We think you should routinely calculate and display them for just about any means that you report from a study. When displayed as error bars on a graph of means, they make it visually obvious how accurate the measures actually are.

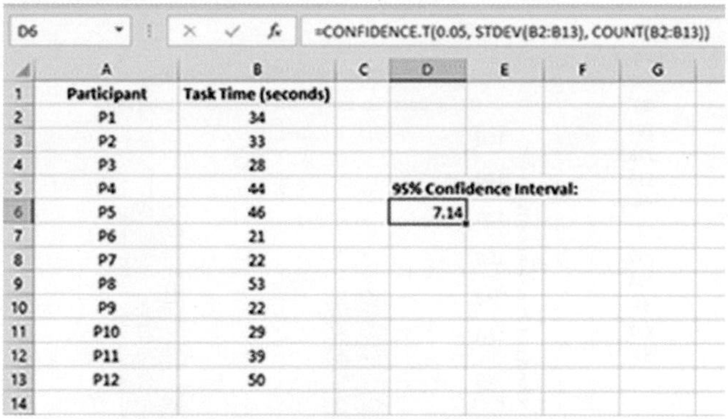
D6 =CONFIDENCE.T(0.05, STDEV(B2:B13), COUNT(B2:B13))

	A	B	C	D	E	F	G
1	Participant	Task Time (seconds)					
2	P1	34					
3	P2	33					
4	P3	28					
5	P4	44		95% Confidence Interval:			
6	P5	46		7.14			
7	P6	21					
8	P7	22					
9	P8	53					
10	P9	22					
11	P10	29					
12	P11	39					
13	P12	50					
14							

Fig. 2.1 Example of how to calculate a 95% confidence interval using the "confidence" function in Excel.

WHAT CONFIDENCE LEVEL SHOULD YOU USE?

How should you decide what confidence level to use? Traditionally, the three commonly used confidence levels are 99%, 95%, and 90% (or their corresponding alpha levels of 1%, 5%, and 10%). The history behind the use of these three levels goes back to the days before computers and calculators, when you had to look up values for confidence levels in printed tables. The people printing these tables didn't want to print a bunch of different versions, so they made just these three. Today, of course, all of these calculations are done for us, so we could choose any confidence level we want. But because of their long-standing use, most people choose one of these three. In the scientific and academic worlds, at least 95% is most commonly used. In the business world, it's common to use 90% or 95%.

The level you choose really does depend upon how certain you need to be that the confidence interval contains the true mean. If you're trying to estimate how long it will take someone to administer a life-saving shock using an automated external defibrillator (AED), you probably want to be very certain of your answer, and would likely choose 99%. But if you're simply estimating how long it will take someone to upload a new photo to their Facebook page, you probably would be satisfied with a 90% confidence level.

2.3.4 Displaying Confidence Intervals as Error Bars

Let's now consider the data in Fig. 2.2, which shows the checkout times for two different designs of a prototype website—the time it took participants to buy a product on the website. In this study, 10 participants performed the checkout task using Design A and another 10 participants performed the checkout task using Design B. Participants were assigned to one group or the other based on the day they came to the study. The means and 90% confidence interval for both groups have been calculated using the AVERAGE and CONFIDENCE functions. The means have been plotted as a bar graph, and the confidence intervals shown

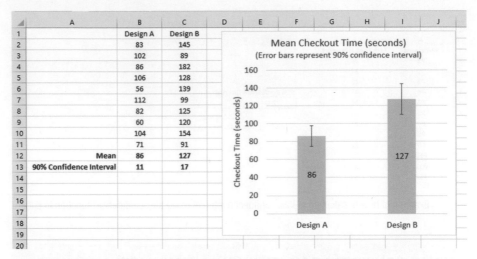

Fig. 2.2 Illustration of displaying confidence intervals as error bars on bar graph.

as error bars on the graph. You can clearly see that the participants who used Design A checked out faster. Even just a quick glance at this bar graph shows that the error bars for these two means don't overlap with each other. When that is the case, you can safely assume that checkout using Design A is significantly faster than using Design B.

EXCEL TIP: ADDING AN ERROR BAR

Once you've created a bar graph showing the means, like Fig. 2.2, you then want to add the error bars to represent the confidence intervals. Here are the steps for that:

1. Click on either of the bars in the chart to select them.

2. In the Excel button bar, choose the "Layout" tab under "Chart Tools."

3. On the "Layout" tab, choose "Error Bars > More Error Bars Options."

4. In the resulting dialog box, select the "Custom" option near the bottom of the dialog box.

5. Click on the "Specify Value" button. The resulting small window allows you to specify the values for the positive and negative portions of the error bars, which will both be the same.

6. Click on the button to specify the Positive Error Value and then select **both** of the values for the 90% confidence interval on the spreadsheet (cells B13 and C13 in Fig. 2.2).

7. Click on the button for the Negative Error Value and select the exact same cells again.

8. Close both windows and your error bars should be on the graph.

2.4 COMPARING MEANS

The data in Fig. 2.2 is an example of comparing means—one of the most useful things you can do with interval or ratio data. We could also have looked at whether Design A has higher satisfaction ratings than Design B, or if the number of errors is higher for Design B. The best approach to all of these questions is through statistics.

There are several ways to compare means, but before jumping into the statistics, you should know the answers to a couple of questions:

1. Is the comparison *within* the same set of users or *across* different users? The data in Fig. 2.2 are from two different groups of 10 participants each. When comparing different samples like that, it's called independent samples. But if you're comparing the *same* group of users on different products or designs, you will use something called paired samples.
2. How many samples are you comparing? If you are comparing two samples, use a *t*-test. If you are comparing three or more samples, use an analysis of variance (also called ANOVA).

2.4.1 Independent Samples

Perhaps the simplest way to compare means from independent samples is using confidence intervals, as shown in the previous section. In comparing the confidence intervals for two means, you can draw the following conclusions:

*   If the confidence intervals *don't overlap*, you can safely assume the two means are significantly different from each other (at the confidence level you chose), which is what we concluded from looking at Fig. 2.2.
*   If the confidence intervals *overlap slightly*, the two means might still be significantly different. Run a *t*-test to determine if they are different.
*   If the confidence intervals *overlap widely*, the two means are not significantly different.

Let's consider the data in Fig. 2.3 to illustrate running a *t*-test for independent samples. This shows the ratings of ease of use on a 1 to 5 scale for two different designs as rated by two different groups of participants (who were randomly assigned to one group or the other). We've calculated the means and confidence intervals and graphed them. But notice that the two confidence intervals overlap slightly: Design 1's interval goes up to 3.8 while Design 2's goes down to 3.5. This is a case where you might want to run a *t*-test to determine if the two means are significantly different (e.g., if you're going to be making a presentation about the results of your study and you want to be sure that the means are significantly different from each other).

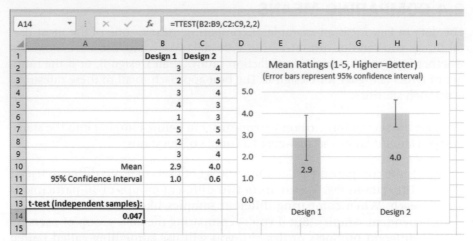

Fig. 2.3 Example of a *t*-test on independent samples.

EXCEL TIP: CALCULATING A T-TEST

As shown in Fig. 2.3, you can use the TTEST function in Excel to run a *t*-test:

$$=TTEST \text{ (Array 1, Array 2, Tails, Type)}$$

Array 1 and Array 2 refer to the sets of values that you want to compare. In Fig. 2.3, Array 1 is the set of ratings for Design 1 and Array 2 is the set of ratings for Design 2. Tails refers to whether your test is one-tailed or two-tailed. This relates to the tails (extremes) of the normal distribution and whether you're considering one end or both ends. From a practical standpoint, this is asking whether it is possible for the difference between these two means to be in either direction (i.e., Design 1 *either* higher or lower than Design 2). In almost all cases that we deal with, the difference could be in either direction, so in those cases the correct choice is "2" for two-tailed. An example where you would use a one-tailed test is one in which you decided before you conducted the study that you want to know if Design 2 is *better than* Design 1, not just which design is best. Finally, Type indicates the type of *t*-test. For these independent samples (not paired), the Type is 2.

This *t*-test returns a value of 0.047. So how do you interpret that? It's telling you that there's a 4.7% chance that this difference is *not* significant. Since we were dealing with a 95% confidence interval, or a 5% alpha level, and this result is less than 5%, we can say that the difference is statistically significant at that level. So you can be confident that this difference is real. Another way of interpreting this is there is a 4.7% chance of saying there is a difference when there really isn't one.

2.4.2 Paired Samples

A paired samples *t*-test is used when you're comparing means within the same set of users. For example, you may be interested in knowing whether there is a difference between two prototype designs. If you have the same set of users perform tasks using prototype A and then prototype B, and you are measuring variables such as self-reported ease of use and time, you will use a paired samples *t*-test.

With paired samples like this, the key is that you're comparing each person to themselves. Technically, you're looking at the difference in each person's data for the two conditions you're comparing. Let's consider the data shown in Fig. 2.4, which shows the "Ease of Use" ratings for an application after its initial use and then again at the end of the session. So there were 10 participants who gave two ratings each. The means and 90% confidence intervals are shown in the graph. Notice that the confidence intervals overlap pretty widely. If these were independent samples, you could conclude that the ratings are not significantly different from each other. However, since these are paired samples, we've done a *t*-test on paired samples (with the "Type" as "1"). That result, 0.0002, shows that the difference is significant.

Let's look at the data in Fig. 2.4 in a slightly different way, as shown in Fig. 2.5. This time we've simply added a third column to the data in which the initial rating was subtracted from the final rating for each participant. Notice that for 8 of the 10 participants, the rating increased by one point while for 2 participants it stayed the same. The bar graph shows the mean of those differences (0.8) as well as the confidence interval for that mean difference. In a paired-samples test like this, you're basically testing to see if the confidence interval for the mean difference includes 0 or not. If not, the difference is significant.

Notice that in a paired samples test, you should have an equal number of values in each of the two sets of numbers that you're comparing (although it is possible to have missing data). In the case of independent samples, the number

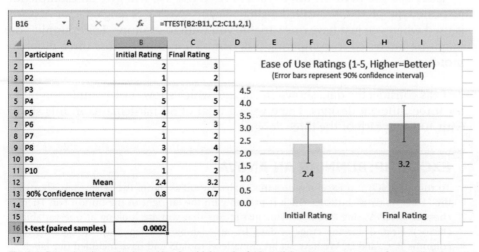

Fig. 2.4 Data showing paired samples, in which each of 10 participants gave an ease-of-use rating (on a 1 to 5 scale) to an application after an initial task and at the end of the study.

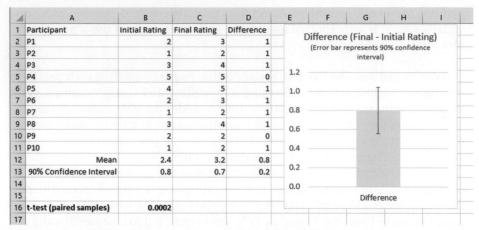

	A	B	C	D	E	F	G	H	I
1	Participant	Initial Rating	Final Rating	Difference					
2	P1	2	3	1					
3	P2	1	2	1					
4	P3	3	4	1					
5	P4	5	5	0					
6	P5	4	5	1					
7	P6	2	3	1					
8	P7	1	2	1					
9	P8	3	4	1					
10	P9	2	2	0					
11	P10	1	2	1					
12	Mean	2.4	3.2	0.8					
13	90% Confidence Interval	0.8	0.7	0.2					
14									
15									
16	t-test (paired samples)	0.0002							
17									

Fig. 2.5 The same data as in Fig. 2.4, but also showing the difference between the initial and final ratings, the mean of those differences, and the 90% confidence interval.

of values does not need to be equal. You might happen to have more participants in one group than the other.

2.4.3 Comparing More Than Two Samples

We don't always compare only two samples. Sometimes we want to compare three, four, or even six different samples. Fortunately, there is a way to do this without a lot of pain. An analysis of variance (commonly referred to as an ANOVA) lets you determine whether there is a significant difference across more than two groups.

Excel lets you perform three types of ANOVAs. We will give an example for just one type of ANOVA, called a single-factor ANOVA. A single-factor ANOVA is used when you just have one variable you want to examine. For example, you might be interested in comparing task completion times across three different prototypes.

Let's consider the data shown in Fig. 2.6, which shows task completion times for three different designs. There were a total of 30 participants in this study, with 10 using each of the three designs.

EXCEL TIP: RUNNING AN ANOVA

To run an ANOVA in Excel requires the Analysis ToolPak. From the "Data" tab, choose the "Data Analysis" button, which is probably on the far right of the button bar. Then choose "ANOVA: Single Factor." This just means that you are looking at one variable (factor). Next, define the range of data. In our example (see Fig. 2.6), the data are in columns B, C, and D. We have set an alpha level to 0.05 and have included our labels in the first row.

	A	B	C	D	E	F	G	H	I	J	K	L
		Design 1	Design 2	Design 3								
1		1	2	3		Anova: Single Factor						
2		34	49	22								
3		33	54	28		SUMMARY						
4		28	52	21		*Groups*	*Count*	*Sum*	*Average*	*Variance*		
5		44	39	30		Design 1	10	335	33.5	43.2		
6		21	60	32		Design 2	10	490	49.0	63.3		
7		40	58	36		Design 3	10	302	30.2	38.6		
8		36	49	27								
9		29	34	40								
10		32	46	37		ANOVA						
11		38	49	29		*Source of Variation*	*SS*	*df*	*MS*	*F*	*P-value*	*F crit*
12	Mean:	33.5	49.0	30.2		Between Groups	2015.3	2	1007.6	20.8	0.000003	3.4
13	90% Confidence Interval:	3.8	4.6	3.6		Within Groups	1306.1	27	48.4			
14												
15						Total	3321.4	29				
16												

Fig. 2.6 Task completion times for three different designs (used by different participants) and the results of a single-factor analysis of variance (ANOVA).

The results are shown in two parts on the right-hand portion of Fig. 2.6. The top part is a summary of the data. As you can see, the average time for Design 2 is quite a bit longer, and the times for Designs 1 and 3 are less. Also, the variance is greater for Design 2 and less for Designs 1 and 3. The second part of the output lets us know whether this difference is significant. The p-value of 0.000003 reflects the statistical significance of this result. Understanding exactly what this means is important: It means that there is a significant effect of the "designs" variable. It does not necessarily mean that each of the design means is significantly different from each of the others—only that there *is* an effect overall. To see if any two means are significantly different from each other, you could do a two-sample *t*-test on just those two sets of values. That would be important if you were making a presentation to a design team and wanted to know if the Design 2 mean was significantly slower than each of the other two designs.

2.5 RELATIONSHIPS BETWEEN VARIABLES

Sometimes it's important to know about the relationship between different variables. We've seen many cases where someone observing a usability test for the first time remarks that what users say and what they do don't always correspond with each other. Many users will struggle to complete just a few tasks with a prototype, but when asked to rate how easy or difficult it was, they often give it good ratings. In this section we provide examples of how to perform analyses that investigate these kinds of relationships (or lack thereof).

2.5.1 Correlations

When you first begin examining the relationship between two variables, it helps to start by visualizing what the data look like. That's easy to do in Excel using a scatterplot. Fig. 2.7 is an example of a scatterplot of actual data from

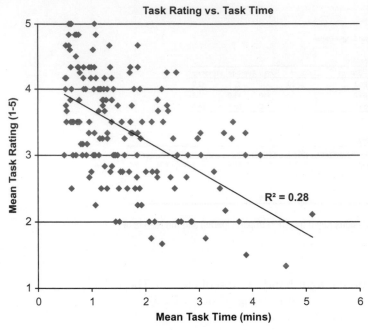

Fig. 2.7 An example of a scatterplot (with trend line) in Excel.

an online user experience study. The horizontal axis shows mean task time in minutes and the vertical axis shows mean task rating (1 to 5, with higher numbers being better). Notice that as the mean task time increases, the average task rating drops. This is called a negative relationship because as one variable increases (task time), the other variable decreases (task rating). The line that runs through the data is called a trend line and is easily added to the chart in Excel by right-clicking on any one of the data points and selecting "Add Trend Line." The trend line helps you to better visualize the relationship between the two variables. You can also have Excel display the R^2 value (a measure of the strength of the relationship) by right-clicking on the trend line, choosing "Format Trend Line," and checking the box next to "Display R-squared value on chart."

EXCEL TIP: CALCULATING CORRELATIONS

You can calculate the strength of the relationship between any two variables (like task time and task rating) using the CORREL function in Excel:

$$= CORREL \text{ (Array 1, Array 2)}$$

Array 1 and Array 2 are the two sets of numbers to be correlated. The result will be a correlation coefficient, or "r." For the data represented in Fig. 2.7, $r = -0.53$. A correlation coefficient is a measure of the strength of the relationship between the two variables and has a range from -1 to $+1$. The stronger the relationship, the closer the value is to -1 or $+1$. The weaker the relationship, the closer the correlation coefficient is to 0. The negative value for "r" signifies the negative relationship between the two variables. If you square the correlation coefficient you get the same value as the R^2 value shown on the scatterplot (0.28).

2.6 NON-PARAMETRIC TESTS

Non-parametric tests are used for analyzing nominal and ordinal data. For example, you might want to know if there is a significant difference between customers and prospects for success and failure on a particular task. Or perhaps you're interested in determining whether there is a difference between experts, intermediates, and novices on how they ranked different websites. To answer questions that involve nominal and ordinal data, you will need to use some type of non-parametric test.

Non-parametric statistics make different assumptions about the data than the statistics we've reviewed for comparing means and describing relationships between variables. For instance, when we run *t*-tests and correlation analysis, we assume that data are normally distributed and the variances are approximately equal. The distribution is not normal for nominal or ordinal data. Therefore, we don't make the same assumptions about the data in non-parametric tests. For example, in the case of (binary) success, when there are only two possibilities, the data are based on the binomial distribution. Some people like to refer to non-parametric tests as "distribution-free" tests. There are a few different types of non-parametric tests, but we will just cover the chi-square test because it is probably the most commonly used. Other non-parametric tests such as the Wilcoxon Signed Rank, Mann-Whitney, or Kruskal-Wallis test for comparing medians. See Hollander et al. (2013) for an extensive review of non-parametric tests.

2.6.1 The Chi-Square Test

The chi-square test is used when you want to compare nominal (or categorical) data. Let's consider an example. Assume you're interested in knowing whether there is a significant difference in task success with a financial application between three different groups: novice, intermediate, and expert Excel users. You run a total of 60 people in your study, 20 in each group. You measure task success or failure on a single task. You count the number of people who were successful in each group. For the novices, only 6 out of 20 were successful, 12 out of 20 intermediates were successful, and 18 out of 20 experts were successful. You want to know if there is a statistically significant difference between the groups—that is, does success with the financial application task increase with Excel experience?

EXCEL TIP: CHI-SQUARE TESTS

To perform a chi-square test in Excel, you use the "CHITEST" function. This function calculates whether the differences between the observed and expected values are simply due to chance. The function is relatively easy is to use:

$$= CHITEST\ (actual\_range,\ expected\_range)$$

The actual range is the number of people who were successful on the task for each group. The expected range is the total number of people successful (33) divided by the number of groups (3), or 11 in this example. The expected value is what you would expect if there were no differences between any of the three groups.

Fig. 2.8 shows what the data look like and the output from the CHITEST function. In this example, the likelihood that this distribution is due to chance is about 2.9% (0.028856). Because this number is less than 0.05 (95% confidence),

C7		f_x	=CHITEST(B2:B4,C2:C4)	
	A	B	C	D
1	Group	Observed	Expected	
2	Novice	6	11	
3	Intermediate	9	11	
4	Experts	18	11	
5	Total	33	33	
6				
7		Chi Test	0.029	
8				

Fig. 2.8 Output from a chi-square test in Excel.

C13		f_x	=CHITEST(B3:C5,B9:C11)		
	A	B	C	D	E
1		*Observed*	*Observed*		
2	Group	Design A	Design B		
3	Novice	4	2		
4	Intermediate	6	3		
5	Expert	12	6		
6					
7		*Expected*	*Expected*		
8	Group	Design A	Design B		
9	Novice	5.5	5.5		
10	Intermediate	5.5	5.5		
11	Expert	5.5	5.5		
12					
13		Chi Test	0.003		
14					

Fig. 2.9 Output from a chi-square test with two variables.

we can reasonably say that there is a difference in success rates between the three groups.

In this example we were just examining the distribution of success rates across a single variable (Excel experience). There are some situations in which you might want to examine more than one variable, such as experience group and design prototype. Performing this type of evaluation works the same way. Fig. 2.9 shows data based on two different variables: group and design. For a more detailed example of using the chi-square to test for differences in live website data for two alternative pages (so-called A/B tests), see Chapter 10.

2.7 PRESENTING YOUR DATA GRAPHICALLY

You might have collected and analyzed the best set of user experience data ever, but it's of little value if you can't communicate it effectively to others. Data tables are certainly useful in some situations, but in most cases you'll want to present your data graphically. A number of excellent books on the design of effective data graphs are available, including those written by Edward Tufte (1990, 1997, 2001, 2006), Stephen Few (2006, 2009, 2012), and Dona Wong (2010). Our intent in this section is simply to introduce some of the most important principles in the design of data graphs, particularly as they relate to user experience data.

We've organized this section around tips and techniques for five basic types of data graphs:

- Column or bar graphs
- Line graphs
- Scatterplots
- Pie and donut charts
- Stacked bar graphs

We will begin each of the following sections with one good example and one bad example of that particular type of data graph.

GENERAL TIPS FOR DATA GRAPHS

Label the axes and units. It might be obvious to you that a scale of 0%–100% represents the task completion rate, but it may not be obvious to your audience. Or you might know that the times being plotted on a graph are minutes, but your audience may be left pondering whether they could be seconds or even hours. And make the labels descriptive and helpful to the viewer. For example, if the bars on a graph represent tasks, it's probably more useful to label them "Login," "Checkout," etc., rather than "Task 1," "Task 2," etc.

Don't imply more precision in your data than it deserves. Labeling your time data with "0.00" seconds to "30.00" seconds is almost never appropriate, nor is labeling your task completion data with "0.0%" to "100.0%." Whole numbers work best in most cases. Exceptions include some metrics with a very limited range and some statistics that are almost always fractional (e.g., correlation coefficients).

Don't use color alone to convey information. Of course, this is a good general principle for the design of any information display, but it's worth repeating. Color is commonly used in data graphs, but make sure it's supplemented by positional information, labels, or other cues that help someone who can't clearly distinguish colors to interpret the graph.

Show confidence intervals whenever possible. This mainly applies to bar graphs and line graphs that are presenting means of individual participant data (times, ratings, etc.). Showing the 95 or 90% confidence intervals for the means via error bars is a good way to visually represent the variability in the data.

Don't overload your graphs. Just because you *can* create a single graph that shows the task completion rate, error rate, task times, and subjective ratings for each of 20 tasks, broken down by novice versus experienced users, doesn't mean you *should*.

Avoid 3D graphs. If you're tempted to use a 3D graph, ask yourself whether it really helps. In many cases, the use of 3D makes it harder to see the values being plotted.

2.7.1 Column or Bar Graphs

Fig. 2.10 shows two column or bar graphs. Column graphs and bar graphs are the same thing; the only difference is their orientation. Technically, column graphs are vertical and bar graphs are horizontal. In practice, most people refer to both types simply as bar graphs, which is what we will do.

Bar graphs are probably the most common way of displaying user experience data. Almost every presentation of data from a usability test that we've seen has included at least one bar graph, whether it was for task completion rates, task times, self-reported data, or something else. The following are some of the principles for using bar graphs:

- Bar graphs are appropriate when you want to present the values of continuous data (e.g., times, percentages, etc.) for discrete items or categories (e.g., tasks, participants, designs, etc.). If both variables are continuous, a line graph is appropriate.

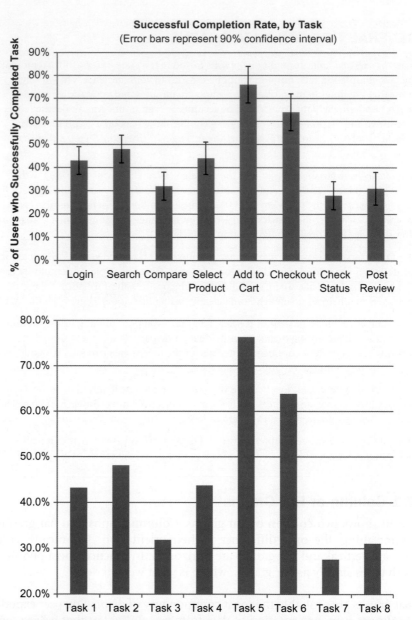

Fig. 2.10 Good *(top)* and bad *(bottom)* examples of bar graphs for the same data. The mistakes in the bad version include failing to label the data, not starting the vertical axis at 0, not showing confidence intervals when you can, and showing too much precision in the vertical axis labels.

- The axis for the continuous variable (the vertical axis in Fig. 2.10) should normally start at 0. The whole idea behind bar graphs is that the lengths of the bars represent the values being plotted. By not starting the axis at 0, you're artificially manipulating their lengths. The bad example in Fig. 2.10 gives the impression that there's a larger difference between the tasks than there really is. A possible exception is when you include error bars, making it clear which differences are real and which are not.

- Don't let the axis for the continuous variable go any higher than the maximum value that's theoretically possible. For example, if you're plotting percentages of users who successfully completed each task, the theoretical maximum is 100%. If some values are close to that maximum, Excel and other packages will tend to automatically increase the scale beyond the maximum, especially if error bars are shown.

2.7.2 Line Graphs

Line graphs (Fig. 2.11) are most commonly used to show trends in continuous variables, often over time. Although not as common as bar graphs in presenting user experience data, they certainly have their place. The following are some of the key principles for using line graphs:

- Line graphs are appropriate when you want to present the values of one continuous variable (e.g., percent correct, number of errors, etc.) as a function of another continuous variable (e.g., age, trial, etc.). If one of the variables is discrete (e.g., gender, participant, task, etc.), then a bar graph is more appropriate.

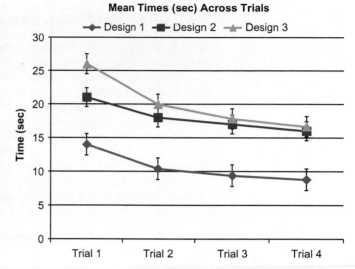

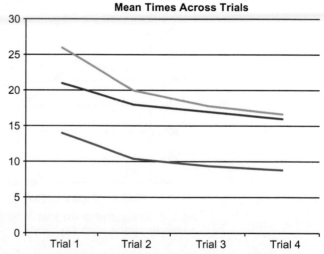

Fig. 2.11 Good *(top)* and bad *(bottom)* examples of line graphs for the same data. The mistakes in the bad version include failing to label the vertical axis, not showing the data points, not including a legend, and not showing confidence intervals.

- Show your data points. Your actual data points are the things that really matter, not the lines. The lines are just there to connect the data points and make the trends more obvious. You may need to increase the default size of the data points in Excel.
- Use lines that have sufficient weight to be clear. Very thin lines are not only hard to see, but it's harder to detect their color and they may imply a greater precision in the data than is appropriate. You may need to increase the default weight of lines in Excel.

LINE GRAPHS VERSUS BAR GRAPHS

Some people have a hard time deciding whether it's appropriate to use a line graph or a bar graph to display a set of data. Perhaps the most common data-graph mistake we see is using a line graph when a bar graph is more appropriate. If you're considering presenting some data with a line graph, ask yourself a simple question: Do the places along the line *between* the data points make sense? In other words, even though you don't have data for those locations, would they make sense if you did? If they don't make sense, a bar graph is more appropriate. For example, it's technically possible to show the data in Fig. 2.11 as a line graph, as shown in Fig. 2.12. However, you should ask yourself whether things like "Task 1½" or "Task 6¾" make any sense, because the lines imply that they should. Obviously, they don't, so a bar graph is the correct representation. The line graph might make an interesting picture, but it's a misleading picture.

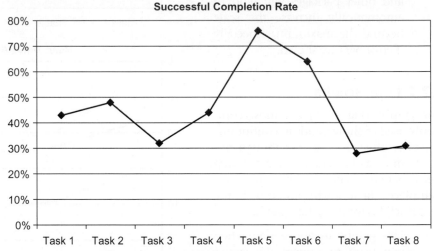

Fig. 2.12 An inappropriate line graph of the data shown in Fig. 2.11. The lines imply that the tasks are a continuous variable, which they are not.

- Include a legend if you have more than one line. In some cases, it may be clearer to manually move the labels from the legend into the body of the graph and put each label beside its appropriate line. It may be necessary to do this in PowerPoint or some other drawing program.
- As with bar graphs, the vertical axis normally starts at 0, but it's not as important with a line graph to always do that. There are no bars whose length is important, so sometimes it may be appropriate to start the vertical axis at a higher value. In that case, you should mark the vertical axis appropriately.

2.7.3 Scatterplots

Scatterplots (Fig. 2.13), or X/Y plots, show pairs of values. Although they're not very common in usability reports, they can be very useful in certain situations, especially to illustrate relationships between two variables. Here are some of the key principles for using scatterplots:

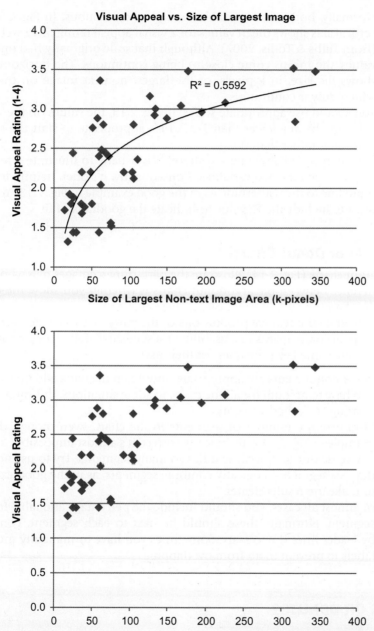

Fig. 2.13 Good and bad examples of scatterplots for the same data. The mistakes in the bad version include an inappropriate scale for the vertical axis, not showing the scale for the visual appeal ratings (1 to 4), not showing a trend line, and not showing the goodness of fit (R^2).

- You must have paired values that you want to plot. A classic example is heights and weights of a group of people. Each person would appear as a data point, and the two axes would be height and weight.

- Normally, both of the variables would be continuous. In Fig. 2.13, the vertical axis shows mean values for a visual appeal rating of 42 web pages (from Tullis & Tullis, 2007). Although that scale originally had only four values, the means come close to being continuous. The horizontal axis shows the size, in k pixels, of the largest nontext image on the page, which truly is continuous.
- You should use appropriate scales. In Fig. 2.13, the values on the vertical axis can't be any lower than 1.0, so it's appropriate to start the scale at that point rather than 0.
- Your purpose in showing a scatterplot is usually to illustrate a relationship between the two variables. Consequently, it's often helpful to add a trend line to the scatterplot, as in the good example in Fig. 2.13. You may want to include the R^2 value to indicate the goodness of fit.

2.7.4 Pie or Donut Charts

Pie or donut charts (Fig. 2.14) illustrate the parts or percentages of a whole. The only difference between pie and donut charts is whether you show the central part of the chart (i.e., the "donut hole"). These charts can be useful any time you want to illustrate the relative proportions of the parts of a whole to each other (e.g., how many participants in a usability test succeeded, failed, or gave up on a task). Here are some key principles for their use:

- Pie or donut charts are appropriate only when the parts add up to 100%. You have to account for all the cases. In some situations, this might mean creating an "other" category.
- Minimize the number of segments in the chart. Even though the bad example in Fig. 2.14 is technically correct, it's almost impossible to make any sense out of it because it has so many segments. Try to use no more than six segments. Logically combine segments, as in the good example, to make the results clearer.
- In almost all cases, you should include the percentage and label for each segment. Normally these should be next to each segment, connected by leader lines if necessary. Sometimes you have to manually move the labels to prevent them from overlapping.

PIES OR DONUTS?

Should you use a pie or donut chart when this type of chart is appropriate? Some data we've recently collected but not yet published suggest that donut charts might be slightly more effective than pie charts. We think it has to do with where the viewer tends to focus in the two kinds of charts. In a pie chart, the viewer's eye is drawn toward the center of the pie, but in a donut chart the eye is drawn more toward the periphery. And it's easier to make judgments about relative sizes from the periphery than the center.

% of Pages With Accessibility Errors

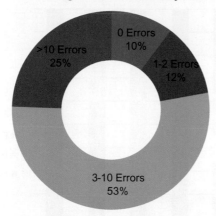

% of Pages With Accessibility Errors

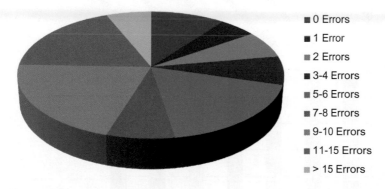

Fig. 2.14 Good and bad examples of pie charts for the same data. The mistakes in the bad version include too many segments, poor placement of the legend, not showing percentages for each segment, and using 3-D, for which the creator of this pie chart should be pummeled with a wet noodle.

2.7.5 Stacked Bar Graphs

Stacked bar graphs (Fig. 2.15) are basically multiple pie charts shown in bar form. They're appropriate whenever you have a series of datasets, each of which represents parts of the whole. Their most common use in user experience data is to show different task completion states for each task. Here are some key principles for their use:

- Like pie charts, stacked bar graphs are only appropriate when the parts for each item in the series add up to 100%.

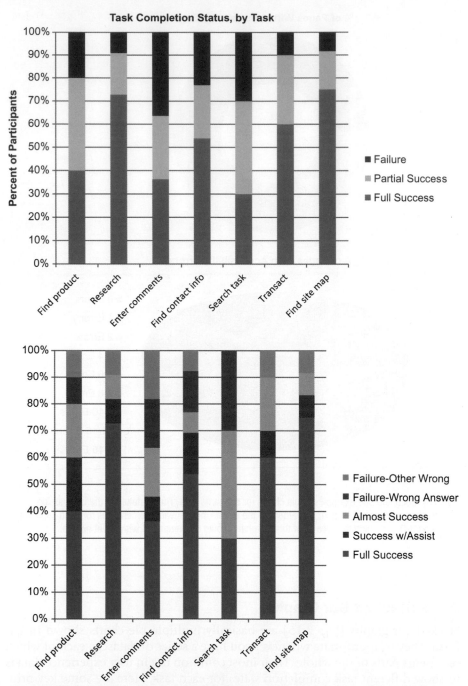

Fig. 2.15 Good and bad examples of stacked bar graphs for the same data. The mistakes in the bad version include too many segments, poor color coding, and failing to label the vertical axis.

- The items in the series are normally categorical (e.g., tasks, participants, etc.).
- Minimize the number of segments in each bar. More than three segments per bar can make it difficult to interpret. Combine segments as appropriate.
- When possible, make use of color-coding conventions that your audience is likely to be familiar with. For many U.S. audiences, green is good, yellow is marginal, and red is bad. Playing off of these conventions can be helpful, as in the good example in Fig. 2.15, but don't rely solely on them.
- Use meaningful labels. The reader can easily tell the nature of the tasks that participants were attempting. For example, there is clearly a problem with the design of the search function.

2.8 SUMMARY

In a nutshell, this chapter is about knowing your data. The better you know your data, the more likely you are to clearly answer your research questions. The following are some of the key takeaways from this chapter:

1. Knowing your data is critical when analyzing your results. The specific type of data you have will dictate what statistics you can (and can't) perform.
2. Nominal data are categorical, such as binary task success or males and females. Nominal data are usually expressed as frequencies or percentages. Chi-square tests can be used when you want to learn whether the frequency distribution is random or there is some underlying significance to the distribution pattern.
3. Ordinal data are rank orders, such as a severity ranking of usability issues. Ordinal data are also analyzed using frequencies, and the distribution patterns can be analyzed with a chi-square test.
4. Interval data are continuous data where the intervals between each point are meaningful but without a natural zero. The SUS score is one example. Interval data can be described by means, standard deviations, and confidence intervals. Means can be compared to each other for the same set of users (paired samples t-test) or across different users (independent samples t-test). ANOVA can be used to compare more than two sets of data. Relationships between variables can be examined through correlations.
5. Ratio data are the same as interval but with a natural zero. One example is completion times. Essentially, the same statistics that apply to interval data also apply to ratio data.
6. Any time you can calculate a mean, you can also calculate a confidence interval for that mean. Displaying confidence intervals on graphs of means helps the viewer to understand the accuracy of the data and to quickly see any differences between means.

7. Use graphs to communicate your data. Take advantage of the flexibility that tools like Excel have to create meaningful and clear labels for graphs, axes, and categories. Don't overload graphs and be careful when using 3-D.

8. When presenting your data graphically, use the appropriate types of graphs. Use bar graphs for categorical data and line graphs for continuous data. Use pie charts or stacked bar graphs when the data sum to 100%.

CHAPTER 3
Planning

CONTENTS

Measuring the User Experience. DOI: http://dx.doi.org/10.1016/B978-0-12-818080-8.00003-0

Preparation is the key to any successful user experience study. If nothing else, we hope this chapter convinces you to plan ahead, particularly where data collection is involved.

When planning any UX research study, a few high-level questions should be answered. First, you need to understand the goals of the study. For example, are you trying to ensure optimal user experience for a new piece of functionality, or are you benchmarking the user experience for an existing product? Are you trying to identify the most significant usability issues or measure preferences around the design? Next, you need to understand the goals of the users. Are users looking to simply complete a task and then stop using the product, or will they use the product many times on a daily basis? What are the business goals that are specific to desired user behavior? Are the business sponsors focused on the adoption of a new technology, increasing user engagement, or decreasing drop-off rates for a key transaction? Knowing the study goals, UX goals, and business goals will lead toward choosing the right metrics.

Many practical details come into play as well. For example, you must decide on the most appropriate evaluation method, how many participants are enough to get reliable feedback, how collecting metrics will impact the timeline and budget, what the best tool is to collect the data, and how the data will be analyzed. By answering these questions, you will be well prepared to carry out any UX research study involving metrics. In the end, you will likely save time and money and have a greater impact on the product.

3.1 STUDY GOALS

The first decision to make when planning a study is how the data will ultimately be used within the product development life cycle. There are essentially two ways to use UX data: formative and summative.

3.1.1 Formative User Research

When running a formative study, a UX researcher is much like a chef who periodically checks a dish while it's being prepared and makes adjustments to positively impact the end result. The chef might add a little salt, then a few more spices, and finally a dash of chili pepper right before serving. The chef is periodically evaluating, adjusting, and reevaluating. The same is true in formative user research. A UX researcher, like a chef, periodically evaluates a product or design while it is being created, identifies pain points, makes recommendations, and then repeats the process, until, ideally, the product comes out as close to perfect as possible.

What distinguishes formative user research is the iterative nature of the evaluation, when it occurs, and the sample size. The goal is to make improvements in the design prior to release. This means identifying or diagnosing the problems, making and implementing recommendations, and then evaluating again.

Formative user research is generally done before the design has been finalized. In fact, the earlier the formative evaluation, the more impact the evaluations will have on the design. Most formative user research involves small sample sizes, typically in the range of 8 to 12 participants. This small sample size is when the researcher's goal is to identify problems. However, if the researcher aims to measure preferences, a much larger sample size is required, typically in the range of at least a few hundred.

Here are a few key questions you will be able to answer with a formative approach:

- What are the most significant issues that are preventing users from accomplishing their goals or that are resulting in inefficiencies?
- What aspects of the product work well for the users? What do users' find most frustrating?
- What are the most common errors or mistakes users are making?
- Are improvements being made from one design iteration to the next?
- What UX issues can you expect to remain after the product is launched?

The most appropriate situation to run a formative usability study is when an obvious opportunity to improve the design presents itself. Ideally, the design process allows for multiple evaluations. If there's no opportunity to impact the design, then running a formative test is probably not a good use of time or money. Generally, though, selling the value of formative usability shouldn't be a problem. Most people will see the importance of it. The biggest obstacles tend to be a limited budget or time rather than a failure to see the value.

3.1.2 Summative User Research

Continuing with our cooking metaphor, summative user research is about evaluating the dish after it comes out of the oven. The UX specialist running a summative user research study is like a food critic who evaluates a few sample dishes at a restaurant or perhaps compares the same meal in multiple restaurants. The goal of summative research is to evaluate how well a product or piece of functionality meets its objectives. Summative research can also be about comparing several products to each other. Although formative research focuses on identifying ways of making improvements, summative testing focuses on evaluating against a set of criteria. Summative evaluations answer these questions:

- Did we meet the UX goals of the project?
- What is the overall UX of our product?
- How does our product compare against the competition?
- Have we made improvements from one product release to the next?

Running a successful summative usability test should always involve some follow-up activities. Just seeing the metrics is usually not enough for most organizations. Potential outcomes of a summative study might be securing funding to enhance functionality on your product, launching a new project to address some outstanding issues, or even benchmarking changes to the user experience against which senior managers will be evaluated. We recommend that follow-up actions be planned along with any summative user research study.

FORMATIVE AND SUMMATIVE USABILITY TESTING

The terms *formative* and *summative* were borrowed from the classroom environment, where formative assessment is done on an ongoing basis by a teacher every day in the classroom (think informal observation and "pop quizzes") while summative assessment is done at the end of some significant period of time (think "final exams"). The earliest application of these terms to usability testing appears to be in a paper presented by Tom Hewett at a conference at the University of York in the UK (Hewett, 1986). This was also when one of us (Tullis) first met Tom Hewett, mainly because we were the only two Americans at the conference! We've been friends ever since.

3.2 UX GOALS

When planning a user research study, you need to understand the users and what they are trying to accomplish. For example, are users required to use the product every day as part of their job? Are they likely to use the product only once or just a few times? Are they using it frequently as a source of entertainment? It's critical to understand what matters to the user. Does the user simply want to complete a task, or is their efficiency the primary driver? Do users care at all about the design aesthetics of the product? All these questions boil down to measuring three critical aspects of the user experience: performance, preferences, and emotions.

3.2.1 User Performance

Performance is all about what the user actually does in interacting with the product. It includes measuring the degree to which users can successfully accomplish a task or set of tasks. Many measures related to the performance of these tasks are also important, including the time it takes to perform each task, the amount of effort to perform each (such as the number of mouse clicks or amount of cognitive effort), the number of errors committed, and the amount of time it takes to become proficient in performing the tasks (learnability). Performance measures are critical for many different types of products and applications, especially those where the user doesn't really have much choice in how they are used (such as a company's internal applications). If users can't successfully perform key tasks when using a product, it's likely to fail. Chapter 4 reviews different types of performance measures.

3.2.2 User Preferences

There is no inherent good or bad or right and wrong when it comes to user preferences. Users may have strong preferences on various aspects of the user experience, such as the aesthetics or visual appeal, usefulness of various functions, or the perceived value of the system. For example, one user might strongly prefer an information-rich system, while a different user has a clear preference for a much more streamlined design. Neither is right or wrong, but rather has a preference on which type of system will be most useful to them. Measuring user preferences is a critical element in designing the best user experiences. While reliably identifying usability issues can be achieved through a small sample size (see Chapter 6), user preferences require a larger sample size. Therefore, when the goal is to measure user preferences, special consideration must be given to the data collection strategy that will easily produce a larger sample size. Chapter 5 reviews various ways to measure user preferences.

3.2.3 User Emotions

It is no longer good enough to design products that are easy and efficient to use. Now, products and services also need to deliver better emotional outcomes to maintain a competitive advantage. User emotions can vary widely depending on the specific product or service, and its context of use. Some products and services aim to build a greater sense of trust and confidence with the user, while other products and services focus on increasing engagement. Some products and services want to build more positive feelings to align with their brand strategy. Depending on the UX goal, there are different UX metrics and data collection techniques. Chapter 8 reviews the latest technologies and metrics to measure various aspects of the emotional user experience.

DO PERFORMANCE AND SATISFACTION CORRELATE?

Perhaps surprisingly, performance and satisfaction don't always go hand-in-hand. We've seen many instances of a user struggling to perform key tasks with an application and then giving it glowing satisfaction ratings. Conversely, we've seen users give poor satisfaction ratings to an application that worked perfectly. So it's important that you look at both performance and satisfaction metrics to get an accurate overall picture of the user experience. We were curious about the correlations we've seen between two measures of performance (task success and task time) and one measure of satisfaction (task ease rating). We looked at the data from 10 online usability studies we've run. The number of participants in each of these studies ranged from 117 to 1036. The correlations between task time and task rating were mostly negative, as you would expect (the longer it takes, the less satisfied you are), but ranged from −0.41 to +0.06. The correlations between task success and task rating were at least all positive, ranging from 0.21 to 0.65. Together, these results suggest that there is a relationship between performance and satisfaction, but not always.

3.3 BUSINESS GOALS

Not only do you need to consider the goals of the study and the user, but you also need to keep in mind the business goals. After all, the business stakeholders are likely sponsoring your study. One of the best places to begin to understand the business goals is to conduct stakeholder interviews where you can gain clarity on what they really care about. The foundation of any interview and especially a stakeholder interview is listening. When you ask about their goals, pay special attention to what they mention first, and where they are most concerned. What keeps them up at night? How is their performance measured, and how does the user experience play a role in their individual or team goals? A stakeholder interview is not just listening, but translating what they care about into your research plan so you are able to capture the data that will provide answers to their questions or address their concerns.

At a more granular level, measuring the user experience should take into account specific elements that are directly tied to achieving business goals. For example, an organization might be trying to increase sales of a specific product or decreasing support costs associated with an important piece of functionality. The UX metrics plan will need to understand how each aspect of the user experience correlates with a specific business goal. By understanding this relationship, the UX researcher will be able to not only prioritize UX metrics but interpret and present them in a way that clearly resonates with the business sponsors.

AGILE DEVELOPMENT AND UX METRICS

One of the core principles of the agile software development process (http://agilemanifesto.org/principles.html) is a focus on customer satisfaction through great design. Luckily, this aligns perfectly with what we do as user experience professionals. However, in practice, it is not so pretty. Many of us who have been a part of an agile development process know that user research is often minimized, or simply cut out of the process altogether. The typical response has something to do with compressed schedules with a focus on product delivery.

So, how can UX "squeeze" into the agile development process while not slowing down the process? The good news is that there are a few simple user research techniques and metrics that can be used which are more "agile friendly." One obvious approach is to recurring 1-day usability tests every 2 to 3 weeks. Capturing both qualitative and quantitative user data on a frequent basis will help the team course correct their design and tell you something about how well the product is achieving is performing in terms of usability. Along these lines, we have also utilized lightweight online surveys to focus on a few key questions such as ranking usefulness for various features, terminology, or design treatments. These surveys can be designed and launched usually within 1 day. With limited analysis answers to key research questions can easily be turned around in less than 2 days. Having easy access to a panel of participants is very helpful in this case. Lastly, negotiate for several "partial-summative" evaluations after every four to six design sprints, or whenever there is enough to evaluate a handful of key use cases. This would provide extremely helpful UX metrics that can be used as part of the design process moving forward, prior to product release. Bottom line—whatever you find works with agile, take advantage of it. Don't let a compressed development schedule discourage you from conducting at least some type of user research. Check out Babich (2018) to learn more about UX and the agile process.

3.4 CHOOSING THE RIGHT UX METRICS

Some of the issues you should consider when choosing UX metrics include the goals of the study and the user, the technology that is available to collect the data, and the budget and time you have to turn around your findings. Because every user study has unique qualities, we can't prescribe the exact metrics to use for every type of user study. Instead, we've identified 10 prototypical categories of user research studies and developed recommendations about metrics for each. The recommendations we offer are simply suggestions that you should consider when running a user research study with a similar set of characteristics. Conversely, metrics that may be essential to your study may not be on the list. Also, we strongly recommend that you explore your raw data and develop new metrics that are meaningful to your project goals. Ten common scenarios are listed in Table 3.1. The metrics that are commonly used or are appropriate for each of the scenarios are indicated. The following sections discuss each of the 10 scenarios.

3.4.1 Completing an eCommerce Transaction

Many UX research studies are aimed at making transactions run as smoothly as possible. These might take the form of a user completing a purchase, registering a new piece of software, or resetting a password. A transaction usually has a well-defined beginning and end. For example, on an e-commerce website or mobile app, a transaction may start when a user places something in his shopping cart and ends when he has completed the purchase on the confirmation screen.

Perhaps the first metric that you will want to examine is task success. Each task is scored as a success or failure. Obviously, the tasks need to have a clear end-state, such as reaching a confirmation that the transaction was successful.

Reporting the percentage of participants who were successful is an excellent measure of the overall effectiveness of the transaction. If the transaction involves a website or mobile app, analytics such drop-off rate from the transaction can be very useful. By knowing where users are dropping off, you will be able to focus your attention on the most problematic steps in the transaction.

Calculating issue severity can help narrow down the cause of specific usability problems with a transaction. By assigning a severity to each usability issue, you will be able to focus on the high-priority problems with any transaction. Two types of self-reported metrics are also very useful: likelihood to return and user expectations. In cases where users have a choice of where to perform their transactions, it's important to know what they thought of their experience. One of the best ways to learn this is by asking participants whether they would use the same product again and whether the product met or exceeded their expectations. Efficiency is an appropriate metric when a user has to complete the same transaction many times. Efficiency is often measured as task completion per unit of time.

UX Study Goal	Task Success	Task Time	Errors	Efficiency Metrics	Learnability	Issues-based Metrics	Self-reported Metrics	Eye Tracking and Biometrics	Combined and Comparative Metrics	Live Website Metrics	Card Sorting/Tree Testing
Completing a transaction	X	X		X		X	X			X	
Comparing products	X	X		X			X		X		
Evaluating frequent use of the same product	X			X	X		X				
Evaluating navigation and/or information architecture	X		X	X							X
Increasing awareness							X	X		X	
Problem discovery						X	X				
Maximizing usability for a critical product	X		X	X							
Designing a highly engaging user experience							X	X			
Evaluating the impact of subtle design changes										X	
Comparing alternative designs	X	X				X	X		X		

Table 3.1 Ten common UX study goals and the metrics that may be most appropriate for each.

3.4.2 Comparing Products

It is always useful to know how your product compares to the competition or to previous releases. By making comparisons, you can determine your product's strengths and weaknesses and whether improvements have been made from one release to another. The best way to compare different products or releases is through the use of various UX metrics. The type of metrics you choose should be based on the product itself. Some products aim to maximize efficiency, whereas others try to create an exceptional user experience.

For most types of products, we recommend three general classes of metrics to get an overall sense of the user experience. First, we recommend looking at some task success measures. Being able to complete a task correctly is essential for most products. It's also important to pay attention to efficiency. Efficiency might be task completion time, number of page views (in the case of some websites), or number of action steps taken. By looking at efficiency, you will get a good sense of how much effort is required to use the product. Some self-reported metrics focused on overall satisfaction, and specific emotions provide a good summary of the user's overall experience. Satisfaction and emotion measures make the most sense with products where people have choices. Finally, one of the best ways to compare the user experience across products is by combined and comparative metrics. This will give an excellent big picture of how the products compare from a UX perspective.

3.4.3 Evaluating Frequent Use of the Same Product

Many products are intended to be used on a frequent or semi-frequent basis. Examples might include microwave ovens, mobile phones, web applications used as part of your job, and even the software program we used to write this book. These products need to be both easy to use and highly efficient. The amount of effort required to send a text message or download an application needs to be kept to a minimum. Most of us have very little time or patience for products that are difficult and inefficient to use.

The first metric we would recommend is task time. Measuring the amount of time required to complete a set of tasks will reveal the effort involved. For most products, the faster the completion time, the better. Because some tasks are naturally more complicated than others, it may be helpful to compare task completion times to expert performance. Other efficiency metrics such as the number of steps or page views (in the case of some websites) can also be helpful. The time for each step may be short, but the separate decisions that must be made to accomplish a task can be numerous.

Learnability metrics assess how much time or effort is required to achieve maximum efficiency. Learnability can take the form of any of the previous efficiency metrics examined over time. In some situations, consider self-reported metrics, such as awareness and usefulness. By examining the difference between users' awareness and perceived usefulness, you will be able to identify aspects of the product that should be promoted or highlighted. For example, users may have low awareness for some parts of the product, but once they use it, they find out it is extremely useful.

3.4.4 Evaluating Navigation and/or Information Architecture

Many user research studies focus on improving the navigation and/or information architecture. This is probably most common for websites, software programs, mobile applications, consumer electronics, voice response systems, or any information-rich product. It may involve making sure that users can quickly and easily find what they are looking for, easily navigate around the product, know where they are within the overall structure, and know what options are available to them. Typically, these studies involve the use of wireframes or partially functional prototypes because the navigation and information mechanisms and information architecture are so fundamental to the design that they have to be figured out before almost anything else.

One of the best metrics to evaluate navigation is task success. By giving participants tasks to find key pieces of information (a "scavenger hunt"), you can tell how well the navigation and information architecture works for them. Tasks should touch on all the different areas of the product. An efficiency metric that's useful for evaluating navigation and information architecture is lostness, which looks at the number of steps the participant took to complete a task (e.g., web page visits) relative to the minimum number to complete the task.

Card sorting is a particularly useful method to understand how participants organize information. One type of card-sorting study is called a closed sort, which has participants put items into predefined categories. A useful metric to come from a closed card sort study is the percentage of items placed into the correct category. Tree Tests are becoming popular, which takes advantage of metrics such as directness and success which measure the efficiency (number of clicks) to find the correct card or piece of information. This metric indicates the intuitiveness of the information architecture. There are some helpful online tools to collect and analyze this type of data, such as Optimal Sort and Treejack (developed by Optimal Workshop in New Zealand).

3.4.5 Increasing Awareness

Not every design that goes through a UX evaluation is about making something easier or more efficient to use. Some design changes are aimed at increasing awareness of a specific piece of content or functionality. This is certainly true for online advertisements, but it's also true for products that have important but underutilized functionality. There can be many reasons why something is not noticed or used, including some aspect of the visual design, labeling, or placement.

First, we recommend monitoring the number of interactions with the element in question. This is not foolproof, since a participant might notice something but not click on it or interact with it in some way. The opposite would not be very likely: interaction without noticing. Because of this, the data can help confirm awareness but not demonstrate a lack of awareness. Sometimes it's useful to ask for self-reported metrics about whether the participants noticed or were aware of a specific design element. Measuring noticeability involves pointing out specific elements to the participants and then asking whether they had noticed those elements during the task. Measuring awareness involves asking the participants if they were aware of the feature before the study began. However, the data are not always reliable (Albert & Tedesco, 2010). Therefore, we don't recommend that this be your sole measure; you should complement it with other data sources.

Memory is another useful self-reported metric. For example, you can show participants several different elements, only one of which they had actually seen previously, and ask them to choose which one they saw during the task. If they noticed the element, their memory should be better than chance. But perhaps the best way to assess awareness, if you have the technology available, is through the use of behavioral and physiological metrics such as eye-tracking data. Using eye-tracking technology, you can determine the average time spent looking at a certain element, the percentage of participants who looked at it, and even the average time it took to first notice it. Another metric to consider, in the case of websites, is a change in live website data. Looking at how traffic patterns change between different designs will help you determine relative awareness. Simultaneous testing of alternative designs (A/B testing) on live sites is an increasingly common way to measure how small design changes impact user behavior.

3.4.6 Problem Discovery

The goal of problem discovery is to identify major user experience pain points. In some situations, you may not have any preconceived ideas about what the significant UX issues are with a product, but you want to know what annoys or most frustrates users. This is often done for a product that is already built but has not gone through an evaluation before or in a long time. A problem discovery study also works well as a periodic checkup to get back in touch with how users are interacting with your product. A discovery study is a little different from other types of user research studies because it is generally open-ended. Participants in a problem discovery study may be generating their own tasks, as opposed to being given a list of specific tasks. It's important to strive for realism as much as possible. This might involve using the live product and their own accounts (if applicable) and performing tasks that are relevant only to them. It might also include evaluating the product in the participants' environments, such as homes or workplaces.

Because they may be performing different tasks and their contexts of use may be different, comparing across participants may be a challenge. Issues-based metrics may be the most appropriate for problem discovery. Assuming you capture all the usability issues, it's fairly easy to convert those data into frequency and type. For example, you might discover that 40% of the usability issues pertain to high-level navigation and 20% of the issues to confusing terminology. Even though the exact problems encountered by each participant might be different, you can still generalize to a higher-level category of issue. Examining the frequency and severity of specific issues will reveal how many repeat issues are being observed. Is it a one-time occurrence or part of a recurring problem? By cataloging all the issues and assigning severity ratings, you may come away with a quick-hit list of design improvements.

3.4.7 Maximizing Usability for a Critical Product

Although some products strive to be easy to use and efficient, such as a mobile phone or washing machine, critical products *have* to be easy to use and efficient, such as a defibrillator, voting machine, or emergency exit instructions on an airplane. What differentiates a critical product from a noncritical product is that the entire reason for the critical product's existence is for the user to complete a very important task with high efficiency, confidence, and effectiveness, oftentimes in stressful situations. Not completing that task will have a significant negative outcome.

Measuring user experience for any critical product is essential. Just running a few participants through the lab is rarely good enough. It's important that user performance be measured against a target goal. Any critical product that doesn't meet its target UX goals should undergo a redesign. Because of the degree of certainty you want from your data, you may have to run relatively large numbers of participants in the study. One very important metric is user errors. This might include the number of errors or mistakes made while performing a specific task. Errors are not always easy to tabulate, so special attention must be given to how you define an error. It's always best to be very explicit about what constitutes an error and what doesn't.

Task success is also important. We recommend using a binary approach to success in this situation. For example, the true test of a portable defibrillator machine is that someone can use it successfully by themselves. In some cases, you may wish to tie task success to more than one metric, such as completing the task successfully within a specific amount of time and with no errors. Other efficiency metrics are also useful. In the example of the defibrillator machine, simply using it correctly is one thing, but doing so in a timely manner is altogether different. Self-reported metrics are relatively less important with critical products. What users think about their use of the product is much less important than their actual success.

3.4.8 Creating an Overall Positive User Experience

Some products strive to create an exceptional user experience. It's simply not enough to be usable. These products need to be engaging, thought-provoking, entertaining, and maybe even slightly addictive. The aesthetics and visual appeal usually play an important role as well. These are products that you tell a friend about and are not embarrassed to mention at a party. Their popularity usually grows at phenomenal rates. Even though the characteristics of what constitutes a great user experience are subjective, they are still measurable.

Although some performance metrics may be useful, what really matters is what the user thinks, feels, and says with respect to his or her experience. In some ways, this is the opposite perspective of measuring the usability of a critical product. If the user struggles a little at first, it may not be the end of the world. What matters is how the user feels at the end of the day. Many self-reported metrics must be considered when measuring the overall user experience.

Satisfaction is perhaps the most common self-reported metric, but it may not always be the best one. Being "satisfied" is usually not enough. One of the most valuable self-reported metrics we've used relates to the participant's expectation. The best experiences are those that exceed a participant's expectations. When the participant says something is much easier, more efficient, or more entertaining than expected, you know you are on to something.

Another set of self-reported metrics relates to future use. For example, you might ask questions related to the likelihood to purchase, recommend to a friend, or use in the future. The net promoter score (NPS) is a widely used metric to measure the likelihood of future use. Another interesting set of metrics relates to physiological reactions that users may be having. For example, if you want to make sure your product is engaging, you can look at physiological metrics such as facial expression analysis and skin conductance (electrodermal activity).

3.4.9 Evaluating the Impact of Subtle Changes

Not all design changes have an obvious impact on user behavior. Some design changes are much more subtle, and their impact on user behavior is less clear. Small trends, given enough users, can have huge implications for a large population of users. The subtle changes may involve different aspects of the visual design, such as font choice and size, placement, visual contrast, color, and image choice. Nonvisual design elements, such as subtle changes to content or terminology, can also have an impact on the user experience.

Perhaps the best way to measure the impact of subtle design changes is through live-site metrics from A/B tests. A/B testing involves comparing a control design against an alternative design. For websites, this usually involves diverting a (usually a small) portion of web traffic to an alternative design and comparing metrics such as traffic or purchases to a control design. An online usability study with a large population can also be very useful. If you don't have access to the technology to run A/B tests or online studies, we recommend using e-mail and online surveys to get feedback from as many representative participants as you can.

3.4.10 Comparing Alternative Designs

One of the most common types of user research studies involves comparing more than one design alternative. Typically, these types of studies take place early in the design process before any one design has been fully developed. (We often refer to these as "design bakeoffs.") Different design teams put together semi-functional prototypes, and we evaluate each design using a predefined set of metrics. Setting up these studies can be a little tricky. Because the designs are often similar, there is a high likelihood of a learning effect from one design to another. Asking the same participant to perform the same task with all designs usually does not yield reliable results, even when counterbalancing design and task order.

There are two solutions to this problem. You can set up the study as purely between subjects whereby each participant only interacts with only one design, which provides a clean set of data but requires significantly more participants. Alternatively, you can ask participants to perform the tasks using one primary design (counterbalancing the designs) and then show the other design alternatives and ask for their preference. This way you can get feedback about all the designs from each participant.

The most appropriate metrics to use when comparing multiple designs may be issues-based metrics. Comparing the frequency of high-, medium-, and low-severity issues across different designs will help shed light on which design or designs are more usable. Ideally, one design ends up with fewer issues overall and fewer high-severity issues. Performance metrics such as task success and task times can be useful, but because sample sizes are typically small, these data tend to be of limited value. A couple of self-reported metrics are particularly relevant. One is asking each participant to choose which prototype they would most like to use in the future (as a forced choice comparison). Also, asking each participant to rate each prototype along dimensions such as ease of use and visual appeal can be insightful.

3.5 USER RESEARCH METHODS AND TOOLS

One of the great features of collecting UX metrics is that you're not restricted to a certain type of user research study. UX metrics can be collected using almost any kind of user research study. This may be surprising because there is a common misperception that metrics can only be collected through large-scale studies or traditional usability evaluations. This is simply not the case. There are a wide variety of user research methods and tools to support the UX researcher. Below are a few examples of common user research methods and tools that are helpful when measuring the user experience.

3.5.1 Traditional (Moderated) Usability Tests

The most common user research method is a lab (or remote) usability test that utilizes a relatively small number of participants (typically 8 to 12). The usability-lab test involves a one-on-one session between a moderator (usability specialist) and a test participant. The moderator asks questions of the participants and gives them a set of tasks to perform on the product in question. The participants are likely to be thinking aloud as they perform the various tasks. The moderator records the participant's behavior and responses to questions. Lab tests are most often used in formative studies where the goal is to make iterative design improvements. The most important metrics to collect are about issues, including issue frequency, type, and severity. Collecting performance data such as task success, errors, and efficiency may also be helpful.

Self-reported metrics can also be collected by having participants answer questions regarding each task or at the conclusion of the study. However, we recommend that you approach performance data and self-reported data very carefully because it's easy to overgeneralize the results to a larger population without an adequate sample size. In fact, we typically only report the frequency of successful tasks or errors. We hesitate even to state the data as a percentage for fear that someone (who is less familiar with usability data or methods) will overgeneralize the data.

Usability tests are not always run with a small number of participants. In some situations, such as comparison tests, you might want to spend some extra time and money by running a larger group of participants (perhaps 15 to 50 users). The main advantage of running a test with more participants is that as your sample size increases, so does your confidence in the data. Also, this will afford you the ability to collect a wider range of data. In fact, all performance, self-reported, and physiological metrics are fair game. But there are a few metrics that you should be cautious about. For example, inferring website traffic patterns from usability-lab data is probably not very reliable, nor is looking at how subtle design changes might impact the user experience. In these cases, it is better to test with hundreds or even thousands of participants in an online study.

FOCUS GROUPS VERSUS USABILITY TESTS

When some people first hear about usability testing, they believe it is the same as a focus group. But in our experience, the similarity between the two methods begins and ends with the fact that they both involve representative participants. In a focus group, the participants commonly watch someone demonstrate or describe a potential product and then react to it. In a usability test, the participants actually try to use some version of the product themselves. We've seen many cases where a prototype got rave reviews from focus groups and then failed miserably in a usability test.

3.5.2 Unmoderated Usability Tests

Online studies involve testing with many participants at the same time. It's an excellent way to collect a lot of UX data in a relatively short amount of time from users who are geographically dispersed. Unmoderated studies are usually set up similarly to a lab test in that there are some background or screener questions, tasks, and follow-up questions. Participants go through a predefined script of questions and tasks, and all their data are collected automatically. You can collect a wide range of data, including many performance metrics and self-reported metrics. It may be difficult to collect issues-based data because you're not directly observing participants. However, the performance and self-reported data can point to issues, and verbatim comments can help infer their causes. Albert and colleagues (2010) go into detail about how to plan, design, launch, and analyze an online usability study.

Unlike other methods, online usability studies provide the researcher a tremendous amount of flexibility in the amount and type of data they collect. Online usability studies can be used to collect both qualitative and quantitative data and can focus on either user preferences or behaviors. The focus of an online study depends largely on the project goals and is rarely limited by the type or amount of data that are collected. While online studies are an excellent way to collect data, it is less ideal when the UX researcher is trying to gain deeper insight into the users' behaviors and motivations. Check out popular tools such as UserZoom (www.userzoom.com), Loop11 (www.loop11.com), UserTest (www.usertest.com), Validately (www.validatley.com), TryMyUI (www.trymyui.com), and Userlytics (www.userlytics.com) to learn more.

WHICH ONE GOES FIRST? LAB OR ONLINE TEST?

We often get questions about which should go first, a traditional lab study, followed by an online study, or vice versa. There are some pretty strong arguments for both sides.

Lab First, Then Online	Online First, Then Lab
Identify/fix "low hanging fruit" and then focus on remaining tasks with a large sample size	Identify the most significant issues online through metrics, then use lab study to gather a deeper qualitative understanding of those issues
Generate new concepts, ideas, questions through lab testing, then test/validate online	Collect video clips or more quotes of users to help bring metrics to life
Validate attitudes/preferences observed in lab testing	Gather all the metrics to validate design – if it tests well, then no need to bring users into the lab

3.5.3 Online Surveys

Many UX researchers think of online surveys strictly for collecting data about preferences and attitudes and firmly in the camp of market researchers. This is no longer the case. For example, many online survey tools allow you to include images, such as a prototype design, within the body of the survey. Including images within a survey will allow you to collect feedback on visual appeal, page layout, perceived ease of use, and likelihood to use, to name just a few metrics. We have found online surveys to be a quick and easy way to compare different types of visual designs, measure satisfaction with different web pages, and even preferences for various types of navigation schemes. As long as you don't require your participants to directly interact with the product, an online survey may suit your needs. Check out survey tools such as Qualtrics (www.qualtrics.com), Survey Monkey (www.surveymonkey.com), Survey Gizmo (www.surveyGizmo .com), and Google Forms.

INTERACTING WITH DESIGNS IN AN ONLINE SURVEY

Some online survey tools let participants have some level of interaction with images. This is exciting because it means you can ask participants to click on different areas of a design that are most (or least) useful, or where they would go to perform certain tasks. Fig. 3.1 is an example of a click map generated from an online survey. It shows different places where participants clicked to begin a task. In addition to collecting data on images, you can also control the time images are displayed. This is very helpful to gather first impressions of a design, or test whether they see certain visual elements (sometimes referred to as a "blink test").

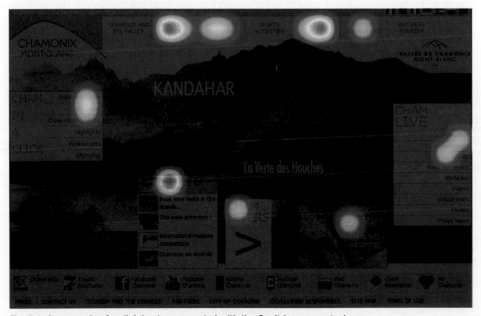

Fig. 3.1 An example of a click heat map created with the Qualtrics survey tool.

3.5.4 Information Architecture Tools

Research tools to measure an information architecture are becoming more popular. Based on formative and summative research goals, there are two ways to look at IA tools. A "formative" approach is all about developing an intuitive information architecture. The most common tools involve sorting items, usually tasks or types of content, into similar groups. They are effective tools that help UX researchers to gain valuable insights into how to develop an intuitive information architecture that supports users in easily finding what they are looking for. This includes not only how related items are grouped together but also the names used to describe each group of items.

Conversely, a "summative" approach is about testing or evaluating the intuitiveness of an existing or proposed information architecture. A "tree-test" is a very popular tool now to measure the intuitiveness of an information architecture. Metrics include success (could they find what they were looking for), directness (the path taken to find what they were looking for), and the time to find the item. Together, these three metrics allow you to compare various proposed information architectures. Check out Optimal Workshop (www.optimal workshop.com), UsabiliTest (www.usabilitest.com), and Simple Card Sort (www.simplecardsort.com) to learn more.

3.5.5 Click and Mouse Tools

Sometimes a UX researcher wants to gain insights into how users are interacting on a digital platform. There are a host of tools such as X, Y, and Z that let researchers track clicks and mouse movements to gain a deeper insight into user behavior, particularly with respect to comparing behavior on various design alternatives. These tools typically allow researchers to monitor what elements are attracting the most attention and which elements are being ignored. Furthermore, the researcher may use the data to infer the priority of actions by analyzing the sequence of movements. The benefit of these tools is the ecological validity (measuring actual user behavior without any interference). However, the downside is that oftentimes it is difficult to know the context of use, specifically what was the user is trying to accomplish. Check out Clicktale (www .clicktale), CrazyEgg (www.crazyegg.com), CanvasFlip (www.canvasflip.com), and Mouseflow (www.mouseflow.com) to learn more.

3.6 OTHER STUDY DETAILS

Many other details must be considered when planning any user research study. Several important issues to consider are budget/timelines, participants, data collection, and data cleanup.

3.6.1 Budgets and Timelines

The cost and time of running a user research study with metrics depend on the evaluation method, metrics chosen, participants, and available tools. It's impossible for us to give even approximate costs or time estimates for any particular type of user research study. The best we can do is to provide a few general rules of thumb for estimating costs and time for some common types of studies. When making these estimates, we recommend that you carefully consider all the variables that go into any user research study and communicate those estimates to business sponsors (or whoever is funding the study) as early as possible. Also, it's wise to add at least a 10% buffer for both costs and time, knowing that there may be some unforeseen costs and delays.

If you are running a formative study with a small number of participants (10 or fewer), collecting metrics should have little, if any, impact on the overall timeline or budget. Collecting and analyzing basic metrics on issue frequency and severity should at most add a few hours to any study. Just allow yourself a little extra time to analyze the data once the study is complete. If you're not yet very familiar with collecting these metrics, give yourself some extra time to set up tasks and agree on a method for making severity ratings prior to starting the test. Because it is a formative study, you should make every attempt to get the findings back to the stakeholders as quickly as possible to influence the next design iteration and not slow down the project.

In the case of running a user research study with a larger number of participants (usually more than a dozen), including metrics may have more of an impact on the budget and timeline. The most significant cost impact may be any additional costs for recruiting and compensating the participants. These costs depend on who they are (e.g., internal to your company versus external), how participants are recruited, and whether the data collection will be moderated sessions (in-person or remotely through a screen-sharing application) or unmoderated such as through an online survey. The most significant impact on the timeline is likely to be the additional time required to run the larger number of participants. Depending on your billing or cost-recovery model, there may also be additional costs because of the increased time for the UX researchers. Keep in mind that you will also need extra time to clean up and analyze the data.

Running an online (unmoderated) study is quite different in terms of costs and time. Typically, about half of the time is usually spent setting up the study, from identifying and validating tasks, creating questions and scales, evaluating the prototypes or designs, identifying and/or recruiting participants, and developing the online script or survey. Unlike traditional lab tests where a lot of time is spent collecting the data, running an online study requires little time on the part of the UX researcher for data collection. With most online technologies you simply flip the switch and then monitor the data as they pour in. Monitoring data collection, particularly with respect to filling certain quota of user groups, is always advisable.

The other half of the time is spent cleaning up and analyzing the data. It is very common to underestimate the time required for this. Data are often not in a format that readily allows analysis. For example, you will need to filter out extreme values (particularly when collecting time data), check for data inconsistencies, and code new variables based on the raw data (such as creating top-2-box variables for self-reported data). We have found that we can run an online study in about 100 to 200 person-hours. This includes everything from the planning phase through data collection, analysis, and presentation. The estimate can vary by up to 50% in either direction based on the scope of the study. Many of these details are covered in the book *Beyond the Usability Lab: Conducting Large-scale Online User Experience Studies* (Albert et al., 2010).

3.6.2 Participants

The specific participants in any user research study have a major impact on its findings. It's critical that you carefully plan how to include the most representative participants as possible in your study. The steps you will go through in recruiting participants are essentially the same whether you're collecting metrics or not.

The first step is to identify the recruiting criteria that will be used to determine whether a specific person is eligible to participate in the study. Criteria should be as specific as possible to reduce the possibility of recruiting someone who does not fit the profile(s). As part of identifying the criteria, you may segment participant types. For example, you may recruit a certain number of new participants as well as ones who have experience with the existing product.

After deciding on the types of participants you want, you need to figure out how many you need. Many factors enter into the decision, including the diversity of the user population, the complexity of the product, and the specific goals of the study. But as a general rule of thumb, testing with about six to eight participants for each iteration in a formative study works well. The most significant usability findings will be observed with the first six or so participants. If there are distinct groups of users, it's helpful to have at least five from each group. Section 6.7 provides more details about determining a sample size for usability testing.

For summative usability studies, we recommend having data from 50 to 100 representative users for each distinct user group. If you're in a crunch, you can go as low as 30 participants, but the variance in the data will be quite high, making it difficult to generalize the findings to a broader population. In the case of studies where you are testing the impact of potentially subtle design changes, having at least 100 participants for each distinct user group is advisable.

After determining the sample size, you will need to plan the recruiting strategy. This is essentially how you are actually going to get people to participate in the study. You might generate a list of possible participants from customer data and then write a screener that a recruiter uses when contacting potential participants. You might send out requests to participate via e-mail distribution lists. You can screen or segment participants through a series of background questions. Or you might decide to use a third party to handle all of the recruiting.

Some of these companies have quite extensive user panels to draw on. Other options exist, such as posting an announcement on the web or e-mailing a specific group of potential participants. Different strategies work for different organizations.

DOES GEOGRAPHY MATTER?

A common question we get from our clients is whether we need to recruit participants from different cities, regions, and countries. The answer is usually no, geography does not matter when collecting user data. It's very unlikely that participants in New York are going to have a different set of issues than participants in Chicago, London, or even Index, Washington. But there are some exceptions. If the product you are evaluating has a large corporate presence in one location, it may bias responses. For example, if you want to evaluate Walmart.com in their hometown of Benton, Arkansas, you might find it hard to get a neutral, unbiased set of results. Also, location can have an impact on user goals for some products. For example, if you are evaluating an ecommerce clothing website, you might collect different data from participants in urban or rural settings, or participants in different countries, where the needs and preferences can vary quite a bit. Even when it doesn't really make sense to conduct user research in different locations, some clients still choose to evaluate products in different regions, simply to prevent senior management from questioning the validity of the results. At the end of the day, it's likely not money well spent, but if it helps get the team bought into the method and results, it might be worth it.

3.6.3 Data Collection

It is important to think about how the data are going to be collected. You should plan well in advance how you are going to capture all the data that you need for your study. The decisions you make may have a significant impact on how much work you have to do further down the road when you begin analysis.

In the case of a method that relies on a small number of participants, Excel probably works as well as anything for collecting data. Make sure you have a template in place for quickly capturing the data during the test. Ideally, this is not done by the moderator but by a note taker or someone behind the scenes who can quickly and easily enter the data. We recommend that data be entered in numeric format as much as possible. For example, if you are coding task success, it is best to code it as a "1" (success) and "0" (failure). Data entered in a text format will eventually have to be converted, with the exception of verbatim comments.

The most important thing when capturing data is for everyone on the UX team to know the coding scheme extremely well. If anyone starts flipping scales (confusing the high and low values) or does not understand what to enter for certain variables, you will have to either recode or throw the data out. We strongly recommend that you offer training to others who will be helping you collect data. Just think of it as cheap insurance to make sure you end up with reliable and useful data.

For studies involving larger numbers of participants, consider using a data-capture tool. If you are running an online study, data are typically collected automatically. You should also have the option of downloading the raw data into Excel or various statistical programs such as R, SAS, or SPSS.

3.6.4 Data Cleanup

Data rarely come out in a format that is instantly ready to analyze. Some sort of cleanup is usually needed to get your data in a format that allows for quick and easy analysis. Data cleanup might include the following:

- **Filtering data**. You should check for extreme values in the data set. The most likely culprit will be task completion times (in the case of online studies). Some participants may have gone out to lunch in the middle of the study, and their task times will be unusually large. Also, some participants may have taken an impossibly short amount of time to complete the task. This is likely an indicator that they were not truly engaged in the study. Some general rules for how to filter time data are included in Section 4.2. You should also consider filtering out data for participants who do not reflect your target audience or where outside factors impacted the results.
- **Creating new variables**. Building on the raw data set is very useful. For example, you might want to create a top-2-box variable for self-reported rating scales by counting the number of participants who gave one of the two highest ratings. Perhaps you want to aggregate all the success data into one overall success average representing all tasks. Or you might want to combine several metrics using a z-score transformation (described in Section 9.1.3) to create an overall UX score.
- **Verifying responses**. In some situations, particularly for online studies, participant responses may need to be verified. For example, if you notice that a large percentage of participants are all giving the same wrong answer, this should be investigated.
- **Checking consistency**. It's important to make sure that data are captured properly. A consistency check might include comparing task completion times and successes to self-reported metrics. If many participants completed a task in a relatively short period of time and were successful but gave the task a very low rating, there may be a problem with either how the data were captured or participants confusing the scales of the question. This is quite common with scales involving self-reported ease of use.
- **Transferring data**. It's common to capture and clean up the data using Excel, then use another program such as SPSS to run some statistics (although all the basic statistics can be done with Excel), and then move back to Excel to create the charts and graphs.

Data cleanup can take anywhere from 1 hour to a couple of weeks. For simple user research studies, with just a couple of metrics, cleanup should be very quick. Obviously, the more metrics you are dealing with, the more time it will take. Also, online studies can take longer because more checks are being done. You want to make sure that the technology is correctly coding all the data.

3.7 SUMMARY

Running a user research study including metrics requires some planning. The following are some of the key points to remember.

- The first decision you must make is whether you are going to take a formative or summative approach. A formative approach involves collecting data to help improve the design before it is launched or released. It is most appropriate when you have an opportunity to positively impact the design of the product. A summative approach is taken when you want to measure the extent to which certain target goals were achieved. Summative evaluations are also used in competitive user research studies.
- When deciding on the most appropriate metrics, three main aspects of the user experience to consider are performance, preferences, and emotion. We strongly recommend considering a variety of UX metrics to gain a more complete picture of the overall user experience.
- There are a host of methods and tools available to help you carry out your user research studies. Some of these methods and tools focus on usability testing (both formative and summative), online surveys to measure user preferences, information architecture, or user behaviors by tracking mouse clicks or movements in a digital context. Each of these methods and tools offer distinct advantages and disadvantages when they are used to measure the user experience.
- Budgets and timelines need to be planned out well in advance when running any user research studies involving metrics. If you are running a formative study with a relatively small number of participants, collecting metrics should have little, if any, impact on the overall timeline or budget. Otherwise, special attention must be paid to estimating and communicating costs and time for larger-scale studies.

CHAPTER 4
Performance Metrics

CONTENTS

Anyone who uses technology has to interact with some type of interface to accomplish their goals. An interface may take many forms, from a graphical interface to a voice or conversational interface or a wearable or tangible interface. For example, a user of a website clicks on different links, a user of a word-processing application enters information via a keyboard, or a user of a microwave oven pushes buttons or turns knobs. No matter the technology, users are behaving or interacting with a product in some way. These behaviors form the cornerstone of performance metrics.

Measuring the User Experience. DOI: http://dx.doi.org/10.1016/B978-0-12-818080-8.00004-2

Every type of user behavior is measurable in some way. For example, you can measure whether users clicking through a website found what they were looking for. You can measure how long it took users to enter and properly format a page of text in a word-processing application or how many buttons users pressed in trying to cook a frozen dinner in a microwave. All performance metrics are calculated based on specific user behaviors.

Performance metrics rely not only on user behaviors but also on the use of scenarios or tasks. For example, if you want to measure success, the user needs to have specific tasks or goals in mind. The task may be to find the price of a sweater or submit an expense report. Without tasks, performance metrics aren't possible. You can't measure success if the user is only aimlessly browsing a website or playing with a piece of software. How do you know if they were successful? But this doesn't mean that the tasks must be something arbitrary given to the users. They could be whatever the users wanted to do on a live website, or something that the participants in a usability study generate themselves.

Performance metrics are among the most valuable tools for any UX research professional. They're the best way to evaluate the effectiveness and efficiency of many different products. If users are making many errors, you know there are opportunities for improvement. If users are taking four times longer to complete a task than what was expected, efficiency can be greatly improved. Performance metrics are the best way of knowing how well users are actually using a product.

Performance metrics are also useful to estimate the *magnitude* of a specific usability issue. Many times it's not enough to know that a particular issue exists. You probably want to know *how many* people are likely to encounter the same issue after the product is released. For example, by calculating a success rate that includes a confidence interval, you can derive a reasonable estimate of how big a usability issue really is. By measuring task completion times, you can determine what percentage of your target audience will be able to complete a task within a specified amount of time. If only 20% of the target users are successful at a particular task, it should be fairly obvious that the task has a usability problem.

Senior managers and other key stakeholders on a project usually pay attention to performance metrics, especially when they are presented effectively. Managers will want to know how many users are able to successfully complete a core set of tasks using a product. They see these performance metrics as a strong indicator of overall usability and a potential predictor of cost savings or increases in revenue.

Performance metrics are not the magical elixir for every situation. Similar to other metrics, an adequate sample size is required. Although the statistics will work whether you have 2 or 100 participants, your confidence level will change dramatically depending on the sample size. If you're only concerned about identifying the lowest of the low-hanging fruit, performance metrics are probably not a good use of time or money. But if you have the time to collect data from at least 10 participants, and ideally more, you should be able to derive meaningful performance metrics with reasonable confidence levels.

Over-relying on performance metrics can be a danger. When reporting task success or completion time, you may lose sight of the underlying issues behind the data. Performance metrics tell the *what* very effectively but not the *why*. Performance data can point to tasks or parts of an interface that were particularly problematic for users. Still, you will usually want to supplement it with other data, such as observational or self-reported data, to understand better why they were problems and how you might fix them.

This chapter covers five basic types of performance metrics.

1. *Task success* is perhaps the most widely used performance metric. It measures how effectively users are able to complete a given set of tasks. Two different types of task success will be reviewed: binary success and levels of success.
2. *Time-on-task* is a common performance metric that measures how much time is required to complete a task.
3. *Errors* reflect the mistakes made during a task. Errors can be useful in pointing out particularly confusing or misleading parts of an interface.
4. *Efficiency* can be assessed by examining the amount of effort a user expends to complete a task, such as the number of clicks in a website or the number of button presses on a mobile phone.
5. *Learnability* is a way to measure how performance changes over time.

4.1 TASK SUCCESS

The most common performance metric is task success, which can be calculated for practically any usability study that includes tasks. It's almost a universal metric because it can be calculated for such a wide variety of *things* being tested—from websites to kitchen appliances. As long as the user has a reasonably well-defined task, you can measure success.

Task success is something that almost anyone can relate to. It doesn't require elaborate explanations of measurement techniques or statistics to get the point across. If your users can't complete their tasks, then you know something is wrong. Seeing users fail to complete a simple task can be compelling evidence that you need to fix something.

To measure task success, each task that users are asked to perform must have a clear end-state, such as purchasing a product, finding the answer to a specific question, or completing an online application form. To measure success, you need to know what constitutes success, so you should define the success criteria for each task prior to the data collection. If you don't predefine the criteria, you run the risk of constructing a poorly worded task and not collecting clean success data. Here are examples of two tasks with clear and not-so-clear end-states:

- Find the 5-year gain or loss for IBM stock (clear end-state)
- Research ways to save for your retirement (not a clear end-state)

Although the second task may be perfectly appropriate in certain types of UX studies, it's not appropriate for measuring task success.

The most common way of measuring success in a lab-based usability test is to have the user verbally articulate the answer after completing the task. Giving the answer is natural for the user, but sometimes it results in answers that are difficult to interpret. Users might give extra or arbitrary information that makes interpreting the answer difficult. In these situations, you may need to probe the users to make sure they completed the task successfully.

Another way to collect success data is by having users provide their answers in a more structured way, such as using an online tool or paper form. Each task might have a set of multiple-choice responses. Users might choose the correct answer from a list of four to five distracters. It's important to make the distracters as realistic as possible. Try to avoid write-in answers if possible. It's much more time-consuming to analyze each write-in answer, and it may involve judgment calls, thereby adding more noise to the data.

In some cases, the correct solution to a task may not be verifiable because it depends on the user's specific situation, and testing is not being performed in person. For example, if you ask users to find the balance in their savings account, there's no way to know what that amount really is unless we're sitting next to them while they do it. So, in this case, you might use a proxy measure of success. For example, you could ask the user to identify the title of the page that shows their balance. This works well if the title of the page is unique and obvious, and you're confident that they are actually able to see the balance if they reached this page.

4.1.1 Binary Success

Binary success is the simplest and most common way of measuring task success. Users either completed a task successfully or they didn't. It's similar to a "pass/fail" course in college. Binary success is appropriate to use when the product's success depends on users completing a task or set of tasks. Getting close doesn't count. The only thing that matters is that they accomplish their tasks. For example, when evaluating the usability of a defibrillator device (to resuscitate people during a heart attack), the only thing that matters is being able to use it correctly without making any mistakes within a certain amount of time. Anything less would be a major problem, especially for the recipient! A less dramatic example might be a task that involves purchasing a book on a website. Although it may be helpful to know where in the process someone failed, if your company's revenue depends on selling those books, task success is what really matters.

Each time users perform a task, they should be given a "success" or "failure" score. Typically, these scores are in the form of 1's (for success) and 0's (for failure). (The analysis is easier if you assign a numeric score rather than a text value of "success" or "failure.") By having a numeric score, you can easily calculate the average as well as other statistics you might need. Simply calculate the average of the 1's and 0's to determine the binary success rate. Assuming you have more than one participant and more than one task, there are always two ways you can calculate task success:

- By looking at the average success rate for each *task* across the participants, or
- By looking at the average success rate for each *participant* across the tasks.

As an example, consider the data in Table 4.1. The averages across the bottom represent the task success rates for each *task*. The averages along the right represent the success rates for each *participant*. As long as no data are missing, the averages of those two sets of averages will always be the same.

Participant	Login	Navigate	Search	Find Category	Find Author	Find Review	Add to Cart	Update Address	Check-out	Check Status	Averages
Participant 1	1	1	1	0	1	1	1	1	0	1	80%
Participant 2	1	0	1	0	1	0	1	0	0	1	50%
Participant 3	1	1	0	0	0	0	1	0	0	0	30%
Participant 4	1	0	0	0	1	0	1	1	0	0	40%
Participant 5	0	0	1	0	0	1	0	0	0	0	20%
Participant 6	1	1	1	1	1	0	1	1	1	1	90%
Participant 7	0	1	1	0	0	1	1	1	0	1	60%
Participant 8	0	0	0	0	1	0	0	0	0	1	20%
Participant 9	1	0	0	0	0	1	1	1	0	1	50%
Participant 10	1	1	0	1	1	1	1	1	0	1	80%
Averages	70%	50%	50%	20%	60%	50%	80%	60%	10%	70%	52.0%

Table 4.1 Task success data for 10 participants and 10 tasks

DOES TASK SUCCESS ALWAYS MEAN *FACTUAL* SUCCESS?

The usual definition of task success is achieving some factually correct or clearly defined state. For example, if you're using the NASA site to find who the Commander of Apollo 12 was, there's a single factually correct answer (Charles "Pete" Conrad, Jr.). Or, if you're using an ecommerce site to purchase a book, then purchasing that book would indicate success. But in some cases, perhaps what's important is not so much reaching a factual answer or achieving a specific goal, but rather the users *being satisfied* they have achieved a certain state. For example, just before the 2008 U.S. Presidential election, we conducted an online study comparing the websites of the two primary candidates, Barack Obama and John McCain. The tasks included things like finding the candidate's position on Social Security. Task success was measured by self-report only (Yes I Found It, No I Didn't Find, or I'm Not Sure), since for this kind of site, the important thing is whether the users *believe* they found the information they were looking for.

The most common way to analyze and present binary success rates is by task. This involves simply presenting the percentage of participants who successfully completed each task. Fig. 4.1 shows the task success rates for the data in Table 4.1. This approach is most useful when you want to compare success rates for each task. You can then do a more detailed analysis of each task by looking at the specific problems to determine what changes may be needed to address them.

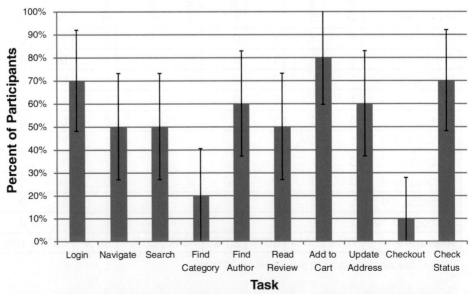

Fig. 4.1 Task success rates for the data in Table 4.1, including a 90% confidence interval for each task.

For example, Fig. 4.1 shows that tasks 4 (find category) and 9 (checkout) appear to be problematic.

Another common way of looking at binary success is by user or type of user. As always, in reporting usability data, you should be careful to maintain the anonymity of the users in the study using numbers or other nonidentifiable descriptors. The main value of looking at binary success data from a user perspective is that you can identify different groups of users who perform differently or encounter different sets of problems. Here are some of the common ways to segment different users:

- Frequency of use (infrequent users versus frequent users)
- Previous experience using the product
- Domain expertise (low-domain knowledge versus high-domain knowledge)
- Age group

Task success for different groups of participants is also used when each group is given a different design to work with. For example, participants in a study might be randomly assigned to use either Version A or Version B of a prototype website. A key comparison will be the average task success rate for the participants using Version A vs. those using Version B.

If you have a relatively large number of users in a study, it may be helpful to present binary success data as a frequency distribution (Fig. 4.2). This is a convenient way to visually represent the variability in binary task success data. For example, in Fig. 4.2, six users in the evaluation of the original website completed 61% to 70% of the tasks successfully, one completed fewer than 50%, and only two completed as many as 81% to 90%. In a revised design, six users had a success rate of 91% or greater, and no user had a success rate below 61%. Illustrating that the two distributions of task success barely overlap is a much more dramatic way of showing the improvement across the iterations than simply reporting the two means.

CALCULATING CONFIDENCE INTERVALS FOR BINARY SUCCESS

One of the most important aspects of analyzing and presenting binary success is including confidence intervals. Confidence intervals are essential because they reflect your trust or confidence in the data. In most usability studies, binary success data are based on relatively small samples (e.g., 5 to 20 users). Consequently, the binary success metric may not be as reliable as we would like it to be. For example, if four out of five users successfully completed a task,

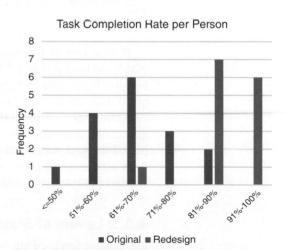

Fig. 4.2 Frequency distributions of binary success rates from usability tests of the original version of a website and the redesigned version. (data from LeDoux, Connor, & Tullis, 2005).

how confident can we be that 80% of the larger population of users will be able to successfully complete that task? Obviously, we would be more confident if 16 out of 20 users successfully completed the task and even more confident if 80 out of 100 did.

Fortunately, there is a way to take this into account. Binary success rates are essentially proportions: the proportion of the users who successfully completed a given task. The appropriate way to calculate a confidence interval for a proportion like this is to use a binomial confidence interval. Several methods are available for calculating binomial confidence intervals, such as the Wald Method and the Exact Method. But as Sauro and Lewis (2005) have shown, many of those methods are too conservative or too liberal in their calculation of the confidence interval when you're dealing with the small sample sizes we commonly have in usability tests. They found that a modified version of the Wald Method, called the Adjusted Wald, yielded the best results when calculating a confidence interval for task success data.

CONFIDENCE INTERVAL CALCULATOR FOR TASK SUCCESS

Jeff Sauro has provided a very useful calculator for determining confidence intervals for binary success on his website: http://www.measuringu.com/wald. When you enter the total number of people who attempted a given task and how many of them successfully completed it, this tool will automatically perform the Wald, Adjusted Wald, Exact, and Score calculations of the confidence interval for the mean task completion rate. You can choose to calculate a 99%, 95%, or 90% confidence interval. Or if you really want to calculate confidence intervals for binary success data yourself, the details are included on our website.

If four out of five users successfully completed a given task, the Adjusted Wald Method yields a 95% confidence interval for that task completion rate ranging from 36% to 98%—a rather large range! On the other hand, if 16 out of 20 users completed the task successfully (the same proportion), the Adjusted Wald Method yields a 95% confidence interval of 58% to 93%. Or if you *really* got carried away and ran a usability test with 100 participants, of whom 80 completed the task successfully, the 95% confidence interval would be 71% to 87%. As is almost always the case with confidence intervals, larger sample sizes yield smaller (or more accurate) intervals.

4.1.2 Levels of Success

Identifying levels of success is useful when there are reasonable shades of gray associated with task success. The user receives some value from partially completing a task. Think of it as partial credit on a homework assignment if you showed your work, even though you got the wrong answer. For example, assume that a user's task is to find the cheapest digital camera with at least 8 megapixel resolution, at least 12× optical zoom, and weighing no more than 3 pounds. What if the user found a camera that met most of those criteria but had a 10× optical zoom instead of 12×? According to a strict binary success approach, that would be a failure. But you're losing some important information by doing that. The user actually came very close to successfully completing the task. In some cases this might be acceptable to a user. For some types of products, coming close to fully completing a task may provide value to the user. Also, it may be helpful for you to know why some users failed a task or with which particular tasks users needed help.

SHOULD YOU INCLUDE TASKS THAT CANNOT BE COMPLETED?

An interesting question is whether a usability study should include tasks that can't be performed using the product being testing. For example, assume you're testing an online bookstore that only carries mystery novels. Would it be appropriate to include a task that involves trying to find a book that the store doesn't carry, such as a science-fiction novel? If one of the goals of the study is to determine how well users can determine what the store does *not* carry, we think it could make sense. In the real world, when you come to a new website, you don't automatically know everything that can or can't be done using the site. A well-designed site not only makes clear what *is* available on the site but also what's *not* available. However, when tasks are presented in a usability study, there's probably an implication that they *can* be done. So we think if you do include tasks that can't be done, you should make it clear up front that some of the tasks may not be possible.

HOW TO COLLECT AND MEASURE LEVELS OF SUCCESS

Collecting and measuring levels of success data are very similar to binary success data, except that you must define the various levels. There are a two approaches to levels of success:

- Levels of success might be based on the user's experience in completing a task. Some users might struggle or require assistance, while others complete their tasks without any difficulty.
- Levels of success might be based on the users accomplishing the task in different ways. Some users might accomplish the task in an optimal way, while others might accomplish it in ways that are less than optimal.

Levels of success based on the degree to which users complete a task typically have between three and six levels. A common approach is to use three levels: complete success, partial success, and complete failure.

Levels of success data are almost as easy to collect and measure as binary success data. It just means defining what you mean by "complete success" and by "complete failure." Anything in between is considered a partial success. A more granular approach is to break out each level according to whether assistance was given or not. Below is an example of six different levels of completion:

- Complete success
    - With assistance
    - Without assistance
- Partial success
    - With assistance
    - Without assistance
- Failure
    - User thought it was complete, but it wasn't
    - User gave up

If you do decide to use levels of success, it's important to clearly define the levels beforehand. Also, consider having multiple observers independently assess the levels for each task and then reach a consensus.

A common issue when measuring levels of success is deciding what constitutes "giving assistance" to the participant. The following are some examples of situations we define as giving assistance:

- Moderator takes the participant back to a home page or resets to an initial (pretask) state. This form of assistance may reorient the participant and help avoid certain behaviors that initially resulted in confusion.
- Moderator asks the participant probing questions or restates the task. This may cause the user to think about their behavior or choices in a different way.
- Moderator answers a question or provides information that helps the participant complete the task.
- Participant seeks help from an outside source. For example, the participant calls a phone representative, uses another website, consults a user manual, or accesses an online help system.

Level of success can also be examined in terms of the user experience. We commonly find that some tasks are completed without any difficulty, and others are completed with minor or major problems along the way. It's important to distinguish between these different experiences. A four-point scoring method can be used for each task:

1 = No problem. The user successfully completed the task without any difficulty or inefficiency.

2 = Minor problem. The user successfully completed the task but took a slight detour. They made one or two small mistakes but quickly recovered and was successful.

3 = Major problem. The user successfully completed the task but had major problems. They struggled and took a major detour in their eventual successful completion of the task.

4 = Failure/gave up. The user provided the wrong answer or gave up before completing the task, or the moderator moved on to the next task before successful completion.

When using this scoring system, it's important to remember that these data are ordinal (see Chapter 2). Therefore, you should not report an average score. Rather, present the data as frequencies for each level of completion. This scoring system is relatively easy to use, and we usually see agreement on the various levels by different usability specialists observing the same interactions. Also, you can aggregate the data into a binary success rate if you need to. Finally, this scoring system is usually easy to explain to your audience. It's also helpful to focus on the 3's and 4's as part of design improvements; there's usually no need to worry about the 1's and 2's.

HOW TO ANALYZE AND PRESENT LEVELS OF SUCCESS

In analyzing levels of success, the first step is to create a stacked bar chart. This will show the percentage of users who fall into each category or level, including failures. Make sure that the bars add up to 100%. Fig. 4.3 is an example of a common way to present levels of success.

4.1.3 Issues in Measuring Success

Obviously, an important issue in measuring task success is simply how you define whether a task was successful. The key is to clearly define beforehand

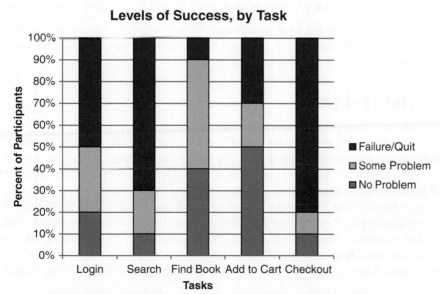

Fig. 4.3 Stacked bar chart showing different levels of success based on task completion.

what the criteria are for *successfully* completing each task. Try to think through the various situations that might arise for each task and decide whether or not they constitute success. For example, is a task successful if the user finds the right answer but reports it in the wrong format? Also, what happens if the user reports the right answer but then restates the answer incorrectly? When unexpected situations arise during the test, make note of them and try to reach a consensus among the observers afterward about those cases.

One issue that commonly arises during a usability evaluation is how or when to end a task if the user is not successful. In essence, this is the "stopping rule" for unsuccessful tasks. Here are some of the common approaches to ending an unsuccessful task:

1. Tell the users at the beginning of the session that they should continue to work on each task until they either complete it or reach the point at which, in the real world, they would give up or seek assistance (from technical support, a colleague, etc.).

2. Apply a "three strikes and you're out" rule. This means that the users get three attempts (or whatever number you decide) to complete a task before you stop them. The main difficulty with this approach is defining what is meant by an "attempt." It could be three different strategies, three wrong answers, or three different "detours" in finding specific information. However you define it, there will be a considerable amount of discretion on behalf of the moderator or scorer.

3. "Call" the task after a predefined amount of time has passed. Set a time limit, such as 5 minutes. After the time has expired, move on to the next task. In most cases, it is better not to tell the user that you are timing them. By doing so, you create a more stressful, "test-like" environment.

Of course, you always have to be sensitive to the user's state in any usability test and potentially end a task (or even the session) if you see that the user is becoming particularly frustrated or agitated.

4.2 TIME-ON-TASK

Time-on-task (sometimes referred to as task completion time or simply task time) is a good way to measure the efficiency of a product. In most situations, the faster a user can complete a task, the better the experience. In fact, it would be fairly unusual for a user to complain that a task took less time than expected. But there are some exceptions to the assumption that faster is better. One could be a game where the user doesn't want to finish too quickly. The main purpose of most games is the experience itself rather than the quick completion of a task. Another exception may be e-learning. For example, if you're putting together an online training course, slower may be better. Users may retain more if they spend more time completing the tasks rather than rushing through the course.

TIME ON TASK VERSUS SESSION DURATION

Our assertion that faster task times are generally better seems at odds with the view from web analytics that you want longer page-views or session durations. From a web-analytics perspective, longer page-view durations (the amount of time each user is viewing each page) and longer session durations (the amount of time each user is spending on the site) are generally considered good things. The argument is that they represent greater "engagement" with the site, or the site is considered "stickier." Part of the reason that our assertion seems at odds with that perspective is that we don't agree with it. Session and page-view duration are examples of metrics that are from the perspective of the site owner rather than the user. We would argue that users generally want to be spending *less* time on the site, not *more*. But there is a way in which the two viewpoints might be reconciled. Perhaps a goal of a site might be to get users to perform more in-depth or complex tasks rather than just superficial ones (e.g., rebalancing their financial portfolio instead of just checking their balances). More complex tasks will generally yield longer times on the site *and* longer task times than superficial tasks.

4.2.1 Importance of Measuring Time-on-Task

Time-on-task is particularly important for products where tasks are performed repeatedly by the user. For example, if you're designing an application for use by customer service representatives of an airline, the time it takes to complete a phone reservation would be an important measure of efficiency. The faster the airline agent can complete a reservation, presumably the more calls they can handle and, ultimately, the more money the airline can save. The more often a task is performed by the same user, the more important efficiency becomes. One of the side benefits of measuring time-on-task is that it can be relatively straight-forward to calculate cost savings due to an increase in efficiency and then derive an actual ROI (Return on Investment). Calculating ROI is discussed in more detail in Chapter 10.

4.2.2 How to Collect and Measure Time-on-Task

Time-on-task is simply the time elapsed between the start of a task and the end of a task, usually expressed in minutes and seconds. Logistically, time-on-task can be measured in many different ways. The moderator or note taker can use a stopwatch or any other time-keeping device that can measure at the minute and second levels. Using a digital watch or application on smart phone, you could simply record the start and end times. When video-recording a usability session, we find it's helpful to use the time-stamp feature of most recorders to display the time and then to mark those times as the task start and stop times. If you choose to record time-on-task manually, it's important to be very diligent about when

AUTOMATED TOOLS FOR MEASURING TIME-ON-TASK

A much easier and less error-prone way of recording task times is using an automated tool. Some tools that can assist in logging of task times include the following:

- The Observer XT from Noldus Information Technology
- Ovo Logger from Ovo Studios
- Morae from TechSmith
- Usability Test Data Logger from UserFocus

Our website, MeasuringUX.com, also includes a simple macro for use in Microsoft Word for logging start and finish times. An automated method of logging has several advantages. Not only is it less error-prone, but it's also much less obtrusive. The last thing you want is a participant in a usability test to feel nervous from watching you press the start and stop button on your stopwatch or smartphone.

to start and stop the clock and/or record the start and stop times. It may also be helpful to have two people record the times.

TURNING ON AND OFF THE CLOCK

Not only do you need a way to measure time, but you also need some rules about *how* to measure time. Perhaps the most important rule is when to turn the clock on and off. Turning on the clock is fairly straightforward: If you have the participants read the task aloud, you start the clock as soon as they finish reading the task.

Turning off the clock is a more complicated issue. Automated time-keeping tools typically have an "answer" button. Users are required to hit the "answer" button, at which point the timing ends, and they are asked to provide an answer and perhaps a few additional questions. If you are not using an automated method, you can have users verbally report the answer, or perhaps even write it down. However, there are many situations in which you may not be sure if they have found the answer. In this situation, it's important for participants to indicate their answer as quickly as possible. In any case, you want to stop timing when the user has stopped interacting with the product.

TABULATING TIME DATA

The first thing you need to do is arrange the data in a table, as shown in Table 4.2. Typically, you will want a list of all the participants in the first column, followed by the time data for each task in the remaining columns (expressed in seconds, or minutes if the tasks are long). Table 4.2 also shows summary data, including the average, median, geometric mean, and confidence intervals for each task.

Participant	Task 1	Task 2	Task 3	Task 4	Task 5
P1	259	112	135	58	8
P2	253	64	278	160	22
P3	42	51	60	57	26
P4	38	108	115	146	26
P5	33	142	66	47	38
P6	33	54	261	26	42
P7	36	152	53	22	44
P8	112	65	171	133	46
P9	29	92	147	56	56
P10	158	113	136	83	64
P11	24	69	119	25	68
P12	108	50	145	15	75
P13	110	128	97	97	78
P14	37	66	105	83	83
P15	116	78	40	163	100
P16	129	152	67	168	109
P17	31	51	51	119	116
P18	33	97	44	81	127
P19	75	124	286	103	236
P20	76	62	108	185	245
Average	**86.6**	**91.5**	**124.2**	**91.35**	**80.3**
Median	**58.5**	**85**	**111.5**	**83**	**66**
Geometric mean	**65.216**	**85.225**	**104.971**	**73.196**	**60.323**
Upper-bound	**119.8**	**108.0**	**159.5**	**116.6**	**110.2**
Lower-bound	**53.4**	**75.0**	**119.9**	**66.1**	**50.4**
Confidence interval	**33.2**	**16.5**	**19.8**	**25.2**	**29.9**

Table 4.2 Time-on-task data for 20 users and 5 tasks.

WORKING WITH TIME DATA IN EXCEL

If you use Excel to log data during a usability test, it's often convenient to use times that are formatted as hours, minutes, and (sometimes) seconds (hh:mm:ss). Excel provides a variety of formats for time data. This makes it easy to enter the times, but it slightly complicates matters when you need to calculate an elapsed time. For example, assume that a task started at 12:46 PM and ended at 1:04 PM. Although you can look at those times and determine that the elapsed time was 18 minutes, how to get Excel to calculate that isn't so obvious. Internally, Excel stores all times as a number reflecting the number of seconds elapsed since midnight. So to convert an Excel time to minutes, multiply it by 60 (the number of minutes in an hour) and then by 24 (the number of hours in a day). To convert to seconds, multiply by another 60 (the number of seconds in a minute).

4.2.3 Analyzing and Presenting Time-on-Task Data

You can analyze and present time-on-task data in many different ways. Perhaps the most common way is to look at the average amount of time spent on any particular task or set of tasks by averaging all the times for each user by task (Fig. 4.4). This is a straightforward and intuitive way to report time-on-task data. One downside is the potential variability across users. For example, if you have several users who took an exceedingly long time to complete a task, it may increase the average considerably. Therefore, you should always report a confidence interval to show the variability in the time data. This will not only show the variability within the same task but also help visualize the difference across tasks to determine whether there is a statistically significant difference between tasks.

Some UX researchers prefer to summarize time-on-task data using the median rather than the mean. The median is the middle point in an ordered list of all the

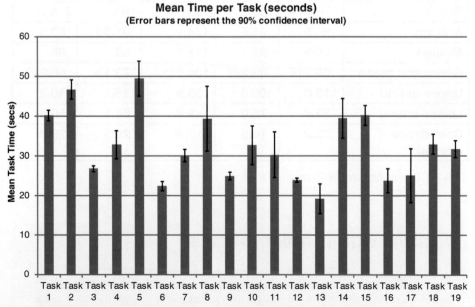

Fig. 4.4 Mean time-on-task for 19 tasks. Error bars represent a 95% confidence interval. These data are from an online study of a prototype website.

times: Half of the times are below the median, and half are above the median. Similarly, some researchers suggest that the geometric mean is potentially less biased. Time data are typically skewed, in which case geometric means may be more appropriate. These alternatives can be calculated in Excel using the "=MEDIAN" or "=GEOMEAN" functions. In practice, we find that using these other methods of summarizing the time data may change the overall level of the times, but the kinds of patterns you're interested in (e.g., comparisons across tasks) usually stay the same; the same tasks still took the longest or shortest times overall.

RANGES

A variation on calculating average completion time by task is to create ranges, or discrete time intervals, and report the frequency of users who fall into each time interval. This is a useful way to visualize the spread of completion times by all users. In addition, this might be a helpful approach to look for any patterns in the type of users who fall within certain segments. For example, you may want to focus on those users who had particularly long completion times to see if they share any common characteristics.

THRESHOLDS

Another useful way to analyze task time data is by using a threshold. In many situations, the only thing that matters is whether users can complete certain tasks within an acceptable amount of time. In many ways, the average is unimportant. The main goal is to minimize the number of users who need an excessive amount of time to complete a task. The main issue is determining what the threshold should be for any given task. One way is to perform the task yourself, keeping track of the time, and then double that number. Alternatively, you could work with the product team to come up with a threshold for each task based on competitive data or even a best guess. Once you have set your threshold, simply calculate the percentage of users above or below the threshold and plot as illustrated in Fig. 4.5.

DISTRIBUTIONS AND OUTLIERS

Whenever analyzing time data, it's critical to look at the distribution. This is particularly true for time-on-task data collected via automated tools (when the moderator is not present). Participants might take a phone call or even go out to lunch in the middle of a task. The last thing you want is to include a task time of 2 hours among other times of only 15 to 20 seconds when calculating an average! It's perfectly acceptable to exclude outliers from your

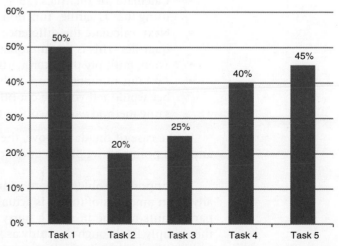

Fig. 4.5 An example showing the percentage of users who completed each task in less than 1 minute.

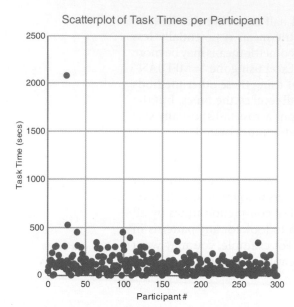

Fig. 4.6 Scatterplot of the time data for one task from an online study with 298 participants. Note the one obvious outlier in the times.

analysis, and many statistical techniques for identifying them are available. Sometimes we exclude any times that are more than two or three standard deviations above the mean. Alternatively, we sometimes set up thresholds, knowing that it should never take a user more than x seconds to complete a task. You should have some rationale for using an arbitrary threshold for excluding outliers.

For example, consider the time data shown in Fig. 4.6. This is the actual time data for one task in an online study with 298 participants. (Note that you can create a scatterplot like this in Excel by simply selecting a single column of times and then inserting a scatterplot. It automatically treats the rows as the data to be plotted on the x-axis.) It's obvious from this figure that there's at least one extreme outlier: the one that's over 2000 seconds while all the others are under about 500 seconds. But are there more outliers? The mean of these times is 115 seconds, with a standard deviation of 145. Using a conservative threshold of the mean plus three standard deviations, or 550 seconds, there are no more outliers at the high end. So the one value of 2081 seconds would be excluded from the analysis.

Another common method to identify and remove outliers is based on the interquartile range. The math is straightforward. Based on this method, you simply do the following:

- Calculate the quartiles (25%, 50%, and 75%). In Excel this can be done using the "Quartile" function.
- Next, calculate the difference between the first (25%) and third (75%) quartiles. This is the interquartile range.
- Then, multiply the interquartile range by 1.5
- Add this number on top of the third quartile (75% quartile). This number would tell you the cut-off point for an outlier at the high level. The same method would work at the lower level.

In the case of the data above, the interquartile method would indicate that any data points above 318 seconds could be considered an outlier.

The opposite problem—participants apparently completing a task in unusually short amounts of time—is actually more common in online studies. Some participants may be in such a hurry or only care about the compensation, so they simply fly through the study as fast as they can. In most cases, it's very easy to identify these individuals through their time data. For each task, determine the fastest possible time. This would be the time it would take someone with perfect knowledge and optimal efficiency to complete the task. For example, if there is no way you, as an expert user of the product, can finish the task in less than 8 seconds, then it is highly unlikely that a typical user could complete the task any faster. Once you have established this minimum acceptable time, you should identify the tasks that have times less than that minimum. These are candidates for removal—not just of the time but of the entire task (including any other data for the task such as success or subjective rating). Unless you can find evidence suggesting otherwise, the time indicates that the participant did not make a reasonable attempt at the task. If a participant did this for multiple tasks, you should consider dropping that participant. You can expect anywhere from 5% to 10% of the participants in an online study to be in it only for the compensation.

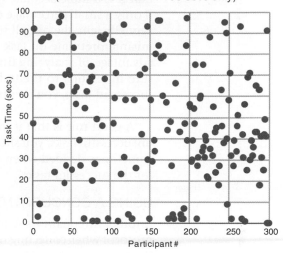

Fig. 4.7 Scatterplot of time data showing task times for participants with less than 100 seconds. This allows the researcher to quickly identify potential data points at the low (fast) end.

Continuing with the same sample time data as shown in Fig. 4.6, consider the graph shown in Fig. 4.7. This shows the same basic data as in Fig. 4.6, but with the y-axis truncated to show only times less than or equal to 100 seconds. This was done to be able to see the data points at the low end. You can see from this graph that there's a "gap" in the data between about 10 and 18 seconds. This is a good indication that the participants who took less than 10 seconds were probably "cheating" and not really attempting the task. This could be further validated by checking the task success data for these participants, which would likely show that they were not successful. These participants would then be candidates for dropping from the analysis. In this example, that's 23 participants at the low end, which is 8% of the total participants.

4.2.4 Issues to Consider When Using Time Data

Some of the issues to think about when analyzing time data is whether to look at all tasks or just the successful tasks, what the impact of using a think-aloud protocol might be, and whether to tell test participants that time is being measured.

ONLY SUCCESSFUL TASKS OR ALL TASKS?

Perhaps the first issue to consider is whether you should include the times for only successful tasks or all tasks in the analysis. The main advantage of only including successful tasks is that it is a cleaner measure of efficiency. For example, time data for unsuccessful tasks are often very difficult to estimate. Some users will keep on trying until you practically unplug the computer. Any task that ends with the participant giving up or the moderator "pulling the plug" is going to result in highly variable time data.

The main advantage of analyzing time data for *all* tasks, successful or not, is that it is a more accurate reflection of the overall user experience. For example, if only a small percentage of users were successful, but that particular group was very efficient, the overall time-on-task is going to be low. Therefore, it is easy to misinterpret time-on-task data when only analyzing successful tasks. Another advantage of analyzing time data for all tasks is that it is an independent measure in relation to the task success data. If you only analyze the time data for successful tasks, you're introducing a dependency between the two sets of data.

A good rule is that if the participant always determined when to give up on unsuccessful tasks, you should include all times in the analyses. If the moderator sometimes decided when to end an unsuccessful task, then use only the times for the successful tasks.

USING A CONCURRENT THINK-ALOUD PROTOCOL

Another important issue to consider is whether to use a concurrent think-aloud protocol when collecting time data (i.e., asking participants to think aloud while they are going through the tasks). Most UX researchers rely heavily on a concurrent think-aloud protocol to gain important insight into the user experience. But sometimes a think-aloud protocol leads to a tangential topic or a lengthy interaction with the moderator. The last thing you want to do is measure time-on-task while a participant is giving a 10-minute diatribe on the importance of fast-loading web pages. A good solution, when you want to capture time-on-task but also use a concurrent think-aloud protocol, is to ask participants to "hold" any longer comments for the time between tasks. Then you can have a dialog with the participant about the just-completed task after the "clock is stopped."

RETROSPECTIVE THINK-ALOUD (RTA)

A technique that is gaining in popularity among many usability professionals is retrospective think-aloud, or RTA (e.g., Birns Joffre, Leclerc, & Paulsen, 2002; Guan, Lee, Cuddihy, Ramey, 2006; Petrie & Precious, 2010). With this technique, participants typically remain silent while they are interacting with the product being tested. Then, after all the tasks, they are shown a "reminder" of what they did during the session and are asked to describe what they were thinking or doing at various points in the interaction. The reminder can take several different forms, including a video replay of screen activity, perhaps with a camera view of the user, or an eye-tracking replay showing what the user was looking at. This technique probably yields the most accurate task time data. Some evidence suggests that the additional cognitive load of concurrent think-aloud causes participants to be less successful with their tasks. For example, van den Haak, de Jong, and Schellens (2004) found that participants in a usability study of a library website were successful with only 37% of their tasks when using concurrent think-aloud, but they were successful with 47% when using retrospective think-aloud. On the other hand, Peute, Keizer, and Jaspers (2015), in studying a physician data query tool, found that concurrent think-aloud performed significantly better in detecting usability problems than did retrospective think-aloud.

SHOULD YOU TELL THE PARTICIPANTS ABOUT THE TIME MEASUREMENT?

An important question to consider is whether or not to tell the participants you are recording their time. It's possible that if you don't, participants won't behave in an efficient manner. It's not uncommon for participants to explore different parts of a website when they are in the middle of a task. On the flip side, if you tell them they are being timed, they may become nervous and feel they are the ones being tested and not the product. A good compromise is asking the participants to perform the tasks as quickly and accurately as possible without volunteering that they are being explicitly timed. If the participant happens to ask (which they rarely do), then simply state that you are noting the start and finish time for each task.

4.3 ERRORS

Some UX professionals believe errors and usability issues are essentially the same thing. Although they are certainly related, they are actually quite different. A usability issue is the underlying *cause* of a problem, whereas one or more errors are possible *outcomes* of an issue. For example, if users are experiencing a problem in completing a purchase on an e-commerce website, the issue (or cause) may be confusing labeling of the products. The error, or the result of the issue, may be the act of choosing the wrong options for the product they want to buy. Essentially, errors are incorrect actions that may lead to task failure.

4.3.1 When to Measure Errors

In some situations it's helpful to identify and classify errors rather than just document usability issues. Measuring errors is useful when you want to understand the specific action or set of actions that may result in task failure. For example, a user may make the wrong selection on a web page and sell a stock instead of buying more. A user may push the wrong button on a medical device and deliver the wrong medication to a patient. In both cases, it's important to know what errors were made and how different design elements may increase or decrease the frequency of errors.

Errors are a useful way of evaluating user performance. While being able to complete a task successfully within a reasonable amount of time is important, the number of errors made during the interaction is also very revealing. Errors can tell you how many mistakes were made, where they were made while interacting with the product, how various designs produce different frequencies and types of errors, and generally how usable something really is.

Measuring errors is not right for every situation. We've found that there are three general situations where measuring errors might be useful:

1. When an error will result in a significant loss in efficiency—for example, when an error results in a loss of data, requires the user to reenter information, or significantly slows the user in completing a task.

2. When an error will result in significant costs to your organization or the end user—for example, if an error will result in increased call volumes to customer support or in increased product returns.
3. When an error will result in task failure—for example, if an error will cause a patient to receive the wrong medication, a voter to accidentally vote for the wrong candidate, or a web user to buy the wrong product.

4.3.2 What Constitutes an Error?

Surprisingly, there is no widely accepted definition of what constitutes an error. Obviously, it's some type of incorrect action on the part of the user. Generally an error is any action that prevents the user from completing a task in the most efficient manner. Errors can be based on many different types of actions by the user, such as the following:

- Entering incorrect data into a form field (such as typing the wrong password during a login attempt)
- Making the wrong choice in a menu or drop-down list (such as selecting "Delete" when they should have selected "Modify")
- Taking an incorrect sequence of actions (such as reformatting their home media server when all they were trying to do was play a recorded TV show)
- Failing to take a key action (such as clicking on a key link on a web page)

Obviously, the range of possible actions will depend on the product you are studying (website, cell phone, media player, etc.). When you're trying to determine what constitutes an error, first make a list of all the possible actions a user can take on your product. Once you have the universe of possible actions, you can then start to define many of the different types of errors that can be made using the product.

4.3.3 Collecting and Measuring Errors

Measuring errors is not always easy. Similar to other performance metrics, you need to know what the correct action should be or, in some cases, the correct set of actions. For example, if you're studying a password reset form, you need to know what is considered the correct set of actions to successfully reset the password and what is not. The better you can define the universe of correct and incorrect actions, the easier it will be to measure errors.

An important consideration is whether a given task presents only a single error opportunity or multiple error opportunities. An error opportunity is basically a chance to make a mistake. For example, if you're measuring the usability of a typical login screen, two error opportunities are possible: making an error when entering the user name and making an error when entering the password. If you're measuring the usability of an online form, there could be as many error opportunities as there are fields on the form.

In some cases there might be multiple error opportunities for a task, but you only care about one of them. For example, you might be interested only in whether users click on a specific link that you know will be critical to completing their task. Even though errors could be made on other places on the page, you're narrowing your scope of interest to that single link. If users don't click on the link, it is considered an error.

The most common way of organizing error data is by task. Simply record the number of errors for each task and each user. If there is only a single opportunity for error, the numbers will be 1's and 0's:

0 = No error
1 = One error

If multiple error opportunities are possible, the numbers will vary between 0 and the maximum number of error opportunities. The more error opportunities, the harder and more time-consuming it will be to tabulate the data. You can count errors while observing the users during a lab study, by reviewing videos after the sessions are over, or by collecting the data using an automated or online tool.

If you can clearly define all the possible error opportunities, another approach could be to identify the presence (1) or absence (0) of each error opportunity for each user and task. The average of these for a task would then reflect the incidence of those errors.

4.3.4 Analyzing and Presenting Errors

The analysis and presentation of error data differ slightly depending upon whether a task has only one error opportunity or multiple error opportunities.

TASKS WITH A SINGLE ERROR OPPORTUNITY

The most common way to analyze errors for tasks with single opportunities is to look at the frequency of the error for each task. This will indicate which tasks are associated with the most errors and thus have the most significant usability issues. This can be done in either of two ways with slightly different forms of interpretation:

- Run a frequency of errors by task and plot out the number of errors. This would show the number of errors made on each task. Note that you do not need to use confidence intervals in this type of analysis because you are not trying to extrapolate to a more general population; you are only interested in seeing which tasks have the most errors.
- Divide the number of errors by the total number of participants for each task. This will tell you the percentage of participants who made

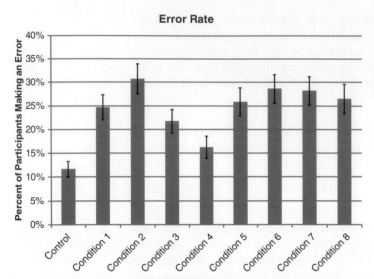

Error Rate

Fig. 4.8 An example showing how to present data for single-error opportunities. In this study, only one error opportunity per task (entering a password incorrectly) was possible, and the graph shows the percentage of participants who made an error for each condition.

an error for each task. This is especially useful if different numbers of participants performed each task. Fig. 4.8 is an example of presenting errors based on a single opportunity. In this example, they were interested in the percentage of participants who experienced an error when using different types of on-screen keyboards (Tullis, Mangan, & Rosenbaum, 2007). The control condition is the current QWERTY keyboard layout.

Another way to analyze and present error metrics for tasks with single opportunities is from an aggregate perspective. You may not always be concerned about a specific task, but about how users performed overall. Here are some options:

- You could average the error rates for each task into a single error rate. This would tell you the overall error rate for the study. For example, you might be able to say that the tasks had an average error rate of 25%. This is a useful bottom-line metric for reporting errors.
- Another way is to take an average of all the tasks that had a certain number of errors. For example, if you are looking at a large number of tasks, you could report that 50% of the tasks had an error rate of 10% or greater. Or you might state that at least one participant made an error on 80% of the tasks.
- You could establish maximum acceptable error rates for each task. For example, you might only be interested in identifying the tasks that have an error rate above a particular threshold, such as 10%. You could then calculate the percentage of tasks above and below this threshold. For example, you might simply state that 25% of the tasks exceeded an acceptable error rate.
- Lastly, you might want to categorize each type of error (Fig. 4.9). For example, you could identify different sources of each error, such as those that are based on navigation, content, terminology, or simple lack of awareness. By categorizing each error, you will now be able to get a sense of how to remedy the various errors, as well as a priority of error type.

TASKS WITH MULTIPLE ERROR OPPORTUNITIES

Here are some of the more common ways to analyze the data from tasks that provide multiple error opportunities:

- A good place to start is to look at the frequency of errors for each task. You will be able to see which tasks are resulting in the most errors. But this may be misleading if each task has a different number of error opportunities. In that case, it might be better to divide the total number of errors for the task by the total number of error opportunities. This creates an error rate that takes into account the number of opportunities.
- You could calculate the average number of errors made by each participant for each task. This will also tell you which tasks are producing the most errors. However, it may be more meaningful because it suggests that a

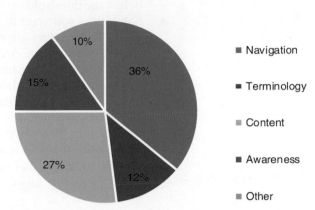

Error Type Averaged Across Tasks

- Navigation
- Terminology
- Content
- Awareness
- Other

Fig. 4.9 The percentage of different types of errors aggregated across all tasks.

typical user might experience *x* number of errors on a particular task when using the product. Another advantage is that it takes into account the extremes. If you are simply looking at the frequency of errors for each task, some users may be the source of most of the errors, whereas many others are performing the task error-free. By taking an average number of errors by each user, this bias is reduced. See Fig. 4.10 as an example of presenting the average number of errors per task.

- In some situations, it might be interesting to know which tasks fall above or below a threshold. For example, for some tasks, an error rate above 20% is unacceptable, whereas for others, an error rate above 5% is unacceptable. The most straightforward analysis is to first establish an

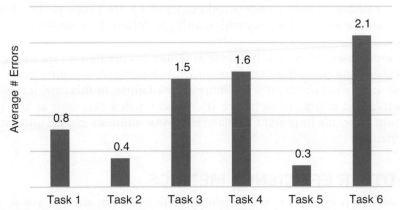

Fig. 4.10 Presenting the average number of errors for each task.

acceptable threshold for each task or each participant. Next, calculate whether that specific task's error rate or user error count was above or below the threshold.

- Sometimes you want to take into account that not all errors are created equal. Some errors are much more serious than others. It's possible to weight each type of error with a different value and then calculate an "error score"—for example, trivial, moderate, and serious. You could then weight each of those errors with a value of 1 (trivial), 2 (moderate), or 3 (serious). Then, simply add up the score for each participant using these weights. Divide all the scores by the number of participants for each task. This will produce an average "error score" for each task. The interpretation is a little different from an error rate. Essentially, you will be able to report that certain tasks have more frequent and/or serious errors than other tasks.

4.3.5 Issues to Consider When Using Error Metrics

Several important issues must be considered when looking at errors. First, make sure you are not double-counting errors. Double-counting happens when you assign more than one error to the same event. For example, assume you are counting errors in a password field. If a user typed an extra character in the password, you could count that as an "extra character" error, but you shouldn't also count it as an "incorrect character" error.

Sometimes you need to know more than just an error rate; you need to know *why* different errors are occurring. The best way to do this is by looking at each type of error. Basically, you want to try to code each error by type of error. Coding should be based on the various types of errors that occurred. For example, continuing with the password example, the types of errors might include "missing character," "transposed characters," "extra character," and so on. Or at a higher level, you might have "navigation error," "selection error," "interpretation error," and so on. Once you have coded each error, you can run frequencies on the error type for each task to better understand exactly where the problems lie. This will also help improve the efficiency with which you collect the error data.

In some cases, an error is the same as failing to complete a task—for example, with a login page. If no errors occur while logging in, it is the same as task success. If an error occurs, it is the same as task failure. In this case, it might be easier to report errors as task failure. It's not so much a data issue as it is a presentation issue. It's important to make sure your audience clearly understands your metrics.

4.4 OTHER EFFICIENCY METRICS

Time-on-task is often used as a measure of efficiency, but another way to measure efficiency is to look at the amount of effort required to complete a task. This is typically done by measuring the number of actions or steps that users took in performing each task. An action can take many forms, such as clicking a link on a web page, pressing a button on a microwave oven or a mobile phone, or flipping a switch on an aircraft. Each action a user performs represents a certain amount of effort. The more actions taken by a user, the more effort involved. In most products, the goal is to minimize the number of discrete actions required to complete a task, thereby minimizing the amount of effort.

What do we mean by effort? There are at least two types of effort: cognitive and physical. Cognitive effort involves finding the right place to perform an action (e.g., finding a link on a web page), deciding what action is necessary (should I click this link?), and interpreting the results of the action. Physical effort involves the physical activity required to take action, such as moving your mouse, inputting text on a keyboard, turning on a switch, and many others.

Efficiency metrics work well if you are concerned not only with the time it takes to complete a task but also the amount of cognitive and physical effort involved. For example, if you're designing an automobile navigation system, you need to make sure that it does not take much effort to interpret its navigation directions, since the driver's attention must be focused on the road. It would be important to minimize both the physical and cognitive effort to use the navigation system.

4.4.1 Collecting and Measuring Efficiency

There are five important points to keep in mind when collecting and measuring efficiency.

Identify the action(s) to be measured: For websites, mouse clicks or page views are common actions. For software, it might be mouse clicks or keystrokes. For appliances or consumer electronics, it could be button presses. Regardless of the product being evaluated, you should have a clear idea of all the possible actions.

Define the start and end of an action: You need to know when an action begins and ends. Sometimes the action is very quick, such as a press of a button, but other actions can take much longer. An action may be more passive in nature, such as looking at a web page. Some actions have a very clear start and end, whereas other actions are less defined.

Count the actions: You must be able to count the actions. Actions must happen at a pace that can be identified visually or, if they are too fast, by an automated system. Try to avoid having to review hours of video to collect efficiency metrics.

Actions must be meaningful: Each action should represent an incremental increase in cognitive and/or physical effort. The more actions, the more effort. For example, each click of a mouse is almost always an incremental increase in effort.

Only look at successful tasks: When measuring efficiency using the number of actions, you should only calculate it for successful tasks. It does not make sense to include task failures. For example, a participant may quit a task after only a few steps when they become hopelessly lost. If you used this data, it may look like they performed at the same level of efficiency as another participant who completed the task successfully with the minimum number of steps required.

Once you have identified the actions you want to capture, counting those actions is relatively simple. You can do it manually, such as counting page views or presses of a button. This will work for fairly simple products, but in most cases, it is not practical. Many times a participant is performing these actions at amazing speeds. There may be more than one action every second, so using automated data collection tools is far preferable.

4.4.2 Analyzing and Presenting Efficiency Data

The most common way to analyze and present efficiency metrics is by looking at the number of actions each participant takes to complete a task. Simply calculate an average for each task (by participant) to see how many actions are taken. This analysis is helpful in identifying which tasks required the most amount of effort, and it works well when each task requires about the same number of actions. However, if some tasks are more complicated than others, it may be misleading. It's also important to represent the confidence intervals (based on a continuous distribution) for this type of chart.

Shaikh, Baker, and Russell (2004) used an efficiency metric based on number of clicks to accomplish the same task on three different weight-loss sites: Atkins, Jenny Craig, and Weight Watchers (WW). They found that users were significantly more efficient (needed fewer clicks) with the Atkins site than with the Jenny Craig or WW sites.

LOSTNESS

Another measure of efficiency sometimes used in studying behavior on the web is called "lostness" (Smith, 1996). Lostness is calculated using three values:

N: The number of *different* web pages visited while performing the task
S: The *total* number of pages visited while performing the task, counting revisits to the same page
R: The *minimum* (optimum) number of pages that must be visited to accomplish the task

Lostness, L, is then calculated using the following formula:

$$L = \mathrm{sqrt}[(N/S - 1)^2 + (R/N - 1)^2]$$

Consider the example shown in Fig. 4.11. In this case, the user's task is to find something on Product Page C1. Starting on the home page, the minimum number of page visits (R) to accomplish this task is three. On the other hand, Fig. 4.12

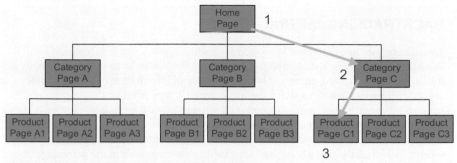

Fig. 4.11 Optimum number of steps (three) to accomplish a task that involves finding a target item on Product Page C1 starting from the home page.

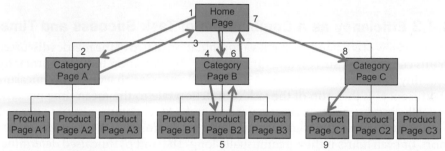

Fig. 4.12 Actual number of steps a user took in getting to the target item on Product Page C1. Note that each revisit to the same page is counted, giving a total of eight steps.

illustrates the path a particular user took in getting to that target item. This user started down some incorrect paths before finally getting to the right place, visiting a total of six different pages (N), or a total of eight page visits (S). So for this example:

$N = 6$
$S = 8$
$R = 3$

$$L = \text{sqrt}[(6/8 - 1)^2 + (3/6 - 1)^2] = 0.56$$

A perfect lostness score would be 0. Smith (1996) found that participants with a lostness score less than 0.4 did not exhibit any observable characteristics of being lost. On the other hand, participants with a lostness score greater than 0.5 definitely did appear to be lost.

Once you calculate a lostness value, you can easily calculate the average lostness value for each task. The number or percent of participants who exceed the ideal number of actions can also be indicative of the efficiency of the design. For example, you could show that 25% of the participants exceeded the ideal or minimum number of steps, and you could break it down even further by saying that 50% of the participants completed a task with the minimum number of actions.

BACKTRACKING METRIC

Treejack is a tool from Optimal Workshop for testing information architectures (IAs). Participants in a Treejack study navigate an information hierarchy to indicate where in the hierarchy they would expect to find a given piece of information or perform some action. Participants can move down the hierarchy, or, if they need to, they can move back up it. Several useful metrics come out of a Treejack study, including traditional ones such as where the participants indicated they would expect to find each function. But a particularly interesting metric is a "backtracking" metric, which indicates the cases where a participant went back *up* the hierarchy. You can then look at the percentage of participants who "backtracked" while performing each task. In our IA studies, we've found this was often the most revealing metric.

4.4.3 Efficiency as a Combination of Task Success and Time

Another view of efficiency is that it's a combination of two of the metrics discussed in this chapter: task success and time-on-task. The Common Industry Format for Usability Test Reports (ISO/IEC 25062:2006) specifies that the "core measure of efficiency" is the ratio of the task completion rate to the mean time per task. Basically, it expresses task success per unit time. Most commonly, time per task is expressed in minutes, but seconds could be appropriate if the tasks are very short, or even hours if they are unusually long. The unit of time used determines the scale of the results. Your goal is to choose a unit that yields a "reasonable" scale (i.e., one where most of the values fall between 1% and 100%). Table 4.3 shows an example of calculating an efficiency metric based on task completion and task time. Fig. 4.13 shows how this efficiency metric looks in a chart. The efficiency measure is simply the ratio of the task completion to the task time in minutes. Of course, higher values of efficiency are better. In this example, users appear to have been more efficient in performing tasks 5 and 6 than other tasks.

A slight variation on this approach to calculating efficiency is to count the number of tasks successfully completed by each participant and divide that by the

	Task Completion Rate (%)	Task Time (min)	Efficiency (%)
Task 1	65	1.5	43
Task 2	67	1.4	48
Task 3	40	2.1	19
Task 4	74	1.7	44
Task 5	85	1.2	71
Task 6	90	1.4	64
Task 7	49	2.1	23
Task 8	33	1.3	25

Table 4.3 Table showing how efficiency is calculated based on task completion rate and task time.

Efficiency (Task Success per Minute)

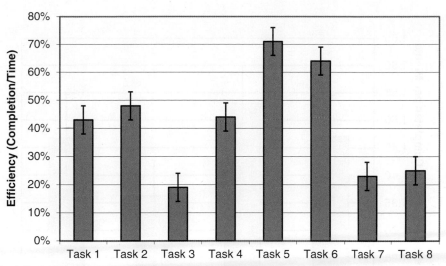

Fig. 4.13 An example showing efficiency as a function of completion rate/time.

total time spent by the participant on *all* the tasks (successful and unsuccessful). This gives you a very straightforward efficiency score for each participant: number of tasks successfully completed per minute (or whatever unit of time you used). If a participant completed 10 tasks successfully in a total time of 10 minutes, then that participant was successfully completing 1 task per minute overall. This works best when all participants attempt the same number of tasks, and the tasks are relatively comparable in terms of their level of difficulty.

Fig. 4.14 shows the data from an online study comparing four different navigation prototypes for a website. This was a between-subjects study, in which each participant used only one of the prototypes, but all participants were asked to perform the same 20 tasks. Over 200 participants used each prototype. We were able to count the number of tasks successfully completed by each participant and divide that by the total time that participant spent. The averages of these (and the 95% confidence intervals) are shown in Fig. 4.14.

4.5 LEARNABILITY

Most products, especially new ones, require some amount of learning. Usually learning does not happen in an instant but occurs over time as experience increases. Experience is based on the amount of time spent using a product and the variety of tasks performed. Learning is sometimes quick and painless, but at other times it is quite arduous and time-consuming. Learnability is the extent to which something can be learned. It can be measured by looking at how much

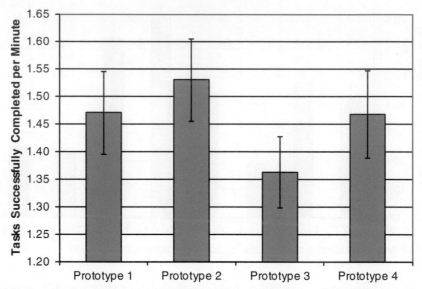

Average Efficiency (Tasks Successfully Completed per Minute)

Fig. 4.14 Average number of tasks successfully completed per minute in an online study of four different prototypes of navigation for a website. Over 200 participants attempted 20 tasks for each prototype. Participants using Prototype 2 were significantly more efficient (i.e., completed more tasks per minute) than those using Prototype 3.

time and effort is required to become proficient and ultimately expert in using something. We believe that learnability is an important metric that does not receive as much attention as it should. It's an essential metric if you need to know how someone develops proficiency with a product over time.

Consider the following example. Assume you're a UX researcher who has been asked to evaluate a time-keeping application for employees within their organization. You could go into the lab and test with 10 participants, giving each participant a set of core tasks. You might measure task success, time-on-task, errors, and even overall satisfaction. Using these metrics will allow you to get some sense of the usability of the application. Although these metrics are useful, they can also be misleading. Because the use of a time-keeping application is not a one-time event, but happens with some degree of frequency, learnability is very important. What really matters is how much time and effort is required to become *proficient* using the time-keeping application. Yes, there may be some initial obstacles when first using the application, but what really matters is "getting up to speed." It's quite common in usability studies to look only at a participant's initial exposure to something, but sometimes it's more important to look at the amount of effort needed to become proficient.

Learning can happen over a short period of time or over longer periods of time. When learning happens over a short period of time, the user tries out different strategies to complete tasks. A short period of time might be several minutes, hours, or days. For example, if users have to submit their timesheets every day using a time-keeping application, they try to quickly develop some type of mental model of how the application works. Memory is not a big factor in learnability; it is more about adapting strategies to maximize efficiency. The hope is that maximum efficiency is achieved within a few hours or days.

Learning can also happen over a longer time period, such as weeks, months, or years. This is the case where there are significant gaps in time between each use. For example, if you only fill out an expense report every few months, learnability can be a significant challenge because you may have to relearn the application each time you use it. In this situation, memory is very important. The more time there is between experiences with the product, the greater the reliance on memory.

4.5.1 Collecting and Measuring Learnability Data

Collecting and measuring learnability data is basically the same as it is for the other performance metrics, but you're collecting the data multiple times. Each instance of collecting the data is considered a trial. A trial might be every 5 minutes, every day, or once a month. The time between trials, or when you collect the data, is based on expected frequency of use.

The first decision is which type of metrics you want to use. Learnability can be measured using almost any performance metric over time, but the most common ones are those that focus on efficiency, such as time-on-task, errors, number of steps, or task success per minute. As learning occurs, you expect to see efficiency improve.

After you decide which metrics to use, you need to decide how much time to allow between trials. What do you do when learning occurs over a very long time? What if users interact with a product once every week, month, or even year? The ideal situation would be to bring the same participants into the lab every week, month, or even year. In many cases, this is not very practical. The developers and the business sponsors might not be very pleased if you tell them the study will take 3 years to complete. A more realistic approach is to bring in the same participants over a much shorter time span and acknowledge the limitation in the data. Here are a few alternatives:

Trials within the same session. The participant performs the task, or set of tasks, one right after the other, with no breaks in between. This is very easy to administer, but it does not take into account significant memory loss.

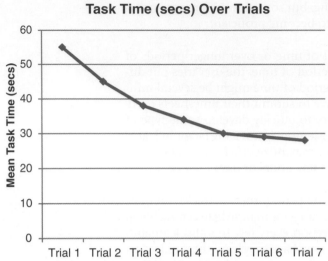

Task Time (secs) Over Trials

Fig. 4.15 An example of how to present learnability data based on time-on-task.

Trials within the same session but with breaks in between each task. The break might be a distracter task or anything that might promote forgetting. This is fairly easy to administer, but it tends to make each session relatively long.

Trials between sessions: The participant performs the same tasks over multiple sessions, with at least 1 day in between. This may be the least practical, but most realistic, if the product is used sporadically over an extended period of time.

4.5.2 Analyzing and Presenting Learnability Data

The most common way to analyze and present learnability data is by examining a specific performance metric (such as time-on-task, number of steps, or number of errors) by trial for each task or aggregated across all tasks. This will show you how that performance metric changes as a function of experience, as illustrated in Fig. 4.15. You could aggregate all the tasks together and represent them as a single line of data, or you could look at each task as separate lines of data. This can help to determine how the learnability of different tasks compare, but it also can also make the chart harder to interpret.

The first aspect of the chart you should notice is the slope of the line(s). Ideally, the slope (sometimes called the learning curve) is fairly flat and low on the y-axis (in the case of errors, time-on-task, number of steps, or any other metric where a smaller number is better). If you want to determine whether a statistically significant difference between the learning curves (or slopes) exists, you need to perform an analysis of variance and see if there is a main effect of trial.

SLOPE FUNCTION IN EXCEL

A useful Excel function for analyzing learnability data is the SLOPE function. The arguments to the SLOPE function are a set of known "x" values and associated "y" values. For example, the "x" values might be trial numbers. The "y" values might be the times associated with each trial. The SLOPE function then returns the slope of the linear regression line through those points (i.e., the slope of the best-fitting straight line through the data).

You should also notice the point of asymptote, or essentially where the line starts to flatten out. This is the point at which users have learned as much as they can, and there is very little room for improvement. Project team members are always interested in how long it will take someone to reach maximum performance.

Finally, you should look at the difference between the highest and lowest values on the y-axis. This will tell you how much learning must occur to reach maximum performance. If the gap is small, users will be able to learn the product quickly. If the gap is large, users may take quite some time to become proficient with the product. One easy way to analyze the gap between the highest and lowest scores is by looking at the ratio of the 2. Here's an example:

- If the average time on the first trial is 80 seconds and on the last trial is 60 seconds, the ratio shows that users are initially taking 1.3 times longer.
- If the average number of errors on the first trial is 2.1 and on the last trial is 0.3, the ratio shows a 7 times improvement from the first trial to the last trial.

It may be helpful to look at how many trials are needed to reach maximum performance. This is a good way to characterize the amount of learning required to become proficient in using the product.

In some cases you might want to compare learnability across different conditions, as shown in Fig. 4.16. In this study (Tullis, Mangan, & Rosenbaum, 2007), they were interested in how speed (efficiency) of entering a password changed over time using different types of on-screen keyboards. As you can see from the data, there is an improvement from the first trial to the second trial, but then the times flatten out pretty quickly. Also, all the on-screen keyboards were significantly slower than the control condition, which was a real keyboard.

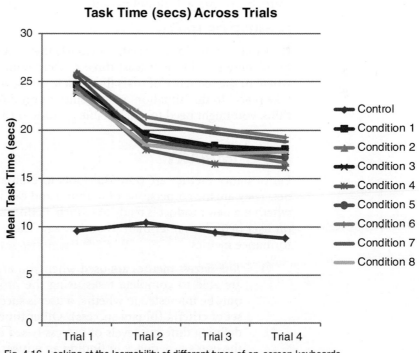

Fig. 4.16 Looking at the learnability of different types of on-screen keyboards.

4.5.3 Issues to Consider When Measuring Learnability

Two of the key issues to address when measuring learnability are (1) what should be considered a trial and (2) how many trials to include.

WHAT IS A TRIAL?

In some situations learning is continuous. This means that the user is interacting with the product fairly continuously without any significant breaks in time. Memory is much less a factor in this situation. Learning is more about developing and modifying different strategies to complete a set of tasks. The whole concept of trials does not make much sense for continuous learning. What do you do in this situation? One approach is to take your measurements at specified time intervals. For example, you may need to take measurements every 5 minutes, 15 minutes, or every hour. In one usability study we conducted, we wanted to evaluate the learnability of a new suite of applications that would be used many times every day. We started by bringing the participants into the lab for their first exposure to the applications and their initial tasks. They then went back to their regular jobs and began using the applications to do their normal work. We brought them back into the lab 1 month later and had them perform basically the same tasks again (with minor changes in details) while we took the same performance measures. Finally, we brought them back one more time after another month and repeated the procedure. In this way, we were able to look at learnability over a 2-month period.

NUMBER OF TRIALS

How many trials do you need? Obviously there must be at least two, but in most cases there should be at least three or four. Sometimes it's difficult to predict where in the sequence of trials the most learning will take place, or even *if* it will take place. In this situation, you should err on the side of more trials than you think you might need to reach stable performance.

4.6 SUMMARY

Performance metrics are powerful tools to evaluate the usability of any product. They are the cornerstone of usability and can inform key decisions, such as whether a new product is ready to launch. Performance metrics are always based on user behavior rather than what they say. There are five general types of performance metrics:

1. *Task success* metrics are used when you are interested in whether users are able to complete tasks using the product. Sometimes you might only be interested in whether a user is successful or not based on a strict set of criteria (binary success). Other times you might be interested in defining different levels of success based on the degree of completion, the user's experience in finding an answer, or the quality of the answer given.

2. *Time-on-task* is helpful when you are concerned about how quickly users can perform tasks with the product. You might look at the time it takes to complete a task for all users, a subset of users, or the proportion of users who can complete a task within a desired time limit.

3. *Errors* are a useful measure based on the number of mistakes users make while attempting to complete a task. A task might have a single error opportunity or multiple error opportunities, and some types of errors may be more important than others.

4. *Efficiency* is a way of evaluating the amount of effort (cognitive and physical) required to complete a task. Efficiency is often measured by the number of steps or actions required to complete a task or by the ratio of the task success rate to the average time per task.

5. *Learnability* involves looking at how any efficiency metric changes over time. Learnability is useful if you want to examine how and when users reach proficiency in using a product.

CONTENTS

Measuring the User Experience. DOI: http://dx.doi.org/10.1016/B978-0-12-818080-8.00005-4

Perhaps the most obvious way to learn about the user's experience with something is to ask users to tell you about that experience. But exactly how to ask so that you get good data is not so obvious. The questions you might ask could take on many forms, including various kinds of rating scales, lists of attributes that the users choose from, and open-ended questions like "List the top three things you liked the most about this application." Some of the attributes you might ask about include overall satisfaction, ease of use, effectiveness of navigation, awareness of certain features, clarity of terminology, visual appeal, trust in a company that sponsors a website, enjoyment in playing a game, and many others. But the common feature of all of these is you're asking the user for information, which is why we think *self-reported* best describes these metrics. And as we will see, one critical type of self-reported data is the verbatim comments made by participants while using a product.

THE EVOLUTION OF USABILITY AND USER EXPERIENCE

One of the historical precedents for the usability field was human factors, or ergonomics, which itself grew primarily out of World War II and a desire to improve airplane cockpits to minimize pilot error. With this ancestry, it's not surprising that much of the early focus of usability was on performance data (e.g., speed and accuracy). But that has been changing, quite significantly we think. Part of the reason for the widespread adoption of the term "user experience," or UX, is the focus that it provides on the entire range of experience that the user has with a product. Even the Usability Professionals Association (UPA) changed its name in 2012 to the User Experience Professionals Association (UXPA). All of this reflects the importance of the kind of metrics we discuss in this chapter and tries to encompass such states as delight, joy, trust, fun, challenge, anger, frustration, and many more. An interesting analysis was done by Bargas-Avila and Hornbæk (2011) of 66 empirical studies in the UX literature from 2005 to 2009 showing how the studies reflect some of these shifts. They found, for example, that emotions, enjoyment, and aesthetics were the most frequently assessed UX dimensions in recent studies.

Two other terms sometimes used to describe this kind of data include *subjective data* and *preference data*. *Subjective* is used as a counterpart to *objective*, which is often used to describe the performance data from a usability study. But this implies that there's a lack of objectivity to the data you're collecting. Yes, it may be subjective to each participant who's providing the input, but from the perspective of the user experience professional, it is completely objective. Similarly, *preference* is often used as a counterpart to *performance*. Although there's nothing wrong with that, we believe that preference implies a choice of one option over another, which is often not the case in UX studies.

5.1 IMPORTANCE OF SELF-REPORTED DATA

Self-reported data give you the most important information about users' *perception* of the system and their interaction with it. At an emotional level, the data may tell you something about how the users *feel* about the system. In many situations, these kinds of reactions are the main thing that you care about. Even if it takes users a long time to perform something with a system, if the experience makes them happy, that may be the only thing that matters.

Your goal is to make the users think of your product first. For example, when deciding what travel-planning website to use for an upcoming vacation, users are more likely to think of the site that they liked the last time they used it. They're much less likely to remember how long the process was or that it took more mouse clicks than it should have. That is why users' subjective reactions to a website, product, or store may be the best predictor of their likelihood to return or make a purchase in the future.

5.2 RATING SCALES

One of the most common ways to capture self-reported data in a UX study is with some type of rating scale. Two of the classic approaches to rating scales are the Likert scale and semantic differential scale.

5.2.1 Likert Scales

A typical item in a Likert scale is a statement to which the respondents rate their level of agreement. The statement may be positive (e.g., "The terminology used in this interface is clear") or negative (e.g., "I found the navigation options confusing"). Usually, a 5-point scale of agreement like the following is used:

1. Strongly disagree
2. Disagree
3. Neither agree nor disagree
4. Agree
5. Strongly agree

In the original version of the scale, Likert (1932) provided "anchor terms" for each point on the scale, such as Agree, and did not use numbers. Some people prefer to use a 7-point scale, but it gets a bit more difficult to come up with descriptive terms for each point as you get to higher numbers. This is one reason many researchers have dropped the intervening labels and just label the two ends (or anchor points) and perhaps the middle, or neutral, point. Many variations on Likert scales are still used today, but most Likert-scale purists would say that the two main characteristics of an item on a Likert scale are: (1) it expresses the degree of agreement with a statement, and (2) it uses an odd number of response options, thus allowing a neutral response. By convention, the "Strongly Agree" end of a Likert scale is generally shown on the right when presented horizontally.

In designing the *statements* for Likert scales, you need to be careful how you word them. You should avoid adverbs like *very, extremely*, or *absolutely* in the statements and use unmodified versions of adjectives. For example, the statement "This website is beautiful" may yield results that are quite different from "This website is absolutely beautiful," which may decrease the likelihood of strong agreement.

WHO WAS LIKERT?

Many people have heard of Likert scales, but not many know where the name came from or even how to pronounce it! It's pronounced "LICK-ert," not "LIKE-ert." This type of scale is named for Rensis Likert, who created it in 1932.

5.2.2 Semantic Differential Scales

The semantic differential technique involves presenting pairs of bipolar, or opposite, adjectives at either end of a series of scales, such as the following:

Weak	o	o	o	o	o	o	o	Strong
Ugly	o	o	o	o	o	o	o	Beautiful
Cool	o	o	o	o	o	o	o	Warm
Amateur	o	o	o	o	o	o	o	Professional

Like the Likert scale, a 5-point or 7-point scale is commonly used. The difficult part about the semantic differential technique is coming up with words that are truly opposites. Sometimes a thesaurus can be helpful since it includes antonyms. However, you need to be aware of the connotations of different pairings of words. For example, a pairing of "Friendly/Unfriendly" may have a somewhat different connotation and yield different results from "Friendly/Not Friendly" or "Friendly/Hostile."

OSGOOD'S SEMANTIC DIFFERENTIAL

The semantic differential technique was developed by Charles E. Osgood (Osgood et al., 1957), who designed it to measure the connotations of words or concepts. Using factor analysis of large sets of semantic differential data, he found three recurring attitudes that people used in assessing words and phrases: evaluation (like "good/bad"), potency (like "strong/weak"), and activity (like "passive/active").

WHICH IS BETTER: LIKERT-STYLE OR SEMANTIC-DIFFERENTIAL-STYLE QUESTIONS?

Some researchers prefer scales of agreement (i.e., Likert-style), while others prefer item-specific endpoints (i.e., semantic-differential-style). But is there any evidence to show that one is better than the other? Jim Lewis (2018) conducted a study to address this question. He argued that scales of agreement might suffer from an "acquiescence bias" in which respondents are slightly more likely to agree with agree/disagree scales. Two hundred respondents completed a survey in which they rated a recent interaction with an auto insurance website. Half of the respondents gave ratings using an agreement format, and half gave ratings using item-specific endpoint anchors. Of 14 comparisons made between metrics using agreement versus item-specific formats, 12 (86%) showed no significant difference. The two statistically significant differences were those for Efficient and Reliable. For both items, the means of the agreement versions were significantly lower than those for the item-specific versions, which is the opposite of the expected result if there were an acquiescence bias. Lewis concludes that both agreement and item-specific formats appeared to work equally well.

5.2.3 When to Collect Self-Reported Data

During a UX study, you might collect self-reported data in the form of verbatim comments from a think-aloud protocol while the participants are interacting with the product. Two additional times when you might want to more explicitly probe for self-reported data are immediately after each task (post-task ratings) and at the end of the entire session (post-study ratings). Post-study ratings tend to be the more common, but both have advantages. Quick ratings immediately after each task can help pinpoint tasks and parts of the interface that are particularly problematic. More in-depth ratings and open-ended questions at the end of the session can provide an effective overall evaluation after the participant has had a chance to interact with the product more fully. It is also common to collect self-reported data in the form of an "exit survey" after users of a website have completed what they came to the site for.

5.2.4 How to Collect Ratings

Logistically, three techniques can be used to collect self-reported data in a UX study: answer questions or provide ratings orally, record responses on a paper form, or provide responses using some type of online tool. Each technique has its advantages and disadvantages. Having the participant provide responses orally is the easiest method from the participant's perspective, but, of course, it means that an observer needs to record the responses and may introduce some bias as participants sometimes feel uncomfortable verbally stating poor ratings. This works best for a single, quick rating after each task.

Paper forms and online forms are suitable for both quick ratings and for longer surveys. Paper forms may be easier to create than online, but they involve manual entry of the data, including the potential for errors in interpreting handwriting. Online forms are getting easier to create, as evidenced by the number of web-based questionnaire tools available, and participants are getting more accustomed to using them. One technique that works well is to have a laptop computer or perhaps a tablet computer with the online questionnaire next to the participant's computer in a UX study. The participant can then easily refer to the application or website while completing the online survey.

ONLINE SURVEY TOOLS

Many tools are available for creating and administering surveys via the web. Doing a search on "online survey tools" turns up a pretty extensive list. Some of them are Google Forms, Qualtrics, SnapSurveys, SoGoSurvey, SurveyGizmo, SurveyMonkey, SurveyShare, TypeForm, and Zoho Surveys. Most of these tools support a variety of question types, including rating scales, checkboxes, drop-down lists, grids, and open-ended questions. These tools generally have some type of free trial or other limited-functionality subscription that lets you try out the service for free.

5.2.5 Biases in Collecting Self-Reported Data

Some studies have shown that people who are asked directly for self-reported data, either in person or over the phone, provide more positive feedback than when asked through an anonymous web survey (e.g., Dillman et al., 2008). This is called the social desirability bias (Nancarrow & Brace, 2000), in which respondents tend to give answers they believe will make them look better in the eyes of others. For example, people who are called on the phone and asked to evaluate their satisfaction with a product typically report higher satisfaction than if they reported their satisfaction levels in a more anonymous way. Telephone respondents or participants in a usability lab essentially want to tell us what they think we want to hear, and that is usually positive feedback about our product.

Therefore, we suggest collecting post-test data in such a way that the moderator or facilitator does not see the user's responses until after the participant has left. This might mean either turning away or leaving the room when the user fills out the automated or paper survey. Making the survey itself anonymous may also elicit more honest reactions. Some UX researchers have suggested asking participants in a usability study to complete a post-test survey after they get back to their office or home and received their incentive. This can be done by giving them a paper survey and a postage-paid envelope to mail it back or by emailing a pointer to an online survey. The main drawback of this approach is that you will typically have some dropoff in terms of who completes the survey. Another drawback is that it increases the amount of time between the user's interaction with the product and their evaluation via the survey, which could have unpredictable results.

5.2.6 General Guidelines for Rating Scales

Crafting good rating scales and questions is hard; it is both an art and a science. So, before you go off on your own, look at existing sets of questions, like those in this chapter, to see if you cannot use those instead. But if you decide that you need to create your own, here are some general points to consider:

- **Multiple scales help "triangulate."** When creating scales to assess a specific attribute such as visual appeal, credibility, or responsiveness, the main thing to remember is that you will probably get more reliable data if you can think of a few different ways to ask participants to assess the attribute. In analyzing the results, you would average those responses together to arrive at the participant's overall reaction for that attribute. Likewise, the success of questionnaires that include both positive and negative statements to which participants respond would suggest the value of including both types of statements.

- **Odd or even number of values?** The number of values to use in rating scales can be a source of heated debate among UX professionals. Many of the arguments center on the use of an even or odd number of points on the scale. An odd number of points has a center, or neutral, point, whereas an even number does not, thus forcing the user slightly toward one end or the other on the scale. We believe that in most real-world situations a neutral reaction is a perfectly valid reaction and should be allowed on a rating scale. So in most cases, we use rating scales with an odd number of points. However, there's some indication that not including a mid-point may minimize the effect of the social desirability bias in the face-to-face administration of rating scales (e.g., Garland, 1991).

- **Total number of points.** The other issue, of course, is the actual number of points to use on the rating scales. Some people seem to believe "more is always better," but we don't really agree with that. The survey literature suggests that any more than nine points rarely provides useful additional information (e.g., Cox, 1980; Friedman & Friedman, 1985). In practice, we use five or seven points.

IS FIVE POINTS ENOUGH FOR A RATING SCALE?

Craig Finstad (2010) did an interesting study comparing 5-point and 7-point versions of the same set of rating scales (the System Usability Scale [SUS], to be discussed later in this chapter). The ratings were administered orally. He counted the number of times that the participant answered with an "interpolation," such as 3.5, 3½, or "between 3 and 4." In other words, the participant wanted to pick a value *between* two of the values given on the scale. He found that the participants using the 5-point version of the scale were significantly more likely to use interpolations than those using the 7-point version. In fact, about 3% of the individual ratings on the 5-point scale were interpolations, while *none* of the ratings on the 7-point scale were. This would suggest that verbal (and perhaps paper-based) rating scales, where the participant could be tempted to use interpolations, might yield more accurate results with 7-point scales. Sauro (2010) also concluded that 7-point scales are slightly better than 5-point scales.

SHOULD YOU NUMBER SCALE VALUES?

One of the issues that comes up in designing rating scales is whether to show the user a numeric value for each scale position. Our sense is that with scales of no more than five or seven values, adding numbers for each position is not necessary. But as you increase the number of scale values, numbers might become more useful in helping the user keep track of where she or he is on the scale. But don't use something like −3, −2, −1, 0, +1, +2, +3. Studies have shown that people tend to avoid using zero or negative values (e.g., Schwarz et al., 1991; Sangster & Willitz, 2001).

5.2.7 Analyzing Rating-Scale Data

The most common technique for analyzing data from rating scales is to assign a numeric value to each of the scale positions and then compute the averages. For example, in the case of a 5-point Likert scale, you might assign a value of 1 to the "Strongly Disagree" end of the scale and a value of "5" to the "Strongly Agree" end. These averages can then be compared across different tasks, studies, user groups, and so on. This is common practice among most UX professionals as well as market researchers. Even though rating-scale data is not technically interval data, many professionals treat it as interval. For example, we assume the distance between a 1 and a 2 on a Likert scale is the same as the distance between a 2 and a 3 on the same scale. This assumption is called *degrees of intervalness*. We also assume that a value *between* any two of the scale positions has meaning. The bottom line is that it is close enough to interval data that we can treat it as such.

When analyzing data from rating scales, it is important to look at the actual frequency distribution of the responses. Because of the relatively small number of response options (e.g., 5 to 9) for each rating scale, it's even more important to look at the distribution than it is for truly continuous data like task times. You might see important information in the distribution of responses that you would totally miss if you just looked at the average. For example, let's assume you asked 20 users to rate their agreement with the statement "This web site is easy to use" on a 1 to 7 scale, and the resulting average rating was 4 (right in the middle). You might conclude that the users were basically just lukewarm about the site's ease of use. But then you look at the distribution of the ratings and you see that 10 users rated it a "1" and 10 rated it a "7." So, in fact, no one was lukewarm. They either thought it was great or they hated it. You might then want to do some segmentation analysis to see if the people who hated it have anything in common (e.g., they had never used the site before) versus the people who loved it (e.g., long-time users of the site).

WHAT NUMBER SHOULD RATING SCALES START WITH?

Regardless of whether you show numbers for each scale value to the *user*, you will normally use numbers *internally* for analysis. But what number should the scales start with, 0 or 1? It generally doesn't matter, as long as you report what the scale is whenever showing mean ratings (e.g., a mean of 3.2 on a scale of 1 to 5). But there are some cases where it's convenient to start the scale at zero, particularly if you want to express the ratings as percentages of the best possible rating. On a scale of 1 to 5, a rating of 5 would correspond to 100%, but a rating of 1 does not correspond to 20%, as some might think (e.g., calculating the percentage by multiplying the rating by 20, which is wrong). On a scale of 1 to 5, 1 is the lowest possible rating, so it should correspond to 0%. Consequently, we often find it's easier to keep our sanity by internally numbering rating scales starting at zero, so that a rating of 0 corresponds to 0%.

Another way to analyze rating-scale data is by looking at top-box or top-2-box scores. Assume you're using a rating scale of 1 to 5, with 5 meaning "Strongly Agree." The sample data in Fig. 5.1 illustrates the calculation of top-box and top-2-box scores. A top-box score would be the percentage of participants who

	C2		f_x	=IF(B2>4,1,0)
	A	**B**	**C**	**D**
1	**Participant**	**Rating (1–5)**	**Top Box?**	**Top 2 Box?**
2	P1	4	0	1
3	P2	5	1	1
4	P3	3	0	0
5	P4	4	0	1
6	P5	2	0	0
7	P6	3	0	0
8	P7	5	1	1
9	P8	4	0	1
10	P9	3	0	0
11	P10	5	1	1
12	**Averages**	**3.8**	**30%**	**60%**

Fig. 5.1 Example of the calculation of top-box and top-2-box scores from ratings in Excel. The "=IF" function in Excel is used to check to see whether an individual rating is greater than 4 (for Top Box) or greater than 3 (for Top 2 Box). If it is, a value of "1" is given. If not, a value of "0" is given. Averaging these 1's and 0's together gives you the percentage of Top-Box or Top-2-Box scores.

gave a rating of 5. Similarly, a top-2-box score would be the percentage who gave a rating of 4 or 5. (Top-2-box scores are more commonly used with larger scales, such as 7 or 9 points.) The theory behind this method of analysis is that it lets you focus on how many participants gave very positive ratings. (Note that the analysis can also be done as a bottom-box or bottom-2-box analysis, focusing on the other extreme.) Keep in mind that when you convert to a top-box or top-2-box score, the data can no longer be considered interval. Therefore, you should just report the data as frequencies (e.g., the percentage of users who gave a top-box rating). Also, keep in mind that you lose information by calculating a top-box or top-2-box score. Lower ratings are essentially ignored by this analysis.

WHERE SHOULD THE "POSITIVE" OR "AGREE" END OF A SCALE BE?

Although there's no hard-and-fast rule about it, we suggest that the positive/agree end of a horizontal scale should usually be on the right. This is because we think of an attribute or agreement increasing as you proceed from left to right (at least in many Western cultures). Similarly, with a vertical scale, we suggest that the positive/agree end should usually be at the top because we commonly think of "top" scores as the best. But whatever approach you adopt, the most important thing is to be consistent.

From a practical standpoint, what difference does it make when you analyze rating scales using means versus top-box or top-2-box scores? To illustrate the difference, we looked at the data from an online usability study conducted on the eve of the 2008 U.S. Presidential election (Tullis, 2008c). There were two leading candidates, Barack Obama and John McCain, both of whom had websites about their candidacy. Participants were asked to perform the same four tasks on one of the sites (which they were randomly assigned to). After each task, they were asked to rate how easy it was on a scale of 1 to 5, with 1 = Very Difficult and 5 = Very Easy. A total of 25 participants performed tasks on the Obama site and 19 on the McCain site. We then analyzed the task ease ratings both by calculating the means, top-box scores, and top-2-box scores. The results are shown in Fig. 5.2.

All three charts seem to indicate that the Obama site got a higher rating than the McCain site for three tasks (Tasks 1, 2, and 4) while the McCain site got a higher rating than the Obama site for one task (Task 3). However, the apparent disparity between the two sites differs depending upon the analysis method. There tends to be a greater difference between the two sites with the top-box and top-2-box scores compared to the means. (And no, that's not an error in the top-box and top-2-box charts for Task 2. *None* of the participants gave that task a top-box or top-2-box rating for the McCain site.) But also note that the error bars tend to be larger with the top-box and top-2-box scores compared to the means.

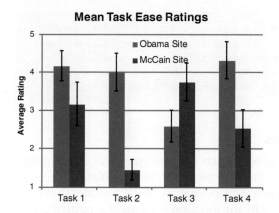

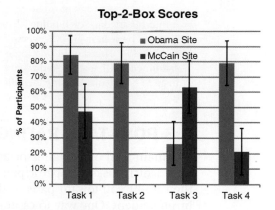

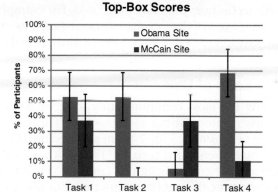

Fig. 5.2 Three different analyses of the task ease ratings from a study of the Obama and McCain websites (Tullis, 2008c): Mean ratings, Top-2-Box scores, and Top-Box scores. Note how similar patterns are revealed in all three analysis methods, but the apparent disparity between the two sites differs. In each chart, error bars represent the 90% confidence interval.

Should you analyze rating scales using means or top-box scores? In practice, we generally use means because they take all the data into account (not ignoring some ratings as in top-box or top-2-box analyses). But some companies or senior executives are more familiar with top-box scores (often from market research), so in some situations, we use top-box scores. (It's important to understand who you're presenting your results to.)

HOW DO YOU CALCULATE CONFIDENCE INTERVALS FOR TOP-BOX SCORES?

If you're calculating means of ratings, then you can calculate confidence intervals in the same way you do for any other continuous data: using the "=CONFIDENCE.T" function in Excel. But if you're calculating top-box or top-2-box scores, it's not so simple. When you calculate a top-box or top-2-box value for each rating, you're turning it into binary data: each rating is either a top-box value (or top-2-box value) or it's not. This can be seen in Fig. 5.1, where each of the top-box (or top-2-box) values is either a "0" or "1." This should ring some mental bells: it's like the task success data that we examined in Chapter 4. And when you're dealing with binary data, confidence intervals need to be calculated using the Adjusted Wald method. See Chapter 4 for details.

5.3 POST-TASK RATINGS

The main goal of ratings associated with each task is to give you some insight into which tasks the participants thought were the most difficult. This can then point you toward parts of the system or aspects of the product that need improvement. One way to capture this information is to ask the participant to rate each task on one or more scales. The next few sections examine some of the specific techniques that have been used. For example, the data shown in Fig. 5.2 show that users of the Obama site rated Task 3 as the most difficult, while users of the McCain site rated Task 2 as the most difficult.

5.3.1 Ease of Use

Probably the most common rating scale involves simply asking users to rate how easy or how difficult each task was. This typically involves asking them to rate the task using a 5- or 7-point scale. Some UX professionals prefer to use a traditional Likert scale, such as "This task was easy to complete" (1 = Strongly Disagree, 3 = Neither Agree nor Disagree, 5 = Strongly Agree). Others prefer to use a semantic differential technique with anchor terms like "Easy/Difficult." Either technique will provide you with a measure of perceived usability on a task level. Sauro and Dumas (2009) tested a single 7-point rating scale, which they coined the "Single Ease Question," or SEQ:

Overall, this task was?

Very Difficult   o   o   o   o   o   o   o   Very Easy

They compared it to several other post-task ratings and found it to be among the most effective.

5.3.2 After-Scenario Questionnaire

Jim Lewis (1991) developed a set of three rating scales—the After-Scenario Questionnaire (ASQ)—designed to be used after the user completes a set of related tasks or a scenario:

1. "I am satisfied with the ease of completing the tasks in this scenario."
2. "I am satisfied with the amount of time it took to complete the tasks in this scenario."
3. "I am satisfied with the support information (online help, messages, documentation) when completing the tasks."

Each of these statements is accompanied by a 7-point rating scale of "Strongly Disagree" to "Strongly Agree." Note that these questions in the ASQ touch upon three fundamental areas of usability: effectiveness (question 1), efficiency (question 2), and satisfaction (all three).

5.3.3 Expectation Measure

Albert and Dixon (2003) proposed a different approach to assessing users' subjective reactions to each task. Specifically, they argued that the most important thing about each task is how easy or difficult it was *in comparison to* how easy or difficult the user *thought* it was going to be. So before the users actually did any of the tasks, they asked them to rate how easy/difficult they *expect* each of the tasks to be based simply on their understanding of the tasks and the type of product. Users expect some tasks to be easier than others. For example, getting the current quote on a stock should be easier than rebalancing an entire financial portfolio. Then, after performing each task, the users were asked to rate how easy/difficult the task *actually was*. The "before" rating is called the *expectation* rating, and the "after" rating is called the *experience* rating. They used the same 7-point rating scales (1 = Very Difficult, 7 = Very Easy) for both ratings. For each task, you can then calculate an average *expectation rating* and an average *experience rating*. You can then visualize these two scores for each task as a scatterplot, as shown in Fig. 5.3.

The four quadrants of the scatterplot provide some interesting insight into the tasks and where you should focus your attention when making improvements:

1. In the lower right are the tasks that the users thought would be *easy* but actually turned out to be *difficult*. These probably represent the tasks that are the biggest dissatisfiers for the users—those that were the biggest disappointment. These are the tasks you should focus on first, which is why this is called the "Fix It Fast" quadrant.

2. In the upper right are the tasks that the users thought would be *easy* and actually *were* easy. These are working just fine. You don't want to "break" them by making changes that would have a negative impact. That's why this is called the "Don't Touch It" quadrant.

Fig. 5.3 Comparison of the average expectation ratings and average experience ratings for a set of tasks in a usability test. Which quadrants the tasks fall into can help you prioritize which tasks to focus on improving. (Modified from Albert and Dixon [2003]; used with permission).

3. In the upper left are the tasks that the users thought would be *difficult* and actually were *easy*. These are pleasant surprises, both for the users and the designers of the system! These could represent features of your site or system that may help distinguish you from the competition, which is why this is called the "Promote It" quadrant.

4. In the lower left are the tasks that the users thought would be *difficult* and actually *were* difficult. There are no big surprises here, but there might be some important opportunities to make improvements. That is why this is called the "Big Opportunities" quadrant.

5.3.4 A Comparison of Post-Task Self-Reported Metrics

Tedesco and Tullis (2006) compared a variety of task-based self-reported metrics in an online usability study. Specifically, they tested the following five different methods for eliciting self-reported ratings after each task.

Condition 1: "Overall, this task was: Very Difficult … Very Easy" This was a very simple post-task rating scale that many usability teams commonly use.

Condition 2: "Please rate the usability of the site for this task: Very Difficult to Use … Very Easy to Use" Obviously, this is very similar to Condition 1 but with an emphasis on the usability of *the site* for the task. Perhaps only usability geeks detect the difference, but we wanted to find out!

Condition 3: "Overall, I am satisfied with the ease of completing this task: Strongly Disagree … Strongly Agree" "Overall, I'm satisfied with the amount of time it took to complete this task: Strongly Disagree … Strongly Agree" These are two of the three questions used in Lewis's (1991) ASQ. The third question in the ASQ asks about the support information such as online help, which was not relevant in this study, so it was not used.

Condition 4: (Before doing all tasks): "How difficult or easy do you expect this task to be? Very Difficult … Very Easy" (After doing each task): "How difficult or easy did you find this task to be? Very Difficult … Very Easy" This is the expectation measure by Albert and Dixon (2003).

Condition 5: "Please assign a number between 1 and 100 to represent how well the website supported you for this task. Remember: 1 would mean that the site was not at all supportive and completely unusable. A score of 100 would mean that the site was perfect and would require absolutely no improvement." This condition was loosely based on a method called Usability Magnitude Estimation (McGee, 2003) in which test participants are asked to create their own "usability scale."

These techniques were compared in an online study. The participants performed six tasks on a live application used to look up information about employees (phone number, location, manager, etc.). Each participant used only one of the five self-report techniques. A total of 1131 people participated in the online study, with at least 210 participants using each self-report technique.

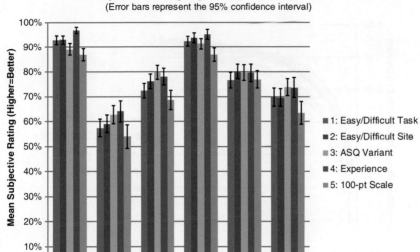

Subjective Ratings by Task for All Conditions
(Error bars represent the 95% confidence interval)

Legend:
- 1: Easy/Difficult Task
- 2: Easy/Difficult Site
- 3: ASQ Variant
- 4: Experience
- 5: 100-pt Scale

Y-axis: Mean Subjective Rating (Higher=Better)

X-axis: Task 1, Task 2, Task 3, Task 4, Task 5, Task 6

Fig. 5.4 Average subjective ratings split by task and condition. All five conditions (self-report techniques) yielded essentially the same pattern of results for the six tasks. (Modified from Tedesco and Tullis [2006]; used with permission.)

The main goal of this study was to see if these rating techniques are sensitive to detecting differences in the perceived difficulty of the tasks. Fig. 5.4 shows the averages of the task ratings for each of the tasks, split out by condition. The key finding is that the pattern of the results was very similar regardless of which technique was used. This is not surprising, given the very large sample (total N of 1131). In other words, at large sample sizes, all five of the techniques can effectively distinguish between the tasks.

But what about the smaller sample sizes more typical of usability tests? To answer that question, we did a subsampling analysis looking at large numbers of random samples of different sizes taken from the full dataset. The results of this are shown in Fig. 5.5, where the correlation between the data from the sub-samples and the full dataset is shown for each subsample size.

The key finding was that one of the five conditions, Condition 1 resulted in better correlations starting at the smallest sample sizes and continuing. Even at a sample size of only seven, which is typical of many usability tests, its correlation with the full dataset averaged .91, which was significantly higher than any of the other conditions. So Condition 1, which was the simplest rating scale ("Overall, this task was Very Difficult … Very Easy"), was also the most reliable

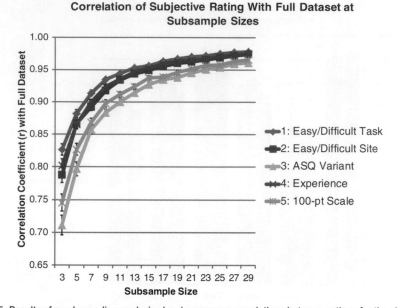

Fig. 5.5 Results of a subsampling analysis showing average correlations between ratings for the six tasks from subsamples of various sizes and the full dataset for each condition. Error bars represent the 95% confidence interval for the mean. *ASQ*, After-Scenario Questionnaire. (Modified from Tedesco and Tullis [2006]; used with permission.)

at smaller sample sizes. Note that this is basically the Single Ease Question (SEQ) as described by Sauro (2012).

RATINGS DURING A TASK?

At least one study (Teague et al., 2001) has indicated that you might get a more accurate measure of the user's experience with a task by asking for ratings *during* the conduct of the task. They found that participants' ratings of ease of use were significantly higher after the task was completed than it was during the task. It could be that task success changes participants' perception of how difficult the task was to complete.

5.4 OVERALL USER EXPERIENCE RATINGS

One of the most common uses of self-reported metrics is as an overall measure of the perceived user experience, typically after interactions with the product. These can be used as an overall "barometer" of the user experience, particularly if you establish a track record with the same measurement technique over time. Similarly, these kinds of ratings can be used to compare multiple design alternatives in a single study or to compare your product, application, or website to the competition.

You might be tempted to develop your own rating scales for assessing the overall user experience, but we would strongly suggest you consider one or more of the standard tools (questionnaires) that are available for this purpose. There are several advantages to using one of these standard tools:

- They have been carefully crafted and validated to yield unbiased data.
- In most cases, there are multiple studies in the UX literature using the tool.
- In many cases, benchmark data from many studies are available for comparison purposes.

There are more standard tools for assessing different aspects of the user experience than we can reasonably cover in this chapter. Instead, we cover in detail a handful of the tools that we have personally used, and then we provide an annotated list of many more. Note that these tools commonly have somewhat different purposes. Some focus purely on usability while others focus on the user experience more generally or on specific aspects like the perceived difficulty of using the product.

5.4.1 System Usability Scale

One of the most widely used tools for assessing the perceived usability of a system or product is the SUS. It was originally developed by John Brooke in 1986 while he was working at Digital Equipment Corporation (Brooke, 1996). As shown in Fig. 5.6, it consists of 10 statements to which users rate their level of agreement. Half of the statements are positively worded and half negatively worded. A 5-point scale of agreement is used for each. A technique for combining the 10 ratings into an overall score (on a scale of 0 to 100) is also given. A SUS score of 0 is the absolute worst possible score, while a score of 100 is the absolute best. Hundreds of studies in the UX literature have reported using SUS.

CALCULATING A SUS SCORE

To calculate a SUS score, first sum the score contributions from each item. Each item's score contribution will range from 0 to 4. For items 1, 3, 5, 7, and 9, the score contribution is the scale position minus 1. For items 2, 4, 6, 8, and 10, the contribution is 5 minus the scale position. Multiply the sum of the scores by 2.5 to obtain the overall SUS score. Consider the sample data in Fig. 5.6. The sum of the values, using these rules, is 22. Multiply that by 2.5 to get the overall SUS score of 55. Or better yet, download our spreadsheet for calculating SUS scores from www.MeasuringUX.com.

SUS has been made freely available for use in UX studies, both for research purposes and industry use. The only prerequisite for its use is that any published report should acknowledge the source of the measure. Since it has been so widely used, many studies in the UX literature have reported SUS scores for

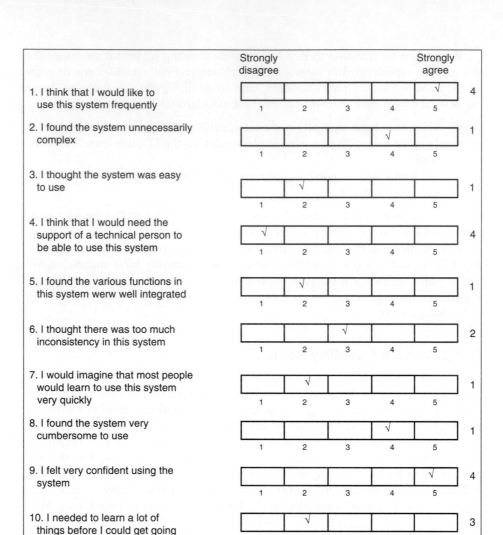

	Strongly disagree				Strongly agree	
1. I think that I would like to use this system frequently	1	2	3	4	5 √	4
2. I found the system unnecessarily complex	1	2	3	4 √	5	1
3. I thought the system was easy to use	1	2 √	3	4	5	1
4. I think that I would need the support of a technical person to be able to use this system	1 √	2	3	4	5	4
5. I found the various functions in this system werw well integrated	1	2 √	3	4	5	1
6. I thought there was too much inconsistency in this system	1	2	3 √	4	5	2
7. I would imagine that most people would learn to use this system very quickly	1	2 √	3	4	5	1
8. I found the system very cumbersome to use	1	2	3	4 √	5	1
9. I felt very confident using the system	1	2	3	4	5 √	4
10. I needed to learn a lot of things before I could get going with this system	1	2 √	3	4	5	3

Total= 22   SUS Score= 22 * 2.5 = 55

Fig. 5.6 The System Usability Scale (SUS), developed by John Brooke at Digital Equipment Corporation and an example of scoring it.

different products and systems, including desktop applications, web sites, voice-response systems, and various consumer products. Tullis (2008a) and Bangor, Kortum, and Miller (2008) both reported analyses of SUS scores from a wide variety of studies. Tullis reported data from 129 different uses of SUS while Bangor et al. reported data from 206. Frequency distributions of the two sets of data are remarkably similar, as shown in Fig. 5.7, with a median study score of 69 for the Tullis data and 71 for the Bangor et al. data. Bangor et al. suggested the following interpretation of SUS scores based on their data:

Frequency Distributions of Mean SUS Scores

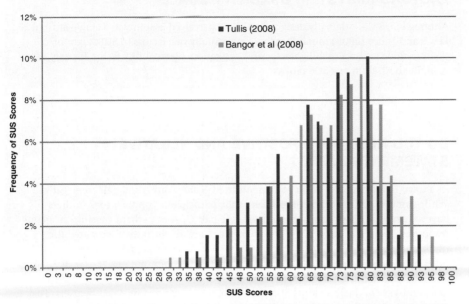

Fig. 5.7 Frequency distributions of mean SUS scores reported by Tullis (2008) and by Bangor et al. (2008). The Tullis data are based on a total of 129 study conditions and the Bangor et al. data is based on 206.

- >70: Acceptable
- 50 to 70: Marginal
- <50: Not acceptable

SYSTEM USABILITY SCALE RESOURCES

We have posted some resources related to SUS on our website at MeasuringUX.com/sus. These include Qualtrics and Google Forms versions of SUS, a spreadsheet for calculating SUS scores, a spreadsheet containing SUS scores for 129 conditions from 50 studies in the literature, and links to many published studies about SUS.

Bangor, Kortum, and Miller (2009) conducted an analysis of nearly 3500 SUS surveys within 273 studies. They developed a "grading scale" that could be useful in conveying the results of a SUS analysis to others. Their analysis suggested the following interpretation:

- 90 to 100: A
- 80 to 89: B
- 70 to 79: C
- 50 to 59: D
- <50: F

FACTORS IN SYSTEM USABILITY SCALE

Although SUS was originally designed to assess perceived usability as a single attribute, Lewis and Sauro (2009) found that there are actually two factors in SUS. Eight of the questions reflect a usability factor and two reflect a learnability factor. It's easy to compute both from raw SUS ratings.

DO YOU NEED BOTH POSITIVE AND NEGATIVE STATEMENTS IN SUS?

As shown in Fig. 5.6, half of the statements in SUS are positive and half are negative. While some argue that this approach keeps the participants "on their toes," others have argued that it also seems to confuse some participants, perhaps causing erroneous responses. Sauro and Lewis (2011) conducted a study in which they compared the traditional version of SUS to an all-positive version. They found no significant difference between the mean SUS scores for the two versions. But in a review of 27 SUS datasets, they found evidence that 11% of the studies had some miscoding of the SUS data, and 13% of the individual SUS questionnaires contained mistakes by users. They suggest using an all-positive version of SUS to avoid some of those possible errors. If you want to use the all-positive version, see Sauro and Lewis (2011) for an example.

5.4.2 Computer System Usability Questionnaire

Jim Lewis (1995), who developed the ASQ technique for post-task ratings, also developed the Computer System Usability Questionnaire (CSUQ) to do an overall assessment of a system at the end of a usability study. The CSUQ is very similar to Lewis's Post-Study System Usability Questionnaire (PSSUQ), with only minor changes in wording. PSSUQ was originally designed to be administered in person, whereas CSUQ was designed to be administered by mail or online. CSUQ consists of the following 19 statements to which the user rates agreement on a 7-point scale of "Strongly Disagree" to "Strongly Agree," plus N/A:

1. Overall, I am satisfied with how easy it is to use this system.
2. It was simple to use this system.
3. I could effectively complete the tasks and scenarios using this system.
4. I was able to complete the tasks and scenarios quickly using this system.
5. I was able to efficiently complete the tasks and scenarios using this system.
6. I felt comfortable using this system.
7. It was easy to learn to use this system.
8. I believe I could become productive quickly using this system.
9. The system gave error messages that clearly told me how to fix problems.
10. Whenever I made a mistake using the system, I could recover easily and quickly.

11. The information (such as online help, on-screen messages, and other documentation) provided with this system was clear.
12. It was easy to find the information I needed.
13. The information provided for the system was easy to understand.
14. The information was effective in helping me complete the tasks and scenarios.
15. The organization of information on the system screens was clear.
16. The interface of this system was pleasant.
17. I liked using the interface of this system.
18. This system has all the functions and capabilities I expect it to have.
19. Overall, I am satisfied with this system.

Unlike SUS, all of the statements in CSUQ are worded positively. Factor analyses of a large number of CSUQ and PSSUQ responses have shown that the results may be viewed in four main categories: System Usefulness, Information Quality, Interface Quality, and Overall Satisfaction.

5.4.3 Product Reaction Cards

A very different approach to capturing post-test subjective reactions to a product was presented by Joey Benedek and Trish Miner (2002) from Microsoft. As illustrated in Fig. 5.8, they presented a set of 118 cards, each containing adjectives (e.g., Fresh, Slow, Sophisticated, Inviting, Entertaining, Incomprehensible). Some of the words are positive and some are negative. The users would then simply choose the cards they felt described the system. After selecting the cards, they were asked to pick the top five cards and explain why they chose each. This technique is intended to be more qualitative in that its main purpose is to elicit commentary from the users. But it can also be used in a quantitative way by counting the number of times each word is chosen by participants. The results can also be visualized using a word cloud (e.g., using Wordle.net), as in Fig. 5.9.

5.4.4 User Experience Questionnaire

The User Experience Questionnaire (UEQ) was developed by a team of German UX researchers, Martin Schrepp, Jörg Thomaschewski, and Andreas Hinderks (e.g., Schrepp, Hinderks, & Thomaschewski, 2017). As shown in Fig. 5.10, UEQ is a semantic differential scale composed of 26 bipolar terms. It is available in more than 20 languages. A complete set of resources related to UEQ is available at https://www.ueq-online.org.

The results from a UEQ analysis are divided into six categories:

- Attractiveness
- Perspicuity
- Efficiency
- Dependability

The complete set of 118 Product Reaction Cards				
Accessible	Creative	Fast	Meaningful	Slow
Advanced	Customizable	Flexible	Motivating	Sophisticated
Annoying	Cutting edge	Fragile	Not Secure	Stable
Appealing	Dated	Fresh	Not Valuable	Sterile
Approachable	Desirable	Friendly	Novel	Stimulating
Attractive	Difficult	Frustrating	Old	Straight Forward
Boring	Disconnected	Fun	Optimistic	Stressful
Business-like	Disruptive	Gets in the way	Ordinary	Time-consuming
Busy	Distracting	Hard to use	Organized	Time-Saving
Calm	Dull	Helpful	Overbearing	Too Technical
Clean	Easy to use	High quality	Overwhelming	Trustworthy
Clear	Effective	Impersonal	Patronizing	Unapproachable
Collaborative	Efficient	Impressive	Personal	Unattractive
Comfortable	Effortless	Incomprehensible	Poor quality	Uncontrollable
Compatible	Empowering	Inconsistent	Powerful	Unconventional
Compelling	Energetic	Ineffective	Predictable	Understandable
Complex	Engaging	Innovative	Professional	Undesirable
Comprehensive	Entertaining	Inspiring	Relevant	Unpredictable
Confident	Enthusiastic	Integrated	Reliable	Unrefined
Confusing	Essential	Intimidating	Responsive	Usable
Connected	Exceptional	Intuitive	Rigid	Useful
Consistent	Exciting	Inviting	Satisfying	Valuable
Controllable	Expected	Irrelevant	Secure	
Convenient	Familiar	Low Maintenance	Simplistic	

Fig. 5.8 The complete set of 118 Product Reaction Cards developed by Joey Benedek and Trish Miner at Microsoft. *Source:* From Microsoft: "Permission is granted to use this Tool for personal, academic and commercial purposes. If you wish to use this Tool, or the results obtained from the use of this Tool for personal or academic purposes or in your commercial application, you are required to include the following attribution: Developed by and © 2002 Microsoft Corporation. All rights reserved."

- Stimulation
- Novelty

The UEQ website provides multiple spreadsheets that will do calculations and create graphs for you, such as the example shown in Fig. 5.11. This shows the use of UEQ to compare two prototypes. The data, confidence intervals, and graphs were all generated using a spreadsheet available on the UEQ website. The spreadsheet also calculates t-tests to compare the data from the two versions. In this example, the scores for Attractiveness, Perspicuity, Efficiency, and Dependability are significantly higher for Prototype #2.

The UEQ website also provides a spreadsheet that will compare the results of your study to their benchmark data from many other studies, as shown in Fig. 5.12. This example shows a comparison of the results from a UEQ study

Fig. 5.9 Sample word cloud of the results from a study using the Product Reaction Cards. Larger words are those that were chosen more frequently by the respondents.

to the benchmarks for each of the six scales. The scores for Dependability and Novelty came out Below Average compared to their benchmarks while all the others were either Above Average or Good.

Note that a short version of the UEQ, called the UEQ-S, is also available, consisting of a subset of only eight rating scales (Schrepp, Hinderks, & Thomaschewski 2017). However, this brevity comes at a price. While the full UEQ gives detailed feedback on six different aspects of the user experience (Attractiveness, Efficiency, Perspicuity, Dependability, Stimulation, Originality), the short version only distinguishes between pragmatic and hedonic quality.

5.4.5 AttrakDiff

Like the UEQ, AttrakDiff was developed by a team of German UX researchers, specifically Marc Hassenzahl, Michael Burmester, and Franz Koller (Hassenzahl, Burmester, & Koller, 2003). AttrakDiff is a semantic differential scale composed of 28 bipolar terms. An AttrakDiff study is built and run using the AttrakDiff website: http://www.attrakdiff.de/index-en.html.

The results of an AttrakDiff analysis are summarized using four scales:

- Pragmatic Quality (PQ): This is what we usually think of as the usability of a product—the extent to which users can achieve their goals with it.

	1	2	3	4	5	6	7		
annoying	O	O	O	O	O	O	O	enjoyable	1
not understandable	O	O	O	O	O	O	O	understandable	2
creative	O	O	O	O	O	O	O	dull	3
easy to learn	O	O	O	O	O	O	O	difficult to learn	4
valuable	O	O	O	O	O	O	O	inferior	5
boring	O	O	O	O	O	O	O	exciting	6
not interesting	O	O	O	O	O	O	O	interesting	7
unpredictable	O	O	O	O	O	O	O	predictable	8
fast	O	O	O	O	O	O	O	slow	9
inventive	O	O	O	O	O	O	O	conventional	10
obstructive	O	O	O	O	O	O	O	supportive	11
good	O	O	O	O	O	O	O	bad	12
complicated	O	O	O	O	O	O	O	easy	13
unlikable	O	O	O	O	O	O	O	pleasing	14
usual	O	O	O	O	O	O	O	leading edge	15
unpleasant	O	O	O	O	O	O	O	pleasant	16
secure	O	O	O	O	O	O	O	not secure	17
motivating	O	O	O	O	O	O	O	demotivating	18
meet expectations	O	O	O	O	O	O	O	does not meet expectations	19
inefficient	O	O	O	O	O	O	O	efficient	20
clear	O	O	O	O	O	O	O	confusing	21
impractical	O	O	O	O	O	O	O	practical	22
organized	O	O	O	O	O	O	O	cluttered	23
attractive	O	O	O	O	O	O	O	unattractive	24
friendly	O	O	O	O	O	O	O	unfriendly	25
conservative	O	O	O	O	O	O	O	innovative	26

Fig. 5.10 The rating scales of the User Experience Questionnaire (UEQ).

- Hedonic Quality-Stimulation (HQ-S): This dimension indicates to what extent the product supports the needs of users to develop and move forward in terms of novel, interesting, and stimulating interactions.
- Hedonic Quality-Identity (HQ-I): This indicates to what extent the product allows the user to identify with it.
- Attractiveness (ATT): This indicates the extent to which the product is considered appealing, inviting, attractive, and pleasant.

Finally, as shown in Fig. 5.13, the AttrakDiff website also presents a graph showing where the results of the study fall on a 3 × 3 grid of Pragmatic Quality vs. Hedonic Quality (with the two hedonic quality scales combined). In this example, the results fall mostly in the center, which is considered the "Neutral" area. The blue rectangle represents the degree of uncertainty around that location, with greater certainty yielding a smaller rectangle.

5.4.6 Net Promoter Score

One self-reported metric that has gained rapidly in popularity, especially among senior executives, is the Net Promoter Score (NPS). It is intended to be a measure of customer loyalty and was originated by Fred Reichheld in his 2003 article in the *Harvard Business Review*: "One Number You Need to Grow" (Reichheld, 2003). The power of NPS seems to derive from its simplicity since it uses only one question: "How likely is it that you would recommend [this company, product, website, etc.] to a friend or colleague?" The respondent answers using an 11-point scale of 0 (Not at all likely) to 10 (Extremely likely). The respondents are then divided into three categories:

- Detractors: Those who gave ratings of 0 to 6.
- Passives: Those who gave ratings of 7 or 8
- Promoters: Those who gave ratings of 9 or 10

Note that the categorization into Detractors, Passives, and Promoters is nowhere near symmetrical. By design, the bar is set pretty high to be a Promoter, while it is very easy to be a Detractor. To calculate the NPS, you subtract the percentage of Detractors (ratings of 0 to 6) from the percentage of Promoters (ratings of 9 or 10). The Passives are ignored in the calculation (except that they add to the overall sample size). In theory, NPSs can range from −100 to +100.

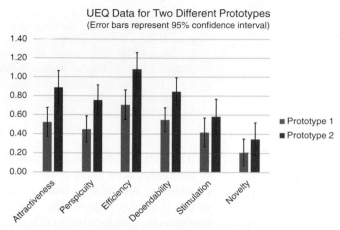

Fig. 5.11 Sample data showing the use of UEQ to compare two prototypes. The data and chart were generated using a spreadsheet from the UEQ website.

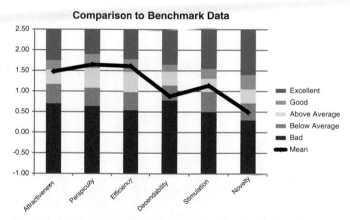

Fig. 5.12 Sample data showing a comparison of the results from a UEQ study to benchmark data. The data and chart were generated using a spreadsheet from the UEQ website.

A NET PROMOTER SCORE CALCULATION TRICK

One of the issues that some people have with NPS is that it is only calculated as an overall score (% Promoters − % Detractors) rather than scores for each respondent.

This makes it a bit more challenging to come up with a confidence interval for the score. However, there is a calculation "trick" you can use, which gives you a score for each respondent plus the exact same overall score as the traditional method. Simply recode each NPS rating so that Promoters are given +100, Passives 0, and Detractors −100. The mean of these scores will be the same as the NPS calculated the normal way. But you also have scores for each individual, which means you can calculate a confidence interval using the CONFIDENCE.T function.

The NPS is not without its own detractors. One criticism is that the reduction of the scores from an 11-point scale to just three categories (Detractors, Passives, Promoters) results in a loss of statistical power and precision. This is similar to the loss of precision when using the "Top Box" or "Top-2-Box" method of analysis discussed earlier in this chapter. But you lose even more precision when you take the *difference* between two percentages (Promoters minus Detractors), which is similar to subtracting "Bottom Box" scores from "Top Box" scores. At least one analysis (Stuchbery, 2010) has indicated that you would need a sample size at least two to four times larger to get an NPS margin of error equivalent to the margin of error for a traditional Top-2-Box score.

DOES PERCEIVED USABILITY PREDICT CUSTOMER LOYALTY?

Jeff Sauro (2010) wanted to know whether usability, as measured by SUS, tended to predict customer loyalty, as measured by NPS. He analyzed data from 146 users who were asked to complete both the SUS questions and the NPS questions for a variety of products, including websites and financial applications. The result was a correlation of $r=.61$, which is highly significant ($P < .001$). He found that Promoters had an average SUS score of 82, while Detractors had an average SUS score of 67.

5.4.7 Additional Tools for Measuring Self-Reported User Experience

As mentioned earlier in this chapter, there are too many tools for measuring the self-reported user experience to cover them all in detail. We have covered some of the more popular ones that we have used. But there are many more, and some of which may be quite well suited to your needs. Note that some of these tools are free while others require a license. Here are some of these additional tools:

- **NASA Task Load Index (NASA-TLX):** The NASA-TLX is a multidimensional assessment tool that rates perceived workload in order to assess a system's effectiveness. It was developed at NASA's Ames Research Center (Hart & Staveland, 1988) and comes from a more traditional human-factors perspective than most of the other tools here. There are six scales for TLX: Mental Demand, Physical Demand, Temporal Demand, Frustration, Effort, and Performance. Administering TLX is a two-step process. First, respondents are asked to judge the importance of the six scales by looking at the 15 paired comparisons of them. Second, they rate the system or process on each of the six dimensions using 7-point scales from Low to High or from Good to Poor. The raw score for each of the six items is multiplied by the weight from the first step to generate an overall workload score. See Sauro (2019) for an overview. Note that there is an Apple iOS app for administering TLX (https://apps.apple.com/us/app/nasa-tlx/id1168110608).

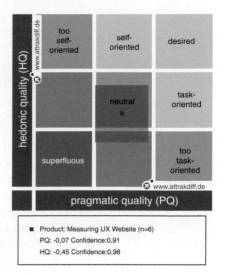

Fig. 5.13 Example showing where the results of an AttrakDiff study fall on a 3 × 3 grid of Pragmatic Quality vs. Hedonic Quality for the MeasuringUX.com website.

- **Post-Study System Usability Questionnaire (PSSUQ)**: PSSUQ was developed by Jim Lewis (1991) and is an 18-item Likert scale that measures users' perceived satisfaction with a product (e.g., "The system gave error messages that clearly told me how to fix problems."). Analysis of the data from PSSUQ results in an overall score and three subscales of System Quality, Information Quality, and Interface Quality.

- **Questionnaire for User Interface Satisfaction (QUIS)**: QUIS was developed by a team at the University of Maryland and has been available since the 1980s (Chi, Diehl, & Norman, 1988). It consists of 27 rating scales of 10 points each divided into five categories: Overall Reaction, Screen, Terminology/System Information, Learning, and System Capabilities.

- **Software Usability Measurement Inventory (SUMI)**: SUMI was developed by Jurek Kirakowski (Kirakowski & Corbett, 1993). There are 50 rating scales (e.g., "This software responds too slowly to inputs"), but the responses required are only "Agree," "Undecided," or "Disagree." The results of a SUMI analysis are divided into six categories: Efficiency, Affect, Helpfulness, Control, Learnability, and Global Usability. The SUMI report also tells you how your product compares to data from more than 2000 responses to commercially available software. SUMI is currently available in 20 languages.

- **Standardized User Experience Percentile Rank Questionnaire (SUPR-Q)**: This tool was developed over five years by Jeff Sauro (2015) using data from 4000 respondents rating their experiences with over 100 websites. The questionnaire is eight items using a Likert scale of agreement (e.g., "It is easy to navigate within the website"). The results contain four factors: usability, trust/credibility, appearance, and loyalty. More information can be found at Sauro (2018).

- **Technology Acceptance Model (TAM)**: TAM has its heritage in the world of Management Information Systems rather than the UX/Usability world that most of the other tools come from. It was originally developed by Fred Davis (1989) as a part of his dissertation at MIT. The basic premise is that products need to be both useful and usable for people to accept them. Although TAM has evolved over the years, the original version used 12 Likert-style rating scales of agreement: Six for Usefulness and six for Ease of Use. (See Sauro, 2019, for an overview.)

- **Usability Metric for User Experience (UMUX)**: UMUX was developed by Kraig Finstad (2010) and is a four-item Likert scale. It was specifically designed to yield results similar to the 10-item SUS but with fewer items. It was also intended to more closely align with the ISO definition of usability, with components for Efficiency, Effectiveness, and Satisfaction. The overall correlation with SUS was quite high ($r=.96$, $P < .001$) (Finstad, 2010). Additional versions of UMUX have also been developed, including UMUX-Lite (Sauro, 2017) with only two items.

- **Usefulness, Satisfaction, and Ease-of-Use (USE) Questionnaire**: Arnie Lund (2001) proposed the Usefulness, Satisfaction, and Ease of Use (USE) questionnaire, which consists of 30 rating scales divided into four categories: Usefulness, Satisfaction, Ease of Use, and Ease of Learning. Each is a positive statement (e.g., "I would recommend it to a friend") to which the respondent rates their level of agreement on a 7-point scale.

- **Microsoft Net Satisfaction (NSAT)**: NSAT was developed at Microsoft for measuring user satisfaction with their own products (Microsoft, n.d.). NSAT is based on one satisfaction question worded something like, "Thinking about your experience in the last few months, rate your overall satisfaction with this product." The rating is on a 4-point scale of "Very Satisfied" to "Very Dissatisfied." The NSAT score is then based on the percentage of "Very Satisfied" responses minus the percentage of "Somewhat Dissatisfied" plus "Very Dissatisfied" responses. Finally, 100 is added to the result to keep the numbers positive. Conceptually this is similar to NPS but with significantly fewer points on the rating scale. Note that there are very few published articles on NSAT.

5.4.8 A Comparison of Selected Overall Self-Reported Metrics

Tullis and Stetson (2004) conducted a study in which we compared a variety of questionnaires for measuring user reactions to websites in an online usability study. We studied the following questionnaires, adapted in the manner indicated for the evaluation of websites.

SUS. It was adapted by replacing the word *system* in every question with *website*.

QUIS. Three of the original rating scales that did not seem to be appropriate to websites were dropped (e.g., "Remembering names and use of commands"). The term *system* was replaced with *website*, and the term *screen* was generally replaced by *web page*.

CSUQ. The term *system* or *computer system* was replaced by *website*.

Microsoft's Product Reaction Cards. Each word was presented with a check box, and the user was asked to choose the words that best describe their interaction with the website. They were free to choose as many or as few words as they wished.

Our Questionnaire. We had been using this questionnaire for several years in usability tests of websites. It was composed of nine positive statements (e.g., "This website is visually appealing") to which the user responds on a 7-point Likert scale from "Strongly Disagree" to "Strongly Agree."

We used these questionnaires to evaluate two web portals in an online usability study. There were 123 participants in the study, with each participant using one of the questionnaires to evaluate both websites. Participants performed two tasks on each website before completing the questionnaire for that site. When we analyzed the data from all the participants, we found that all five of the questionnaires revealed that Site 1 got significantly better ratings than Site 2. The data were then analyzed to determine what the results would have been at different sample sizes from 6 to 14, as shown in Fig. 5.14. At a sample size of 6, only 30% to 40% of the samples would have identified that Site 1 were significantly preferred. But at a sample size of 8, which is relatively common in many lab-based usability tests, we found that SUS would have identified Site 1 as the preferred site 75% of the time—a significantly higher percentage than any of the other questionnaires.

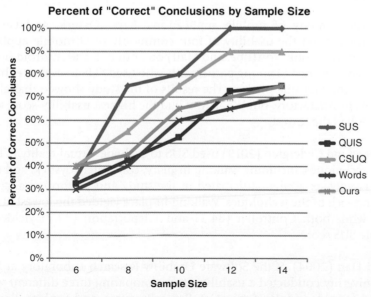

Fig. 5.14 Data illustrating the accuracy of the results from random subsamples ranging from size 6 to 14. This graph shows what percentage of the random samples yielded the same answer as the full dataset at the different sample sizes. *CSUQ,* Computer System Usability Questionnaire; *QUIS,* Questionnaire for User Interface Satisfaction; *SUS,* System Usability Scale. *Source:* Adapted from Tullis and Stetson (2004); used with permission.

It is interesting to speculate why SUS appears to yield more consistent ratings at relatively small sample sizes. One reason may be its use of both positive and negative statements with which users must rate their level of agreement. This may keep participants more alert. Another possible reason may be that it does not try to break down the assessment into more detailed components (e.g., ease of learning and ease of navigation). All 10 of the rating scales in SUS are simply asking for an assessment of the product as a whole, just in slightly different ways.

5.5 USING SUS TO COMPARE DESIGNS

A number of studies that involved comparing different designs for accomplishing similar tasks have used the SUS questionnaire as one of the techniques for making the comparison (typically in addition to performance data).

Kortum and Sorber (2015) used SUS to compare the usability of applications on two kinds of mobile platforms—phones and tablets—across both iOS and Android systems. A total of 3575 users rated the usability of 10 applications that had been selected based on their popularity, as well as five additional applications that users had identified as using frequently. The average SUS rating for the top 10 apps across all platforms was 77.7, with a nearly 20-point spread (67.7 to 87.4) between the highest- and lowest-rated apps. Overall, applications on phone platforms were judged to be more usable than applications on the tablet platforms.

In another study of mobile applications, Kaya, Ozturk, and Gumussoy (2019) investigated the usability of four commonly used mobile applications (WhatsApp, Facebook, YouTube, and Mail) on both iOS and Android operating systems. There were 222 young participants who used SUS to evaluate the applications on their mobile phones. The results of the study showed that all applications were satisfactory, but WhatsApp had the highest usability score whereas Facebook had the lowest.

Boletsis and Cedergren (2019) used SUS to evaluate virtual reality (VR) locomotion techniques, including walking-in-place, controller/joystick, and teleportation. Twenty-six adults participated in the study and performed a game-like task using each of the techniques. Walking-in-place yielded the lowest SUS score (67.6), while both Controller (84.3) and Teleportation (82.7) yielded quite favorable SUS scores.

Traci Hart (2004) of the Software Usability Research Laboratory at Wichita State University conducted a usability study comparing three different websites designed for older adults: SeniorNet, SeniorResource, and Seniors-Place. After attempting tasks on each website, the participants rated each of them using the SUS questionnaire. The average SUS score for the SeniorResource site was 80, which was significantly better than the average scores for SeniorNet and Seniors-Place, both of which averaged 63.

Sarah Everett, Michael Byrne, and Kristen Greene (2006), from Rice University, conducted a usability study comparing three different types of paper ballots: bubble, arrow, and open response. These ballots were based on actual ballots used in the 2004 U.S. elections. After using each of the ballots in a simulated election, the 42 participants used the SUS questionnaire to rate each one. They found that the bubble ballot received significantly higher SUS ratings than either of the other two ($P < .001$).

There's also some evidence that participants who have more experience with a product tend to give it higher SUS ratings than those with less experience. In testing two different applications (one web-based and one desktop-based), McLellan, Muddimer, and Peres (2012) found that the SUS scores from users who had more extensive experience with a product tended to be about 15% higher compared to users with either no or limited experience with the product.

5.6 ONLINE SERVICES

More and more companies are learning the value of getting feedback from the users of their websites. The currently in-vogue term for this process is listening to the "*Voice of the Customer*," or VoC studies. This is essentially the same process as in post-session self-reported metrics. The main difference is that VoC studies are typically done on live websites. The common approach is that a randomly selected percentage of live-site users get offered a pop-up survey asking for their feedback at a specific point in their interaction with the site—usually on logout, exiting the site, or completing a transaction. Another approach is to provide a standard mechanism for getting this feedback at various places in the site. The following sections present some of these online services. This list is not intended to be exhaustive, but it is at least representative.

5.6.1 Website Analysis and Measurement Inventory

The Website Analysis and Measurement Inventory (WAMMI—www.wammi.com) is an online service that grew out of the earlier SUMI, both of which were developed in the Human Factors Research Group (HFRG) of the University College Cork in Ireland (Kirakowski, Claridge, & Whitehand, 1998; also see Kirakowski & Cierlik, 1998). Although SUMI is designed for the evaluation of software applications, WAMMI is designed for the evaluation of websites.

WAMMI is composed of 20 statements (e.g., "It is difficult to move around this website") in a Likert scale, with 5-point scales of agreement. Like SUS, some of the statements are positive and some are negative. WAMMI is available in most European languages. The primary advantage that a service like WAMMI has over creating your own questionnaire and associated rating scales is that WAMMI has already been used in the evaluation of hundreds of websites worldwide. When used on your site, the results are delivered in the form of a comparison against their reference database built from tests of these hundreds of sites.

Results from a WAMMI analysis are divided into five areas: Attractiveness, Controllability, Efficiency, Helpfulness, and Learnability, plus an overall usability score. Each of these scores is standardized (from comparison to their reference database), so a score of 50 is average and 100 is perfect.

5.6.2 American Customer Satisfaction Index

The American Customer Satisfaction Index (ACSI—www.TheACSI.org) was developed at the Stephen M. Ross Business School of The University of Michigan. It covers a wide range of industries, including retail, automotive, and manufacturing. The analysis of websites using the ACSI methodology is done by Foresee Results (www.ForeseeResults.com). The ACSI has become particularly popular for analyzing U.S. government websites. For example, their 2018 ACSI Federal Government Report (ACSI, 2019a) found that the Departments of Defense and Interior (both 78 on their 100-point scale) had the highest ACSI scores, while the Department of Housing and Urban Development had the lowest (54). Similarly, their Retail and Consumer Shipping Report for 2018 to 2019 (ACSI, 2019b) showed that Costco took the lead position away from Amazon with a score of 83. After holding the top spot since 2010, Amazon dropped to second place with a score of 82. Tied at 81 were Etsy, Kohl's, Nordstrom, and Nike. Walmart and Sears anchored the bottom of the category with scores of 74 and 73, respectively.

The ACSI questionnaire for websites is composed of a core set of 14 questions. Each asks for a rating on a 10-point scale of different attributes, such as the quality of information, freshness of content, clarity of site organization, overall satisfaction, and likelihood to return. Specific implementations of the ACSI commonly add additional questions or rating scales. The ACSI results for a website are divided into six quality categories: Content, Functionality, Look and Feel, Navigation, Search, and Site Performance, plus an overall satisfaction score. In addition, they provide average ratings for two "Future Behavior" scores: Likelihood to Return and Recommend to Others. All the scores are a 100-point scale.

Finally, they also make assessments of the impact that each of the quality scores has on overall satisfaction. This allows you to view the results in four quadrants, plotting the quality scores on the vertical axis and the impact on overall satisfaction on the horizontal axis. The scores in the lower right quadrant (high impact, low score) indicate the areas where you should focus your improvements.

5.6.3 OpinionLab

A somewhat different approach is taken by OpinionLab (www.OpinionLab.com), which provides page-level feedback from users. In some ways, this can be thought of as a page-level analog of the task-level feedback discussed earlier.

A common way for OpinionLab to allow for this page-level feedback is through a floating icon that always stays at the bottom right corner of the page regardless of the scroll position.

Clicking on that icon then leads to a method for capturing the feedback. Their scales use five points that are marked simply as: $- -$, $-$, $+-$, $+$, and $++$. OpinionLab provides a variety of techniques for visualizing the data for a website, allowing you to easily spot the pages that are getting the most negative feedback and those that are getting the most positive feedback.

5.6.4 Issues With Live-Site Surveys

The following are some of the issues you will need to address when you use live-site surveys.

- *Number of questions.* The fewer questions you have, the higher your response rate is likely to be. That's one reason that companies like OpinionLab keep the number of questions to a minimum. You need to try to strike a balance between getting the information you need and "scaring off" potential respondents. With every question you consider adding, ask yourself if you absolutely must have the information. Some researchers believe that about 20 is the maximum number of questions you should ask in this type of survey.
- *Self-selection of respondents.* Because respondents decide whether or not to complete the survey, they are self-selecting. You should ask yourself if this biases the responses in any way. Some researchers argue that people who are unhappy with the website are more likely to respond than those who are happy (or at least satisfied). If your main purpose is to uncover areas of the site to improve, that may not be a problem.
- *Number of respondents.* Many of these services work on the basis of a percentage of visitors to offer the survey. Depending on the amount of traffic your site gets, this percentage could be quite small and still generate a large number of responses. You should closely monitor responses to see if you need to increase or decrease the percentage.
- *Nonduplication of respondents.* Most of these services provide a mechanism for noting (typically via a browser cookie or IP address) when the survey has already been offered to someone. As long as the user doesn't clear their cookies and is using the same computer, the survey won't be presented to them again for a specified time period. This prevents duplicate responses from an individual and also prevents annoying those users who don't want to respond.

5.7 OTHER TYPES OF SELF-REPORTED METRICS

Many of the self-report techniques described so far have sought to assess users' reactions to products or websites as a whole or to tasks performed using them.

But depending on the objectives of a usability study, you might want to assess users' reactions to specific *attributes* of the product overall or specific *parts* of the product.

5.7.1 Assessing Attribute Priorities

A common need, especially early in the development of a new product, is to determine the relative priorities of features or attributes of the product. You might be trying to decide what feature combinations to offer in a product or you might be trying to determine what filters to offer for use in narrowing a long list of alternatives.

One approach could be to simply list all the attributes and ask respondents to rate the importance of each. Although this might work, there's also a chance that the respondents will indicate that ALL the attributes are extremely important. While that may be true, in reality, there probably are some that are more important than others.

Another approach could be to show all pairs of attributes to the respondents and ask them to indicate which is more important to them. However, this can get unwieldy very quickly. The formula for calculating the number of pairwise combinations is $n!/(n-2)!2!$, where n is the number of attributes. So, for example, with 10 attributes there are $10!/8!2!$, or $3,628,800/(40,320 \times 2) = 45$ pairwise combinations. Although there are many ways of analyzing the data from pairwise comparisons, a very simple technique is to look at the percentage of time each item is chosen over its pair.

Conjoint analysis is a method from market research that can also be used to identify priorities (e.g., Green & Rao, 1971; Green & Srinivasan, 1978). Conjoint analysis helps determine how people value different attributes (feature, function, benefits) that make up an individual product or service. Note that the focus of conjoint analysis is really on the products or services defined by a set of attributes rather than the attributes themselves. A controlled set of potential products or services is shown to respondents, and by analyzing how they make choices between these products, the implicit value of the individual elements making up the product or service can be determined.

Very similar to conjoint analysis is a method called MaxDiff, or best-worst scaling (e.g., Louviere & Woodworth, 1983). MaxDiff simply involves respondents indicating the "Best" and the "Worst" options out of each of a series of sets of attributes or features. The usual recommendation is that each set should have no more than about five attributes. Then, different sets of five attributes are presented to the respondents. Having enough sets so that each attribute is shown more than once will result in the best data. The results of a MaxDiff analysis include a rank ordering of the attributes as well as an importance score for each attribute (which is a Bayesian average).

A different approach to identifying priorities is taken by the Kano Model (Kano, Seraku, Takahashi, & Tsuji, 1984). Noriaki Kano and his colleagues believed that not all attributes of a product or service performance are equal in the eyes of the customer and that some attributes create higher levels of customer loyalty than others. Specifically, they identified five categories of attributes:

- **Must-be Quality**: Requirements that the customers expect and are taken for granted.
- **Performance Quality**: Attributes that result in satisfaction when fulfilled and dissatisfaction when not fulfilled.
- **Attractive Quality**: Attributes that provide satisfaction when achieved fully but do not cause dissatisfaction when not fulfilled.
- **Indifferent Quality**: Attributes that refer to aspects which are neither good nor bad and do not result in either customer satisfaction or customer dissatisfaction.
- **Undesired Quality**: Attributes that result in dissatisfaction, sometimes due to the fact that not all customers are alike.

Customer's perspectives on the product features are measured by assessing two items for each feature: how you would feel if the product *had* the feature and how you would feel if the product *did not have* the feature, each on a scale of "I Like It," "I Expect It," "I'm Neutral," "I Can Live With It," or "I Dislike It." Analysis of the data from a Kano Model study results in the placement of each of the product features onto a two-dimensional space of four quadrants: Attractive, Performance, Indifference, and Must-be. For a good overview of conducting a Kano Model study, including analyzing the data, see the article by Daniel Zacarias (n.d.).

5.7.2 Assessing Specific Attributes

Here are some of the attributes of a product or website that you might be interested in assessing:

- Visual appeal
- Perceived efficiency
- Confidence
- Usefulness
- Enjoyment
- Credibility
- Appropriateness of terminology
- Ease of navigation
- Responsiveness

Covering in detail the ways you might assess all the specific attributes you are interested in is beyond the scope of this book. Instead, we describe some examples of studies that have focused on assessing specific attributes.

Gitte Lindgaard and her associates at Carleton University were interested in learning how quickly users form an impression of the visual appeal of a web page (Lindgaard et al., 2006). They flashed images of web pages for either 50 ms or 500 ms to the participants in their study. Each web page was rated on an overall scale of visual appeal and on the following bipolar scales: Interesting/Boring, Good Design/Bad Design, Good Color/Bad Color, Good Layout/Bad Layout, and Imaginative/Unimaginative. They found that the ratings on all five of these scales correlated very strongly with visual appeal ($r^2 = 0.86$ to 0.92). They also found that the results were consistent across the participants at both the 50 and 500 ms exposure levels, indicating that even at 50 ms (or 1/20th of a second), users can form a consistent impression about the visual appeal of a webpage.

Bill Albert and his associates at Bentley University (Albert, Gribbons, & Almadas, 2009) extended this research to see if users could quickly form an opinion about their trust of websites based on very brief exposures to images of the web pages. They used 50 screenshots of popular financial and health-care websites. After viewing a page for only 50 ms, participants were asked to give a rating of their trust of the site on a 1 to 9 scale. After a break, they repeated the procedure in a second trial with the same 50 images. They found a significant correlation ($r = 0.81$, $P < .001$) between the trust ratings in the two trials.

Pengnate and Sarathy (2017) manipulated the designs of four websites along two dimensions: High or Low Visual Appeal and High or Low Ease of Use. A total of 192 participants completed the study; each was randomly assigned to one of the four study conditions (websites). A number of different rating scales were used after participants completed tasks using their assigned site. These scales included the TAM (described earlier), four scales related to visual appeal adapted from Cyr, Head, and Ivanov (2006), four scales of trust adapted from McKnight and Chervany (2001), and four scales of intention to act adapted from Jarvenpaa, Tractinsky, and Vitale (2000). They found that perceived visual appeal significantly influenced perceived ease of use, and that perceived visual appeal produced a much stronger effect on trust than perceived ease of use.

B. J. Fogg and his associates at the Stanford Persuasive Technology Lab conducted a series of studies to learn more about what makes a website *credible* (Fogg et al., 2001). For example, they used a 51-item questionnaire to assess how believable a website is. Each item was a statement about some aspect of the site, such as "This site makes it hard to distinguish ads from content," and an associated 7-point scale from "Much less believable" to "Much more believable," on which the users rated the impact of that aspect on how believable the site is. They found that data from the 51 items fell into seven scales, which they labeled as Real-World Feel, Ease of Use, Expertise, Trustworthiness, Tailoring, Commercial Implications, and Amateurism. For example, one of the 51 items that weighted strongly in the "Real-World Feel" scale was "The site lists the organization's physical address."

5.7.3 Assessing Specific Elements

In addition to assessing specific *aspects* of a product or website, you might be interested in assessing specific *elements* of it, such as instructions, FAQs, or online help; the homepage; the search function; or the site map. The techniques for assessing subjective reactions to specific elements are basically the same as for assessing specific aspects. You simply ask the user to focus on the specific element and then present some appropriate rating scales.

The Nielsen Norman Group (Stover, Coyne, & Nielsen, 2002) conducted a study that focused specifically on the site maps of 10 different websites. After interacting with a site, the users completed a questionnaire that included six statements related to the site map:

- The site map is easy to find.
- The information on the site map is helpful.
- The site map is easy to use.
- The site map made it easy to find the information I was looking for.
- The site map made it easy to understand the structure of the website.
- The site map made it clear what content is available on the website.

Each statement was accompanied by a 7-point Likert scale of "Strongly Disagree" to "Strongly Agree." They then averaged the ratings from the six scales to get an overall rating of the site map for each of the ten sites. This is an example of getting more reliable ratings of a feature of a website by asking for several different ratings of the feature and then averaging them together.

Tullis (1998) conducted a study that focused on possible homepage designs for a website. (In fact, the designs were really just templates containing "placeholder" or "Lorem Ipsum" text.) One of the techniques used for comparing the designs was to ask participants in the study to rate the designs on three rating scales: page format, attractiveness, and use of color. Each was rated on a 5-point scale (−2, −1, 0, 1, 2) of "Poor" to "Excellent." (Note to self and others: Don't use that scale again. It tends to bias respondents away from the ratings associated with the negative values and zero. But the results are still valid if the main thing we are interested in is the relative *comparison* of the ratings for the different designs.) The results for the five designs are shown in Fig. 5.15. The design that received the best ratings was Template 1, and the design that received the worst ratings was Template 4. This study also illustrates another common technique in studies that involve a comparison of alternatives. The participants were asked to rank-order the five templates from their most preferred to least preferred. In this study, 48% of the participants ranked Template 1 as their first choice, while 57% ranked Template 4 as their last choice.

5.7.4 Open-Ended Questions

Most questionnaires in usability studies include some open-ended questions in addition to the various kinds of rating scales that we've discussed in this chapter.

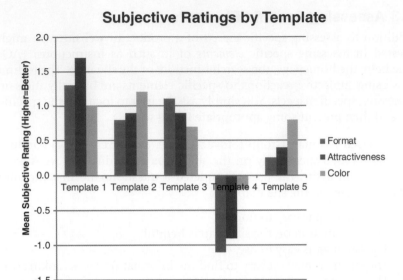

Fig. 5.15 Data in which five different designs for a website's homepage were each rated on three scales: format, attractiveness, and use of color. *Source:* Adapted from Tullis (1998); used with permission.

In fact, one common technique is to allow the user to add comments related to any of the individual rating scales. Although the utility of these comments to the calculation of specific metrics may be limited, they can be very helpful in identifying ways to improve the product.

Another flavor of open-ended questions commonly used in UX studies is to ask the users to list three to five things they like the *most* about the product and three to five things they like the *least*. These can be translated into metrics by counting the number of instances of essentially the same thing being listed and then reporting those frequencies. Of course, you could also treat the remarks that participants offer while thinking aloud as these kinds of verbatim comments.

Entire books have been written about analyzing these kinds of verbatim responses using what's generally called text mining (e.g., Ignatow & Mihalcea, 2017; Ignatow, 2016; Liu, 2015; Miner et al. 2012), and a wide variety of tools are available in this space (e.g., NVivo, Clarabridge, IBM SPSS Text Analysis, to name a few). We just describe a few simple techniques for collecting and summarizing these kinds of verbatim comments.

Summarizing responses from open-ended questions is always a challenge. We've never come up with a magic solution to doing this quickly and easily. One thing that helps is to be relatively specific in your open-ended questions. For example, a question that asks participants to describe anything they found confusing about the interface is going to be easier to analyze than a general "comments" field.

One very simple analysis method that we like is to copy all the verbatim responses to a question into a tool for creating word clouds, such as Wordle.net. For example, Fig. 5.16 shows a word cloud of the responses to a question asking participants to describe anything they found particularly challenging or frustrating about using the NASA website about the Apollo Space Program (Tullis, 2008b). In a word cloud, larger text is used to represent words that appear more frequently. It's apparent from this word cloud that participants were frequently commenting on the "search" on the site and the "navigation." (Some frequent words, like "Apollo," are certainly not surprising given the subject matter.)

Fig. 5.16 Word cloud created with Wordle.net of the responses in an online study of the NASA website about the Apollo Space Program to a question asking for anything they found particularly frustrating or challenging about the site.

FINDING ALL COMMENTS THAT INCLUDE A SPECIFIC WORD

After studying a word cloud (and the accompanying word frequencies that most of these tools can generate), it's sometimes helpful to find all the verbatim comments that included specific words anywhere in the comment. For example, after seeing the word cloud in Fig. 5.18, it might be helpful to find all the comments that included the word "navigation." This can be done in Excel using the =SEARCH function. You can then sort on the column containing the results of the SEARCH function. Entries containing the target word will have numeric values (actually the character position where the target word starts), and those that don't contain the target word will give a "#VALUE!" error.

In our experience, analyzing verbatim comments often comes down to manual analysis. (We have recently seen job postings in the UX field for people whose primary job is to analyze verbatim comments!) Two common approaches to manual text analysis include categorizing and tagging. Either approach can be done in Excel, where each row in a spreadsheet is a comment. Note that you will often need to start by identifying any comments that are really multiple comments and splitting them up. Of course, you will want to maintain any demographic data associated with the comment since it's sometimes useful to slice verbatim comments by demographics.

In categorizing comments, you go through all the comments and assign a single category to each (e.g., account opening and font size). It's useful to quickly scan a sample of the comments first to help you identify the categories. Tagging comments is similar, but you can associate multiple tags (similar to categories) with each comment. Logistically, when categorizing comments, you would typically add one column to the spreadsheet to contain the categories (often in a drop-down list). In tagging, you would add as many columns as you have tags and then simply put an "X" (or something) in each column you want to tag for a comment. For a good overview of manual coding and analysis of comments, see Sauro (2017).

5.7.5 Awareness and Comprehension

A technique that somewhat blurs the distinction between self-reported data and performance data involves asking the users some questions about what they saw or remember from interacting with the application or website after they have performed some tasks with it and not being allowed to refer back to it. One flavor of this is a check for awareness of various features of a website. For example, consider the NASA homepage shown in Fig. 5.17. First, the user would be given a chance to explore the site a little and complete a few very general tasks like reading the latest news from NASA and finding how to get images from the Hubble Space Telescope. Then, with the site no longer available to the user, a questionnaire is given that lists a variety of specific pieces of content that the site may or may not have had.

These would generally be content and *not* directly related to the specific tasks that the user was asked to perform. You're interested in whether some of these other pieces of content "stood out to the user. The user then indicates which of the pieces of content on the questionnaire he or she remembers seeing on the site. For example, two of the items on the questionnaire might be "JAXA Spacecraft Launch Scrubbed" and "Name NASA's Next Mars Rover," both of which are links on the homepage. One of the challenges in designing such a questionnaire is that it must include logical "distracter" items as well—items that were not on the website (or page, if you limit the study to one page) but that look like they could have been.

A closely related technique involves testing for the users' learning and comprehension related to some of the content of the website. After interacting with

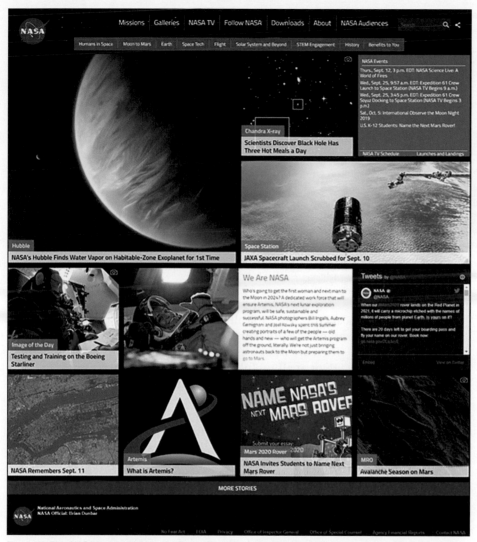

Fig. 5.17 This NASA homepage illustrates one technique for assessing how "attention-grabbing" various elements of a web page are. After letting users interact with the site, you ask them to identify from a list of content items which ones were actually on the site.

a site, users are given a quiz to test their comprehension of some of the information on the site. If the information is something that some of the participants might have already known prior to using the site, it would be necessary to administer a pretest to determine what they already know and then compare their results from the post-test back to that. When the users are not overtly directed to the information during their interaction with the site, this is usually called an "incidental learning" technique.

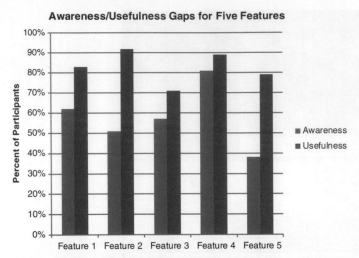

Awareness/Usefulness Gaps for Five Features

- ■ Awareness
- ■ Usefulness

Fig. 5.18 Data from a study looking at awareness-usefulness gaps. Items with the greatest difference between the awareness and usefulness ratings, such as Tasks 2 and 5, are those you should consider making more obvious in the interface.

5.7.6 Awareness and Usefulness Gaps

One type of analysis that can be very valuable is to look at the difference between users' *awareness* of a specific piece of information or functionality and their perceived *usefulness* of that same piece of information or functionality once they are made aware of it. For example, if a vast majority of users are unaware of some specific functionality, but once they notice it, they find it very useful and suggest you should promote or highlight that functionality in some way.

To analyze awareness-usefulness gaps, you must have both an awareness and usefulness metric. We typically ask users about awareness as a yes/no question—for example, "Were you aware of this functionality prior to this study? (yes or no)." Then we ask: "On a 1 to 5 scale, how useful is this functionality to you?" (1 = Not at all useful; 5 = Very useful). This assumes that they have had a couple of minutes to explore the functionality. Next, you will need to convert the rating-scale data into a top-2 box score so that you have an apples-to-apples comparison. Simply plot the percent of users who are aware of the functionality next to the percent of users who found the functionality useful (percent top-2 box). The difference between the two bars is called the *awareness-usefulness gap* (Fig. 5.18).

5.8 SUMMARY

Many different techniques are available for getting UX metrics from self-reported data. Here is a summary of some of the key points to remember:

1. Consider getting self-reported data at both a task level and overall. Task-level data can help you identify areas that need improvement. Overall data can help you get a sense of the complete user experience.

2. Consider using one of the standard questionnaires for assessing subjective reactions to a system. The SUS has been shown to be robust even with relatively small numbers of participants (e.g., 8 to 10).

3. If you are interested in benchmarking your product in comparison to others, consider using one of the tools that has a large comparison dataset or available published literature, such as SUS, UEQ, SUPR-Q, WAMMI, or ACSI.

4. To learn about the priorities that users have for various features or functions, consider using conjoint analysis, MaxDiff, or the Kano Model.
5. Be creative but also cautious in the use of other techniques in addition to simple rating scales. When possible, ask for ratings on a given topic in several different ways and average the results to get more consistent data. Carefully construct any new rating scales. Make appropriate use of open-ended questions and consider techniques like checking for awareness or comprehension after interacting with the product.

CHAPTER 6
Issues-Based Metrics

153

CONTENTS

Many UX researchers consider identifying usability issues and providing design recommendations the most important part of their job. A usability issue might involve confusion around a particular term or piece of content, method of navigation, or just not noticing something that should be noticed. These types of issues, and many others, are typically identified as part of an iterative process in which designs are being evaluated and improved throughout design and

Measuring the User Experience. DOI: http://dx.doi.org/10.1016/B978-0-12-818080-8.00006-6

development. This process provides tremendous value to product design and is a cornerstone of UX research.

Usability issues are generally thought of as purely qualitative. They typically include the identification and description of a problem one or more participants experienced and, in many cases, an assessment of the underlying cause of the problem. Most UX professionals also include specific recommendations for remedying the problem, and many report positive findings as well (i.e., something that worked particularly well).

Most UX professionals don't strongly associate metrics with usability issues. This may be because of the gray areas in identifying issues or because identifying issues is part of an iterative design process, and metrics are perceived as adding little value. However, not only is it possible to measure usability issues, but doing so also adds value in product design while not slowing down the iterative design process.

In this chapter we review some simple metrics around usability issues. We will also discuss different ways of identifying usability issues, prioritizing the importance of different types of issues, and factors you need to think about when measuring usability issues.

6.1 WHAT IS A USABILITY ISSUE?

What do we mean by usability issues? Usability issues are based on behavior in using a product. As a UX professional, you interpret the cause of these issues, such as confusing terminology or hidden navigation. Examples of usability issues include:

- Behaviors that prevent task completion
- Behaviors that takes someone "off course"
- An expression of frustration by the participant
- Not seeing something that should be noticed
- A participant says a task is complete when it is not
- Performing an action that leads away from task success
- Misinterpreting some piece of content
- Choosing the wrong link to navigate through web pages

A key point to consider in defining usability issues is how they will be addressed. The most common use is in an iterative design process focused on improving the product. In that context, the most useful issues are those that point to possible improvements in the product. In other words, it helps if issues are reasonably actionable. If they don't directly point to a part of the interface that was causing a problem, they should at least give you some hint of where to begin looking. For example, we once saw an issue in a usability test report that said, "The mental model of the application does not match the user's mental model." Notice that no behavior was mentioned. And that was it. Although this may be an interesting interpretation of some behavior in a theoretical sense, it does very little to guide designers and developers in addressing the issue.

On the other hand, consider an issue like this: "Many participants were confused by the top-level navigation menu (which is the interpretation of the behavior), often jumping around from one section to another trying to find what they were looking for (the behavior)." This comment could be very helpful, particularly if this issue is followed by a variety of detailed examples describing what happened. It tells you where to start looking (the top-level navigation), and the more detailed examples of additional behaviors may help focus on some possible solutions. Molich, Jeffries, and Dumas (2007) conducted an interesting study of usability recommendations and ways to make them more useful and usable. They suggest that all usability recommendations improve the overall user experience of the application, consider business and technical constraints, and are specific and clear.

Of course, not all usability issues are things to be avoided. Some usability issues are positive. These are sometimes called usability "findings," since the term *issues* often has negative connotations. Here are some examples of positive usability issues:

- All participants were able to log into the application.
- There were no errors in completing the search task.
- Participants were faster at creating a report.

The main reason for reporting positive findings, in addition to providing some positive reinforcement for the project team, is to make sure that these aspects of the interface don't get "broken" in future design iterations.

6.1.1 Real Issues Versus False Issues

One of the most difficult parts of a UX researcher's job is determining which usability issues are real and which are merely an aberration. Obvious issues are those that most, if not all, participants encounter. For example, it may be obvious when participants select the wrong option from a poorly worded menu, get taken down the wrong path, and then spend a significant amount of time looking for their target in the wrong part of the application. These are behaviors with causes that are usually a "no-brainer" for almost anyone to identify.

Some usability issues are much less obvious, or it's not completely clear whether something is a real issue. For example, what if only 1 out of 10 participants expresses some confusion around a specific piece of content or terminology on a website? Or if only 1 out of 12 participants doesn't notice something he should have? At some point, you must decide whether what he observed is likely to be repeatable with a larger population. In these situations, ask yourself whether the participant's behavior, thought process, perception, or decisions during the task were logical. In other words, is there a consistent story or reasoning behind his actions or thoughts? If so, then it may be an issue, even if only one participant encountered it. On the other hand, no apparent rhyme or reason behind the behavior may be evident. If the participant can't explain his logic, and it only happened once, then it's likely to be idiosyncratic and should probably be ignored.

For example, assume that you observed one participant click on a link on a web page that started them down the wrong path for accomplishing the task. At the end of the task, you might ask the user why he/she clicked on that link. If he/she says that he/she clicked on it simply because it was there in front of them, some researchers may consider this to be a false issue. On the other hand, if the participant says that the wording of the link made it seem like a reasonable place to begin the task, some researchers will say this is a genuine usability issue.

6.2 HOW TO IDENTIFY AN ISSUE

The most common way to identify usability issues is during a study in which you are directly interacting with a participant. This might be in person or over the phone using remote testing technology. A less common way to identify usability issues is through some automated techniques, such as an online study, or by observing a video from a participant, similar to what is generated from a site like usertesting.com. This is where you don't have an opportunity to directly observe participants but only have access to their behavioral and self-reported data. Identifying issues through this type of data is more challenging but still quite possible.

Possible usability issues might be predicted beforehand and tracked during test sessions. But be careful that you're really *observing* the issues and not just finding them because you expect to. Your job is certainly easier when you know what to look for, but you might also miss other issues that you never considered. In our testing, we typically have an idea of what to look for, but we also try to keep an open mind to spot the surprise issues. There's no "right" approach; it all depends on the goals of the evaluation. When evaluating products that are in an early conceptual stage, it's more likely that you won't have preset ideas about what the usability issues are. As the product is further refined, you may have a clearer idea of what specific issues you're looking for.

THE ISSUES YOU EXPECT MAY NOT BE THE ONES YOU FIND

One of the earliest sets of guidelines for designing software interfaces was published by Apple. It was called the *Apple IIe Design Guidelines*, and it contained a fascinating story of an early series of usability tests Apple conducted. They were working on the design of a program called *Apple Presents Apple*, which was a demonstration program for customers to use in computer stores. One part of the interface to which the designers paid little attention was asking users whether their monitor was monochrome or color. The initial design of the question was "Are you using a black-and-white monitor?" (They had predicted that users might have trouble with the word *monochrome*.) In the first usability test, they found that a majority of the participants who used a monochrome monitor answered this question incorrectly because their monitor actually displayed text in green, not white!

What followed was a series of hilarious iterations involving questions such as "Does your monitor display multiple colors?" or "Do you see more than one color on the screen?"—all of which kept failing for some participants. In desperation, they were considering including a developer with every computer just to answer this question, but then they finally hit on a question that worked: "Do the words above appear in several different colors?" In short, the issues you expect may not be the issues you find.

You can use many of the metrics we've been discussing in this book to triangulate on usability issues. Typically, task-level data are the most helpful. For example, consider the task success data shown in Fig. 6.1. These are data from Team L's report in the Comparative Usability Evaluation study number 8 (Molich, 2010).

It's clear from Fig. 6.1 that users were having significantly more difficulty with Task 4 (Damages) relative to the others. This is reinforced by the data from the same report showing the percentage of participants who gave up on each of

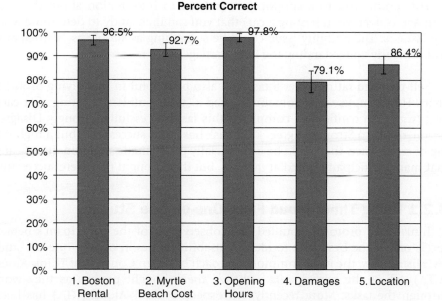

Fig. 6.1 Task success data from Team L's test report in CUE-8 (Molich, 2010).

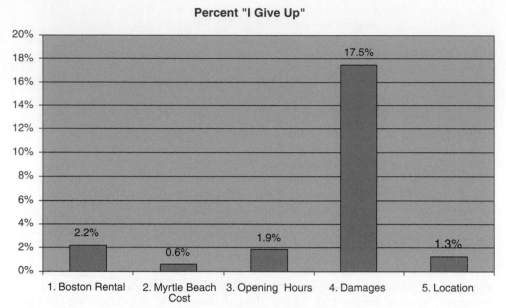

Fig. 6.2 Give-up rates from Team L's test report in CUE-8 (Molich, 2010).

the tasks (Fig. 6.2). Far more participants gave up on Task 4 than they did on any of the other tasks.

This points you to a specific task (related to information about the Loss Damage Waiver when renting a car) that you can then study to determine what the issue is. The usability issue could be something as simple as "Participants had difficulty understanding the Loss Damage Waiver."

Self-reported ratings after a task can also be helpful in identifying problem areas. For example, we've sometimes used a "task confidence" rating after each task (e.g., "I'm confident I completed this task successfully: Strongly Disagree o o o o o Strongly Agree"). If a task has a low success rate but a high rating of confidence, that could be an especially problematic situation. It indicates that many participants failed at the task, but they thought they were successful.

6.2.1 Using Think-Aloud From One-on-One Studies

A think-aloud protocol, coupled with observation of the participant's behavior, is one of the best ways to identify usability issues in one-on-one UX studies. Historically, the most common approach has been Concurrent Think-Aloud (CTA), where the participants verbalize their thought process as they work through the tasks. More recently, Retrospective Think-Aloud (RTA) has been studied as an alternative, mainly due to a concern that CTA might be altering the participant's behavior. For example, Van Den Haak, de Jong, and Schellens (2003) found that CTA had a negative effect on task performance, particularly for complex tasks. In RTA, participants work in silence and verbalize their thoughts afterwards, typically while watching a recording of their task performance. Sometimes this is augmented with eye-tracking gaze replay (e.g., Elling, Lentz, & de Jong, 2011). At this point it's not totally clear whether CTA or RTA is more effective. Both have been shown to uncover usability problems. For example, Van Den Haak et al. (2003) found that the issues revealed by CTA were based more on observation while those revealed by RTA were based more on verbalization.

Regardless of which protocol you use, the participants are typically reporting what they are doing, what they are trying to accomplish, how confident they are about their decisions, their expectations, and why they performed certain actions. Essentially, it's a stream of consciousness focusing on their interaction with the product. During a think-aloud protocol, you might observe the following:

- Verbal expressions of confusion, frustration, dissatisfaction, pleasure, or surprise
- Verbal expressions of confidence or indecision about a particular action that may be right or wrong
- Participants *not* saying or doing something that they should have done or said
- Nonverbal behaviors such as facial expressions or body language

In addition to listening to participants, it's important to observe their behavior. Watching what they are doing, where they struggle, and how they succeed provides a rich source of usability issues.

6.2.2 Using Verbatim Comments From Automated Studies

Identifying usability issues through automated studies requires careful data collection. The key is to allow participants to enter verbatim comments at a page or task level. In most of these studies, several data points are collected for each task: success, time, ease-of-use rating, and verbatim comments. The verbatim comments are the best way to understand possible issues. Continuing with the CUE-8 example from before (see Fig. 6.1), Team J reported the following verbatim comment related to Task 4 (Damages): "I am not sure if I actually got this right or not. It was hard to find a good explanation of the LDW, and once I found an explanation, I was not sure exactly what it actually said" (Molich, 2010).

One way to collect verbatim comments is to require the participant to provide a comment at the conclusion of each task. This might yield some interesting results, but it doesn't always yield the best results. An alternative that seems to work better is to make the verbatim comment conditional. If the participant provides a low ease-of-use score for a task (e.g., not one of the two highest ratings), then she is asked to provide feedback about why she rated the task that way. Having a more pointed question usually yields more specific, actionable comments. For example, participants might say that they were confused about a particular term or that they couldn't find the link they wanted on a certain page. This type of task-level feedback is usually more valuable than one question after they complete all the tasks (post-study). The only downside of this approach is the participant may adjust his/her rating system after several questions in order to avoid the open-ended questions.

6.2.3 Using Web Analytics

If you're studying a website, some usability issues or potential problem areas can be identified from web analytic data. For example, Hasan, Morris, and Probets (2009) used Google Analytics to try to identify usability issues on three different e-commerce websites. They compared the usability findings indicated by Google Analytics to a heuristic evaluation of the sites conducted by experts. They looked at thirteen key metrics, including page views per visit, bounce rate, order conversion rate, searches per visit, and checkout completion rate. They found that two of the sites had relatively high numbers of page views per visit (17 and 13 respectively) compared to the third site, which had a much lower number (6). This was interpreted as indicating potential navigation problems with the third site, which was consistent with the findings of the heuristic evaluators, who found 42 navigation problems with the third site but only 7 and 11 with the other two sites. The authors conclude that web analytics can be useful for quickly finding general usability problem areas and specific pages in a website that have usability problems; however, web analytics can't provide details about specific problems on a page.

6.2.4 Using Eye-Tracking

As discussed in Chapter 7, eye-tracking technology is becoming more widely available and used in UX studies. Consequently, its use in identifying usability issues is growing, but exactly how to correlate eye-tracking data with usability issues is not that clear. For example, if users fixate on an element, such as a graph, for a relatively long time, is that a good thing or a bad thing? It could mean that they find the graph very useful and are extracting information from it, but it could also mean that they are confused by it and are trying to understand it.

Ehmke and Wilson (2007) addressed this question of how eye-tracking data can be used to identify usability issues by studying two different websites. After having 19 participants attempt tasks on the two sites, with eye-tracking, they first identified usability problems from the raw data using a set of clearly defined criteria. This was done based on the directly observable data, not using the eye-tracking information. They then correlated these usability problems with the eye-tracking data. They found that usability problems were connected to not just a single eye-tracking pattern but to specific sequences of patterns. For example, the usability problem of "Overloaded, ineffective presentation" was correlated with eye-tracking data showing short fixations on single areas followed by longer saccades and regressions (back-tracking) to elements.

6.3 SEVERITY RATINGS

Not all usability issues are the same: Some are more serious than others. Some usability issues mildly annoy or frustrate users, whereas others cause them to make the wrong decisions or lose data. Obviously, these two different types of usability issues have a very different impact on the user experience, and severity ratings are a useful way to deal with them.

Severity ratings help focus attention on the issues that really matter. There's nothing more frustrating for a developer or business analyst than being handed a list of 82 usability issues that all need to be fixed immediately. By prioritizing usability issues, you're much more likely to have a positive impact on the design and decrease the likelihood of making enemies with the rest of the design and development team.

The severity of usability issues can be classified in many ways, but most severity rating systems can be boiled down to two different types. In one type of rating system, severity is based purely on the impact on the user experience: The worse the user experience, the higher the severity rating. A second type of severity rating system tries to bring in multiple dimensions or factors, such as business goals and technical implementation costs.

6.3.1 Severity Ratings Based on the User Experience

Many severity ratings are based solely on the impact on the user experience. These rating systems are easy to implement and provide very useful information. They usually have three levels—often something like low, medium, and high severity. Occasionally there is a "catastrophe" level, which is essentially a showstopper (delaying product launch or release—Nielsen, 1993).

When choosing a severity rating system, it's important to look at your organization and the product you are evaluating. Often, a three-level system works well in many situations:

Low: Any issue that annoys or frustrates participants but does not play a role in task failure. These are the types of issues that may lead someone off course, but he still recovers and completes the task. This issue may only reduce efficiency and/ or satisfaction a small amount, if any.

Medium: Any issue that contributes to significant task difficulty but does not cause task failure. Participants often develop workarounds to get to what they need. These issues have an impact on effectiveness and most likely efficiency and satisfaction.

High: Any issue that directly leads to task failure. Basically, there is no way to encounter this issue and still complete the task. This type of issue has a significant impact on effectiveness, efficiency, and satisfaction.

Notice that this scheme is a rating of task failure—one of the measures of user experience. In a test in which there are no task failures, there can be no high severity issues.

AN EXAMPLE OF THE ULTIMATE ISSUE SEVERITY

Tullis (2011) described an example of what we consider the ultimate in issue severity. In the early 1980s, he conducted a usability test of a prototype of a handheld device for detecting high voltage on a metallic surface. The device had two indicator lights: one simply indicated that the device is working and the other indicated that there is high voltage present which could be fatal. Unfortunately, both indicator lights were green. They were also right next to each other, and neither were labeled. After pleading with the designers to change the design, he finally decided to do a quick usability test. He had 10 participants perform 10 simulated tasks with the device. The prototype was rigged to signal the hazardous voltage condition 20% of the time. Out of 100 participant tasks, the indicator lights were interpreted correctly 99 times, but that one error was when it was signaling hazardous voltage. This usability issue could have resulted in serious injury or death to the user. The designers were convinced, and the design was significantly changed.

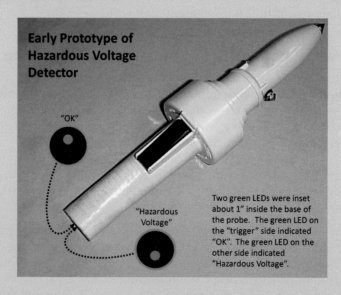

Early Prototype of Hazardous Voltage Detector

"OK"

"Hazardous Voltage"

Two green LEDs were inset about 1" inside the base of the probe. The green LED on the "trigger" side indicated "OK". The green LED on the other side indicated "Hazardous Voltage".

6.3.2 Severity Ratings Based on a Combination of Factors

Severity rating systems that use a combination of factors usually are based on the impact on the user experience coupled with frequency of use and/or impact on the business goals. Nielsen (1993) provides an easy way to combine the impact on the user experience and frequency of use on severity ratings. This severity rating system is intuitive and easy to explain (Table 6.1).

Alternatively, it's possible to consider three, or even four dimensions, such as impact to the user experience, predicted frequency of occurrence, impact on the business goals, and technical/implementation costs. For example, you might combine four different 3-point scales:

	Few users experiencing a problem	Many users experiencing a problem
Small impact to the user experience	Low severity	Medium severity
Large impact to the user experience	Medium severity	High severity

Table 6.1 Severity rating scale taking into account problem frequency and impact on the user experience. *Source.* Adapted from Nielsen (1993).

- Impact on the user experience (0 = low, 1 = medium, 2 = high)
- Predicted frequency of occurrence (0 = low, 1 = medium, 2 = high)
- Impact on the business goals (0 = low, 1 = medium, 2 = high)
- Technical/implementation costs (0 = high, 1 = medium, 2 = low)

By adding up the four scores, you now have an overall severity rating ranging from zero to eight. Of course, a certain amount of guesswork is involved in coming up with the levels, but at least all four factors are being taken into consideration. Or, if you really want to get fancy, you can weight each dimension based on some sort of organizational priority.

Sauro (2013) points out that in prioritizing UX issues we can borrow a methodology called Failure Mode and Effects Analysis (FMEA), developed in the 1950s for reliability engineering. This method involves estimating three factors related to each UX issue:

- Frequency of the problem (1 to 10), with the least common problems getting a 1 and the most common a 10
- Severity of the problem (1 to 10), with a cosmetic issue getting a 1 and total task failure, loss of money, or loss of life getting a 10
- Difficulty of detecting the problem (1 to 10), with issues that are easy to detect getting a 1 and those that are hard to detect getting a 10

The Risk Priority Number (RPN) is then the product of those three ratings:

$$RPN = Frequency \times Severity \times Difficulty\ of\ detecting$$

In theory, this Risk Priority Number could range from 1 to 1,000. Part of the overall process is then to try to identify the root causes of each of the UX issues.

6.3.3 Using a Severity Rating System

Once you have settled upon a severity rating system, you still need to consider a few more things. First, be consistent. Decide on one severity rating system, and use it for all your studies. By using the same severity rating system, you will be able to make meaningful comparisons across studies, as well as help train your audience on the differences between the severity levels. The more your audience internalizes the system, the more persuasive you will be in promoting design solutions.

Second, clearly communicate what each level means. Provide examples of each level as much as possible. This is particularly important for other usability specialists on your team who might also be assigning ratings. It's important that developers, designers, and business analysts understand each severity level. The more the "non-usability" audience understands each level, the easier it will be to influence design solutions for the highest-priority issues.

Third, try to have more than one UX researcher assign severity ratings to each issue. One approach that works well is to have the researchers independently assign severity ratings to each of the issues, then discuss any of the issues where they gave different ratings and try to agree on the appropriate level.

Finally, there's some debate about whether usability issues should be tracked as part of a larger bug-tracking system (Wilson & Coyne, 2001). Wilson argues that it is essential to track usability issues as part of a bug-tracking system because it makes the usability issues more visible, lends more credibility to the usability team, and makes it more likely that the issues will be remedied. Coyne suggests that usability issues, and the methods to fix them, are much more complex than typical bugs. Therefore, it makes more sense to track usability issues in a separate database. Either way, it's important to track the usability issues and make sure they are addressed and not simply forgotten.

6.3.4 Some Caveats About Rating Systems

Not everyone believes in severity ratings. Kuniavsky (2003) suggests letting your audience provide their own severity ratings. He argues that only those who are deeply familiar with the business model will be able to determine the relative priority of each usability issue.

Bailey (2005) strongly argues against severity rating systems altogether. He cites several studies that show there is very little agreement between usability specialists on the severity rating for any given usability issue (Catani & Biers, 1998; Cockton & Woolrych, 2001; Jacobsen, Hertzum, & John, 1998; Molich & Dumas, 2008). All of these studies generally show that there is very little overlap in what different usability specialists identify as a high-severity issue. Obviously, this is troubling given that many important decisions may be based on severity ratings.

Hertzum et al. (2002) highlight another possible problem in assigning severity ratings. In their research, they found that when multiple usability specialists are working as part of the same team, each usability specialist rates the issues she personally identifies as more severe than issues identified by the other usability specialists on their own team. This is one aspect known as an evaluator effect, and it poses a significant problem in relying on severity ratings by a single UX professional. As a profession, we don't yet know why severity ratings are not consistent between specialists.

So where does this leave us? We believe that severity ratings are far from perfect, but they still serve a useful purpose. They help direct attention to at least some of the most pressing needs. Without severity ratings, the designers or developers will simply make their own priority list, perhaps based on what's easiest or least expensive to implement. Even though there is subjectivity involved in assigning severity ratings, they're better than nothing. We believe that most key stakeholders understand that there is more art than science involved, and they interpret the severity ratings within this broader context.

6.4 ANALYZING AND REPORTING METRICS FOR USABILITY ISSUES

Once you've identified and prioritized the UX issues, it's helpful to do some analyses of the issues themselves. This lets you derive some metrics related to the issues. Exactly how you do this will largely depend on the type of questions you have in mind. Three general questions can be answered by looking at metrics related to usability issues:

- How is the overall usability of the product? This is helpful if you simply want to get an overall sense of how the product did.
- Is the usability improving with each design iteration? Focus on this question when you need to know how the usability is changing with each new design iteration.
- Where should you focus your efforts to improve the design? The answer to this question is useful when you need to decide where to focus your resources.

All of the analyses we will examine can be done with or without severity ratings. Severity ratings simply add a way to filter the issues. Sometimes it's helpful to focus on the high-severity issues. Other times it might make more sense to treat all the usability issues equally.

6.4.1 Frequency of Unique Issues

The simplest way to measure usability issues is to count the unique issues. Analyzing the frequency of unique issues is most useful in an iterative design process when you want some high-level data about how the usability is changing with each new design iteration. For example, you might observe that the number of unique issues decreased from 24 to 12 to 4 through the first three design iterations. These data are obviously trending in the right direction, but they're not necessarily iron-clad evidence that the design is significantly better. Perhaps the four remaining issues are so much bigger than all the rest that, without addressing them, everything else is unimportant. Therefore, we suggest a thorough analysis and explanation of the issues when presenting this type of data.

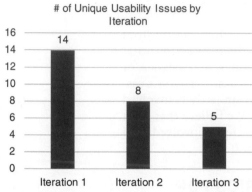

Fig. 6.3 Example data showing the number of unique usability issues by design iteration.

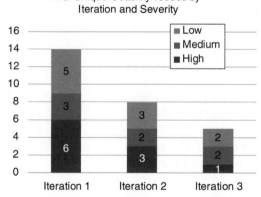

Fig. 6.4 Example data showing the number of unique usability issues by design iteration, categorized by severity rating. The change in the number of high-severity issues is probably of key interest.

Keep in mind that this frequency represents the number of *unique issues*, not the *total number of issues* encountered by all participants. For example, assume Participant A encountered ten issues, whereas Participant B encountered 14 issues, but 6 of those issues were the same as those from Participant A. If A and B were the only participants, the total number of unique issues would be 18. Fig. 6.3 shows an example of how to present the frequency of usability issues when comparing more than one design.

The same type of analysis can be performed using usability issues that have been assigned a severity rating. For example, if you have classified your usability issues into three levels (low, medium, and high severity), you can easily look at the number of issues by each type of severity rating. The most telling data item would be the change in the number of high-priority issues with each design iteration. Looking at the frequency of usability issues by severity rating, as illustrated in Fig. 6.4, can be very informative, since it is an indicator of whether the design effort between each iteration addresses the most important usability issues.

6.4.2 Frequency of Issues per Participant

It can also be informative to look at the number of (non-unique) issues each participant encountered. Over a series of design iterations, you would expect to see this number decreasing along with the total number of unique issues. For example, Fig. 6.5 shows the average number of issues encountered by each participant for three design iterations. Of course, this analysis could also include the average number of issues per participant broken down by severity level. If the average number of issues per participant is steady over a series of iterations, but the total number of unique issues is declining, then you know there is more consistency in the issues that the participants are encountering. This would indicate that the issues encountered by fewer participants are being fixed whereas those encountered by more participants are not.

6.4.3 Percentage of Participants

Another useful way to analyze usability issues is to observe the percentage of participants who encountered a specific issue. For example, you might be interested in whether participants correctly used some new type of navigation element on your website. You report that half of the participants encountered a specific issue in the first design iteration, and only 1 out of 10 encountered the same issue in the second design iteration. This is a useful metric when you need to focus on whether you are improving the usability of specific design elements as opposed to making overall usability improvements.

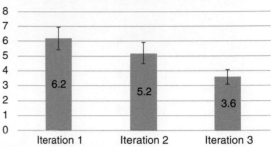

Mean # of Usability Issues per Participant by Iteration (Error bars represent 90% confidence interval)

Fig. 6.5 Example data showing the average number of usability issues encountered by participants in each of three usability tests.

With this type of analysis, it's important that your criteria for identifying specific issues be consistent between participants and designs. If a description of a specific issue is a bit fuzzy, your data won't mean very much. It's a good idea to explicitly document the issue's exact nature, thereby reducing any interpretation errors across participants or designs. Fig. 6.6 shows an example of this type of analysis.

The use of severity ratings with this type of analysis is useful in a couple of ways. First, you could use the severity ratings to focus your analysis only on the high-priority issues. For example, you could report that there are five outstanding high-priority usability issues. Furthermore, the percentage of participants who are experiencing these issues is decreasing with each design iteration. Another form of analysis is to aggregate all the high-priority issues to report the percentage of participants who experienced any high-priority issue. This helps you to see how overall usability is changing with each design iteration, but it is less helpful in determining whether to address a specific usability problem.

6.4.4 Issues by Category

Sometimes it's helpful to know where to focus design improvements from a tactical perspective. Perhaps you feel that only certain areas of the product are causing the most usability issues, such as navigation, content, terminology, and so forth. In this situation, it can be useful to aggregate usability issues into categories. Simply examine each issue and then categorize it into a type of issue. Next, look at the frequencies of issues that fall into each category. Issues can be categorized in many different ways. Just make sure the categorization makes sense to you and your audience, and use a limited number of categories, typically three to eight. If there are too many categories, it won't provide much direction. Fig. 6.7 provides an example of usability issues analyzed by category.

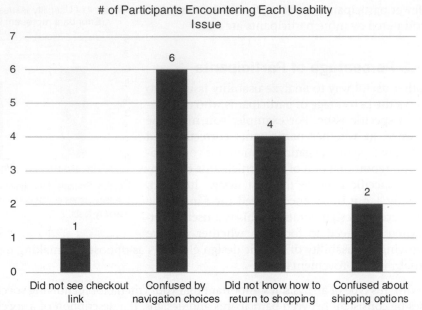

Fig. 6.6 Example data showing the frequency of participants who experienced specific usability issues.

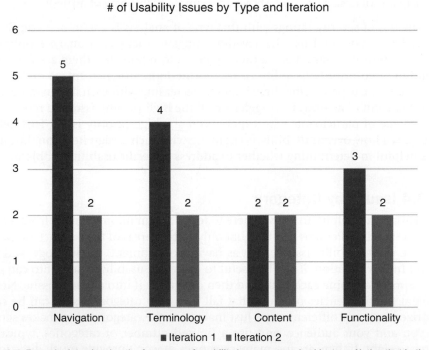

Fig. 6.7 Example data showing the frequency of usability issues categorized by type. Notice that both navigation and terminology issues were improved from the first to the second design iteration.

6.4.5 Issues by Task

Issues can also be analyzed at a task level. You might be interested in which tasks lead to the most issues, and you can report the number of unique issues that occur for each. This will identify the tasks you should focus on for the next design iteration. Alternatively, you can report the frequency of participants who encounter any issue for each task. This will tell you the pervasiveness of a particular issue. The greater the number of issues for each task, the greater the concern should be.

If you have assigned a severity rating to each issue, it might be useful to analyze the frequency of high-priority issues by task. This is particularly effective if you want to focus on a few of the biggest problems and your design efforts are oriented toward specific tasks. This is also helpful if you are comparing different design iterations using the same tasks.

6.5 CONSISTENCY IN IDENTIFYING USABILITY ISSUES

Much has been written about consistency and bias in identifying and prioritizing usability issues. Unfortunately, the news is not so good. Much of the research shows that there is very little agreement about what a usability issue is or how severe it is.

Perhaps the most exhaustive set of studies, called Comparative Usability Evolution (CUE), have been coordinated by Rolf Molich. To date, 10 separate CUE studies have been conducted, dating back to 1998 (Molich, 2018). Most of the studies were set up in a similar manner. Different teams of usability experts all evaluated the same design. Each team reported their findings, including the identification of the usability issues, along with their design recommendations. The first study, CUE-1 (Molich et al., 1998), showed very little overlap in the issues identified. In fact, only 1 out of the 141 issues was identified by all four teams participating in the study, and 128 out of the 141 issues were identified by single teams. Several years later, in CUE-2, the results were no more encouraging: 75% of all the issues were reported by only one of nine usability teams (Molich et al, 2004). CUE-4 (Molich & Dumas, 2008) showed similar results: 60% of all the issues were identified by only 1 of the 17 different teams participating in the study. At least some of the inconsistency in the findings can be attributed to the different tasks that teams selected for their evaluations, but certainly not all.

CUE-9 (Molich, 2018) focused on the evaluator effect, or the Rashomon Effect (named after Akira Kurosawa's 1950 film *Rashomon*, in which the same event is described in four contradictory ways by four witnesses). The evaluator effect in usability studies was first reported by Jacobsen, Hertzum, and John (1998) in which they had four evaluators watch the same videos of a usability test. They found that only 20% of the 93 unique issues were found by all four evaluators, while 46% were detected by only individual evaluators.

One of the goals of CUE-9 was to see if the usability and UX research field had matured to a point where the evaluator effect had either disappeared or was at least less pronounced. CUE-9 was different from the previous CUE studies in that all the teams were given the same five 30-minute videos of test sessions to analyze. These sessions were tests of the U-Haul website. Thirty-five leading UX research professionals participated in CUE-9, each independently writing up a test report based on their viewing of the five videos. Across the 35 teams, 223 unique usability issues were identified. Only four issues were reported by at least 75% of the teams while 90 (or 40%) of the issues were reported by individual teams only. Unfortunately, the evaluator effect was still quite prominent.

Hertzum, Molich, and Jacobsen (2014) studied the details of CUE-9 to identify some of the causes of the evaluator effect. They concluded that there were five main reasons for the evaluator effect in CUE-9:

- The detection, rating, and reporting of usability issues involve human judgments in the face of uncertainty. They came to the same conclusion as Hertzum and Jacobsen (2003, p. 201) who said that "the principal cause for the evaluator effect is that usability evaluation is a cognitive activity, which requires that the evaluators exercise judgment."
- Domain knowledge may be required to assess whether certain parts of a user's interaction with a system are appropriate, and some evaluators may not have that knowledge.
- Some evaluators may have reported only a subset of the issues they uncovered, based on the assumption that they wanted to focus on what they perceived as the most important issues.
- The exact goals of the evaluation may not have been clear or may have been contested. This could have caused some evaluators to adopt a different role from other evaluators (e.g., advocating for the user vs. achieving the client's upselling objective).
- Some evaluators may have reported issues that they considered problematic, but which weren't directly supported by the test sessions. Their logic was that other users would likely encounter these issues.

We won't be able to completely eliminate the evaluator effect but being aware of some of these causes can help to reduce it.

6.6 BIAS IN IDENTIFYING USABILITY ISSUES

Many different factors can influence how usability issues are identified. Carolyn Snyder (2006) provides a review of many of the ways usability findings might be biased. She concludes that bias cannot be eliminated, but it must be understood. In other words, even though our methods have flaws, they are still useful. We've distilled the different sources of bias in a usability study into seven general categories:

Participants: Your participants are critical. Every participant brings a certain level of technical expertise, domain knowledge, and motivation. Some participants may be well targeted, and others may not. Some participants are comfortable in a lab setting, whereas others are not. All of these factors make a big difference in what usability issues you ultimately discover.

Tasks: The tasks you choose have a tremendous impact on what issues are identified. Some tasks might be well defined with a clear end-state, whereas others might be open-ended, and yet others might be self-generated by each participant. The tasks basically determine what areas of the product are exercised and the ways in which they are exercised. Particularly with a complex product, this can have a major impact on what issues are uncovered.

Method: The method of evaluation is critical. Methods might include traditional lab testing or some type of expert review. Other decisions you make are also important, such as how long each session lasts, whether the participant thinks aloud, or how and when you probe.

Artifact: The nature of the prototype or product you are evaluating has a huge impact on your findings. The type of interaction will vary tremendously whether it is a paper prototype, functional or semi-functional prototype, or production system.

Environment: The physical environment also plays a role. The environment might involve direct interaction with the participant, indirect interaction via a conference call or behind a one-way mirror, or even interaction in someone's home. Other characteristics of the physical environment, such as lighting, seating, observers behind a one-way mirror, and videotaping, can all have an impact on the findings.

Moderators: Different moderators will also influence the issues that are observed. A UX professional's experience, domain knowledge, and motivation all play a key role.

Expectations: Norgaard and Hornbaek (2006) found that many usability professionals come into testing with expectations about the most problematic areas of the interface. These expectations have a significant impact on what they report, often missing many other important issues.

An interesting study that sheds some light on these sources of bias was conducted by Lindgaard and Chattratichart (2007). They analyzed the reports from the nine teams in CUE-4 who conducted actual usability tests with real users. They looked at the number of participants in each test, the number of tasks used, and the number of usability issues reported. They found no significant correlation between the number of *participants* in the test and the percentage of usability problems found. On the other hand, they did find a significant correlation between the number of *tasks* used and the percentage of usability problems found ($r = 0.82$, $P < .01$). When looking at the percentage of *new* problems uncovered, the correlation with the number of tasks was even higher ($r = 0.89$, $P < .005$). As Lindgaard and Chattratichart concluded, these results suggest "that with careful participant recruitment, investing in wide task coverage is more fruitful than increasing the number of users."

One technique that works well to increase the task coverage in a usability test is to define a set of tasks that all participants must complete and another set that is derived for each participant. These additional tasks might be selected based on characteristics of the participant (e.g., an existing customer or a prospect), or they might be selected at random. Care must be exercised when making comparisons across participants, since not all participants had the same tasks. In this situation, you may want to limit certain analyses to the core tasks.

THE SPECIAL CASE OF MODERATOR BIAS IN AN EYE TRACKING STUDY

One of the more difficult aspects of moderating a usability study is controlling where you look during the session. Moderators usually are looking at the participant or their interaction on a screen, or some other interface. This works well, except in the case of an eye-tracking study. Most eye-tracking studies measure where participants look, and whether participants are noting key elements on the interface. As a moderator, it can be difficult *not* to look at the target when the participant is scanning the interface. Participants can easily pick up on this and notice where *you* are looking, using that information as a guide to the target. It happens very quickly and subtly. While this behavior has not been reported in the user experience literature, we have observed it during our own eye-tracking studies. The best thing to do is to be aware of it, and if you find your eyes starting to wander to the target, simply re-focus on the participant, what they are doing, or some other element on the page. Another option may be to not sit in the room with the participant. When you're sitting with the participant in an eye-tracking study, there's also a greater chance that the participant will naturally look at you and away from the screen.

6.7 NUMBER OF PARTICIPANTS

There has been much debate about how many participants are needed in a usability test to reliably identify usability issues. (See Barnum et al., 2003, for a summary of the debate.) Nearly every UX professional seems to have an opinion. Not only are many different opinions floating around, but quite a few compelling studies have been conducted on this very topic. From this research, two different camps have emerged: those who believe that five participants are enough to identify most of the usability issues and those who believe that five is nowhere near enough.

6.7.1 Five Participants Is Enough

One camp believes that a majority, or about 80%, of usability issues will be observed with the first five participants (Lewis, 1994; Nielsen & Landauer, 1993; Virzi, 1992). This is known as the "magic number 5." One of the most important ways to figure out how many participants are needed in a usability test is to measure p, or the probability of a usability issue being detected by a single test participant. It's important to note that this p is different from the p-value that is used in tests of significance. The probabilities vary from study to study, but they tend to average around 0.3, or 30%. (See Turner, Nielsen, and Lewis, 2002, for a review of different studies.) In the seminal paper, Nielsen and Landauer (1993) found an average probability of 31% based on 11 different studies. This basically means that each participant only observed about 31% of the usability problems.

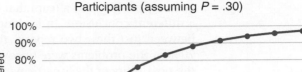

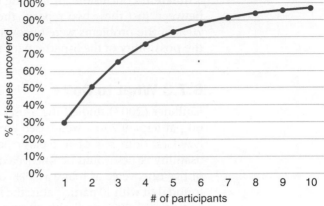

Fig. 6.8 shows how many issues are observed as a function of the number of participants when the probability of detection is 30%. (Notice that this assumes all issues have an equal probability of detection, which may be a big assumption.) As you can see, after the first participant, 30% of the problems are detected; after the third participant, about 66% of the problems are observed; and after the fifth participant, about 83% of the problems have been identified. This claim is backed up not only by this mathematical formula but by anecdotal evidence as well. Many UX professionals only test with five or six participants during an iterative design process. In this situation, it is relatively uncommon to test with more than a dozen, with a few exceptions. If the scope of the product is particularly large or if there are distinctly different audiences, then a strong case can be made for testing with more than five participants.

Fig. 6.8 Example showing how many users are required to observe the total number of issues in a usability study, given a 30% probability of detection.

6.7.2 Five Participants Is *Not* Enough

Other researchers have challenged this idea of the magic number 5 (Molich et al., 1998; Spool & Schroeder, 2001; Woolrych & Cockton, 2001). Spool and Schroeder (2001) asked participants to purchase various types of products, such as CDs and DVDs, at three different electronics websites. They discovered only 35% of the usability issues after the first five participants—far lower than the 80% predicted by Nielsen (2000). However, in this study the scope of the websites being evaluated was very large, even though the task of buying something was very well defined. Woolrych and Cockton (2001) discount the assertion that five participants are enough, primarily because it does not take into account individual differences.

The analyses by Lindgaard and Chattratichart (2007) of the nine usability tests from CUE-4 also raise doubts about the magic number 5. They compared the results of two teams, A and H, that both did very well, uncovering 42% and 43%, respectively, of the full set of usability problems. Team A used only 6 participants, whereas Team H used 12. At first glance, this might be seen as evidence for the magic number 5, since a team that tested only 6 participants uncovered as many problems as a team that tested 12, but a more detailed analysis reveals a different conclusion. In looking specifically at the overlap of usability issues between just these two reports, they found only 28% in common. More than 70% of the problems were uncovered by only one of the two teams, ruling out the possibility of the 5-participant rule applying in this case.

6.7.3 What to Do?

Faulkner (2003) studied the 5-user assumption by conducting test sessions with 60 participants on a web-based employee time-reporting system. She then analyzed random sets of five participants or more to see what percentage of the usability issues would be uncovered by each set. While some of the random sets of five uncovered as many as 99% of the issues, others uncovered only 55%. She found that with 10 participants, the lowest percentage of problems revealed by any one set was 80%, and with 20 participants it reached 95%. She's quick to point out that this is consistent with the original findings of Virzi (1992) and Nielsen (1993), who couched their findings in probabilities and confidence intervals, but which has been widely ignored by advocates of the simple 5-user assumption.

Macefield (2009) provided a good summary of the literature on both sides of this argument. He concludes:

There is no "one size fits all" solution to the challenge here. However, for studies related to problem discovery a group size of 3–20 participants is typically valid, with 5–10 participants being a sensible baseline range. In these scenarios, the group size should typically be increased along with the study's complexity and the criticality of its context. In scenarios concerned with discovering severe ("show stopping") problems in early conceptual prototypes a group size of five participants is typically valid. For comparative studies where statistically significant findings are being sought, a group size of 8–25 participants is typically valid, with 10–12 participants being a sensible baseline range. (Macefield, 2009, p. 43)

Obviously, there's not a simple answer to this question. The bottom line comes back to a point we've been making in various ways throughout this book: to a large extent, the answer depends upon how confident you need to be that you've found a given percentage of the usability issues. In early stages of an iterative product development process, you can probably afford to be less confident, but in later stages you will want to be more confident. The product context clearly makes a difference too: the consequences of missing some usability issues are less for a photo-sharing app than they are for an Automated External Defibrillator (AED). Many other factors will also influence the sample size you choose, including the complexity of the system being evaluated, the diversity of the target users, how you plan to use the data, the number of tasks you plan to use, and, of course, practical considerations like budget and time.

6.7.4 *Our* Recommendation

We recommend being flexible about sample sizes in usability tests. The minimum number needed will be different depending upon the circumstances. It can be acceptable to test with 5 to 10 participants and one UX team when the following conditions are met:

- It's OK to potentially miss some significant usability issues. You're more interested in capturing some of the big issues, iterating on the design, and then retesting. Any improvements are welcome.
- There's only one main user group, and you believe those users will think about the design and tasks in a reasonably similar way.
- The scope of the design is limited. There's a manageable number of screens, pages, or tasks.

We recommend increasing the number of participants to perhaps 10 to 25, and also having multiple UX researchers independently identify the usability issues, when the following conditions apply:

- You must capture as many UX issues as possible. There will be significant negative repercussions if you miss major usability issues.
- You're trying to make statistical comparisons (e.g., between designs or compared to a baseline).
- There is more than one user group, or the users are particularly diverse.
- The scope of the design is large. In this case we would also recommend using a broad set of tasks.

We fully realize that not everyone has access to multiple UX researchers. In that case, try to solicit feedback from any others who can observe the test sessions. No one can see everything, so be ready to acknowledge that you could have missed some of the significant usability issues.

6.8 SUMMARY

Many UX researchers make their living by identifying usability issues and providing actionable recommendations for improvement. Providing metrics around usability issues is not commonly done, but it can easily be incorporated into anyone's routine. Measuring usability issues helps you answer some fundamental questions about how good (or bad) the design is, how it is changing with each design iteration, and where to focus resources to remedy the outstanding problems. You should keep the following points in mind when identifying, measuring, and presenting usability issues.

1. Usability issues can be uncovered using UX metrics (e.g., low success rates), observations and comments from a think-aloud protocol, verbatim comments from online studies, web analytic data, and even eye-tracking data. The more you understand the domain, the easier it will be to spot the issues. Having multiple observers is very helpful in identifying issues.

2. When trying to figure out whether an issue is real, ask yourself whether there is a consistent story behind the user's thought process and behavior. If the story is reasonable, then the issue is likely to be real.
3. The severity of an issue can be determined in several ways. Severity always should take into account the impact on the user experience. Additional factors, such as frequency of use, impact on the business, and persistence, may also be considered. Some severity ratings are based on a simple high/medium/low rating system. Other systems are number based.
4. Some common ways to measure usability issues are measuring the frequency of unique issues, the percentage of participants who experience a specific issue, and the frequency of issues for different tasks or categories of issue. Additional analysis can be performed on high-severity issues or on how issues change from one design iteration to another.
5. When identifying usability issues, questions about consistency and bias may arise. Bias can come from many sources, and there can be a general lack of agreement on what constitutes an issue. Therefore, it's important to work collaboratively as a team, focusing on high-priority issues, and to understand how different sources of bias impact conclusions. Maximizing task coverage may be key.
6. There's no simple answer to how many participants you need in order to uncover the majority of the usability issues. If your focus is on problem discovery and it's a relatively simple non-critical system, 5 to 10 participants is probably a reasonable range. More participants will be needed if the system is complex/critical or you're making statistical inferences. Having multiple UX researchers identifying issues can be very helpful.

CHAPTER 7
Eye Tracking

CONTENTS

Eye tracking is a powerful tool in user research to gain insights into how individuals visually examine different scenes, such as web pages, mobile applications, grocery store shelves, or even billboards on subway platforms. As a UX researcher, eye tracking is a valuable method to better understand how someone visually interacts with any stimuli, answering fundamental questions such as:

- What do they notice?
- How long do they look at it?
- What do they see first?
- What don't they notice (that they should)?

Measuring the User Experience. DOI: http://dx.doi.org/10.1016/B978-0-12-818080-8.00007-8

Eye tracking has been around since the early 1900s. Huey (1908) devised a system whereby someone would wear a contact lens with a small hole for the pupil. The contact lens was then physically attached to a pointing device which would allow researchers to observe eye movements while reading text. Thankfully, we have come a long way since then. Eye tracking is now affordable (for most budgets), highly accurate, able to measure eye movements across a wide variety of stimuli and scenes, portable (through glasses), and the analysis and visualization tools are powerful and easy to use. Plus, there is no need to inject ink into anyone's eye!

Eye tracking is typically performed in one of two ways in the context of user research. In one way, eye tracking is based on a set of research questions that necessitate the need to analyze eye movements. This might involve comparing the visual attention patterns of two different web designs. In order to answer this question, the researcher must collect and analyze eye movement data. In this case, the "hit ratio" would tell them the percentage of participants who notice (or fixate) on an object in one web design compared to another web design.

Another way in which eye tracking is often used in user research is simply to generate real-time qualitative insights. A stakeholder might be interested in observing the eye movements in real time or as part of a participant recording, without any intention of analyzing the data. Observing eye movements provides an additional layer of data to gain a more complete picture of the user experience. Sometimes, the only associated deliverable is a heat map, with any associated metrics. No matter what approach you take with eye tracking, it is critical to determine the goals and the desired output before any work begins.

The information provided by an eye tracking system can be remarkably useful as part of user research. Simply enabling observers to see where the participant is looking in real time is extremely valuable. Even if you do no further analyses of the eye tracking data, just this real-time display provides insight that would not be possible otherwise. For example, assume a participant is performing a task on a website and there's a link on the homepage that would take him directly to the page required to complete the task. The participant keeps exploring the website, going down dead ends, returning to the homepage, but never reaching the required page. In a situation like this, you would like to know whether the participant ever saw the appropriate link on the homepage or whether he saw the link but dismissed it as not what he wanted (e.g., because of its wording). Although you could subsequently ask participants that question, their memory may not be completely accurate. With an eye tracking system, you can tell whether the participant at least fixated on the link long enough to read it.

7.1 HOW EYE TRACKING WORKS

Although a few different technologies are used, many eye tracking systems, such as the one shown in Fig. 7.1, use some combination of an infrared video camera and infrared light sources to track where the participant is looking. The infrared light sources create reflections on the surface of the participant's eye (called the corneal reflection), and the system compares the location of that reflection to the location of the participant's pupil. The location of the corneal reflection relative to the pupil changes as the participant moves his eyes.

The first activity in any eye tracking study is to calibrate the system by asking the participants to look at a series of known points; then the system can subsequently interpolate where a participant is

Fig. 7.1 An eye tracking system from Tobii. This eye tracking hardware is easily portable and plugs into the computer's USB port.

looking based on the location of the corneal reflection. Typically, the researcher can check the quality of the calibration, usually expressed as degrees that deviate from the X and Y visual planes. Deviations less than one degree are generally considered to be acceptable, and less than one-half of a degree is very good. Most eye tracking systems tell you something about the quality of the calibration and an opportunity to attempt another calibration to improve the accuracy. It is critical that the calibration is satisfactory; otherwise, all the eye movement data should not be recorded or analyzed. Without a good calibration, there will be a disconnect between what the participant is *actually* looking at and what you assume he/she is looking at. Following calibration, the moderator makes sure the eye movement data are being recorded. The biggest issue tends to be participants who move around in their seat. Occasionally, the moderator is required to ask the participant to move back/forward, left/right, or raise/lower their seat to recapture the participant's eyes.

INSTRUCTIONS FOR CALIBRATING

In our experience, there are a few simple instructions that can go a long way toward making the experience easy for both participants and researchers, and provide reliable eye tracking data.

1. Make sure the participants are sitting at the right height and distance from the monitor or whatever device (interface) you are tracking. Chairs should ideally be on wheels, with adjustable heights.

2. Let the participants know that the calibration process is quick, simple, and nothing will be touching them.

3. When you display the dynamic calibration point (typically a small circle), tell them to visually follow or trace the circle as it moves around the screen. When the circle momentarily stops at each position, make sure they are looking at the center of the circle.

4. Depending on the quality of the calibration, you may have to ask the participant to go through the process a second time. Simply say something "thanks for doing that—we are going to do it once more so we can make sure we have the most accurate capture of your eye movements." We typically don't go through a third time, unless it is necessary for the study.

5. During the course of the study, participants may move so you no longer are tracking them. Simply ask them to readjust their position so their eyes are again being tracked. If they move around a lot, you might consider asking them to keep still as best they can.

PARTICIPANTS WHO ARE DIFFICULT TO CALIBRATE

It is easy to get a good calibration from most participants. However, there are a few instances that can pose particular challenges. If someone has very narrow framed glasses, the system will have difficulty distinguishing the frames of the glasses from the pupil. Also, if someone is wearing heavy eye make-up, specifically if it is reflective, this will make for a challenging calibration. Lastly, if someone is very fidgety in the chair, such as a child, this will mean that many times you will lose the eye, and you will need them to reposition themselves in a proper position. There is not a lot you can do, other than to specify your requirements during your recruit, as well as give clear instructions during the warm-up. Don't let this discourage you, though. In our experience, we get a good calibration with well over 90% of our participants, even those with glasses.

7.2 MOBILE EYE TRACKING

Contributed by Andrew Schall, Modernizing Medicine.

Users interact with mobile devices very differently than those in a desktop environment. Think about the kind of tasks that you perform when using your smartphone versus using a laptop. Also consider where you are performing these activities and how the environment affects your experience. Mobile experiences often occur when people are on the go and need to accomplish tasks quickly, and this can be significantly impacted by their context of use. Eye tracking provides eye gaze behavior that is ideal for understanding how people view content on their mobile devices, as well as usability metrics such as glanceability.

Fig. 7.2 An example of the use of eye tracking technology with a mobile device.

7.2.1 Measuring Glanceability

Glanceability is defined as being able to quickly *view* and *understand* information. Mobile experiences often rely on the user noticing subtle visual cues that occur within a mobile app and then promptly acting on them. Some of the questions that can be addressed when measuring glanceability include:

- How long does it take a user to notice and read a notification on their smartwatch while they are out for a run?
- How quickly can a user find departure times to determine the next subway train to board to get to their destination?
- During a meeting, how quickly can a user identify an incoming call and determine whether to answer it or not?

An interface with a high degree of glanceability can be identified by relatively low fixation counts, short fixation durations, and short saccades. These eye tracking metrics should be paired with task performance data to determine how quickly the user was able to successfully complete a task based on the information that was observed.

Fig. 7.2 shows a participant using a mobile app to compare prices in the store with those found online. This eye gaze video showed that this user quickly skimmed over the product name (indicated by the red circle) to make sure that it matched the in-store item.

7.2.2 Understanding Mobile Users in Context

Eye tracking can provide insights into how your user's environment and situation impact their experience. Some of the questions that eye tracking can help us to answer include:

- How do the distractions and disruptions on a subway train impact how users consume social media content on their phone?
- How easy is it to set up and use two-factor authentication when checking your bank account balance on your smartwatch while waiting in line at a coffee shop?
- While texting with a friend, what information does a user look at to determine the highest-rated pub within walking distance of their current location?

Fig. 7.3 shows the variety of contexts in which eye tracking can be used in the real environment. Eye tracking glasses provided a first-person perspective as this participant attempted to set up and use the Alaska Airlines iPhone and Apple Watch apps while waiting for her flight.

All of these situations require researchers to get out of the UX lab and take eye trackers into the field to see how mobile applications are used in a real-world

Fig. 7.3 An example of mobile eye tracking across multiple devices and media.

environment. Eye tracking can tell us how these situations affect what the user looks at while performing tasks with their mobile devices.

7.2.3 Mobile Eye Tracking Technology

Conducting eye tracking research with mobile devices presents a few unique challenges. First, consider that neither the participant nor the device nor the eye tracker are stationary. This can impact the eye tracker's ability to track participants accurately and consistently, and also potentially make it difficult to capture eye tracking data across multiple participants. In addition, mobile technology has grown to include many other devices besides a smartphone. Researchers need to evaluate the users' experience on tablet devices, smart watches, and other wearables.

There are several technologies that can be used to track mobile devices:

- **Glasses and wearable eye trackers**: Eyewear containing eye tracking hardware worn by a participant that is paired with a portable recording device.
- **Device stand**: A platform and arm that is used to affix a mobile device and eye tracker unit.
- **Software**: A software app that uses the embedded camera within a mobile device.

7.2.4 Glasses

Eye tracking glasses (Fig. 7.4) can show us exactly what a person is looking at as they move freely in any real-world setting. The glasses provide a first-person perspective that helps us to understand what a user is looking at in their environment and to provide added context to their experience when using their mobile device.

While the glasses provide a high degree of freedom for the participant, it makes it very challenging to compare eye tracking data across participants. It is recommended to use the glasses for only qualitative research insights and to rely on eye gaze recordings to tag key observational findings.

7.2.5 Device Stand

A mobile device stand is best used when it is most important to standardize the testing environment where your users will be interacting with the device (Fig. 7.5). The stand is used by attaching the mobile device to a platform or cradle, along with an eye tracking unit. A camera is fixed to the stand using an arm and is directed at the face of the mobile device. By restricting the movement of the device and eye tracker, it is possible to overlay eye tracking data from different participants to produce aggregated visualizations such as heatmaps and eye gaze plots.

Fig. 7.4 An example of how eye tracking glasses can be used to understand how users consume news on their phone while sipping a latte at their local coffee shop. (This image may be used for editorial purposes with credits to Tobii AB. https://www.tobiipro.com/imagevault/publishedmedia/e317fzptqw0jk3svfn4t/TobiiPro-Glasses2-Mobile-Devseice-Usability-Cafe-150.jpg?download=1)

Fig. 7.5 The Tobii mobile device stand can be paired with a Tobii ×2 eye tracker and the device platform can be used with any model tablet or smartphone.

It is important to note that this configuration creates an artificial situation for using a mobile device. Participants interact with the device while it is sitting on the stand instead of holding it in their hands.

7.2.6 Software-Based Eye Tracking

Eye movement behavior can vary widely from person to person. In order to generalize eye gaze patterns, we need tracking data from a lot of eyes. Using a software-based eye tracking solution allows any smartphone to become an eye tracking device. This allows researchers to collect eye tracking data from hundreds, if not thousands, of participants while they interact with a mobile website or app.

To use this solution, participants will need to install an app on their smartphone, or the software provider will need to embed the code within their app using an SDK. This solution relies on using the camera built into the smartphone, and tracking accuracy can be dependent on sufficient ambient lighting conditions.

Strengths and Limitations of Mobile Eye Tracking Solutions		
Technology	Strength	Limitation
Glasses	• Total freedom of movement • Highly portable • Best for qualitative insights	• Expensive compared to other eye tracking solutions • Difficult to compare results across participants • No quantitative metrics
Stand	• Consistent configuration allows for easier comparison across participants • Can produce eye tracking visualizations	• Less natural experience for the participant • Not very portable • Limited quantitative analysis capabilities
Software	• No additional hardware needed • Potential for large-scale data collection • Eye tracking visualizations that can be aggregated across participants	• Less accurate than traditional eye tracking systems • Tracking accuracy can be affected by variability in ambient lighting conditions

ACCURACY OF WEBCAM–BASED EYE TRACKING

Burton, Albert, and Flynn (2014) conducted research comparing the accuracy of traditional infrared eye tracking systems with webcam-based eye tracking systems. Webcam-based eye tracking systems hold great promise for user researchers because of significantly lower cost, but also the ability to capture eye movement data from a large number of geographically dispersed users, without having to come into a lab.

The study was very simple. Participants were presented a set of images (large and small size) on a 3 × 3 grid on the screen using both an infrared and webcam eye tracking system. Participants were instructed to look at each of the images as they were presented in different locations on the screen. The results clearly showed that both the infrared and webcam-based eye tracking systems were adequate for capturing eye movement data when looking at larger images in the center of the screen. However, the webcam-based eye tracking system was not as accurate when capturing eye movements specific to smaller images, or any size images as they moved toward the edges of the screen, regardless of their size.

7.3 VISUALIZING EYE TRACKING DATA

There are many ways to visualize eye tracking data. These visualizations tell the story about where people were looking and when. They might be the only thing that your stakeholders really care about. All eye tracking visualizations are either at an individual level, showing eye movements for one participant, or at an aggregate level, showing eye movements for more than one participant.

Fig. 7.6 shows the series or sequence of fixations that an individual participant made on the Emirates Airlines website, also known as a scan path. This is perhaps the most common way to visually represent the eye movements for a single participant. A fixation is defined by a pause in the eye's movement within a well-defined area. Eye fixations are typically around 200 ms to 250 ms (1/5th or 1/4th of a second) but are highly variable (Galley, Betz, & Biniossek, 2015). The fixations are usually numbered to indicate their sequence. The size of each circle is proportional to the length or duration of the fixation. The *saccades*, or movements between fixations, are shown by the lines. In Fig.7.6 it is easy to notice that the participant was focused primarily on holiday graphics at the top of the screen and the tabs directly below. However, he did not look at the logo at the top left or the content towards the bottom of the screen. Scan paths are an excellent way to show how a participant looked at the page, and what elements they saw in what order.

By far the most common way to visually represent eye movement for multiple participants is through a heat map (Fig. 7.7). In this visualization, the brightest areas *(red)* represent greater density of fixations. It is an excellent way to get a sense of what areas of the page attract more (and less) visual attention. As you can see, visual attention on the REI outdoor website was concentrated on

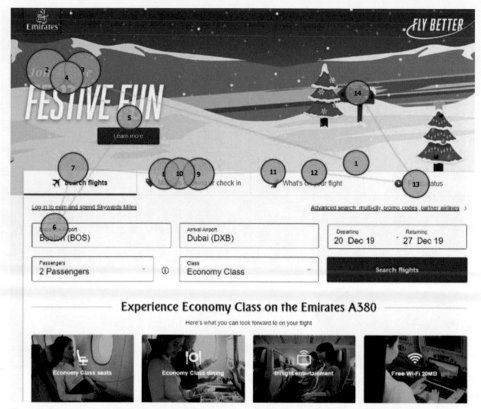

Fig. 7.6 Example of one individual's scan path of eye movements on the Emirates Airlines website.

the woman's face and the 40% offer to the left, with very little visual attention afforded to the top navigation elements.

It is important to keep in mind that the analysis software allows the researcher to define the scale of what is considered "red" versus "orange," etc. So, beware that the researcher can easily exaggerate heat maps to show more or less color. We recommend using the default settings on most software; however, it is important to experiment with using different scales.

7.4 AREAS OF INTEREST

The most common way to analyze eye tracking data is by measuring visual attention on specific elements or regions. Most researchers are not just interested in how visual attention is generally distributed across an entire web page or scene, but whether participants noticed certain objects and how much time was spent looking at them. This is particularly the case in marketing, whereby the success of an ad campaign is directly tied to getting customers to notice something. Also, it's a concern when there are certain elements that are critical to task

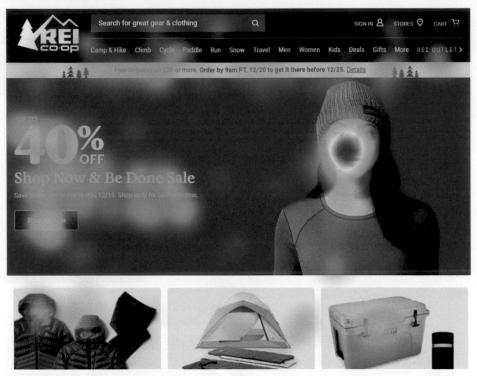

Fig. 7.7 Example of a heat map of the REI outdoor website.

success or having a positive experience. When the users don't see them, you can be sure that is a problem.

Fig. 7.8 is an example of how to define specific regions on the page. These regions are typically referred to as "look zones" or "areas of interest" (AOIs). AOIs are essentially those objects (or collection of objects) that you want to measure, as defined by a set of x,y coordinates. In Fig. 7.8 there, are four AOIs, with the associated statistics for each AOI:

- TTTF: This is "time to first fixation," or the average amount of time to first notice the object. As you can see from Fig. 7.8, the large text next to the women was noticed first, after less than 1 second, whereas the button to watch a video took nearly 5 seconds on average to first notice.
- Time Spent: This is the average dwell time, or the average "time spent" looking at the AOI. As you can see, nearly 2 seconds on average were spent looking at the large image/text block in the center of the screen (AOI 1), and a ½ second looking at the four calls to action (AOI 2) on the upper right.
- Ratio: The ratio is simply the number of participants who fixated, at least one time, within the AOI. All 9 participants (9/9) fixated within the large image/text block, whereas only 5 out of the 9 participants fixated on the logo in the upper left.

Fig. 7.8 Example of common eye tracking statistics for different areas of interest.

When analyzing the time spent looking at different regions, keep the following in mind:

- Carefully define each region. Ideally there will be a small amount of white space in between regions to make sure the eye movements don't get caught in between two AOIs right next to each other.
- Each region should be fairly homogeneous, such as navigation, content, ads, legal information, and so forth. If you prefer to subdivide your AOIs into individual elements, you can always aggregate as part of post-hoc analysis.
- When presenting data by AOIs, the question about where participants actually looked within the region typically comes up. Therefore, we recommend including a heat map, as in Fig. 7.8, that shows the continuous distribution of fixations.

7.5 COMMON EYE TRACKING METRICS

There are many metrics associated with eye tracking data. The following are some of the most common eye tracking metrics used by UX researchers. It's important that all of these metrics are associated with specific AOIs. Fig. 7.8 is an example of the type of metrics derived from a single AOI.

7.5.1 Dwell Time

The dwell time is the total amount of time spent looking within an AOI. This includes all fixations and saccades within the AOI, including revisits. Dwell time is an excellent metric that conveys the level of interest with a certain AOI.

2019). Without considering the emotional user experience, you will be missing a critical element.

In this chapter, we define the emotional user experience, identify specific challenges associated with emotional metrics, and cover some of the more common ways to measure emotion, including coding verbal expressions, self-reported metrics, facial expression analysis, and galvanic skin response (GSR). We wrap up the chapter by integrating several of the biometrics in a case study. Together, these methods will provide you a way to incorporate emotional measurement into your research toolkit.

8.1 DEFINING THE EMOTIONAL USER EXPERIENCE

Many UX researchers speak about the importance of the emotional user experience but often lack specifics. It is as if there is a single emotion, or all relevant emotions are clumped together, or perhaps emotions are only thought in terms of valence (negative or positive feeling). For example, many journey maps depict emotion in its most general form as being positive or negative. In order to measure emotion, you need to specify the emotion, such as joy, stress, or engagement, in order to have a focus or direction for your research and design strategy. Alternatively, you can group various emotions as being either positive or negative in nature and look at an experience from that particular lens.

As we all know, there is a wide range of human emotions. Many of these do not play a role in the user experience. These are typically based on emotions between people, such as jealousy, guilt, shame, grief, and love. However, many do play a role in the user experience, largely depending on the context of use. For example, it is easy to imagine some users who feel insecure when using a complex application for the first time as part of their job, or delight when they complete a task quickly, that they assumed would take much longer. Based on our many years of UX research, we believe there are seven distinct emotions that come up frequently in user experience:

> **Engagement**: Engagement is the degree to which a user is emotionally involved with your product. In other words, is there high or low arousal, for any emotion with your product? We can observe engagement easily just in the way people sit—are they leaning forward in their chair, or slumped? Both behaviors say a lot about their level of interest or level of engagement. It is important to remember that engagement may mean any type of emotion, whether it is delight, stress, surprise, or frustration. The lack of engagement is boredom or apathy. We don't recommend measuring engagement in isolation, as there could be many distinct emotions that drive high levels of engagement, such as surprise, stress, or joy.
>
> **Trust:** Trust is about the relationship that an individual has with another person or organization. In the context of user experience, trust is how your interests align, or perhaps don't align, with an organization. When a user is feeling

trust with an organization, through using their product or service, there is a reasonable level of transparency. The product or service provides all the necessary information to the user, even at the potential expense of their own interests. For example, are there hidden fees during the checkout process, or are the fees disclosed immediately and are easy to see and understand?

Stress: Stress is how much pressure or tension someone feels during, or as a result of, an experience. On one end, someone might not feel any stress at all, or feel peaceful or calm. On the other end of the spectrum, someone might feel a lot of stress, all the way up to panic. For example, think about potential stress when using a poorly designed mobile application to get tickets to a very popular concert, or the feeling of calm when a website carefully walks you through a complicated process, providing status updates throughout, and reconfirms the final transaction.

Joy: Joy is the feeling of well-being or happiness. Joy, in terms of user experience, is usually associated when successfully completing a difficult task, specifically where expectations are far exceeded. Joy is also tied to the amount of effort required to complete a task. The less the cognitive load, relative to expectations, the greater the joy or happiness. The opposite of joy or happiness is sadness. Rarely does sadness play a role in the user experience. Perhaps the closest emotion to sadness that is relevant in UX is disappointment. Therefore, we are usually measuring joy, or the absence of joy.

Frustration: Frustration is the feeling of being annoyed due to not being able to change or accomplish something. Frustration is very relevant in user experience because it is one of the most frequent feelings as a result of poor usability. Frustration may come from confusion or inefficiency. One way to think about frustration is the amount of cognitive effort that is required to complete a task. The more the cognitive effort, typically the more likely the frustration.

Confidence: Confidence is the degree to which the user knows something to be true. For example, a user might know that they just completed a transaction because there was a very clear, concise, and well-designed confirmation screen. Alternatively, a user might not be at all confident if there is a poorly worded confirmation screen, or none at all. Confidence is a critical element when interacting with any product or service. Without confidence there is self-doubt, often leading to behaviors that are inefficient for the individual, such as redoing work, or costing a company by reaching out to confirm the status of their transaction.

Surprise: Surprise is the feeling of something happening that is unexpected. In user experience, this can come from a novel workflow, images, content, or a new way of interacting with the product. Surprise in UX is usually at a lower level of intensity, rather than astonishment or shock. Because surprise could be positive or negative, it is important to collect data about the valence. In other words, is the surprise welcome (positive) or unwarranted (negative)?

There are certainly more than the seven emotions above that are relevant to user experience. Depending on the product, and context of use, other emotions might play a significant role in the experience. For example, emotions such as anticipation, disgust, or anger might be relevant for some products and services. Depending on what emotions you want to measure may mean different data collection methods. For example, anger and disgust can be reliably captured through facial expressions but typically don't play a role in user experience research (Filko & Martinović, 2013).

AROUSAL AND VALENCE

There are two aspects to any emotion: arousal and valence (Feldman & Russell, 1999). The easiest way to think of arousal is the level of excitement of any emotion. For example, both joy and stress may have high levels of arousal, depending on the situation of course. Other emotions such as feeling relaxed or sadness have lower levels of arousal. You might notice that these examples are emotions that have both positive or negative effects. This is called valence, and it is the other way to think about emotion. Most emotions fall along a positive to negative dimension.

For example, most of us would probably say joy is a positive emotion and stress is usually a negative emotion. But, as you can easily imagine, stress might be a positive emotion, such as when watching a scary movie and playing a video game. Fig. 8.1 shows a way to plot most emotions along these two dimensions. As a UX researcher, you should think about what emotions are most relevant for your product, and then plot those dimensions along these scales. This will help you identify potential situations in which certain emotions can move along these scales, depending on the context, such as in the case with stress, potentially having a negative or positive valence. The following is an example of plotting two emotions (joy and stress) along two dimensions: arousal and valence. Keep in mind that this is not absolute, but an example of how certain emotions might map on an arousal and valence scale for a particular person in a specific context.

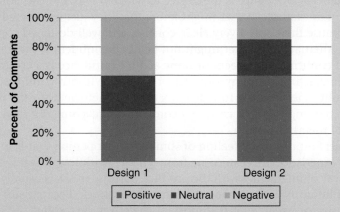

Fig. 8.1 Example comparing the ratio of positive, neutral, and negative comments across two different designs.

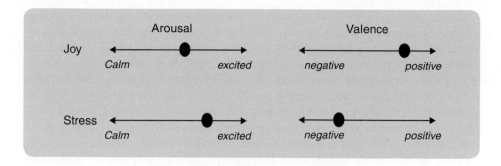

8.2 METHODS TO MEASURE EMOTIONS

There are many ways to measure the emotional user experience. Some methods involve the use of technology (such as facial expression analysis), while other methods don't require anything special, such as surveys or coding verbal responses. Perhaps the most important thing to know is which methods to use for different emotions. So, the emotions you intend to measure would dictate different data collection strategies.

Table 8.1 shows how various UX emotions might be measured with various technologies or approaches. As you can tell, self-report and verbal expressions are both useful for potentially measuring a wide variety of emotions. Other approaches, such as eye tracking and GSR, are much more limited, focusing on engagement and stress (GSR only). While facial expression analysis is very useful, it is somewhat limited, only measuring facial expressions that are tied to specific emotions such as joy (smiling), surprise, and engagement (a combination of facial expressions).

	Self-Report	Eye Tracking	Galvanic Skin Response	Facial Expressions	Verbal Expressions
Engagement	X	X	X	X	X
Trust	X				X
Confidence	X				X
Joy	X			X	
Frustration	X				X
Stress	X		X		X
Surprise	X			X	X

Table 8.1 How Different Methods and Technologies Are Used to Measure Different Emotions

When you consider different ways to measure emotion, we strongly recommend you consider more than one method if possible. For example, if you are interested in measuring engagement, ask some survey questions (self-report), but also integrate eye tracking or facial expression analysis if available. Alternatively, if you want to measure stress levels, we would recommend using GSR, but also relying on self-report and possibly verbal expressions. Over time, you will no doubt get a feel of which methods you trust more for measuring various emotions. Ideally, you will observe the same pattern of results across the various methods. However, there will certainly be cases in which you have conflicting results. In these situations, we recommend diving deeper into each approach, potentially looking at their limitations and biases. All things considered, we tend to trust self-reported and verbal expressions more than the other technical biometrics.

8.2.1 Five Challenges in Measuring Emotions

We have identified five unique challenges to measuring emotion in a UX context. While each of these challenges is significant, there are ways to overcome them. The following section reviews the most significant challenges, along with recommendations to mitigate their adverse effects on your research.

1. **Fleeting Emotions**—Many emotions arise very quickly and don't last very long. Consider emotions such as surprise or frustration and how quickly these feelings come and go. It is very difficult to identify and measure something that has the potential to change so quickly. If you use self-reported metrics, it is likely that the participant will not recall all the emotions that came and went. Rather, they will be responding to the residual emotions left after the experience, which may or may not correlate with the feelings during the experience itself.

   Recommendation: Use technologies such as facial expression analysis, GSR, and eye tracking to capture emotions in real time. Verbal expression coding may also be used, although it is not quite as reliable, since many emotions are not articulated in real time.

2. **Highly Contextual**—When we measure someone's emotional experience with a product or service, there is a broader context in which the measurement is happening. For example, is the participant in a good or bad mood, are they nervous, or are they generally a pessimistic person? Everything that the participant brings to the study will be reflected, to a certain degree, in the data you collect.

   Recommendation: As much as possible, only compare an individual's data to their own (see Chapter 2 for within-subject designs). This provides a natural baseline, so each person is only compared to themselves and not across individuals.

3. **Weak signals**—Many emotions in user experience operate at a fairly low intensity. When you compare most digital experiences in terms of the magnitude of the emotion, they don't compare to other experiences,

such as watching a scary movie trailer or a commercial that makes you want to cry. Therefore, most UX researchers struggle when trying to accurately measure weaker emotional signals.

Recommendation: Ideally, you are measuring a product or service that has a moderate to strong emotional quality. If you feel this is not the case, use methods such as facial expression analysis, eye tracking, and GSR to measure emotion and engagement. In addition, considering self-reported instruments that allow participants to rate their emotional experiences relative to one another, such as comparing more than one product in terms of confidence or stress levels.

4. **Driven by Content**—Participants in UX studies often react much more strongly to the content, rather than design or interaction. For example, a participant could be telling you they love the product, but what they really love is to see how much their retirement fund has increased in the last month. Because of this, it is important to be able to separate their emotional experience into the design and the content (that you may have no control over).

Recommendation: If you are using automated technologies such as GSR, facial expression analysis, or eye tracking, you will not be able to tell reactions to the design versus content apart. Therefore, complement these technologies with self-reported instruments that are more precisely focused on the aspects of the experience you care about and are part of your design. When coding verbal expressions, isolate those comments or expressions that are specific to the design.

5. **Noisy Data**—If all these challenges weren't enough, we often have to deal with noisy data. When we ask participants about emotion, we need to use specific terms, such as joy and delight, or stress and tension. As you might already guess, there is a lot of conceptual overlap in these and many more descriptions of emotion. Because of this, participants do not always share the same level of understanding for each emotion and we cannot fully rely on the data.

Recommendation: Ask about the same type of emotion using different terms. Likely, you will see a high correlation between the ratings of each of the terms. If you have the opportunity, probe to better understand what they are feeling to validate the words they choose to describe it.

INTERACTING WITH PARTICIPANTS WHEN USING BIOMETRICS

If you are going to be using biometrics (eye tracking, facial expression software, or GSR), you will need to be very thoughtful in how you interact with participants. We highly recommend that you do not interact at all with your participants while collecting biometric data. This means no talking at all, e.g., eye contact. Simply be invisible, because every interaction will have a direct impact on the biometrics. For example, if you ask the participant a thought-provoking question, or say something nice to them, you will see their reaction reflected in the biometrics and nothing to do with the product or service you are studying. Therefore, simply save all of your questions and comments until after you have stopped collecting the biometrics. Using the retrospective think-aloud should still be fine, just no discussion at all.

8.3 MEASURING EMOTIONS THROUGH VERBAL EXPRESSIONS

Unprompted verbal expressions provide valuable insight into a participant's emotional and mental state while they are using a product. The participant will probably make many comments without being asked; some negative ("This is hard" or "I don't like this design") and some positive ("Wow, this is much easier than I expected" or "I really like the way this looks"). Some comments are neutral or just hard to interpret, such as "This is interesting" or "This is not what I expected."

One useful metric related to verbal expressions is the ratio of positive to negative comments. To do this type of analysis, you first need to catalog all verbal expressions or comments and then categorize each one as positive, negative, or neutral. Once this is complete, simply look at the ratio of positive to negative comments, as illustrated in Fig. 8.1. Only knowing that positive comments outnumbered negative comments by a 2:1 ratio does not say a lot by itself. However, it is much more meaningful if the ratios are compared across different design iterations or between different products. For example, if the ratio of positive to negative comments has increased significantly with each new design iteration, this would be one indication of an improved design. Also, if a participant is interacting with more than one design, the same ratio can be calculated for each individual participant, assuming of course that the time spent with each product is the same.

It is also possible to get more granular by differentiating among different types of unprompted verbal comments, such as the following:

- Strongly positive comments (e.g., "This is terrific!")
- Other positive comments (e.g., "That was pretty good.")
- Strongly negative comments (e.g., "This website is terrible!")
- Other negative comments (e.g., "I don't much like the way that worked.")
- Suggestions for improvement (e.g., "It would have been better if.")
- Questions (e.g., "How does this work?")
- Variation from expectation (e.g., "This isn't what I was expecting to get.")
- Stated confusion or lack of understanding (e.g., "This page doesn't make any sense.")
- Stated frustration (e.g., "At this point I'd just leave the website!")

These types of data are analyzed by examining the frequency of comments within each category. Like the previous example, comparing across design iterations or products is the most useful. Categorizing verbal comments beyond just the positive, negative, or neutral can be challenging. It's helpful to work with another UX researcher to reach some level of agreement about categorizing each comment. Make good use of video recording. Even the best note-takers can miss something important. Also, we recommend that these comments be viewed within a larger context. For example, if a participant said that they would never use the product, under any circumstance, yet say something positive about the colors, this needs to be accounted for in other metrics, as well as how the findings are presented. While these metrics are seldom collected because it is fairly time consuming, they can offer valuable insight into the underlying feelings about a particular design.

8.4 SELF-REPORT

Asking participants how they feel about their use of a product or service is by far and away the most common method. We refer to these under the broad category of "self-report" metrics because the participants in our studies are telling us how they feel, as opposed to measuring some aspect of their behavior or physiological response.

In Chapter 5 (self-reported metrics), we cover some metrics that have an emotional quality to them, such as the CSUQ (5.4.2), Product Reaction Cards (5.4.3), UEQ (5.4.4), and AttrakDiff (5.4.5). It is important to note that these self-reported instruments are measuring the emotional qualities of a design, such as interesting, attractive, or friendly. They are not directly measuring one's feelings or emotions as a result of an experience. In this chapter, we are focused on measuring emotion, as opposed to the emotional aspects of a design.

Self-reported metrics are the easiest to collect, and certainly the most budget-friendly. They can tell us a lot about what someone is feeling without any technical requirements. Self-reported metrics focused on the emotional experience are typically postsession, after several tasks have been performed. Self-reported metrics capture the essence of the emotional user experience, not specific to any particular part of the product or service. There are many ways to capture this data. Table 8.2 is an example of the type of Likert-scale statements that could be used to measure engagement, stress, and joy (affect). Table 8.3 is an example of Likert-scale statements that could be used to measure frustration, trust, and confidence. As you will see in these examples, there are both positive and negatively worded statements. Also, terms appear that describe both ends of the spectrum of a particular emotion, such as fun and boredom or stressful and relaxing.

There are a few validated survey instruments that focus on the emotional user experience. One particular survey we really like is the emotional metric outcome

Engagement	Stress	Joy (Affect)
This <system> is fun to use	Using this <system> makes me stressed	This <system> makes me mad/angry
I would look forward to using this <system> in the future	I feel anxious (or nervous) when I use this <system>	I like using this <system>
I would rather use this <system> than <other>	This <system> has a calm or peaceful feel to it	Using this system brings me joy/happiness
I would want to use this <system> in my free-time	My tension increases when I use this <system>	When I am finished using this <system> I feel good
I am bored when I use this <system>	I feel relief when I use this <system>	I don't like using this <system>

Table 8.2 Example of Likert Statements That Could Be Used to Measure Engagement, Stress, and Joy (Affect)
Note: These are only examples and have not been validated.

Frustration	Trust	Confidence
I feel frustrated when I use this <system>	I would feel comfortable sharing my personal information with this <system>	I feel confident when I use this <system>
This <system> is easy to use	I would feel comfortable giving my credit card to this <system>	I feel I am making the right choices when using this <system>
I feel annoyed when I use this <system>	I feel this company is trustworthy	I feel unsure about the terminology
I feel I am efficient when I use this <system>	I feel this company has my best interests in mind	I feel confident when I am looking for information
This <system> is delightful to use	This <system> is transparent, with nothing to hide	I feel I have to guess when I use this <system>

Table 8.3 Example of Likert Statements That Could Be Used to Measure Frustration, Trust, and Confidence
Note: These are only examples and have not been validated.

(EMO) questionnaire by Lewis and Mayes (2014). In their questionnaire, they have identified four distinct factors, with four questions related to each factor:

- **Positive relationship affect** (company values my business, looks out for my interest, provides personalized services, and responds to questions quickly).

- **Negative relationship affect** (company stretches the truth, apprehensive about the company's intent, company cares more about selling than satisfying, and others do not trust this company).
- **Positive personal affect** (I felt confident, content, satisfied, and pleased).
- **Negative personal affect** (I felt irritated, tense, annoyed, and frustrated).

Through their extensive research, they have found the EMO is a stronger predictor of overall user experience, likelihood to recommend, and loyalty.

The Self-Assessment Manikin (SAM) scale is another common technique to measure emotion (Bradley & Lang, 1994). SAM is a pictorial assessment that directly measures valence (happy and unhappy), arousal (excited and calm), and dominance (feeling controlled or being controlled). Because it is a pictorial representation, it works well for low-literacy populations, children, and claims to be relevant across cultures. However, there are some concerns that the pictures are difficult to interpret, particularly around dominance (Broekens & Brinkman, 2015). While SAM was not designed specific to measuring emotion around the user experience, it can easily be applied in a UX context.

INTRODUCING YOUXEMOTIONS BY SARAH GARCIA

youXemotions provides a quick and accurate way of quantifying emotions during product or CX journeys, usability testing, diary studies, focus groups, market research, ethnography, and a variety of other standard research techniques (Garcia & Hammond, 2016). youXemotions was developed by usability researchers as a way to augment the traditional UX metrics, without needing to invest in expensive and intimidating biometric options. youXemotions relies on the unbiased self-reporting of emotions by giving participants a way of expressing themselves, either with words or colors. Participants make their selections on a tablet, phone, or web interface during the study, and values are assigned based on multiple factors including the emotion itself and intensity, giving the researcher a quantifiable emotional journey output.

Researchers have found the tool to be extremely helpful in adding a "z-axis" to traditional rating metrics, which has led to deeper, more nuanced insights. Incorporating emotions has allowed researchers to have richer conversations with participants and clients/stakeholders as a better way of understanding the emotion behind impressions. Emotions are a critical but often overlooked factor in fully understanding the customer experience. youXemotions offers an agile and natural approach to understanding the overall journey and inflection points customers experience while using a product.

INTRODUCING THE PREMO TOOL BY DR. PIETER DESMET

Pictorial self-report measures have the advantage of requiring relatively little effort from the respondent and, when carefully developed, they enable the measurement of low-intensity emotions, and can be used with a variety of respondent populations, including children and respondents with different languages (Laurans & Desmet, 2008). An example is PrEmo, which features an animated character that expresses 14 emotions (Desmet, Hekkert, & Jacobs, 2000; Laurans & Desmet, 2012, 2017). The questionnaire is administered through a web interface. When a participant clicks on a character, it plays a 1-second animation of the emotional expression with body movement and sound (IMAGE). PrEmo measures seven positive and seven negative emotions that were based on the work of Ortony, Clore, and Collins (1990) and represents four relevant emotional domains: general well-being emotions (joy, hope, sadness, fear); expectation-based emotions (satisfaction, dissatisfaction); social context emotions (pride, admiration, shame, contempt); material context emotions (fascination, attraction, boredom, disgust). Respondents are asked to consider the emotions represented by the animated cartoon and, for each emotion, to indicate the extent to which it corresponds to their current experience using a five-point scale. PrEmo can be used to measure emotions evoked by separate aspects of products, like appearance or fragrance, but also by product usage.

PrEmo character stills (from Laurans & Desmet, 2017). Top row: joy, admiration, pride, hope, satisfaction, fascination, and attraction. Bottom row: sadness, fear, shame, contempt, dissatisfaction, boredom, and disgust.

8.5 FACIAL EXPRESSION ANALYSIS

Facial expression analysis is a useful technique to measure emotions. In the 1970s, Paul Ekman and Wallace Friesen (1975) developed a taxonomy for characterizing every conceivable facial expression. They called it the Facial Action

Coding System, which included 46 specific actions involving the facial muscles. From his research, Ekman identified six basic emotions: happiness, surprise, sadness, fear, disgust, and anger. Each of these emotions exhibits a distinct set of facial expressions that can be reliably identified automatically through computer vision algorithms.

Fig. 8.2 is an example of how facial expressions are coded based on the Affdex facial expression recognition system (from Affectiva—www.affectiva.com).

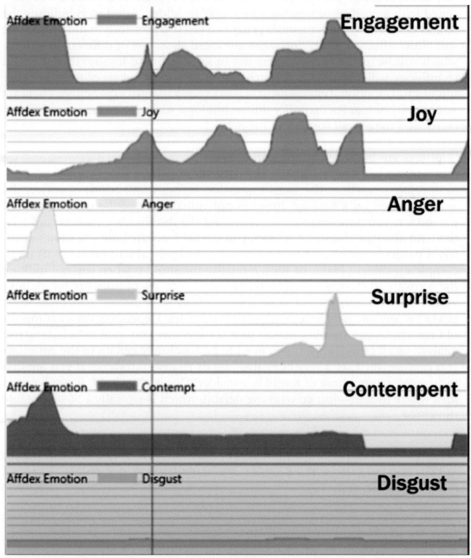

Fig. 8.2 Example of facial expression monitoring using the Affdex SDK within the iMotions platform. The vertical line represents the current moment, and each color represents a separate emotion derived from the facial expression analysis.

Affdex is a passive web-based platform that can take streaming video as an input and predict the presence of facial expressions in close to real-time. Affdex facial expression recognition indicates the type of experience associated with the state of arousal represented by the heights (or peaks) of each emotion. Also, you may notice that Affdex does not capture sadness but does capture both engagement and contempt.

Facial expressions are captured through a standard web camera on the participant's computer. This provides a rich data set, as peaks in arousal can be associated with a positive or negative valence. With Affdex, Affectiva is building the largest database of spontaneously generated facial expressions in the world. This will allow Affectiva to develop more advanced classifiers of different emotions, which will be used to predict increases in sales or brand loyalty. This powerful technology will arm the UX researcher with an additional set of tools to better understand emotional engagement across a wide variety of experiences. There are additional companies that offer this technology, such as Noldus (www.noldus.com), and the overall cost is coming down.

If you are interested in measuring emotion through facial expressions, we recommend you start by having the participant perform some "neutral" tasks to develop a baseline. The facial expression software will adjust or correct the analysis based on a baseline for each individual. One of the most important parameters you have control over is around the thresholds (absolute and relative). An absolute threshold is when you tell the software how you want to classify a particular emotion based on being completely absent (value of 0) up to completely present (value of 100). A relative threshold is when you can indicate the software to classify emotions based on the top $x\%$ of intensity for an individual. For example, you could say that you only want the top 20% of all smile peaks for any one person to be classified as smiles. Depending on what threshold you chose, you should consider how conservative you want to be in how you analyze facial expressions. If you need to be absolutely certain in the emotions you capture, then set a very high absolute or relative threshold. If you are in a more exploratory phase of research, consider a lower threshold. If you have no idea where to start—just go with the default, which is typically a 50% absolute threshold.

THE MECHANICS OF FACIAL EXPRESSIONS BY JOHN FARNSWORTH

Facial expression analysis has emerged as one of the few tools available for gathering information about the emotions of individuals in a UX context. While an indirect measure, it is able to provide information about a user's outwardly expressed emotional state. Data collection can be carried out either through manual or automatic scoring of facial muscle movements or through facial electromyography (although this has restrictions in terms of the number of muscles that can be tracked at any one given time). Most individuals working within UX will find that automatic scoring is most suitable for their needs due to the quick and noninvasive manner in which this methodology is carried out.

Prior to testing, the facial movements of interest should be defined so that relevant data can be captured. In a UX context, two facial muscles can be of particular interest: the zygomaticus major and the corrugator supercilii.

The zygomaticus major is the muscle primarily involved in a smile. Sitting atop the zygomatic bone (the cheekbone), it stretches from the corner of the lips to the edge of the cheekbone. While common sense would dictate that this is typically involved in displaying a positive emotion, it is of course possible that the movement is artificially created (known as a Duchenne smile). Research has shown, however, that increased activation of this muscle is associated with positive affect when a positively rated stimulus is presented. Detecting movement of the muscles within this area can therefore be an indication of positive emotion as long as the stimulus is assumed to be positively rated. Measurement of positive emotions through the zygomaticus major can therefore help in an understanding of the user experience in contexts that are carefully controlled for. Additionally, the corrugator supercilii, the muscle sitting in the corner of the inner brow is able to relay information about the user's display of negative affect. Involved in the process of frowning, this muscle, in the absence of other stimuli (such as sun glare, which triggers a contraction of this muscle) has been shown to be associated with feelings of negative emotion in the presence of negatively rated stimuli.

These two cases illustrate how the areas of interest for facial expression change should be carefully selected, necessitating a focused approach. While the two aforementioned facial muscles are of particular interest for their clear involvement in positive and negative affect, there are 18 to 19 other muscles (depending on how they are counted) that have distinct roles and unique involvements in displaying emotional states. This ultimately means that a more direct research question can be posed, and the analysis determining significant changes in muscle activation can be simplified by only using those areas of interest.

IS A SMILE ALWAYS JOY?

Facial expression software can accurately classify a smile based on a raise of the lip corners or edges of the mouth, along with other facial muscle movements. However, we have seen many times in our user experience product research that a smile does not always equate with joy. If a participant smiles, is it because they are nervous? Or, if the participant laughed, was it because the website displayed something that didn't make sense and was quite funny? Basically, there are many reasons to smile other than simple joy or delight. Therefore, if you are analyzing joy from facial expressions, take extra caution and, if you have the time, try to review and potentially filter out these instances in your analysis to get a cleaner set of data.

TIPS TO MEASURE JOY

UX researchers often want to measure how happy (or not) their users are when using a particular product. Based on our experience, we have a few helpful tips to effectively measure joy (or happiness):

- When using facial expression software, measure joy (smiles) over an extended period of time (a minimum of several minutes, and ideally much longer). If you measure joy over a brief period of time, there are other factors that could drive the smiles, or lack thereof (see the previous sidebar).

- Always include self-report metrics, such as in the form of several Likert-scale questions. See Table 8.2 for some potential examples. Also, consider other methods such as the PremoTool or youXemotions (described earlier in the chapter).

- Try to compare the joy or happiness metrics across various products or experiences. This will provide a useful baseline from which to compare. Focus on the delta, or gap between the baseline, and the product of interest.

- If time permits, consider classifying verbal expressions as positive, negative, and neutral. Compare the ratio of comments across products or experiences.

8.6 GALVANIC SKIN RESPONSE

GSR, or sometimes referred to as electrodermal activity (EDA) or skin conductance, is a method to measure the electrical conductivity of the skin in response

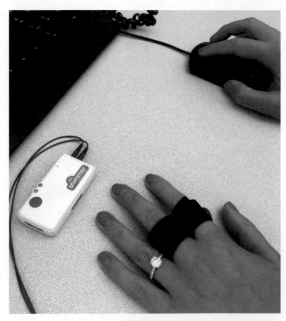

to some stimuli. When we experience something particularly emotional in some way, we trigger our sweat glands in very small ways that we are not aware of, whereby our skin becomes more conductive to electricity. So, GSR is essentially measuring small variations in the electrical conductivity of our skin as a response to some stimuli.

Unlike other aspects of measuring emotion, rapid changes in skin conductance are automatic, happening without conscious awareness or control, since it is part of our autonomic nervous system. While we might be able to control where we look and even our facial expressions, we cannot control our sweat glands. This makes GSR a very attractive tool because we can measure someone's arousal level without requiring them to articulate their feelings, or potentially hiding them as well.

The setup process for using a GSR device is pretty straightforward. Fig. 8.3 shows how a GSR

Fig. 8.3 Example of the setup with a Shimmer galvanic skin response.

sensor works. This GSR is made by Shimmer (www.shimmersensing.com). The device is connected via Bluetooth to the computer. There are two fingers sensors that attach via Velcro to the index and middle fingers. As you can see in Fig. 8.3, the sensors are attached to the nondominant hand (not using the mouse). It is very unobtrusive and easily forgotten by the participant.

When using a GSR sensor, it is important that participants breathe normally and keep their movement to a minimum and sit comfortably. Similar to using facial expression software, do not engage in conversation while collecting GSR data.

The analysis of GSR data is fairly straightforward. Essentially, you are measuring the number of GSR "peaks" over a period of time, or during an exposure. A peak is typically defined as a burst or a peak in the phasic response approximately 1 to 5 seconds after exposure to emotional stimuli. The greater the number of peaks, the greater the arousal during that experience.

It is useful to analyze GSR in a comparative way. Fig. 8.4 is an example from a case study (described in detail in Section 8.7) that compares the average number of GSR peaks per minute across three different websites. In this example, there was not a statistically significant difference between any of the three websites. Because exposure time varied across individuals and website, we analyzed the average number of GSR peaks per minute.

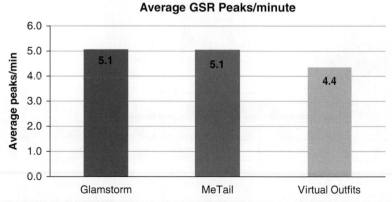

Fig. 8.4 Example comparing the average number of galvanic skin response peaks per minute across three different virtual dressing room websites. The differences are not statistically significant.

One of the main concerns in using GSR data is that you are essentially measuring emotional arousal, without knowing anything about the valence. Basically, you might see a GSR peak but not know whether it was a positive or negative experience. For that reason, we do not recommend you use GSR as a standalone measure. Rather, you should include GSR along with other metrics to have further insight into what prompted the emotional reaction.

8.7 CASE STUDY: THE VALUE OF BIOMETRICS

The Bentley University User Experience Center (www.bentley.edu/uxc) presented a case study in which they wanted to know if biometrics added new insights above and beyond more traditional user research methods (Albert & Marriott, 2019). In other words, what is the value of biometrics for UX researchers?

In this study, Albert and Marriott (2019) compared three different virtual dressing room websites. Virtual dressing rooms allow users to build an avatar of their body shape and overall look, and then visualize how different outfits might look on them. Virtual dressing rooms were chosen as the topic of the case study because of the emotional aspects of data privacy (sharing body dimensions) and issues related to body image.

In the study, all participants were given the same task—find a dress for a friend's wedding. All participants used the same three websites (Glamstorm, MeTail, and Virtual Outfits). After participants used each website for about 10 minutes, they completed a short survey. The iMotions platform was used to collect all biometrics, including facial expressions, eye tracking, and GSR (skin conductance) (Fig. 8.5).

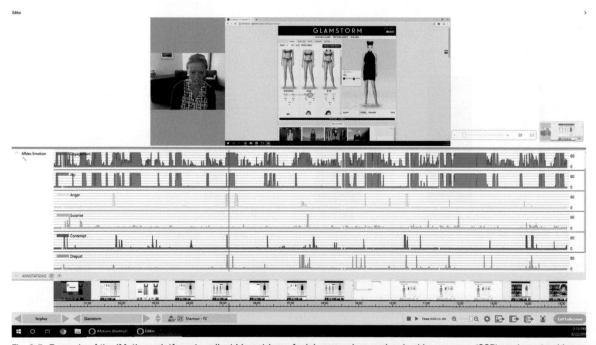

Fig. 8.5 Example of the iMotions platform to collect biometrics—facial expressions, galvanic skin response (GSR), and eye tracking. The upper-left of the image shows the calibration of the facial expressions, the upper-right shows the stimuli and eye movements in real-time. The lower half displays the peaks for each of the facial expressions and GSR.

The first analysis performed was analyzing the survey results and the verbal expressions made by the participants while using the three different websites. The survey results showed that there were no differences in how the participants rated the three websites in terms of the comfort level of using the website, confidence, and usefulness. Verbal expressions were coded as positive, negative, or neutral. Fig. 8.6 shows the distributions of verbal expressions across the three sites. While the frequency of positive comments was not different for the three websites, there were more negative comments about the Glamstorm website compared to the other two websites. This was largely because many of the female participants felt that the default body shape of the Glamstorm avatar was unrealistic. So, based on the frequency of negative and positive comments alone, we would be more likely to conclude the Glamstorm provided a poorer emotional experience compared to the other two websites.

Average Number of Postive/Negative Verbal Expressions by Site

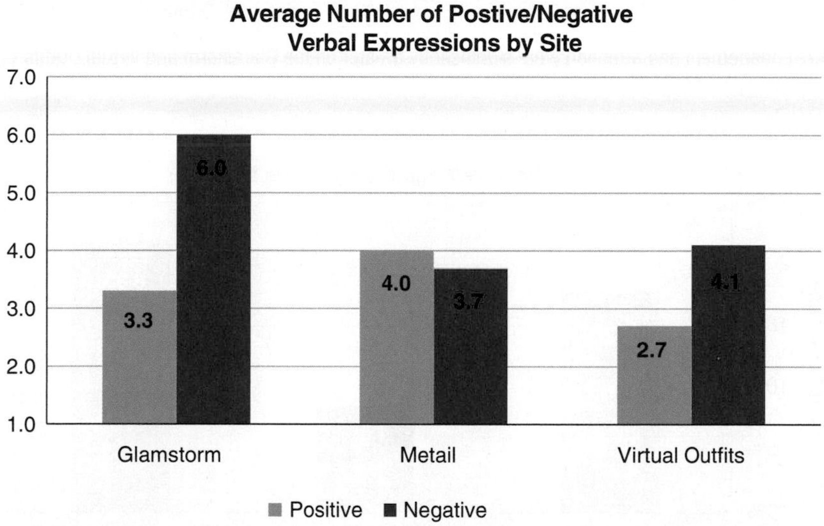

Fig. 8.6 The distribution of positive and negative comments for each of the three websites.

The next level of analysis was to look at the levels of engagement and attention for the three websites. Engagement is the aggregation of all emotions together (positive and negative). Attention is the amount of time spent visually engaged with each website. Fig. 8.7 shows that both the Glamstorm and Virtual Outfits websites had significantly more engagement and attention than the MeTail website ($P < 05$). We speculated that the level of interaction and visuals on the Glamstorm and Virtual Outfits websites was far better than the MeTail website.

In the iMotions platform, you can aggregate emotions by valence (positive and negative). Joy and surprise are considered positive valence, while anger, disgust, and contempt are classified as negative emotions. Fig. 8.8 shows the distribution of positive and negative emotions overall for the three sites. As you

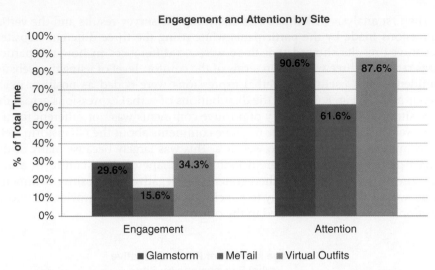

Fig. 8.7 Engagement and attention were significantly greater on the Glamstorm and Virtual Outfits websites, compared to MeTail.

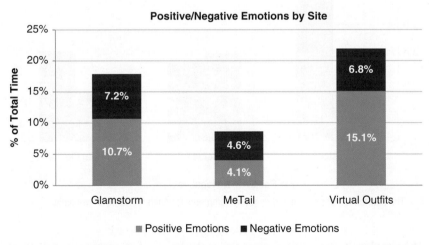

Fig. 8.8 There were significantly more positive emotions associated with the Glamstorm and Virtual Outfits websites compared to the MeTail website.

can see, there are significantly higher positive emotions for the Glamstorm and Virtual Outfits websites. This is very helpful to get an overall sense of the emotional experience of the three websites.

A more detailed look into Joy (Fig. 8.9) shows a similar pattern as positive emotions in Fig. 8.8. There was significantly higher joy in both Glamstorm and Virtual Outfits compared to MeTail ($P < 05$). More precisely, the average percentage of total time in which the participant was joyful was 11% with Glamstorm, 15% for Virtual Outfits, and only 4% of MeTail.

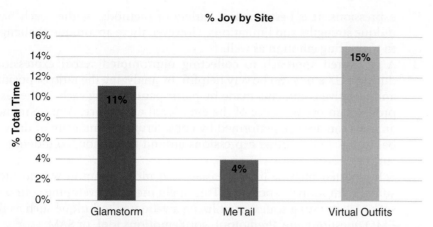

% Joy by Site

Fig. 8.9 The Glamstorm and Virtual Outfits websites had a significantly higher percentage of time with participants expressing joy (smiling), compared to the MeTail website.

This case study was focused on assessing the value of biometrics, above and beyond more traditional user research methods. Based on the analysis of the survey results and verbal expressions, we would conclude that there isn't a big difference between the three websites. If anything, Glamstorm was more negatively perceived. However, when we consider biometrics, we see a very different pattern of results. We see that engagement, attention, and joy are significantly greater in both Glamstorm and Virtual Outfits relative to MeTail. Therefore, in this case study, the biometrics provided a more nuanced perspective by teasing apart the emotional experience across the three websites. The Virtual Outfits may be seen to provide the best overall experience, having the highest levels of engagement, attention, and overall positive emotions.

8.8 SUMMARY

In this chapter, we covered a variety of ways to measure user emotions. This provides potentially valuable insights into the deeper user experience that is often very easy to miss in the course of a usability test. These tools are becoming much easier to use, more accurate, more versatile and powerful, and even quite affordable. Despite these many advances, we strongly recommend taking advantage of other UX metrics and not relying solely on this technology to tell you everything about the user experience. Here's a summary of some of the key points to remember.

1. We define seven unique aspects of the emotional user experience: engagement, trust, stress, joy, frustration, confidence, and surprise. One very useful way to analyze any emotion is based on valence (whether an emotion is positive or negative) and arousal (the intensity of that emotion from low to high).

2. There are different ways to measure emotion in a UX context, including self-report, eye tracking, facial expressions, GSR, and coding verbal

expressions. It is best to use a variety of methods, as they each have unique strengths and limitations. However, there are unique challenges to measuring emotion as well.

3. A structured approach to collecting unprompted verbal expressions during a UX study can be very helpful. By analyzing the ratio of positive and negative comments made by participants during each of the tasks provides an overall sense of the emotional experience. A more refined analysis can also be performed by considering the intensity of the verbal expression, or other expressions around frustration, confidence, or surprise.

4. Self-reported metrics are the easiest and most common way to measure the emotional experience. This might include developing your own set of Likert rating scales, or utilizing a validated technique such as the EMO questionnaire, Premotool, youXemotions tool, or SAM.

5. Facial expression software is a very helpful tool to identify emotions in real time, such as engagement, joy, anger, contempt, disgust, and surprise. Facial expressions are classified according to the movement of many facial muscles. The thresholds you set will determine the reliability of the data.

6. GSR measures arousal levels through small changes in the electrical conductivity of the skin. GSR data are analyzed by the number of peaks over a specified period of time. While GSR is helpful to measure overall arousal levels, it is limited because there is no valence.

7. A case study demonstrated that biometrics may provide additional value beyond more traditional user research methods.

CONTENTS

UX metrics such as task completion rates, task times, and self-reported metrics are certainly useful and informative, but sometimes you want an overall sense of how good (or bad) a user experience is. Perhaps you need something to easily and clearly convey the state of a user experience to the project team or stakeholders. That's where combined and comparative metrics come in. Not only can these metrics be handy when presenting the results of a UX evaluation, but they can also be helpful for tracking changes across iterations or releases and for comparing different designs (e.g., comparing different prototypes or comparing your design to the competition).

Two of the common ways to derive new UX metrics from existing data are (1) by combining more than one metric into a single metric and (2) by comparing existing data to expert or ideal results. We will review both methods in this chapter.

9.1 SINGLE UX SCORES

Many UX researchers collect more than one metric, such as task completion rate, task time, and perhaps a self-reported metric such as a System Usability Scale (SUS) score. In most cases, you don't care so much about the results for each of

Measuring the User Experience. DOI: http://dx.doi.org/10.1016/B978-0-12-818080-8.00009-1

those metrics individually as you do about the total picture of the experience of the product as reflected by *all* of these metrics. This section covers the various ways you can combine or represent different metrics to get an overall view of the UX of a product or different aspects of a product, perhaps as revealed by different tasks.

A common question asked after a UX evaluation is, "How did it do?" The people who ask this question (often the product manager, developer, or other members of the project team) usually don't want to hear about task completion rates, task times, or questionnaire scores. They want an overall score of some type: Did it pass or fail? How did it do in comparison to the last round of usability testing? Making these kinds of judgments in a meaningful way involves combining the metrics from a study into some type of single score. The challenge is figuring out how to combine scores from different scales in a meaningful way (e.g., task completion rates in percentages and task times in minutes or seconds).

9.1.1 Combining Metrics Based on Target Goals

Perhaps the easiest way to combine different metrics is to compare each data point to a target goal and represent one single metric based on the percentage of users who achieved a combined set of goals. For example, assume that the goal is for users to successfully complete at least 80% of their tasks in no more than 70 seconds each on average. Given that goal, consider the data in Table 9.1, which shows the task completion rate and average time per task for each of eight participants in a study.

Table 9.1 shows some interesting results. The average values for task completion (82%) and task time (67 seconds) would seem to indicate that the goals for this test were met. Even if you look at the number of users who met the task completion goal (six participants, or 75%) or the task time goal (five participants,

Participant #	Task Completion	Task Time	Goal Met?
1	85%	68	1
2	70%	59	0
3	80%	79	0
4	75%	62	0
5	90%	72	0
6	80%	60	1
7	80%	56	1
8	95%	78	0
Average:	**82%**	**67**	**38%**

Table 9.1 Sample task completion and task time data from eight participants.
Also shown are the averages for task completion and time and an indication of whether each participant met the objective of completing at least 80% of the tasks in no more than 70 seconds.

or 62%), you would still find the results reasonably encouraging. However, the most appropriate way to look at the results is to see if each individual participant met the stated goal (i.e., the *combination* of completing at least 80% of the tasks in no more than 70 seconds). It turns out, as shown in the last column of Table 9.1, that only three, or 38%, of the participants actually met the goal. This demonstrates the importance of looking at individual participant data rather than just looking at averages. This can be particularly true when dealing with relatively small numbers of participants.

This method of combining metrics based on target goals can be used with any set of metrics. The only real decision is what target goals to use. Target goals can be based on business goals and/or comparison to ideal performance. The math is easy (each person just gets a 1 or 0), and the interpretation is easy to explain (the percentage of users who had an experience that met the stated goal during the test).

Microsoft researchers Van Waardhuizen, McLean-Oliver, Perry, and Munko (2019) conducted an analysis of 36 studies that reported various UX metrics such as task completion rates, task times, and self-reported ratings. This included data for almost 500 tasks across 13 platforms and 800 users. Their primary goal was to identify a single usability metric that could be used to enable comparisons across products and iterations as well as to facilitate communication with stakeholders. After encountering issues with identifying meaningful rules for handling the individual metrics, they came to the conclusion that the kind of analysis just described (comparison to target goals) was the simplest and easiest to communicate to stakeholders.

9.1.2 Combining Metrics Based on Percentages

Although we're well aware that we should have measurable target goals for our UX studies, in practice, many of us don't have them. So what can you do to combine different metrics when you don't have target goals? One simple technique for combining scores on different scales is to convert each score to a percentage and then average them. For example, consider the data in Table 9.2, which shows the results of a study with 10 participants.

One way to get an overall sense of the results from this study is to first convert each of these metrics to a percentage. In the case of the number of tasks completed and the subjective rating, it's easy because we know the maximum ("best") possible value for each of those scores: There were 15 tasks, and the maximum possible subjective rating on the scale was 4. So we just divide the score obtained for each participant by the corresponding maximum to get the percentage.

In the case of the time data, it's a little trickier, since there's not a predefined "best" or "worst" time—the ends of the scale are not known beforehand. One way of handling this would be to have several experts do the task and treat the average of their times as the "best" time. Another way is to treat the fastest time

Participant #	Time per Task (s)	Tasks Completed (of 15)	Rating (0–4)
1	65	7	2.4
2	50	9	2.6
3	34	13	3.1
4	70	6	1.7
5	28	11	3.2
6	52	9	3.3
7	58	8	2.5
8	60	7	1.4
9	25	9	3.8
10	55	10	3.6

Table 9.2 Sample data from a study with 10 participants.

Time per Task is the average time to complete each task, in seconds. Tasks Completed is the number of tasks (out of 15) that the user successfully completed. Rating is the average of a 5-point task ease rating for each task, where higher is better.

obtained from the participants in the study as the "best" (25 seconds, in this example), the slowest time as the "worst" (70 seconds, in this example), and then express the other times in relation to those. Specifically, you divide the difference between the longest time and the observed time by the difference between the longest and shortest times. This way, the shortest time becomes 100%, and the longest becomes 0%. Using that method of transforming the data, you get the percentages shown in Table 9.3.

Participant #	Time (%)	Tasks (%)	Rating (%)	Average (%)
1	11	47	60	39
2	44	60	65	56
3	80	87	78	81
4	0	40	43	28
5	93	73	80	82
6	40	60	83	61
7	27	53	63	48
8	22	47	35	35
9	100	60	95	85
10	33	67	90	63

Table 9.3 Data from Table 7.2 transformed to percentages.

For the Task Completion data, the score was divided by 15. For the Rating data, the score was divided by 4. For the Time data, the difference between the longest time (70) and the observed time was divided by the difference between the longest (70) and shortest (25) times.

When transforming time data in this manner, it's important that any outliers in the time data be removed before doing the transformation. For example, assume that most of the times from a study were between 20 and 60 s, but there was one time that was 3490 s! That's an obvious outlier by any definition that we know. Keeping that outlier in the data, and using it as the longest time for the transformations, would radically impact the transformation. Specifically, it would cause the percentage for that outlier to be 0% and all the other time percentages to cluster near 98% to 100%.

TRANSFORMING TIME DATA IN EXCEL

Here are the steps for transforming time data to percentages using these rules in Excel:

1. Enter the raw times into a single column in Excel. For this example, we will assume they are in column "A" and that you started on row "1." Make sure there are no other values in this column, such as an average at the bottom.

2. In the cell to the right of the first time, enter the formula:

   =(MAX(A:A)-A1)/(MAX(A:A)-MIN(A:A))

3. Copy this formula down as many rows as there are times to be transformed.

Table 9.3 also shows the average of these percentages for each of the participants. If any one participant had successfully completed all the tasks in the shortest average time and had given the product a perfect score on the subjective rating scales, that person's average would have been 100%. On the other hand, if any one participant had failed to complete any of the tasks, had taken the longest time per task, and had given the product the lowest possible score on the subjective rating scales, that person's average would have been 0%. Of course, rarely do you see either of those extremes. Like the sample data in Table 8.3, most participants fall between those two extremes. In this case, the averages range from a low of 28% (Participant 4) to a high of 85% (Participant 9), with an overall average of 58%.

CALCULATING PERCENTAGES ACROSS ITERATIONS OR DESIGNS

One of the valuable uses of this kind of overall score is in making comparisons across iterations or releases of a product or across different designs. But it's important to do the transformation across *all* of the data at once, not separately for each iteration or design. This is particularly important for time data, where the times that you've collected are determining the best and worst times. That selection of the best and worst times should be made by looking across all of the conditions, iterations, or designs that you want to compare.

So if you had to give an overall score to the product whose test results are shown in Tables 9.2 and 9.3, you could say it got 58% overall. Most people wouldn't be too happy with 58%. Many years of grades from school have probably conditioned most of us to think of a percentage that low as a "failing grade." But you should also consider how accurate that percentage is. Since it's an average based on the individual scores from 10 different participants, you can construct a confidence interval for that average, as explained in Chapter 2. The 90% confidence interval, in this case, is ±11%, meaning that the confidence interval extends from 47% to 69%. Running more participants would probably give you a more accurate estimate of this value, whereas running fewer would probably have made it less accurate.

One thing to be aware of is that when we averaged the three percentages together (from the task completion data, task time data, and subjective ratings), we gave equal weight to each of those measures. In many cases, that's a perfectly reasonable thing to do, but sometimes the business goals of the product may indicate a different weighting. In this example, we're combining two performance measures (task completion and task time) with one self-reported measure (rating). By giving equal weight to each, we're actually giving twice as much weight to performance as to the self-reported measure. That can be adjusted by using weights in calculating the averages, as shown in Table 9.4.

Participant #	Time (%)	Weight	Tasks (%)	Weight	Rating (%)	Weight	Weighted Average (%)
1	38	1	47	1	60	2	51
2	50	1	60	1	65	2	60
3	74	1	87	1	78	2	79
4	36	1	40	1	43	2	40
5	89	1	73	1	80	2	81
6	48	1	60	1	83	2	68
7	43	1	53	1	63	2	55
8	42	1	47	1	35	2	40
9	100	1	60	1	95	2	88
10	45	1	67	1	90	2	73

Table 9.4 Calculation of weighted averages.
Each individual percentage is multiplied by its associated weight, these products are summed, and that sum divided by the sum of the weights (4, in this example).

In Table 9.4, the subjective rating is given a weight of 2, and each of the two performance measures is given a weight of 1. The net effect is that the subjective rating gets as much weight in the calculation of the average as the two performance measures together. The result is that these weighted averages for each participant tend to be closer to the subjective ratings than the equal-weight averages in Table 9.3. The exact weights you use for any given product should be determined by the business goals for the product. For example, if you're testing a website for use by the general public, and the users have many other competitors' websites to choose from, you might want to give more weight to self-reported measures because you probably care more about the users' *perception* of the product than anything else.

On the other hand, if you're dealing with an application where speed and accuracy are more important, such as a stock-trading application, you would probably want to give more weight to performance measures. You can use any weights that are appropriate for your situation, but remember to divide by the sum of those weights in calculating the weighted average.

These basic principles apply to transforming any set of metrics from a UX study. For example, consider the data in Table 9.5, which includes the number of tasks successfully completed (out of 10), the number of webpage visits, an overall satisfaction rating, and an overall usefulness rating.

Participant #	Tasks Completed (of 10)	# of Page Visits (Min = 20)	Satis-faction Rating (0–6)	Useful-ness Rating (0–6)	Tasks (%)	Page Visits (%)	Satis-faction (%)	Useful-ness (%)	Average (%)
1	8	32	4.7	3.9	80	63	78	65	71
2	6	41	4.1	3.8	60	49	68	63	60
3	7	51	3.4	3.7	70	39	57	62	57
4	5	62	2.4	2.3	50	32	40	38	40
5	9	31	5.2	4.2	90	65	87	70	78
6	5	59	2.7	2.9	50	34	45	48	44
7	10	24	5.1	4.8	100	83	85	80	87
8	8	37	4.9	4.3	80	54	82	72	72
9	7	65	3.1	2.5	70	31	52	42	49

Table 9.5 Sample data from a study with nine participants.

Tasks completed is the number of tasks (out of 10) that the user successfully completed. Number of page visits is the total number of web pages that the user visited in attempting the tasks. (Typically, each revisit to the same page is counted as another visit.) The two ratings are average subjective ratings of satisfaction and usefulness, each on a 7-point scale (0 to 6).

Calculating percentages from these scores is very similar to the previous example. The number of tasks completed is divided by 10, and the two subjective ratings are each divided by 6 (the maximum rating). The other metric, the number of webpage visits, is somewhat analogous to the time metric in the previous example. But in the case of webpage visits, it is usually possible to calculate the minimum number of page visits that would be required to accomplish the tasks. In this example, it was 20. You can then transform the number of page visits by dividing 20 (the fewest possible) by the actual number of page visits. The closer the number of page visits is to 20, the closer the percentage will be to 100%. Table 9.5 shows the original values, the percentages, and then the equal-weight averages. In this case, note that the equal weighting (normal average) results in the same weight being given to performance data (task completion and page visits) and subjective data (the two ratings).

CONVERTING RATINGS TO PERCENTAGES

What if the subjective ratings you used were on a scale that started at 1 instead of 0? Would that make a difference in how you transform the ratings to a percentage? Most definitely. Let's assume the ratings were on a scale of 1–7 instead of 0–6, with higher numbers better. Both are 7-point scales. In both cases, you want the lowest possible rating to become 0% and the highest possible rating to become 100%. When the ratings are on a 0–6 scale, simply dividing each rating by 6 (the highest possible rating) gives the desired range (0%–100%). But when the ratings are on a 1–7 scale, there's a problem. If you divide each rating by 7 (the highest possible rating), you get a maximum score of 100%, which is OK, but the minimum score is 1/7, or 14%, not the 0% that you want. The solution is to first subtract 1 from each rating (rescaling it to 0–6) and then dividing by the new maximum score (6, in this case). So, the lowest score becomes $(1-1)/6$, or 0%, and the highest becomes $(7-1)/6$, or 100%.

To look at transforming another set of metrics, consider the data in Table 9.6. In this case, the number of errors is listed, which would include specific errors the users made, such as data-entry errors. Obviously, it is possible (and desirable) for a user to make no errors, so the minimum possible is 0. But there's usually no predefined maximum number of errors that a user could make. In a case like this, the best way to transform the data is to divide the number of errors obtained by the maximum number of errors and then subtract from 1. In this example, the maximum is 5, the number of errors made by participant 4. This is how the error percentages in Table 9.6 were obtained. If any user had no errors (optimum), their percentage would be 100%. The percentage for the user(s) with the highest number of errors would be 0%. Notice that in calculating any of these percentages, we always want higher percentages to be better—to reflect better usability. So in the case of errors, it makes more sense to think of the resulting percentage as an "accuracy" measure.

Participant #	Tasks Completed (of 10)	# of Errors	Satisfaction Rating (0–6)	Tasks (%)	Accuracy (%)	Satisfaction (%)	Average (%)
1	8	2	4.7	80	60	78	73
2	6	4	4.1	60	20	68	49
3	7	0	3.4	70	100	57	76
4	5	5	2.4	50	0	40	30
5	9	2	5.2	90	60	87	79
6	5	4	2.7	50	20	45	38
7	10	1	5.1	100	80	85	88
8	8	1	4.9	80	80	82	81
9	7	3	3.1	70	40	52	54
10	9	2	4.2	90	60	70	73
11	7	1	4.5	70	80	75	75
12	8	3	5.0	80	40	83	68

Table 9.6 Sample data from a study with 12 participants.

Tasks Completed is the number of tasks (out of ten) that the user successfully completed. Number of errors is the number of specific errors that the user made, such as data-entry errors. Satisfaction Rating is on a scale of 0 to 6.

WATCH OUT FOR OUTLIERS

Like we said earlier about time data, when transforming any data where you're letting the observed values determine the minimum or maximum (e.g., times, errors, page visits), you need to be particularly cautious about outliers. For example, in the data shown in Table 9.6, what if Participant #4 had made 20 errors instead of 5? The net effect would have been that his transformed percentage would still have been 0%, but all of the others would have been pushed much higher. One of the standard ways of detecting outliers is by calculating the mean and standard deviation of all your data, then consider any values more than *twice* or *three times* the standard deviation away from the mean as outliers. (Most people use twice the standard deviation, but if you want to be really conservative, use three times.) For the purpose of transforming the data, those outliers should be excluded. In this modified example, the mean plus twice the standard deviation of the number of errors is 14.2, while the mean plus three times the standard deviation is 19.5. By either criterion, you should treat 20 errors as an outlier and exclude it.

When transforming any UX metric to a percentage, the general rule is to first determine the minimum and maximum values that the metric can possibly have. In many cases, this is easy; they are predefined by the conditions of the study. Here are the various cases you might encounter:

- If the minimum possible score is 0 and the maximum possible score is 100 (e.g., a SUS score), then you've basically already got a percentage. Just divide by 100 to make it a true percentage.
- In many cases, the minimum is 0, and the maximum is known, such as the total number of tasks or the highest possible rating on a rating scale. In that case, simply divide the score by the maximum to get the percentage. (This is why it's generally easier to code rating scales starting with 0 as the worst value.)
- In some cases, the minimum is 0, but the maximum is not known, such as the example of errors. In that situation, the maximum would need to be defined by the data—the highest number of errors any participant made. Specifically, the number of errors would be transformed by dividing the number of errors obtained by the maximum number of errors any participant made and subtracting that from 1.
- Finally, in some cases, neither the minimum nor maximum possible scores are predefined, as with time data. In this case, you can use your data to determine the minimum and maximum values. Assuming higher values are worse, as is the case with time data, you would divide the difference between the highest value and the observed value by the difference between the highest and lowest values.

WHAT IF HIGHER NUMBERS ARE WORSE?

Although higher numbers are better in cases like task success rates, in other cases, they're worse, such as time or errors. Higher numbers could also be worse in a rating scale if it was defined that way (e.g., 0–6, where 0 = Very Easy and 6 = Very Difficult). In any of these cases, you must reverse the scale before averaging these percentages with other percentages where higher numbers are better. For example, with the rating scale just shown, you would subtract each value from 6 (the maximum) to reverse the scale. So 0 becomes 6, and 6 becomes 0.

9.1.3 Combining Metrics Based on Z-Scores

Another technique for transforming scores on different scales so that they can be combined is using z-scores. (See, for example, Martin & Bateson, 1993, 124.) These are based on the normal distribution and indicate how many units above or below the mean of the distribution any given value is. When you transform a set of scores to their corresponding z-scores, the resulting distribution by definition has a mean of 0 and a standard deviation of 1. This is the formula for transforming any raw score to its corresponding z-score:

$$z = (x - \mu)/\sigma$$

where

x = the score to be transformed
μ = the mean of the distribution of those scores
σ = the standard deviation of the distribution of those scores

This transformation can also be done using the "standardize" function in Excel. The data in Table 9.2 could also be transformed using z-scores, as shown in Table 9.7.

Participant #	Time per Task (s)	Tasks Completed (of 15)	Rating (0–4)	z-time	z-time* (−1)	z-tasks	z-rating	Average
1	65	7	2.4	0.98	−0.98	−0.91	−0.46	−0.78
2	50	9	2.6	0.02	−0.02	0.05	−0.20	−0.06
3	34	13	3.1	−1.01	1.01	1.97	0.43	1.14
4	70	6	1.7	1.30	−1.30	−1.39	−1.35	−1.35
5	28	11	3.2	−1.39	1.39	1.01	0.56	0.99
6	52	9	3.3	0.15	−0.15	0.05	0.69	0.20
7	58	8	2.5	0.53	−0.53	−0.43	−0.33	−0.43
8	60	7	1.4	0.66	−0.66	−0.91	−1.73	−1.10
9	25	9	3.8	−1.59	1.59	0.05	1.32	0.98
10	55	10	3.6	0.34	−0.34	0.53	1.07	0.42
Mean				**0.0**	**0.0**	**0.0**	**0.00**	**0.00**
Standard Deviation				**1.0**	**1.0**	**1.0**	**1.00**	**0.90**

Table 9.7 Sample data from Table 9.2 transformed using **z**-scores.

For each original score, the z-score was determined by subtracting the mean of the score's distribution from it and then dividing by the standard deviation. This z-score tells you how many standard deviations above or below the mean that score is. Since you need all the scales to have higher numbers better, the scale of the z-scores of times is reversed by multiplying by (−1).

STEP-BY-STEP GUIDE TO CALCULATING Z-SCORES

Here are the steps for transforming any set of raw scores (times, percentages, clicks, whatever) into z-scores:

1. Enter the raw scores into a single column in Excel. For this example, we will assume they are in column "A" and that you started on row "1." Make sure there are no other values in this column, such as an average at the bottom.

2. In the cell to the right of the first raw score, enter the formula:

   = STANDARDIZE(A1,AVERAGE(A:A),STDEV(A:A))

3. Copy this "standardize" formula down as many rows as there are raw scores.

4. As a double-check, calculate the mean and standard deviation for this z-score column. The average should be 0, and the standard deviation should be 1 (both within rounding error).

The bottom two rows of Table 9.7 show the mean and standard deviation for each set of z-scores, which should always be 0 and 1, respectively. Note that in using z-scores, we didn't have to make any assumptions about the maximum or minimum values that any of the scores could have. In essence, we let each set of scores define its own distribution and rescale them so those distributions would each have a mean of 0 and a standard deviation of 1. In this way, when they are averaged together, each of the z-scores makes an equal contribution to the average z-score. Notice that when averaging the z-scores together, each of the scales must be going the same direction—in other words, higher values should always be better. In the case of the time data, the opposite is almost always true. Since z-scores have a mean of 0, this is easy to correct simply by multiplying the z-score by (-1) to reverse its scale.

If you compare the z-score averages in Table 9.7 to the percentage averages in Table 9.3, you will find that the ordering of the participants based on those averages is nearly the same: Both techniques yield the same top three participants (9, 5, and 3) and the same bottom three participants (4, 8, and 1).

One disadvantage of using z-scores is that you can't think of the overall average of the z-scores as some type of overall usability score, since, by definition, that overall average will be 0. So when would you want to use z-scores? They are mainly useful when you want to compare one set of data to another, such as data from iterative usability tests of different versions of a product, data from different groups of users in the same usability test, or data from different conditions or designs within the same usability test. You should also have a reasonable sample size (e.g., at least 10 participants per condition) to use the z-score method.

For example, consider the data shown in Fig. 9.1 from Chadwick-Dias, McNulty, and Tullis (2003), which shows z-scores of performance for two iterations of a prototype. This research was studying the effects of age on performance in using a website. Study 1 was a baseline study. Based on their observations of the participants in Study 1, and especially the problems encountered by the older participants, they made changes to the prototype and then conducted Study 2 with a new group of participants. The z-scores were equal-weighted combinations of task time and task completion rate.

It's important to understand that the z-score transformations were done using the *full set* of data from Study 1 and Study 2 combined. They were then plotted appropriately to indicate from which study each z-score was derived. The key finding was that the performance z-scores for Study 2 were significantly higher than the performance z-scores for Study 1, and the effect was the same regardless of age (as reflected by the fact that the two lines are parallel to each other). If the z-score transformations had been done *separately* for Study 1 and Study 2, the results would have been meaningless because the means for Study 1 and Study 2 would both have been forced to 0 by the transformations.

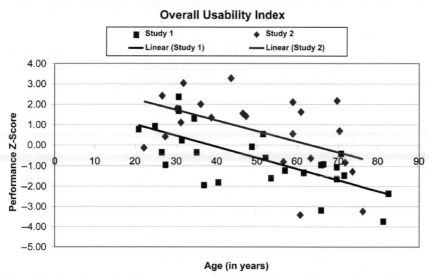

Fig. 9.1 Data showing performance **z**-scores from two studies of a prototype with participants over a wide range of ages. The performance **z**-score was an equal-weighted combination of task time and task completion rate. Changes were made to the prototype between Study 1 and Study 2. The performance **z**-scores were significantly better in Study 2, regardless of the participant's age. Adapted from Chadwick-Dias et al. (2003); used with permission.

9.1.4 Using SUM: Single Usability Metric

Jeff Sauro and Erika Kindlund (2005) developed a quantitative model for combining usability metrics into a single usability score. (Also see Sauro, 2012.) Their focus is on task completion, task time, error counts per task, and post-task satisfaction rating (similar to ASQ described in Chapter 5). Note that all of their analyses are at the task level, whereas the previous sections have described analyses at the "study" level. At the task level, task completion is typically a binary variable for each participant: that person either completed the task successfully or did not. At the study level, task completion, as we have seen in the previous sections, indicates how many tasks each person completed, and it can be expressed as a percentage for each participant.

Sauro and Kindlund used techniques derived from Six Sigma methodology (e.g., Breyfogle, 1999) to standardize their four usability metrics (task completion, time, errors, and task rating) into a Single Usability Metric (SUM). Conceptually, their techniques are not that different from the z-score and percentage transformations described in the previous sections. In addition, they used Principal Components Analysis, a statistical technique that looks at the correlations between variables, to determine if all four of their metrics were significantly contributing to the overall calculation of the single metric. They found that all four were significant and, in fact, that each contributed about equally. Consequently, they decided that each of the four metrics (once standardized) should contribute equally to the calculation of the SUM score.

Jeff Sauro (2019c) provides an Excel spreadsheet that calculates the SUM score from a study (https://measuringu.com/sum-2/). For each task and each participant in the study, you must enter the following:

- Whether the participant completed the task successfully (0 or 1).
- Number of errors committed on that task by that participant. (You also specify the number of error opportunities for each task.)
- Task time in seconds for that participant.
- Post-task satisfaction rating, which is an average of three post-task ratings on five-point scales of task ease, satisfaction, and perceived time—similar to ASQ.

After entering these data for all the tasks, the tool standardizes the scores and calculates the SUM score for each task. The standardized data shown for each task is illustrated in Table 9.8. Notice that a SUM score is calculated for each task, which allows for overall comparisons of tasks. In this sample data, the participants did best on the "Cancel reservation" task and worst on the "Check restaurant hours" task. An overall SUM score, 68% in this example, is also calculated,

| Task | SUM | | | | | | |
	Low (%)	Mean (%)	High (%)	Completion (%)	Satisfaction (%)	Time (%)	Errors (%)
Reserve a room	62	75	97	81	74	68	76
Find a hotel	38	58	81	66	45	63	59
Check room rates	49	66	89	74	53	63	74
Cancel reservation	89	91	99	86	91	95	92
Check restaurant hours	22	46	68	58	45	39	43
Get directions	56	70	93	81	62	66	71
Overall SUM	**53**	**68**	**88**				

Table 9.8 Sample standardized data from a usability test.
After entering data for each participant and each task, these are the standardized scores calculated by SUM, including an overall SUM score and a confidence interval for it.

as is a 90% confidence interval (53% to 88%), which is the average of the confidence intervals of the SUM score for each task.

The online tool also provides the option to graph the task data from a usability study, including the SUM scores. Fig. 9.2 shows a sample graph from the SUM calculator.

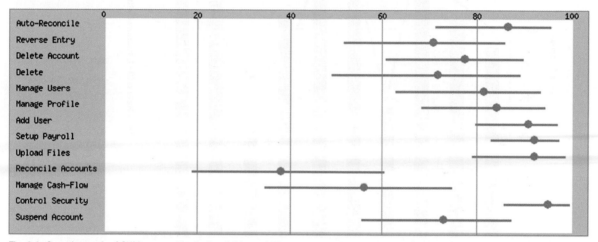

Fig. 9.2 Sample graph of SUM scores. The tasks of this usability test are listed down the left. For each task, the orange circle shows the mean SUM score, and the bars show the 90% confidence interval for each. In this example, it's apparent that the "Reconcile Accounts" and "Manage Cash-Flow" tasks are the most problematic.

9.2 UX SCORECARDS AND FRAMEWORK

Two other techniques for summarizing the results of a UX study are scorecards and frameworks. A UX scorecard is an attempt to graphically present the results of the study in a summary chart. A UX framework is a structured way of summarizing and presenting the results of the study.

9.2.1 UX Scorecards

An alternative to combining different metrics to derive an overall score is to graphically present the results of the metrics in a summary chart. This type of chart is often called a UX Scorecard. The goal is to present the data from the study in such a way that overall trends and important aspects of the data can be easily detected, such as tasks that were particularly problematic for the users. If you only have two metrics that you're trying to represent, a simple combination graph from Excel may be appropriate. For example, Fig. 9.3 shows the task completion rate and task ease rating for each of ten tasks in a usability test.

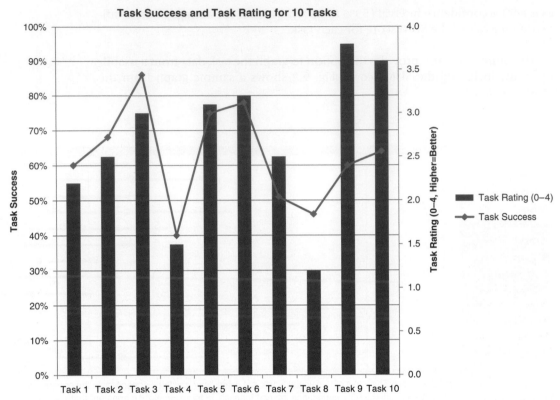

Fig. 9.3 A sample combination column and line chart for ten tasks. Task rating is shown via the columns and labeled on the right axis. Task success is shown via the lines and is labeled on the left axis.

The combination chart in Fig. 9.3 has some interesting features. It clarifies which tasks were the most problematic for the participants (Tasks 4 and 8) because they have the lowest values on both scales. It's also obvious where there were significant disparities between the task success data and task ease ratings, such as Tasks 9 and 10, which had only moderate task completion rates but the highest task ratings. (This is an especially troubling finding because it might indicate that some of the users did not successfully complete the task but thought they did.) Finally, it's easy to distinguish the tasks that had reasonably high values for both metrics, such as Tasks 3, 5, and 6.

This type of combination chart works well if you have only two metrics to represent, but what if you have more? One way of representing summary data for three or more metrics is using radar charts. Fig. 9.4 shows an example of a radar chart for summarizing the results of a study with five factors: task completion, page visits, accuracy (lack of errors), satisfaction rating, and usefulness rating. In this example, although the task completion, accuracy, and usefulness

HOW TO CREATE A COMBINATION CHART IN EXCEL

Using Excel, here's what you do:

1. Enter your data into two columns in the spreadsheet (e.g., one column for task success and the other for task rating). Create a column chart like you normally would for both variables. This will look strange because the two variables will be plotted on the same axis, with one scale greatly overshadowing the other.

2. Right-click on one of the columns in the chart and choose "Format Data Series." In the resulting dialog box, choose "Series Options." In the "Plot Series On" area, choose "Secondary Axis."

3. Close that dialog box. The chart will still look odd because now the two columns are on top of each other.

4. Right-click on a column being charted on the primary (left) axis and select "Change Series Chart Type."

5. Change that variable to a line graph. Close that dialog box.

(Yes, we know this type of combination chart breaks the rule about only using line graphs for continuous data, like times. But you have to break the rule to make it work in Excel. And rules are made to be broken anyway!)

rating were relatively high (good), the page visits and satisfaction rating were relatively low (poor).

Although radar charts can be useful for a high-level view, it's not really possible to represent task-level information in them. The example in Fig. 9.4 averaged the data across the tasks. What if you want to represent summary data for three or more metrics but also maintain task-level information? One technique for doing that is using what are called Harvey Balls. A variation on this technique has been popularized by *Consumer Reports*. For example, consider the data shown earlier in Table 9.7, which presents the results for six tasks in a usability test, including task completion, time, satisfaction, and errors. These data could be summarized in a comparison chart as shown in Fig. 9.5. This type of comparison chart allows you to see at a glance how the participants did for each of the tasks (by focusing on the rows) or how the participants did for each of the metrics (by focusing on the columns).

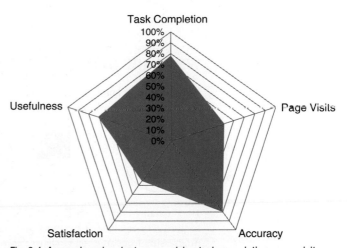

Fig. 9.4 A sample radar chart summarizing task completion, page visits, accuracy (lack of errors), satisfaction rating, and usefulness rating from a usability test. Each has been transformed to a percentage using the techniques outlined earlier in this chapter.

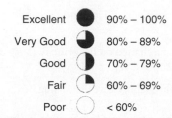

Task	SUM Score	Completion	Satisfaction	Time	Errors
Cancel reservation	91%	◔	●	●	●
Reserve a room	75%	◔	◐	◔	◐
Get directions	70%	◕	◔	◔	◐
Check room rates	66%	◐	○	◔	◐
Find a hotel	58%	◔	○	◔	○
Check restaurant hours	46%	○	○	○	○

Excellent	●	90% – 100%
Very Good	◕	80% – 89%
Good	◐	70% – 79%
Fair	◔	60% – 69%
Poor	○	< 60%

Fig. 9.5 A sample comparison chart using the data from Table 9.7. The tasks have been ordered by their SUM score, starting with the highest. For each of the four standardized scores (task completion, satisfaction, task time, and errors), the value has been represented by coded circles (known as Harvey Balls), as shown in the key.

WHAT ARE HARVEY BALLS?

Harvey Balls are small, round pictograms typically used in a comparison table to represent values for different items:

They're named for Harvey Poppel, a Booz Allen Hamilton consultant who created them in the 1970s as a way of summarizing long tables of numeric data. There are five levels, progressing from an open circle to a completely filled circle. Typically, the open circle represents the worst values, and the completely filled circle represents the best values. Links to images of Harvey Balls of different sizes can be found on our website, www.MeasuringUX.com. Harvey Balls shouldn't be confused with Harvey Ball, who was the creator of the smiley face ☺ !

BENTLEY'S EXPERIENCE SCORECARD

At the Bentley University User Experience Center (www.bentley.edu/uxc), we developed a new way to measure the overall user experience of any product. With my colleague Heather Wright Karlson, we created an experience scorecard that is unique in a few ways:

- We take a very broad, holistic view of the user experience, including usability, design/content, brand, and emotional experience.

- Rather than have all participants perform the same set of tasks, participants self-select from a limited list of tasks that are most relevant to them.

- Participants indicate which of the four attributes (usability, design/content, brand, and emotion) they value most in their experience, and scores are then weighted for each person.

Similar to many UX scorecards, there is an overall number or score that represents the user experience. In one case study, the Ikea website had an overall score of 87, compared to the target of 79.9. The primary contribution was from usability, and the least contribution was from the emotional experience.

By plotting the importance (as reflected by the average weights) and the average experience for each of the four elements, we can get a sense of the design priorities. In the figure below, the emotion dimension falls within the medium priority. Even though the average weight or importance isn't too high (around 20), the average experience rating isn't great (falling below a 4.0). Therefore, the emotion dimension (frustration, stress, confidence, and trust) is something that should be looked at more carefully.

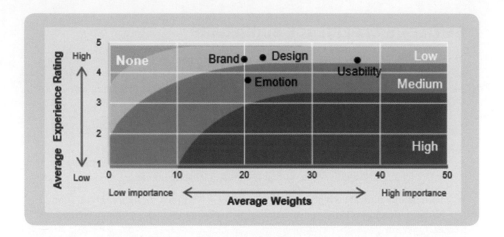

9.2.2 UX Frameworks

A UX framework is a way of thinking about, summarizing, and presenting the results of several different UX metrics from a study. These kinds of frameworks are not particularly new, although the terminology may be. Perhaps the classic framework for UX metrics is the official ISO 9241-11 definition of usability: "the extent to which a product can be used by specified users to achieve specified goals with effectiveness, efficiency and satisfaction in a specified context of use" (International Standards Organization [ISO], 2018). This definition provides a simple framework of three categories of UX metrics: effectiveness, efficiency, and satisfaction. Metrics for each of those areas can then be used as a framework for considering and comparing the results of UX studies. For example, task completion rate could be used for effectiveness, task time for efficiency, and a System Usability Scale score for satisfaction. Using these consistently could allow for meaningful comparisons among different designs or across iterations. This could also support clearer communications with stakeholders.

A UX framework designed primarily for web applications, which has gained some attention, is the Google "HEART" framework (Rodden, Hutchinson, & Fu, 2010). It includes five types of metrics:

- Happiness: A self-reported measure of the users' attitudes or satisfaction, commonly measured with a standard survey.
- Engagement: A measure of how much users interact with the product on their own, often measured by the regularity of use or level of interaction over a given time period.
- Adoption: A measure of the number of new users within a specific time-frame, which indicates how successful the product is in attracting new business.

- Retention: A measure of how well the product keeps existing users within a given time period.
- Task Completion: A measure of how well users are accomplishing their tasks using the product. This includes any of the performance metrics we have discussed (e.g., task success, time, errors).

The authors point out that not all projects will use all these metrics. An example they cite is that Engagement may not be relevant with enterprise applications where users don't really have a choice about using the application or not. They also describe a process for identifying metrics based on business goals. This process involves articulating a product's or feature's goals, then identifying *signals* that indicate success, and finally, building specific *metrics* to track. They found that the HEART metrics helped product teams make better decisions that are both data-driven and user-centered.

9.3 COMPARISON TO GOALS AND EXPERT PERFORMANCE

Although the previous sections focused on ways to summarize UX data without reference to an external standard, in some cases, you may have an external standard that can be used for comparison. The two main flavors of an external standard are predefined goals and expert, or optimum, performance.

9.3.1 Comparison to Goals

Perhaps the best way to assess the results of a study is to compare those results to goals that were established before the test. These goals may be set at the task level or an overall level. Goals can be set for any of the metrics we've discussed, including task completion, task time, errors, and self-reported measures. Here are some examples of task-specific goals:

- At least 90% of representative users will be able to successfully reserve a suitable hotel room.
- Opening a new account online should take no more than 8 minutes on average.
- At least 95% of new users will be able to purchase their chosen product online within 5 minutes of selecting it.

Similarly, examples of overall goals could include the following:

- Users will be able to successfully complete at least 90% of their tasks.
- Users will be able to complete their tasks in less than 3 minutes each, on average.
- Users will give the application an average SUS rating of at least 80%.

Typically, usability goals address task completion, time, accuracy, and/or satisfaction. The key is that the goals must be measurable. You must be able to determine whether the data in a given situation supports the attainment of the goal. For example, consider the data in Table 9.9.

	Target # of Page Visits	Actual # of Page Visits
Task 1	5	7.9
Task 2	8	9.3
Task 3	3	7.3
Task 4	10	11.5
Task 5	4	7
Task 6	6	6.9
Task 7	9	9.8
Task 8	7	10.2

Table 9.9 Sample data from eight tasks showing the target number of page visits and the mean of the actual number of page visits.

This table shows data for eight tasks in a study of a website. For each task, a target number of page visits has been predetermined (ranging from 4 to 10). Fig. 9.6 graphically depicts the target and actual page views for each task. This chart is useful because it allows you to visually compare the actual number of page visits for each task, and its associated confidence interval, to the target number of page views. In fact, all the tasks had significantly more page views than the targets. What's perhaps not so obvious is how the various tasks performed relative to each other—in other

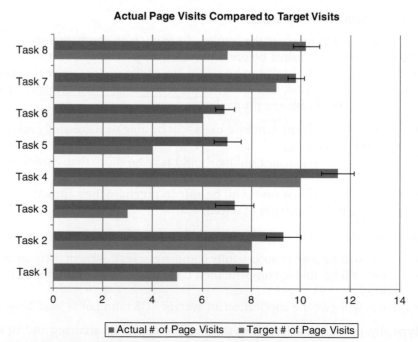

Fig. 9.6 Target and actual number of page visits for each of eight tasks. Error bars represent the 90% confidence interval for the actual number of page visits.

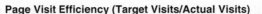

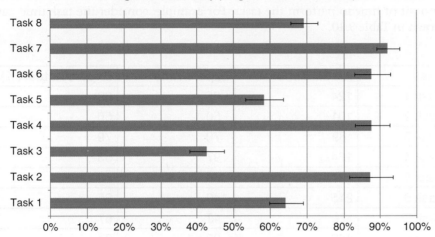

Fig. 9.7 Ratio of target to actual page views for each of eight tasks.

words, which ones came out better and which ones were worse. To make that kind of comparison easier, Fig. 9.7 shows the ratio of the target to actual page views for each task. This can be thought of as a "page view efficiency" metric: the closer it is to 100%, the more efficient the participants were being. This makes it easy to spot the tasks where the participants had trouble (e.g., Task 3) versus the tasks where they did well (e.g., Task 7). This technique could be used to represent the percentage of participants who met any particular objective (e.g., time, errors, SUS rating, etc.) either at the task level or the overall level.

9.3.2 Comparison to Expert Performance

An alternative to comparing the results of a usability test to predefined goals is to compare the results to the performance of experts. The best way to determine the expert performance level is to have one or more presumed experts actually perform the tasks and to measure the same things that you measure in the study. Obviously, your experts really need to be experts—people with subject-matter expertise, in-depth familiarity with the tasks, and in-depth familiarity with the product, application, or website being tested. And your data will be better if you can average the performance results from more than one expert. Comparing the results of a study to the results for experts allows you to compensate for the fact that certain tasks may be inherently more difficult or take longer, even for an expert. The goal, of course, is to see how close the performance of the participants in the test actually comes to the performance of the experts.

Although you could theoretically make a comparison to expert performance for any performance metric, it's most commonly used for time data. With task success data, the usual assumption is that a true expert would be able to perform all the tasks successfully. Similarly, with error data, the assumption is that an expert would not make any errors. But even an expert would require some amount of time to perform the tasks. For example, consider the task time data shown in Table 9.10.

Task	Actual Time	Expert Time	Expert/Actual (%)
Task 1	124	85	69
Task 2	101	50	50
Task 3	89	70	79
Task 4	184	97	53
Task 5	64	40	63
Task 6	215	140	65
Task 7	70	47	67
Task 8	143	92	64
Task 9	108	98	91
Task 10	92	60	65

Table 9.10 Sample time data from 10 tasks in a usability test, showing the average actual time per task (in seconds), the expert time per task, and the ratio of expert to actual time

Graphing the ratio of expert to actual times, as shown in Fig. 9.8, makes it easy to spot the tasks where the test participants did well in comparisons to the experts (Tasks 3 and 9) and the tasks where they did not do so well (Tasks 2 and 4).

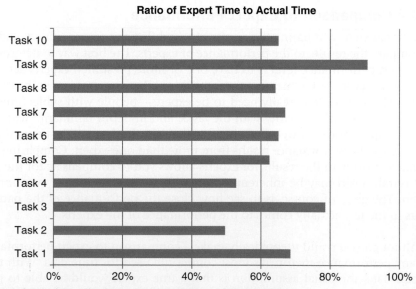

Fig. 9.8 Graph of the ratio of the expert to actual times from Table 9.9.

9.4 SUMMARY

Some of the key takeaways from this chapter are as follows:

1. An easy way to combine different usability metrics is to determine the percentage of users who achieve a combination of goals. This tells you the overall percentage of users who had a good experience with your product (based on the target goals). This method can be used with any set of metrics and is easily understood by stakeholders.

2. One way of combining different metrics into an overall "UX score" is to convert each of the metrics to a percentage and then average them together. This requires being able to specify, for each metric, an appropriate minimum and maximum score.

3. Another way to combine different metrics is to convert each metric to a z-score and then average them together. Each metric gets equal weight when they are combined using z-scores. But the overall average of the z-scores will always be 0. The key is in comparing different subsets of the data to each other, such as data from different iterations, different groups, or different conditions.

4. The SUM technique is another method for combining different metrics, specifically task completion, task time, errors, and task-level satisfaction rating. The method requires the entry of individual task and participant data for the four metrics. The calculations yield a SUM score, as a percentage, for each task, and across all the tasks, including confidence intervals.

5. Various types of graphs and charts can be useful for summarizing the results of a study in a "scorecard." A combination line and column chart is useful for summarizing the results of two metrics for the tasks in a test. Radar charts are useful for summarizing the results of three or more metrics overall. A comparison chart using Harvey Balls to represent different levels of the metrics can effectively summarize the results for three or more metrics at the task level. UX frameworks, such as Google's HEART framework, can also be a useful way of consistently evaluating, presenting, and comparing designs or iterations.

6. Perhaps the best way to determine the success of a study is to compare the results to a set of predefined goals. Typically these goals address task completion, time, accuracy, and satisfaction. The percentage of users whose data met the stated goals can be a very effective summary.

7. A reasonable alternative to comparing with predefined goals, especially for time data, is to compare the actual performance results to the results for experts. The closer the actual performance is to expert performance, the better.

CHAPTER 10
Special Topics

CONTENTS

This chapter introduces a number of topics related to the measurement or analysis of user experience data that are not traditionally thought of as part of "mainstream" UX data. These include information you can glean from web analytics; data from card-sorting studies, tree-testing studies, and "first click" studies; data related to the accessibility of a website; and UX Return on Investment (ROI). These topics didn't fit neatly into the other chapters, but we believe they are an important part of a complete UX metrics toolkit.

10.1 WEB ANALYTICS

If you're dealing with a live website, there's a potential treasure trove of data about what the visitors to your site are actually doing—what pages they're visiting, what links they're clicking, and what paths they're following through the site. The challenge usually isn't getting the raw data but making sense of it. Unlike lab studies with perhaps a dozen participants or online studies with perhaps 100 participants, live sites have the potential to yield data from thousands or even hundreds of thousands of users.

Measuring the User Experience. DOI: http://dx.doi.org/10.1016/B978-0-12-818080-8.00010-8

Entire books have been written on the subject of web metrics and web analytics (e.g., Clifton, 2012; Kaushik, 2009; Beasley, 2013). There's even a *For Dummies* book on the topic (Sostre & LeClaire, 2007). So obviously, we are not able to do justice to the topic in just one section of one chapter in this book. What we'll try to do is introduce you to some of the things you can learn from live website data and specifically some of the implications they might have for the user experience of your site.

10.1.1 Basic Web Analytics

Some websites get huge numbers of visitors every day. But regardless of how many visitors your site gets (assuming it gets some), you can learn from what they're doing on the site. Here are the meanings of some of the terms commonly used in web analytics:

- **Visitors**: The people who have visited your website. Usually, a visitor is counted only once during the time period of a report. Some analytics packages use the term "unique visitor" to indicate that they're not counting the same person more than once. Some also report "new visitors" to distinguish them from the ones who have been to your site before.
- **Visits**: The individual times that your website was accessed. Sometimes also called "sessions." An individual *visitor* can have multiple *visits* to your site during the time period of the report.
- **Page Views**: The number of times individual pages on your site are viewed. If a visitor reloads a page, that typically counts as a new page view; likewise, if visitors navigate to another page in your site and then return to a page, that will count as a new page view. Page views let you see which pages on your site are the most popular.
- **Landing Page or Entrance Page**: The first page that a visitor visits on your site. This is often the home page but might be a lower-level page if they found it through a search engine or had bookmarked it.
- **Exit Page**: The last page that a visitor visits on your site.
- **Bounce Rate**: The percentage of visits in which the visitor views only one page on your site and then leaves the site. This could indicate a lack of engagement with your site, but it could also mean that they found what they were looking for from that one page.
- **Exit Rate** (for a page): The percentage of visitors who leave your site from a given page. *Exit rate*, which is a metric at an individual page level, is often confused with *bounce rate*, which is an overall metric for a site.
- **Conversion Rate**: The percentage of the visitors to a site who convert from being simply a casual visitor to taking some action, such as making a purchase, signing up for a newsletter, or opening an account.

A number of tools are available for capturing web analytics. Most web hosting services provide basic analytics as a part of the hosting service, and other web analytics services are available for free. Perhaps the most popular free analytics service is Google Analytics (http://www.google.com/analytics/). Fig. 10.1 shows a screenshot from Google Analytics Data Studio

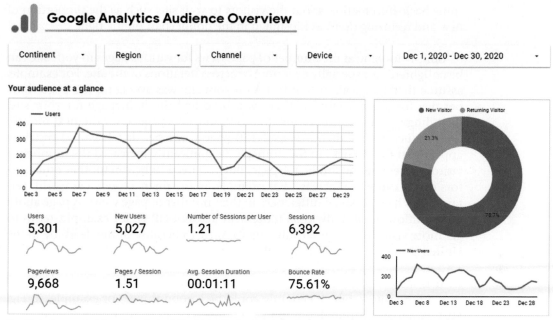

Fig. 10.1 Screenshot from Google Analytics Data Studio showing relevant statistics focused on the audience.

As can be seen in Fig. 10.2 (see also Fig. 10.1), you can look at many of the metrics for your site over time, such as the line graphs for the number of users, average session duration, and page views. The graphs of visits and page views show a pattern that's typical for some websites, which is a difference in the number of visitors, visits, and page views for the weekend vs. the weekdays. You also can capture

Fig. 10.2 Screenshot from Google Analytics Data Studio showing relevant statistics focused on user behavior.

some basic information about the visitors to your site, such as the proportion of new and recurring users, as illustrated in the donut chart on the right.

Simply looking at the number of page views for various pages in your site can be enlightening, especially over time or across iterations of the site. For example, assume that a page about Product A on your site was averaging 100 page views per day for a given month. Then, you modified the homepage for your site, including the description of the link to Product A's page. Over the next month, the Product A page then averaged 150 page views per day. It would certainly appear that the changes to the homepage significantly increased the number of visitors accessing the Product A page. But you need to be careful that other factors didn't cause the increase. For example, in the financial services world, certain pages have seasonal differences in their number of page views. A page about contributions to an individual retirement account (IRA), for example, tends to get more visits in the days leading up to April 15 because of the deadline in the United States for contributing to the prior year's IRA.

It is also possible that something caused your site as a whole to start getting more visitors, which certainly could be a good thing. For example, in Fig. 10.1, you may see a small bump in the number of users in early December. This aligned with a small marketing campaign highlighting new content on the website. But it could also be due to factors not related to the content, such as news events related to the subject matter of your site. This also brings up the issue of the impact that search "bots" can have on your site's statistics. Search bots, or spiders, are automated programs used by most of the major search engines to "crawl" the web by following links and indexing the pages they access. One of the challenges, once your site becomes popular and is being "found" by most of the major search engines, is filtering out the page views due to these search bots. Most bots (e.g., Google) usually identify themselves when making page requests and thus can be filtered out of the data.

What analyses can be used to determine if one set of page views is significantly different from another set? Consider the data shown in Table 10.1, which shows the number of page views per day for a given page over two different weeks. Week 1 was before a new homepage with a different link to the page in question was launched, and Week 2 was after.

These data can be analyzed using a paired t-test to see if the average for Week 2 (519) is significantly different from the average for Week 1 (454). It's important to use a paired t-test because of the variability due to the days of the week; comparing each day to itself from the previous week takes out the variability due to days. A paired t-test shows that this difference is statistically significant ($p < 0.01$). If you had not used a paired t-test and just used a t-test for two independent samples, the result ($p = 0.41$) would not have been anywhere near significant. (See Chapter 2 for details on how to run a paired t-test in Excel.)

	Week 1	Week 2
Sun	237	282
Mon	576	623
Tue	490	598
Wed	523	612
Thu	562	630
Fri	502	580
Sat	290	311
Averages	454	519

Table 10.1 Numbers of Page Views for a Given Web Page Over Two Different Weeks
Week 1 was before a new homepage was launched, and week 2 was after. The new homepage contained different wording for the link to this page.

10.1.2 Click-Through Rates

Click-through rates can be used to measure the effectiveness of different ways of presenting a link or button. They indicate the percentage of visitors who are shown a particular link or button who then actually click on it. If a link is shown 100 times and it is clicked on 1 of those times, its click-through rate is 1%. Most commonly the term is used to measure the effectiveness of web ads, but the concept applies to any link, button, or clickable image (Fig. 10.3).

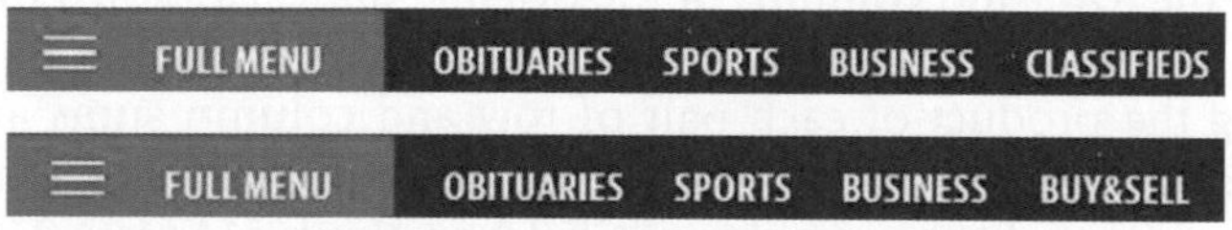

Fig. 10.3 Example of two tab (navigation) designs tested on a product page.

What analyses can be used to determine if the click-through rate for one link is significantly different from that for another link? One appropriate analysis is the chi-square test. A chi-square test lets you determine whether an observed set of frequencies is significantly different from an expected set of frequencies. (See Chapter 2 for more details.) For example, consider the data shown in Table 10.2 that represent click rates for two different links. The click-through rate for Link #1 is 1.4% [145/(145 + 10,289)]. The click-through rate for Link #2 is 1.7% [198/(198 + 11,170)]. But are these two significantly different from each other? Link #2 got more clicks, but it was also presented more times. To do a chi-square test, you must first construct a table of expected frequencies as if there were no difference in the click-through rates of Link #1 and Link #2. This is done using the sums of the rows and columns of the original table, as shown in Table 10.3.

What analyses can be used to determine if the click-through rate for one link is significantly different from that for another link? One appropriate analysis is the chi-square test. A chi-square test lets you determine whether an observed set

	Click	No Click
Link #1	145	10,289
Link #2	198	11,170

Table 10.2 Click Rates for Two Different Links: The Number of Times Each Link Was Clicked and the Number of Times Each Was Presented but Not Clicked

Observed	Click	No Click	Sum
Link #1	145	10,289	10,434
Link #2	198	11,170	11,368
Sum	343	21,459	21,802

Table 10.3 The Same Data as Table 10.2 but With the Sums of the Rows and Columns Added
These are used to calculate the expected frequencies if there were no differences in the click-through rates.

of frequencies is significantly different from an expected set of frequencies. (See Chapter 2 for more details.) For example, consider the data shown in Table 10.2, which represent click rates for two different links. The click-through rate for Link #1 is 1.4% [145/(145 + 10,289)]. The click-through rate for Link #2 is 1.7% [198/(198 + 11,170)]. But are these two significantly different from each other? Link #2 got more clicks, but it was also presented more times. To do a chi-square test, you must first construct a table of expected frequencies as if there were no difference in the click-through rates of Link #1 and Link #2. This is done using the sums of the rows and columns of the original table, as shown in Table 10.3.

By taking the product of each pair of row and column sums and dividing that by the grand total, you get the expected values as shown in Table 10.4. For example, the expected frequency for a "Click" on "Link #1" (164.2) is the product of the respective row and column sums divided by the grand total: $(343 \cdot 10{,}434)/21{,}802$. The "CHITEST" function in Excel can then be used to compare the actual frequencies in Table 10.2 to the expected frequencies in Table 10.4. The resulting value is $p = 0.04$, indicating that there is a significant difference between the click-through rates for Link #1 and Link #2.

Expected	Click	No Click
Link #1	164.2	102,610.8
Link #2	178.8	111,810.2

Table 10.4 The Expected Frequencies If There Were No Difference in the Click-through Rates for Link #1 and Link #2, Derived From the Sums Shown in Table 10.3

You should keep two important points about the chi-square test in mind. First, the chi-square test must be done using raw frequencies or counts, *not* percentages. You commonly think of click-through rates in terms of percentages, but that's not how you test for significant differences between them. Also, the categories used must be *mutually exclusive* and *exhaustive*. That's why the preceding example used "Click" and "No Click" as the two categories of observations for each link. Those two categories are mutually exclusive, and they account for all possible actions that could be taken on the link; either the user clicked on it or didn't.

10.1.3 Drop-off Rates

Drop-off rates can be a particularly useful way of detecting where there might be some usability problems on your site. The most common use of drop-off rates is to identify where in a sequence of pages users are dropping out of or abandoning a process, such as opening an account or completing a purchase. For example, assume that the user must fill out the information on a sequence of five pages to open some type of account. Table 10.5 reflects the percentage of users who started the process that actually completed each of the five pages.

Page #1	89%
Page #2	80%
Page #3	73%
Page #4	52%
Page #5	49%

Table 10.5 The Percentage of Users Who Started a Multipage Process That Actually Completed Each of the Steps

In this example, all of the percentages are relative to the number of users who started the entire process—that is, who got to Page #1. So 89% of the users who got to Page #1 successfully completed it, 80% of that original number completed Page #2, and so on. Given the data in Table 10.5, which of the five pages do the users seem to be having the most trouble with? The key is to look at how many users dropped off from each page—in other words, the difference between how many got to the page and how many completed it. Those "drop-off percentages" for each of the pages are shown in Table 10.6.

Page #1	11%
Page #2	9%
Page #3	7%
Page #4	21%
Page #5	3%

Table 10.6 The Drop-off Percentages for Each Page Shown in Table 10.5: The Difference Between the Percentage Who Got to the Page and the Percentage Who Successfully Completed It

This makes it clear that the largest drop-off rate, 21%, is associated with Page #4. If you are going to redesign this multipage process, you would be well advised to learn what is causing the drop-off at Page #4 and then try to address that in the redesign.

10.1.4 A/B Tests

A/B tests are a special type of live-site study in which you manipulate elements of the pages that are presented to the users. The traditional approach to A/B testing on a website involves posting two alternative designs for a given page or elements of a page. Some visitors to the site see the "A" version and others see the "B" version. In many cases, this assignment is random, so about the same number of visitors sees each version. In some cases, the majority of visitors see the existing page, and a smaller percentage see an experimental version that is being tested. Although these studies are typically called A/B tests, the same concept applies to any number of alternative designs for a page.

WHAT MAKES A GOOD A/B TEST

A good A/B test requires careful planning. Here are some tips to keep in mind:

- Make sure the method you're using to "split" visitors between the "A" and "B" versions really is random. If someone tells you it's good enough to just send all visitors in the morning to version "A" and all visitors in the afternoon to version "B," don't believe it. There could be something different about the morning vs. afternoon visitors.

- Test small changes, especially at first. It might be tempting to design two completely different versions of a page, but you'll learn much more by testing small differences. If the two versions are completely different from each other and one performs significantly better than the other, you still don't know why that one was better. If the only difference is, for example, the wording of the call-to-action button, then you know the difference is due to that wording.

- Test for significance. It might look like one version is beating the other one, but do a statistical test (e.g., chi-square) to make sure.

- Be agile. When you're confident that one version is outperforming the other, then "promote" the winning version (i.e., send all visitors to it) and move on to another A/B test.

- Believe the data, not the highest paid person's opinion (HIPPO). Sometimes the results of A/B tests are surprising and counterintuitive. One of the advantages that UX researchers bring to the mix is that you can follow up on these surprising findings using other techniques (e.g., surveys, lab, or online studies) to try to understand them better.

Technically, visitors to a page can be directed to one of the alternative pages in a variety of ways, including based on random number generation, the exact time (e.g., an even or odd number of seconds since midnight), or several other techniques. Typically, a cookie is set to indicate which version the visitor was shown so that if he or she returns to the site within a specified time period, the same version will be shown again. Keep in mind that it's important to test the alternative versions *at the same time* because of the external factors mentioned before that could affect the results if you tested at different times.

Carefully designed A/B tests can give you significant insight into what works and what doesn't work on your website. Many companies, including Amazon, eBay, Google, Microsoft, Facebook, and others, are constantly doing A/B tests on their live sites, although most users don't notice it (Kohavi, Deng, Frasca, Longbotham, Walker, & Xu, 2012; Kohavi, Crook, & Longbotham, 2009; Tang, Agarwal, O'Brien, Meyer, 2010). In fact, as Kohavi and Round (2004) explained, A/B testing is constant at Amazon, and experimentation through A/B testing is the main way they make changes to their site.

A/B TESTING WITH A NAVIGATION MENU

Deborah O'Malley from GuessTheTest (www.GuessTheTest.com) was kind enough to share a case study of an A/B test from The McClatchy Company. McClatchy owns many newspapers across the US, and is interested in learning how changes to their top-level navigation impact user behavior. First, McClatchy conducted a small sample qualitative study and found that navigation was improved when they changed the term "Classifieds" to "Buy & Sell."

However, management was not convinced and wanted to conduct an A/B test utilizing a much larger sample size. Based on more than 400 K visitors, the "Classifieds" link outperformed "Buy & Sell" by more than 75% (at a 99% confidence level). They speculate that the core audience of McClatchy newspapers is more familiar with the traditional "Classifieds" compared to "Buy & Sell." I recommend www.GuessTheTest. com to check out more fascinating case studies.

10.2 CARD-SORTING DATA

Card-sorting as a technique for organizing the elements of an information system in a way that makes sense to the users has been around at least since the early 1980s. For example, Tullis (1985) used the technique to organize the menus of a mainframe operating system. More recently, the technique has become popular as a way of informing decisions about the information architecture of a website (e.g., Maurer & Warfel, 2004; Spencer, 2009, Nawaz, 2012). Over the years, the technique has evolved from a true card-sorting exercise using index cards to an online exercise using virtual cards. Although many UX professionals seem to be familiar with the basic card-sorting techniques, fewer seem to be aware that various metrics can be used in the analyses of card-sorting data.

The two major types of card-sorting exercises are (1) open card-sorts, where you give users the cards that are to be sorted but let them define their own groups that the cards will be sorted into, and (2) closed card-sorts, where you give users the cards to be sorted as well as the names of the groups to sort them into. Although some metrics apply to both, others are unique to each.

CARD-SORTING TOOLS

A number of tools are available for conducting card-sorting exercises. Some are desktop applications, and others are web-based. Most of these include basic analysis capabilities (e.g., hierarchical cluster analysis). Here are some of the ones we're familiar with:

- OptimalSort (http://www.optimalworkshop.com/optimalsort) (a web-based service)
- UsabiliTest Card-sorting (http://www.usabilitest.com/CardSorting) (a web-based service)
- UserZoom Card-sorting (https://www.userzoom.com/user-research-methods/#ia-research) (a web-based service)
- UzCardSort (http://uzilla.mozdev.org/cardsort.html) (a Mozilla extension)
- XSort (https://xsortapp.com/) (a Mac OS X application)

Although not a card-sorting tool, you could also use PowerPoint or similar programs to do card-sorting exercises when the number of cards is relatively small. Create a slide that has the cards to be sorted along with empty boxes and then email that to participants, asking them to put the cards into the boxes and to name the boxes. Then, they simply e-mail the file back. Of course, you're on your own for the analysis in this case.

10.2.1 Analyses of Open Card-Sort Data

One way to analyze the data from an open card-sort is to create a matrix of the "perceived distances" (also called a dissimilarity matrix) among all pairs of cards in the study. For example, assume you conducted a card-sorting study using 10 fruits: apples, oranges, strawberries, bananas, peaches, plums, tomatoes, pears, grapes, and cherries. Assume one participant in the study created the following names and groupings:

- "Large, round fruits": apples, oranges, peaches, tomatoes
- "Small fruits": strawberries, grapes, cherries, plums
- "Funny-shaped fruits": bananas, pears

You can then create a matrix of "perceived distances" among all pairs of the fruits for each participant by using the following rules:

- If this person put a pair of cards in the same group, it gets a distance of 0.
- If this person put a pair of cards into different groups, it gets a distance of 1.

Using these rules, the distance matrix for the preceding participant would look like what's shown in Table 10.7.

Fruit	Apples	Oranges	Strawberries	Bananas	Peaches	Plums	Tomatoes	Pears	Grapes	Cherries
apples	—	0	1	1	0	1	0	1	1	1
oranges		—	1	1	0	1	0	1	1	1
strawberries			—	1	1	0	1	1	0	0
bananas				—	1	1	1	0	1	1
peaches					—	1	0	1	1	1
plums						—	1	1	0	0
tomatoes							—	1	1	1
pears								—	1	1
grapes									—	0
cherries										—

Table 10.7 Distance Matrix for One Participant in the Fruit Card-Sorting Example

We're only showing the top half of the matrix for simplicity, but the bottom half would be exactly the same. The diagonal entries are not meaningful because the distance of a card from itself is undefined. (Or it can be assumed to be zero if needed in the analyses.) So for any one participant in the study, the entries in this matrix will only be 0 or 1. The key is to then combine these matrices for all the participants in the study. Let's assume you had 20 participants do the card-sorting exercise with the fruits. You can then sum the matrices for the 20 participants. This will create an overall distance matrix whose values can, in theory, range from 0 (if all participants put that pair into the same group) to 20 (if all participants put that pair into different groups). The higher the number, the greater the distance. Table 10.8 shows an example of what that might look like.

Fruit	Apples	Oranges	Strawberries	Bananas	Peaches	Plums	Tomatoes	Pears	Grapes	Cherries
apples	—	5	11	16	4	10	12	8	11	10
oranges		—	17	14	2	12	15	11	12	14
strawberries			—	17	16	8	18	15	4	8
bananas				—	17	15	20	11	14	16
peaches					—	9	11	6	15	13
plums						—	12	10	9	7
tomatoes							—	16	18	14
pears								—	12	14
grapes									—	3
cherries										—

Table 10.8 Overall Distance Matrix for 20 Participants in the Fruit Card-Sorting Study

will give you a measure of the goodness of fit for your derived groups relative to the original data.

10.2.1.2 MULTIDIMENSIONAL SCALING

Another way of analyzing and visualizing the data from a card-sorting exercise is using multidimensional scaling, or MDS. Perhaps the best way to understand MDS is through an analogy. Imagine that you had a table of the mileages between all pairs of major U.S. cities but not a map of where those cities are located. An MDS analysis could take that table of mileages and derive an approximation of the map showing where those cities are relative to each other. In essence, MDS tries to create a map in which the distances between all pairs of items match the distances in the original distance matrix as closely as possible.

The input to an MDS analysis is the same as the input to hierarchical cluster analysis—a distance matrix, like the example shown in Table 10.9. The result of an MDS analysis of the data in Table 10.8 is shown in Fig. 10.5. The first thing that's apparent from this MDS analysis is how the tomatoes and bananas are isolated from all the other fruit. That's consistent with the hierarchical cluster analysis, where those two fruits were the last two to join all the others. In fact, our four-cluster "slice" of the hierarchical cluster analysis (see Fig. 10.4) had these two fruits as groups unto themselves. Another thing apparent from the MDS analysis is how the strawberries, grapes, cherries, and plums cluster together on the left and the apples, peaches, pears, and oranges cluster together on the right. That's also consistent with the hierarchical cluster analysis.

Card	Group A	Group B	Group C	Max
Card #1	17%	78%	5%	78%
Card #2	15%	77%	8%	77%
Card #3	20%	79%	1%	79%
Card #4	48%	40%	12%	48%
Card #5	11%	8%	81%	81%
Card #6	1%	3%	96%	96%
Card #7	46%	16%	37%	46%
Card #8	57%	38%	5%	57%
Card #9	20%	75%	5%	75%
Card #10	4%	5%	92%	92%
			Average	73%

Table 10.9 The Percentage of Participants in a Closed Card-Sort Who Put Each of 10 Cards Into Each of the Three Groups Provided

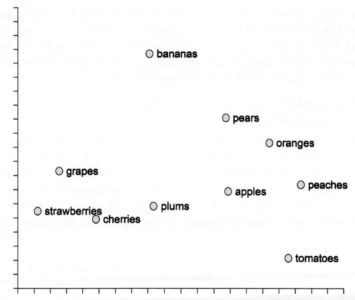

Fig. 10.5 Multidimensional scaling analysis of a distance matrix in Table 10.9.

Notice that it's also possible to use more than two dimensions in an MDS analysis, but we've rarely seen a case where adding even just one more dimension yields particularly useful insights into card-sorting data. Another point to keep in mind is that the orientation of the axes in an MDS plot is arbitrary. You could rotate or flip the map any way you want, and the results would still be the same. The only thing that's actually important is the relative distances between all pairs of the items.

The most common metric that's used to represent how well an MDS plot reflects the original data is a measure of "stress" sometimes referred to as *Phi*. Most of the commercial packages that do MDS analysis can also report the stress value associated with a solution. Basically, it's calculated by looking at all pairs of items, finding the difference between each pair's distance in the MDS map and its distance in the original matrix, squaring that difference, and summing those squares. That measure of stress for the MDS map shown in Fig. 10.5 is 0.04. The smaller the value, the better. But how small does it really need to be? A good rule of thumb is that stress values under 0.10 are excellent, whereas stress values above 0.20 are poor.

We find it useful to do both a hierarchical cluster analysis and an MDS analysis. Sometimes you see interesting things in one that is not apparent in the other. In addition, they are different statistical analysis techniques, so you shouldn't expect them to give exactly the same answers. For example, one thing that's sometimes easier to see in an MDS map is which cards are "outliers"—those that don't obviously belong to a single group. There are at least two reasons why a card could be an outlier: (1) It could truly be an outlier—a function that really is different from all the others; or (2) it could have been "pulled" toward two or more groups. When designing a website, you would probably want to make these functions available from *each* of those clusters.

10.2.1.3 HOW MANY PARTICIPANTS ARE ENOUGH FOR A CARD-SORTING STUDY?

Tullis and Wood (2004) conducted a card-sorting study in which they addressed the question of how many people you need for a card-sorting study if you want to get reliable results from your analyses. They did an open sort with 46 cards and 168 participants. They then analyzed the results for the full dataset (168 participants) as well as many random subsamples of the data from 2 to 70 participants. The correlations of the results for those subsamples to the full dataset are shown in Fig. 10.6.

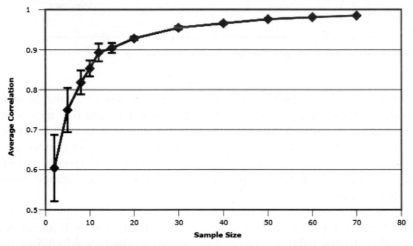

Fig. 10.6 Results from Tullis and Wood (2004) that analyzed how many participants are needed for a card-sorting study.

The "elbow" of that curve appears to be somewhere between 10 and 20, with a sample size of 15 yielding a correlation of .90 with the full dataset. Although it's hard to know how well these results would generalize to other card-sorting studies with different subject matter or different numbers of cards, they at least suggest that about 15 may be a good target number of participants.

10.2.2 Analyses of Closed Card-Sort Data

Closed card-sorts, where you not only give participants the cards but also the names of the groups into which to sort them, are probably done less often than open card-sorts. Typically, you would start with an open sort to get an idea of the kinds of groups that users would naturally create and the names they might use for them. Sometimes it is helpful to follow up an open sort with one or more closed sorts, mainly as a way of testing your ideas about organizing the functions and naming the groupings. With a closed card-sort, you have an idea about how you want to organize the functions, and you want to see how close users come to matching the organization you have in mind.

We used closed card-sorting to compare different ways of organizing the functions for a website (Tullis, 2007). We first conducted an open sort with 54 functions. We then used those results to generate six different ways of organizing the functions that we then tested in six simultaneous closed card-sorting exercises. Each closed card-sort used the same 54 functions but presented different groups to sort the functions into. The number of groups in each "framework" (set of group names) ranged from three to nine. Each participant only saw and used one of the six frameworks.

In looking at the data from a closed card-sort, the main thing you're interested in is how well the groups "pulled" the cards to them that you intend to belong to those groups. For example, consider the data in Table 10.9, which shows the percentage of the participants in a closed card-sorting exercise who put each card into each of the groups.

The other percentage, shown on the right in Table 10.9, is the highest percentage for each card. This is an indicator of how well the "winning" group pulled the appropriate cards to it. What you hope to see are cases like Card #10 in this table, which was very strongly pulled to Group C, with 92% of the participants putting it in that group. The more troubling ones are cases like Card #7, where 46% of the participants put it in Group A, but 37% put it in Group C—so participants were very "split" in terms of deciding where that card belonged in this set of groups.

One metric you could use for characterizing how well a particular set of group names fared in a closed card-sort is the average of these maximum values for all the cards. For the data in Table 10.9, that would be 73%. But what if you want to compare the results from closed card-sorts with the same cards but different sets of groups? That average maximum percentage will work well for comparisons as long as each set contains the same number of groups. But if one set had only three groups and another had nine groups, as in the Tullis (2007) study, it's not a fair metric for comparison. If participants were simply acting randomly in doing the sorting with only three groups, by chance they would get a maximum percentage of 33%. But if they were acting randomly in doing a sort with nine groups, they would get a maximum percentage of only 11%. So using this metric, a framework with more groups is at a disadvantage in comparison to one with fewer groups.

We experimented with a variety of methods to correct for the number of groups in a closed card-sort. The one that seems to work best is illustrated in Table 10.10. These are the same data as shown earlier in Table 10.9 but with two

Card	Category A	Category B	Category C	Max	2nd Place	Difference
Card #1	17%	78%	5%	78%	17%	61%
Card #2	15%	77%	8%	77%	15%	62%
Card #3	20%	79%	1%	79%	20%	60%
Card #4	48%	40%	12%	48%	40%	8%
Card #5	11%	8%	81%	81%	11%	70%
Card #6	1%	3%	96%	96%	3%	93%
Card #7	46%	16%	37%	46%	37%	8%
Card #8	57%	38%	5%	57%	38%	18%
Card #9	20%	75%	5%	75%	20%	55%
Card #10	4%	5%	92%	92%	5%	87%
			Average	73%		52%

Table 10.10 The Same Data as Shown in Table 10.10 but With an Additional Two Columns
"2nd Place" refers to the next-highest percentage after the maximum percentage, and "Difference" indicates the difference between the maximum percentage and the 2nd-place percentage.

additional columns. The "2nd Place" column gives the percentage associated with the group that had the next-highest percentage. The "Difference" column is simply the difference between the maximum percentage and the 2nd-place percentage. A card that was pulled strongly to one group, such as Card #10, gets a relatively small penalty in this scheme. But a card that was more evenly split, such as Card #7, takes quite a hit.

The average of these differences can then be used to make comparisons between frameworks that have different numbers of groups. For example, Fig. 10.7 shows the data from Tullis (2007) plotted using this method. We call this a measure of the percent agreement among the participants about which group each card belongs to. Obviously, higher values are better.

The data from a closed card-sort can also be analyzed using hierarchical cluster analysis and MDS analysis, just like the data from an open card-sort. These give you visual representations of how well the framework you presented to the participants in the closed card-sort actually worked for them.

10.3 TREE TESTING

A technique that's closely related to closed card-sorting is tree testing. This is a technique where you provide an interactive representation of the proposed information organization for a site, typically in the form of menus that let the user traverse the information hierarchy. For example, Fig. 10.8 shows a sample study in TreeJack (www.optimalworkshop.com/treejack/) from the participant's perspective.

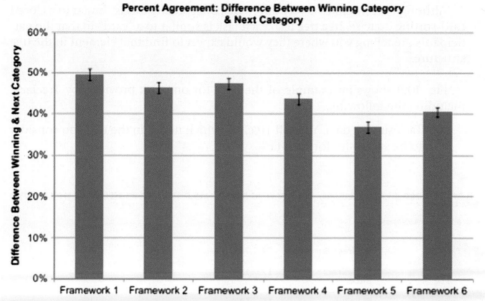

Fig. 10.7   A comparison of six frameworks in six parallel closed card-sorts. Since the frameworks had different numbers of groups, a correction was used in which the percentage associated with the 2nd-place group was subtracted from the winning group. (Adapted from Tullis (2007); used with permission.)

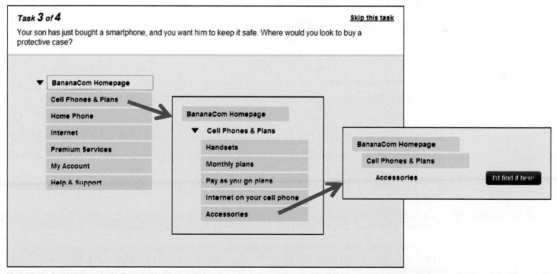

Fig. 10.8   Sample study in TreeJack. The task is shown at the top. Initially, the participant sees only the menu on the left. After selecting "Cell Phones & Plans" from that menu, a sub-menu is shown. This continues until the participant chooses the "I'd find it here" button. The participant can go back up the tree at any time.

Although the interface is very different, conceptually this is similar to a closed card-sorting exercise. In a tree test, each task is similar to a "card" in that the participants are telling you where they would expect to find that element in the tree structure.

Fig. 10.9 shows an example of the data for one task provided by TreeJack, including the following:

- Task success data. You tell TreeJack which nodes in the tree you consider to be successful for each task.

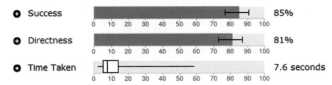

Task 2
8
OVERALL
Your son has just bought a smartphone, and you want him to keep it safe. Where would you look to buy a protective case?

Cell Phones & Plans → Accessories

■ Direct Success	77	70%
■ Indirect Success	17	15%
■ Failure	15	14%
■ Skip	1	1%

✳ View the Pietree for this task

⊕ Success — 85%
   0 10 20 30 40 50 60 70 80 90 100

⊕ Directness — 81%
   0 10 20 30 40 50 60 70 80 90 100

⊕ Time Taken — 7.6 seconds
   0 10 20 30 40 50 60 70 80 90 100

Click the + to learn more about a specific score

Fig. 10.9 Sample data for one task in TreeJack, including task success, directness, and time taken.

- Directness. This is the percentage of participants who didn't backtrack up the tree at any point during the task. This can be a useful indication of how confident the participants in making their selections.
- Time taken. The average time taken by the participants to complete the task.

And all three of these metrics are shown with 95% confidence intervals!

TreeJack also provides an interesting visualization of the data for each task, called a "PieTree," shown in Fig. 10.10. In this visualization, the size of each node reflects the number of participants who visited that node for this task. The colors within each node reflect the percentage of participants who continued down a correct path, an incorrect path, or nominated a "leaf" node as the correct answer. In the online version of the PieTree, hover information for each node gives you more details about what the participants did at that node.

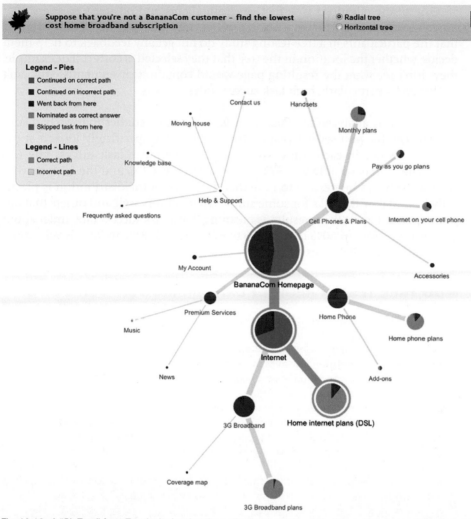

Fig. 10.10 A "PieTree" from TreeJack showing the paths that participants took in performing a single task, in this case indicating where they would expect to find information about the lowest cost home internet plans. Green highlights the correct path, starting from the center.

SOME TREE-TESTING TOOLS

The following are some of the tree-testing tools that we're aware of:

- C-Inspector (http://www.c-inspector.com)
- Optimal Workshop's TreeJack (http://www.optimalworkshop.com/treejack.htm)
- UserZoom Tree Testing (http://www.userzoom.com/products/tree-testing)

One of the questions we often get from clients and business partners after a tree-testing study is "What's a good overall task success rate?" Keep in mind that the participants in a tree-testing study do not get any feedback to help them decide whether the location in the tree that they selected is correct. For example, they don't see what the resulting page would contain. Consequently, you can't really expect particularly high task success rates.

We recently analyzed the data from 98 tree-testing studies that we had conducted over the past several years using TreeJack. We specifically looked at the task success rate in each study. We found that the mean task success rate was 60%. The 25th percentile was 37%, the median was 62%, and the 75th percentile was 83%. It's interesting to note that the shape of the distribution is practically bimodal, with peaks for some studies that did very well and others that did poorly. We interpret these results as meaning that a task success rate under about 40% is poor, 40% to 60% is fair, 61% to 80% is good, 81% to 90% is very good, and greater than 90% is excellent.

DO TREE TESTS PREDICT PERFORMANCE ON A LIVE SITE?

Albert (2016) wanted to know how the state of a prototype predicted actual performance on a live (production) website. In the study, they gave participants one of five different types of prototypes based on the level of interactivity (from low to high) and visual treatment (from low to high). Participants were then given the same set of tasks for each prototype, with the goal being to find the correct page. Four different metrics were analyzed: success in finding the right page, time to complete the task, total number of clicks, and the number of unique pages. The results showed that tree tests were only fair predictors of performance on a live site, while design comps and high-fidelity prototypes were much better predictors of how participants would perform on a live site. Basically, as a prototype gets refined both visually and in terms of the interaction, the better sense you will have of how your users will perform on the live site. Another way to think about it is that if the results from your tree test aren't great–not to worry, it's not a strong predictor of where you will end up.

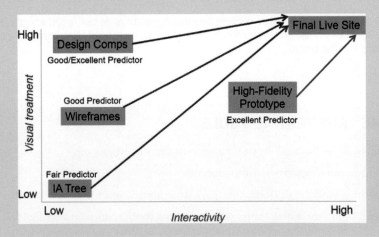

10.4 FIRST CLICK TESTING

First click testing, as its name implies, involves showing participants images of a web page or application and asking them where they would click to begin a given task. The image might be a screenshot from a live website, a new design concept, or a low-fidelity prototype (as is the case in Fig. 10.11). For example, consider the page shown in Fig. 10.11 from Chalkmark, the first click testing tool from Optimal Workshop (https://www.optimalworkshop.com/chalkmark/). Participants are given a task "try to buy a Bluetooth headset for your cell phone." The location of the first click is recorded, as is the time to click. Fig. 10.12 shows a typical visualization of a click test, highlighting the distribution of first clicks for a given task. It is helpful to see the distribution of clicks, particularly whether the distribution of clicks is fairly concentrated or more dispersed. A more dispersed set of first clicks would indicate greater confusion, as more links could potentially be potential choices to begin a task. In some sense, this is a visual version of a tree test, albeit only at the first level, because only the first click is captured.

The analysis of first click testing is straightforward. The primary metric that most researchers are typically focused on is success. In the context of a first click test, success is the percentage of participants who correctly clicked on the right link. In Fig. 10.13, the success rate was 58%. It is also useful to see the links that also received a substantial number of clicks (usually more than 5% or 10%); in this case, it was "monthly plans" (35%) and "which plan" (23%). The second metric that is of interest is the time to first click. In Fig. 10.13, the time to

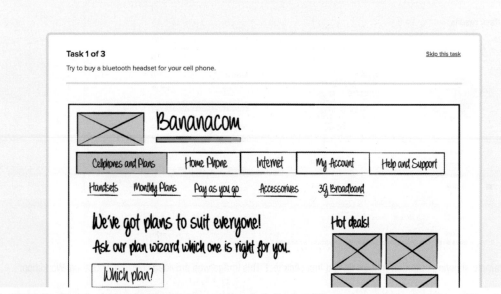

Fig. 10.11 An example of a low-fidelity prototype used in a first click test. This is a typical screen that the participant would see. This image was provided courtesy of Optimal Workshop.

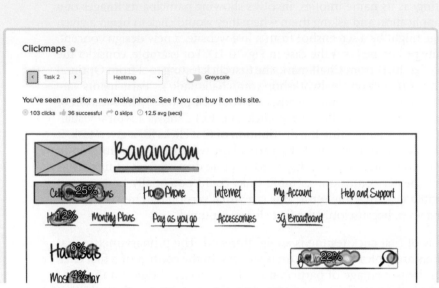

Fig. 10.12 An example showing the distribution of clicks from a first click test. This image was provided courtesy of Optimal Workshop.

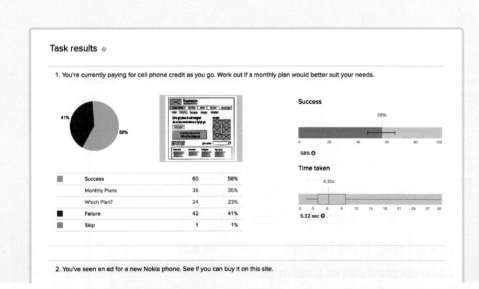

Fig. 10.13 An example showing common metrics from a first click test. This image was provided courtesy of Optimal Workshop.

first click was 6.32 seconds. Typically, a shorter time to click is an indication of greater confidence. Although not shown in Fig. 10.13, an interesting analysis is comparing the time taken for successful versus unsuccessful clicks. If there is no difference, this may suggest that the incorrect (unsuccessful) links are equally as attractive or enticing to the participants as the successful links. This is often the case when they are misleading, or there is a high degree of conceptual overlap.

SOME FIRST CLICK TOOLS

The following are some of the first click tools that we are aware of:

- Optimal Workshop's Chalkmark (https://www.optimalworkshop.com/chalkmark)

- UserZoom's Click and Timeout Testing (https://www.userzoom.com/user-research-methods/)

- UsabilityHub's First click Testing (https://usabilityhub.com/product/first click-tests)

You might wonder whether the first click that a user makes on a webpage or application really matters. After all, if they didn't start down the right path initially, they could always go back and start down another path. Bob Bailey and Carl Wolfson (2013) did an analysis of the data from 12 usability studies done on U.S. government websites. (The details of this study were also presented as Case Study 10.3 in the first edition of this book.) They found that if the user's first click for a task was correct, the probability of getting the task correct was 87%. If the first click was incorrect, the chance of eventually getting the task correct was only 46%. So participants were almost twice as likely to get the task correct if their first click was right. Andrew Mayfield (2015) did a follow-up analysis of millions of tree-testing responses in their TreeJack database. He found that if the first click was correct, the chance of getting the entire scenario correct was 70%. If the first click was incorrect, the chance of eventually getting the scenario correct was only 24%. So he found that participants were almost three times as likely to complete a task successfully if their first click was right. These results certainly seem to point to the importance of getting the first click right.

10.5 ACCESSIBILITY METRICS

Accessibility usually refers to how effectively someone with disabilities can use a particular system, application, or website (e.g., Cunningham, 2012; Henry, 2007; Kirkpatrick et al., 2006). We believe that accessibility is really just usability for a particular set of users. When viewed that way, it becomes obvious that most of the other metrics discussed in this book (e.g., task completion rates and times, and self-reported metrics) can be applied to measure the usability of any system for users with different types of disabilities. For example, Nielsen

(2001) reported four usability metrics from a study of 19 websites with three groups of users: blind users, who accessed the sites using screen-reading software; low-vision users, who accessed the sites using screen-magnifying software; and a control group who did not use assistive technology. Table 10.11 shows the results for the four metrics.

	Screen-Reader Users	Screen-Magnifier Users	Control Group (no disabilities)
Success rate	12.5%	21.4%	78.2%
Time on task	16:46	15:26	7:14
Errors	2.0	4.5	0.6
Subjective rating (1–7 scale)	2.5	2.9	4.6

Table 10.11 Data From Usability Tests of 19 Websites With Blind Users, Low-Vision Users, and Users With Normal Vision

Adapted from Nielsen (2001); used with permission.

These results point out that the usability of these sites is far worse for the screen-reader and screen-magnifier users than it is for the control users. But the other important message is that the best way to measure the usability of a system or website for users with disabilities is to actually test with representative users. Although that's a very desirable objective, most designers and developers don't have the resources to test with representative users from all the disability groups that might want to use their product. That's where accessibility guidelines can be helpful.

Perhaps the most widely recognized web accessibility guidelines are the Web Content Accessibility Guidelines (WCAG), Version 2.0, from the World-wide Web Consortium (W3C) (http://www.w3.org/TR/WCAG20/). These guidelines are divided into four major categories:

1. Perceivable
   a. Provide text alternatives for non-text content.
   b. Provide captions and other alternatives for multimedia.
   c. Create content that can be presented in different ways, including by assistive technologies, without losing meaning.
   d. Make it easier for users to see and hear content.
2. Operable
   a. Make all functionality available from a keyboard.
   b. Give users enough time to read and use the content.
   c. Do not use content that causes seizures.
   d. Help users navigate and find content.

3. Understandable
   a. Make text readable and understandable.
   b. Make content appear and operate in predictable ways.
   c. Help users avoid and correct mistakes.
4. Robust
   a. Maximize compatibility with current and future user tools.

One way of quantifying how well a website meets these criteria is to assess how many of the pages in the site fail one or more of each of these guidelines.

Some automated tools can check for certain obvious violations of these guidelines (e.g., missing "Alt" text on image). Although the errors they detect are generally true errors, they also commonly miss many errors. Many of the items that the automated tools flag as *warnings* may in fact be true errors, but it takes a human to find out. For example, if an image on a web page has null Alt text defined (ALT=""), that may be an error if the image is informational, or it may be correct if the image is purely decorative. The bottom line is that the only really accurate way to determine whether accessibility guidelines have been met is by manual inspection of the code or by evaluation using a screen-reader or other appropriate assistive technology. Often, both techniques are needed.

AUTOMATED ACCESSIBILITY-CHECKING TOOLS

Some of the tools available for checking web pages for accessibility errors include the following:

- Compliance Sheriff® Cynthia Says™ Portal (http://www.cynthiasays.com/)

- WebAIM's WAVE tool (http://wave.webaim.org/)

- University of Toronto Web Accessibility Checker (http://achecker.ca/checker/)

- TAW Web Accessibility Test (http://www.webdevstuff.com/103/taw-web-accessibility-test.html)

- Several accessibility checkers are also available as extensions to Google's Chrome browser, such as:
  - Siteimprove Accessibility Checker
  - WAVE Evaluation Tool
  - axe - Web Accessibility Testing

Once you've analyzed the pages against the accessibility criteria, one way of summarizing the results is to count the number of pages with errors. For example, Fig. 10.14 shows the results of a hypothetical analysis of a website against the WCAG guidelines. This shows that only 10% of the pages have no errors, whereas 25% have more than 10 errors. The majority (53%) have 3 to 10 errors.

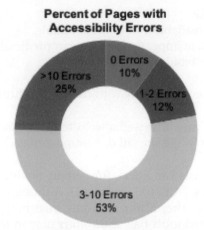

Percent of Pages with Accessibility Errors

0 Errors 10%

>10 Errors 25%

1-2 Errors 12%

3-10 Errors 53%

Fig. 10.14 Results of analysis of a website against the WCAG guidelines.

In the United States, another important set of accessibility guidelines is the so-called Section 508 guidelines, or, technically, the 1998 Amendment to Section 508 of the 1973 Rehabilitation Act (Section 508, 1998; also see Mueller, 2003). This law requires federal agencies to make their electronic and information technology accessible to people with disabilities, including their websites. The law applies to all federal agencies when they develop, procure, maintain, or use electronic and information technology. An updated set of Section 508 requirements became effective in 2018.

10.6 RETURN-ON-INVESTMENT METRICS

A book about usability metrics wouldn't be complete without at least some discussion of ROI, since the usability metrics discussed in this book often play a key role in calculating ROI. But because entire books have been written on this topic (Bias & Mayhew, 2005; Mayhew & Bias, 1994; Nielsen Norman Group, 2009), our purpose is just to introduce some of the concepts.

The basic idea behind usability ROI, of course, is to calculate the financial benefit attributable to usability enhancements for a product, system, or website. These financial benefits are usually derived from such measures as increased sales, increased productivity, or decreased support costs that can be attributed to the usability improvements. The key is to identify the cost associated with the usability improvements and then compare those to the financial benefits.

As Bias & Mayhew (2005) summarize, there are two major categories of ROI, with different types of returns for each:

- Internal ROI:
  - Increased user productivity
  - Decreased user errors

- Decreased training costs
- Savings gained from making changes earlier in the design life cycle
- Decreased user support

- External ROI
  - Increased sales
  - Decreased customer support costs
  - Savings gained from making changes earlier in the design life cycle
  - Reduced cost of providing training (if training is offered by the company)

To illustrate some of the issues and techniques in calculating usability ROI, we look at an example from Diamond Bullet Design (Withrow, Brinck, & Speredelozzi, 2000). This case study involved the redesign of a state government web portal. They conducted usability tests of the original website and a new version that had been created using a user-centered design process. The same 10 tasks were used to test both versions. A few of them were as follows:

- You are interested in renewing a {state} driver's license online.
- How do nurses get licensed in {the state}?
- To assist in traveling, you want to find a map of {state} highways.
- What 4-year colleges are located in {the state}?
- What is the state bird of {the state}?

In addition, 20 residents of the state participated in the study, which was a between-subjects design (with half using the original site and half using the new). The data collected included task times, task completion rates, and various self-reported metrics. They found that the task times were significantly shorter for the redesigned site, and the task completion rates were significantly higher. Fig. 10.15 shows the task times for the original and redesigned sites. Table 10.12 shows a summary of the task completion rates and task times for both versions of the site, as well as an overall measure of efficiency for both (task completion rate per unit time).

So far, everything is straightforward and simply illustrates some of the usability metrics we've discussed in this book. But here's where it gets interesting. To begin calculating ROI from the changes made to the site, Withrow et al. made the following assumptions and calculations related to the *time savings*:

- Of the 2.7 million residents of the state, we might "conservatively estimate" a quarter of them use the website at least once per month.
- If each of them saved 79 seconds (as was the average task savings in this study), then about 53 million seconds (14,800 hours) are saved per year.
- Converting this to labor costs, we find 370 person-weeks (at 40 hours per week) or 7 person-years are saved per month. Eighty-four person-years are saved each year.
- On average, a citizen in the target state had an annual salary of $14,700.
- This leads to a yearly benefit of *$1.2 million* based only on the time savings.

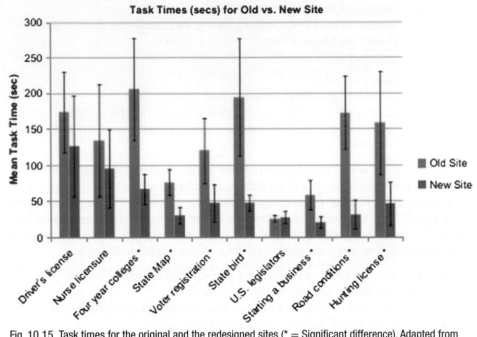

Fig. 10.15 Task times for the original and the redesigned sites (* = Significant difference). Adapted from Withrow et al. (2000); used with permission.

	Original Site	Redesigned Site
Average task completion rate (%)	72	95
Average task time (min)	2.2	0.84
Average efficiency (%)	33	113

Table 10.12 Summary of the Task Performance Data
Adapted from Withrow et al. (2000); used with permission.
Average efficiency is the task completion rate per unit of time (task completion rate/task time).

Notice that this chain of reasoning had to start with a pretty big assumption: that a quarter of the residents of the state use the site at least once per month. So that assumption, which all the rest of the calculations hinge upon, is certainly up for debate. A better way of generating an appropriate value with which to start these calculations would have been from actual usage data for the current site.

They went on to calculate an increase in revenue due to the increased task completion rate for the new site:

1. The task failure rate of the old portal was found to be 28%, whereas the new site was 5%.
2. We might assume that 100,000 users would pay a service fee on the order of $2 per transaction at least once a month.

3. Then the 23% of them who are succeeding on the new site, whereas formerly they were failing, are generating an additional $552,000 in revenue per year.

Again, a critical assumption had to be made early in the chain of reasoning: that 100,000 users would pay a service fee to the state on the order of $2 per transaction at least once a month. A better way of doing this calculation would have been to use data from the live site specifically about the frequency of fee-generating transactions (and the amounts of the fees). These could then have been adjusted to reflect the higher task completion rate for the redesigned site. If you agree with their assumptions, these two sets of calculations yield a total of about $1.75 million annually, either in time savings to the residents or increased fees to the state. Although Withrow et al. don't specify how much was spent on the redesign of this portal, we can safely assume it was dramatically less than $1.75 million!

This example points out some of the challenges associated with calculating usability ROI. In general, there are two major classes of situations where you might try to calculate a usability ROI: when the users of the product are *employees* of your company, and when the users of the product are your *customers*. It tends to be much more straightforward to calculate ROI when the users are employees of your company. You generally know how much employees are paid, so time savings in completing certain tasks (especially highly repetitive ones) can be directly translated to dollar savings. In addition, you may know the costs involved in correcting certain types of errors, so reductions in the rates of those errors could also be translated to dollar savings.

Calculating usability ROI tends to be much more challenging when the users are your customers (or really anyone not an employee of your company). Your benefits are much more indirect. For example, it might not make any real difference to your bottom line that your customers can complete a key income-generating transaction in 30% less time than before. It probably does *not* mean that they will then be performing significantly more of those transactions. But what it *might* mean is that over time those customers will remain your customers and others will become your customers who might not have otherwise (assuming the transaction times are significantly shorter than they are for your competitors), thus increasing revenue. A similar argument can be made for increased task completion rates.

SOME ROI CASE STUDIES

A variety of other case studies of usability ROI are available. Here's just a sampling:

- The Nielsen Norman Group did a detailed analysis of 72 usability ROI case studies and found increases in key performance indicators of 0% to over 6,000%. The case studies covered a wide variety of websites, including Macy's, Bell Canada, New York

Life, OpenTable, a government agency, and a community college (Nielsen, Berger, Gilutz, & Whitenton, 2008).

- A redesign of the BreastCancer.org discussion forums resulted in a 117% increase in site visitors, 41% increase in new memberships, 53% reduction in time taken to register, and 69% reduction in monthly help desk costs (Foraker, 2010).

- After a redesign of Move.com's home search and contact an agent features, users' ability to find a home increased from 62% to 98%, sales lead generation to real estate agents increased over 150%, and their ability to sell advertising space on the site improved significantly (Vividence, 2001).

- A user-centered redesign of Staples.com resulted in 67% more repeat customers and a 10% improvement in ratings of ease of placing orders, overall purchasing experience, and the likelihood of purchasing again. Online revenues went from $94 million in 1999 to $512 million after implementation of the new site (Human Factors International, 2002).

- A major computer company spent $20,700 on usability work to improve the sign-on procedure in a system used by several thousand employees. The resulting productivity improvement saved the company $41,700 the first day the system was used (Bias & Mayhew, 1994).

- After a redesign of the navigational structure of Dell.com, revenue from online purchases went from $1 million per day in September 1998 to $34 million per day in March 2000 (Human Factors International, 2002).

- A user-centered redesign of a software product increased revenue by more than 80% over the initial release of the product (built without usability work). The revenues of the new system were 60% higher than projected, and many customers cited usability as a key factor in deciding to buy the new system (Wixon & Jones, 1992, as reported in Bias & Mayhew, 1994).

10.7 SUMMARY

Here are some of the key takeaways from this chapter:

1. If you're dealing with a live website, you should be studying what your users are doing on the site as much as you can. Don't just look at page views. Look at click-through rates and drop-off rates. Whenever possible, conduct live A/B tests to compare alternative designs (typically with small differences). Use appropriate statistics (e.g., chi-square) to make sure any differences you're seeing are statistically significant.

2. Card-sorting can be immensely helpful in learning how to organize some information or an entire website. Consider starting with an open sort and then following up with one or more closed sorts. Hierarchical cluster analysis and multidimensional scaling (MDS) are useful techniques for summarizing and presenting the results. Closed card-sorts can be used to compare how well different information architectures work for the users.

3. Tree-testing can also be a useful way to test a candidate organization. In this type of study, users get to interact with an actual menu system, navigating freely in the hierarchy. Measures of task success and directness can help you compare the effectiveness of different hierarchies.

4. First click testing is a good way to determine whether the design of a webpage helps users to decide where they would start to perform various tasks. There's evidence suggesting that users are two to three times more likely to be successful with a task if their first click is correct.

5. Accessibility is just usability for a particular group of users. Whenever possible, try to include older users and users with various kinds of disabilities in your usability tests. In addition, you should evaluate your product against published accessibility guidelines or standards, such as WCAG or Section 508.

6. Calculating ROI data for usability work is sometimes challenging, but it usually can be done. If the users are employees of your company, it's generally easy to convert metrics like reductions in task times into dollar savings. If the users are external customers, you generally have to extrapolate metrics like improved task completion rates or improved overall satisfaction to decreases in support calls, increases in sales, or increases in customer loyalty.

CONTENTS

Measuring the User Experience. DOI: http://dx.doi.org/10.1016/B978-0-12-818080-8.00011-X

Chapter 11 presents five case studies, all focusing on a unique aspect of UX measurement. In the first case study, Zach Schendel from Netflix demonstrates how eye tracking metrics can be used to drive design decisions. The second case study by Sandra Teare, Linda Borghesani, and Stuart Martinez from Endurance International Group presents a framework for competitive benchmarking. The third case study by JD Buckley at JD Usability shares a study on the UX profit chain model. The fourth case study by Kuldeep Kalkar from UserZoom walks us through a competitive benchmarking study of four insurance websites based on their unique UX metric. The final case study by Eric Benoit, Sharon Lee, and Juhan Sonin at GoInvo explains how to use UX metrics as part of the design of a mobile application.

11.1 THINKING FAST AND SLOW IN THE NETFLIX TV USER INTERFACE

By Zach Schendel, Product Consumer Insights, Netflix

11.1.1 Background

Netflix is a global subscription streaming video service that allows members to find and watch a wide variety of TV series, documentaries, and feature films across genres and languages anytime, anywhere, on any internet-connected screen. Regardless of location, time of day, or device they are watching on, there are two primary situations that Netflix members typically find themselves in when they first launch the experience:

1. Destination:

The member knows exactly what they are going to watch. They want Netflix to serve up this content as quickly as possible. Netflix helps to reduce friction by saving bookmarks, surfacing the Continue Watching row, or using lexical matches in Search.

2. Discovery:

The member has some-to-no idea of what they are going to watch. They want to be inspired to try new content. Netflix tries to help by emphasizing the newest and most buzzworthy shows, notifying a member that something they had been wanting to watch has just arrived, or by recommending X "Because you watched...Y".

While the Netflix Product team works to satisfy both contexts of use, discovery remains the largest innovation opportunity by far. According to our members, this process can be time consuming and challenging—"I don't know what to watch", "I haven't heard of these movies," "Why are you recommending THIS to ME?"

The purpose of this foundational study was to inspire innovations that could significantly improve the content discovery user experience on Netflix. This research specifically focuses on *evidence*—the information Netflix provides to help members make a watch/no-watch decision (e.g., artwork, synopsis, trailer, etc.). The team sought to clarify the processes members use to make content decisions in ambiguity: how do members behave when they are attempting to discover what to watch, what evidence do they pay attention to, and what evidence is differentially valuable? The insights have resulted in multiple innovations, including evidence personalization, which will be specifically discussed below.

11.1.2 Methods

The team chose to triangulate insights using two methods: in-depth interviews (qualitative) and eye tracking (quantitative). These methods provide implicit and explicit signals that can be used in tandem to model the content discovery process.

PARTICIPANT INTERVIEWS

Content consumption patterns tend to evolve with product exposure, so three groups of participants were recruited with different Netflix tenures: Never members, Early members, and Tenured members. Twenty-five adults (18+) from the Richmond, VA area who had never been members or used Netflix before were recruited (Never members). They were signed up for a free trial and then were exposed to the Netflix TV UI for the first time. They all had access to Netflix at home after they left the research facility, and then most of them returned 45 days later (Early members) to repeat the study. We also recruited 25 adults who had been Netflix members for at least six months. All participants owned and were familiar with a PlayStation 3 (PS3) and had used the controller. They were paid for participation in the study.

MATERIALS

The TV user interface (seen in Fig. 11.1, from 2014) was chosen for this research as it was the only Netflix UI where the majority of evidence was available on the surface—members weren't required to click to gain access.

A living room setup was created in a research facility. A couch was pointed at a large, mounted flat-screen high-definition TV (HDTV). An internet-connected PS3 was used to display Netflix onto the HDTV through an HDMI cable. A game controller was used to navigate.

PROCEDURE

Each participant completed an hour-long in-depth interview (IDI). After a brief introduction and warm-up, participants were asked to imagine that they were at

Fig. 11.1 The Netflix TV UI in 2014 (the large top image rotated through three images).

home in their own living room. They were then given 5 to 10 discovery scenarios (examples below), and their goal was to find something to watch on Netflix in each scenario. They could take as much or little time as they needed. Each scenario ended when the participant pressed play. The researcher simply observed and noted behaviors (silent discovery).

The same procedure was then repeated with 5 to 10 *additional* scenarios. This time, each participant narrated their behaviors out loud: what they were doing, what they were pausing on, what they were reading, etc. No detail was too inconsequential. The researcher asked questions as they went along: why did you pause there, why did you reject that title? The scenario order was randomized, and the number of scenarios depended on browse time.

EXAMPLE SCENARIOS

- You are alone, choose something you have never heard of that looks good.
- You want to catch up on something your friends are all talking about.

EYE-TRACKING

Forty-three participants from the San Jose, CA area completed a very similar study using a PS4 in a research facility. All were adult (18+) Netflix members that had recently watched Netflix through their PS4 on TV. Portions of the IDI's silent discovery procedure were repeated. The primary difference between the IDIs and this study was that each participant wore Tobii 2 eye-tracking glasses while they were performing the tasks and that the participants completed fewer tasks. They were paid for participation in the study.

11.1.3 Results

Participants navigated quickly through the UI. During this navigation, they were consistently referencing the artwork found in the lower third of the screen (the "boxart"). They specifically talked about what the boxart was conveying: a genre, tone, or mood; an actor; something familiar they had seen before or were planning to watch in the future; or even a collection of artwork that felt like it matched a cohesive theme (e.g., a row of adult animation is bright and colorful).

Participants tended to pause when something familiar or trustworthy caught their eye - "I have seen two of these movies in this row", "I like everything she is in", "This is my favorite genre." They also tended to pause when they landed on something they wanted to dig deeper into. In these moments the top two-thirds of the screen became viable, they referenced specific words in the synopsis or actors they saw in the larger imagery. They rarely mentioned the rest of the evidence (e.g., stars, maturity ratings).

The IDIs led to hypotheses about the process members used to make watch/no-watch decisions. The proposed process is illustrated in Fig. 11.2.

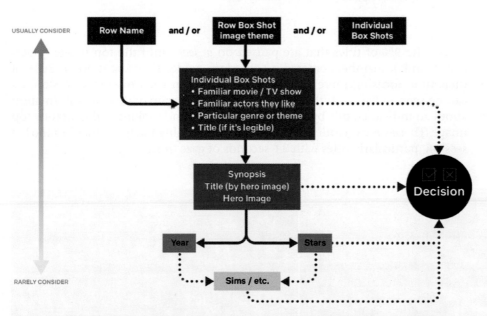

Fig. 11.2 A qualitative model of evidence hierarchy in discovery moments Netflix (2014). (The Netflix TV UI is much different now than it was in 2014. For example, video trailers play automatically at the top of the screen, there is a navigation menu on the left to surface search and other functions, thumbs have replaced stars, and not all rows/boxarts are the same size and shape, to name a few. The insights here are historically accurate, but do not all apply to the latest UI.)

Eye tracking was used to test these hypotheses. The results brought quantitative depth to our burgeoning understanding of the content discovery process. First, members spent about 70% of their gaze time rapidly scrolling and "judging books by their covers." Ninety-one percent of rejection decisions were made in less than 1 second based entirely on a quick glance at the boxart. As seen in Fig. 11.3, about 75% of gaze time is spent looking at boxart. In many instances, they were scrolling so quickly that the evidence loading at the top of the page was not loaded fast enough to display. For this part of the discovery process, the rest of the UI, including text evidence, row names, and other images, were mostly irrelevant.

Fig. 11.3 Proportion of gaze time during content discovery on Netflix, Thinking Fast.

For the 9% of titles that are paused on *at least* until the top image rotates (~2 seconds), members entered a secondary mode. They spent about 30% of their time focusing more in-depth at ~5 titles on each discovery session. As can be seen in Fig. 11.4, they dive more deeply to gain additional information about an individual title by reading text evidence and looking at the rotating top image. These were the titles that members were highly likely to "play" in the lab session, particularly titles with 3+ seconds of gaze time.

Fig. 11.4 Proportion of gaze time during content discovery on Netflix, Thinking Slow.

11.1.4 Discussion

Combining the qualitative evidence hierarchy model with the gaze measures obtained through eye tracking, it was concluded that different areas of the TV UI were serving two distinct user decision processes that mirror those discussed in *Thinking Fast and Thinking Slow* (Kahneman, 2011).

THINKING FAST

System 1 or "Thinking Fast" decisions are immediate, lazy, gut reactions. These decisions mirror the process members used when quickly considering the boxart. The boxart quickly conveys high-level critical information through images rather than text. It is possible from a glance to at least guess what the genre and tone are and sometimes who is in the title. System 1 relies more on "associative activation," where quick, tight associations form between an image (man + woman smiling at each other) and a concept (romance). However, System 1 is prone to judgment errors. A boxart for a title you *would* have loved is ignored when it doesn't quickly convey critical information. Another one might look like a period drama (which you love), but it is actually an irreverent historical comedy (which you hate). As discussed below, the primary impact of this research was to highlight just how critical it was to optimize artwork chosen for boxart.

THINKING SLOW

On Netflix, System 1 decisions act as the primary gateway to System 2 evaluation. System 2 or "Thinking Slow" decisions are very different than System 1. They take time. They are thoughtful, contemplative, and measured. They can also act as a check and balance for error-prone System 1 evaluations. On Netflix, members were using the synopsis, star rating, and other text information on the top two-thirds of the screen as a secondary filter for titles that made it past the System 1 judgment from the boxart. For example, they could look up and read more in-depth about the "period drama" to discover it's actually a comedy. They could also look up to confirm from other text data that the image is, in fact, Keanu Reeves. Since there were so few titles that made it to this stage, the conclusion from the research was that evidence above the boxart was a secondary place for innovation after boxarts were optimized.

11.1.5 Impact

Image personalization is the latest innovation Netflix has used to leverage the associative activation between System 1 canvases like the boxart and important evidence like genre and cast, etc. As a result of a series of A/B tests (Chandrashekar, 2016), Netflix no longer assumes that a single image is enough to facilitate a fruitful discovery process (Nelson, 2016). Multiple images are created for each title to help all global members make smart, fast watch/no-watch decisions. As seen in Fig. 11.5, impactful image sets emphasize variety—variety in genre, cast, tone, and style. *Stranger Things* is fantasy, sci-fi, and horror, there are strong relationships formed between the kids, and it's set in the 1980s.

Fig. 11.5 Example boxart options for *Stranger Things*.

A personalized image is then chosen from these sets for each member—they are algorithmically matched with the image that is most likely to lead to a *quality* play based on their own view history (Chandrashekar et al., 2017). For example, someone who watches romance movies might receive the *Good Will Hunting* image in Fig. 11.6 that emphasizes the romantic plot with Matt Damon and Minnie Driver versus a member who watches more comedies seeing Robin Williams. The algorithms seek to remove misrepresentative images that drive up click bait or title abandonment. The goal is to give members enough evidence in the image so that their decision will result in a clear *hit* or *correct rejection*. The subsequent reduction in *misses* and *false positives* will make the discovery process more efficient and enjoyable.

Fig. 11.6 Examples of how different view histories might result in boxart personalization.

BIOGRAPHY

Zach Schendel is the Director of UX Research at Netflix. His team of consumer insights experts seeks to give our members a front-row seat at the Netflix Product Innovation table. We bring joy to our members through tactical and strategic UI, feature, and algorithmic optimization, helping 100+ million global users of all ages find something great to watch. Previously, after receiving his PhD in Cognitive Psychology from the Ohio State University, Zach led insights work across all five senses for other billion-dollar brands at Unilever and Altria.

11.2 PARTICIPATE/COMPETE/WIN (PCW) FRAMEWORK: EVALUATING PRODUCTS AND FEATURES IN THE MARKETPLACE

By Sandra Teare, Linda Borghesani, and Stuart Martinez, Constant Contact, Inc.

11.2.1 Introduction

In 2018, senior leadership at our company (Sue Mildrum, Damon Dimmick, Sherrie Fernandez) came up with the idea of assigning each new product development initiative with a goal to either simply Participate in the marketplace, to be Competitive, or to Win (PCW) (See Figure 11.7). By designating each initiative with a goal, they hoped to get better team alignment in terms of communication to better understand the feature set and robustness required and the level of resources and time that should be expended on each initiative. Our UX Research challenge was to define and measure the initiatives.

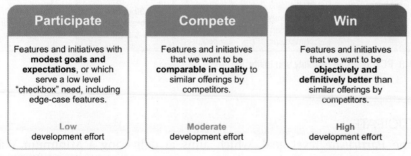

Participate	Compete	Win
Features and initiatives with **modest goals and expectations**, or which serve a low level "checkbox" need, including edge-case features.	Features and initiatives that we want to be **comparable in quality** to similar offerings by competitors.	Features and initiatives that we want to be **objectively and definitively better** than similar offerings by competitors.
Low development effort	Moderate development effort	High development effort

Fig. 11.7 PCW definition.

As part of our process, each project team is required to write a Discovery brief for their initiative that outlines the business and user goals and defines success metrics, many of which are business metrics that are not able to be measured until after the feature has been released. The UX Research team was asked to outline objective criteria that could be used to give teams an *early* idea of whether they were getting close to achieving their PCW goals. We defined our criteria to include both usability and utility metrics, since user experience and feature set differentiation are both important to the competitiveness of a product (Porter, 1985).

In 2018, we performed feature analyses and summative testing on various initiatives, providing both quantitative and qualitative feedback that helped the project teams decide whether and where their initiatives needed further improvements. Our PCW testing was meant to be one of many KPIs but was certainly the one we could measure the earliest in the development process.

11.2.2 Outlining Objective Criteria

In outlining and defining objective goals, we referenced some industry experts to determine our desired success rates and sample sizes (See Figure 11.8).

PCW Quality Goal	Usability			Utility
	Task Success	**Customer Ratings**	**# of Participants/ Prototypes**	**Functionality**
Participate (Minimum Viable Product)	Minimum 80% success rate*	Average 3 out of 5 or better	**10 users/** 1 prototype	Has minimal feature set
Compete (all Participate criteria plus)	~ equal to competitor	~ equal to competitor	**15-20 users/** 2 prototypes/sites (Ours & Competitor)	Feature set comparable to competitors
Win	Statistically significantly better than competitor	Statistically significantly better than competitor	**30 users/** 2 prototypes/sites (Ours & Competitor)	Feature set includes more or better features

Fig. 11.8 PCW goals for usability and utility.

PARTICIPATE

For the *Participate* level goal, which aims at delivering a Minimum Viable Product (MVP), we wanted to make sure there were no critical usability issues, so we chose a success rate of 80%, which is roughly equivalent to the industry average of 78% found by MeasuringU (Sauro, 2011). We also wanted to aim for at least an average (three out of five) customer ratings for usability, trust, and learnability. By testing with 10 participants, we can uncover 97% of moderately frequent problems (those with a likelihood of detection of 30%) and 63% of low-frequency problems (those with a likelihood of detection of 10%) as well as provide a baseline Task Success rate (Sauro, 2010).

COMPETE

For the *Compete* level criteria, we want to achieve roughly equivalent task success and customer ratings as our competition. By testing specific features against competitive products, we can better understand our strengths and weaknesses to help identify what these competitive tools do well to help inform our evolving design. We suggested running about 15-20 participants if running a within-subjects design and slightly more, ~25 participants, for a between-subjects design. Screening of participants is very important for the comparison to be valid. When running the comparison, it is important for participants to either be equally unfamiliar with the feature in both products or have comparable experiences in each product with the feature being evaluated.

WIN

For the *Win* level criteria, we want to aim for a meaningful and statistically significant difference in both task success and customer ratings. To confirm that the selected features provide more value than the competitor, we chose a 30% difference as being meaningful and detectable. In order to be able to detect a difference of that magnitude, we need to run about 30 people in a within-subjects design or 64 people in a between-subjects design (Sauro, 2015). In practice, due to constraints, knowledge of the product is important, so we often end up running between-subjects rather than within-subject studies.

11.2.3 Feature Analysis

GENERATING THE FEATURE LIST

We work with the product and UX teams to identify direct and indirect competitors to start generating the competitive feature set for each initiative (See Figure 11.9). In addition, we collect important features by exploring competitor websites, reviews/blogs, third-party comparisons, and marketing materials and performing product evaluations.

CALCULATING A FEATURE IMPORTANCE SCORE

Having a larger number of features does not necessarily make a product better or more useful for customers. Using the list of features from the feature analysis, we then conduct a Feature Prioritization study, identifying which features are most important to both our customers and prospective customers. Using Optimal Sort, participants sort features into one of three buckets: "Must have," "Nice to have," and "Not important" to help us focus on features that are most valuable/important to our customers (See Figure 11.10).

From this data, we calculate a Feature Importance Score using the following formula (see Figure 11.11):

$$\text{Feature importance score} = (3 \times \text{Must Have}) + (2 \times \text{Nice2 Have}) - (1 \times \text{Not Important})$$

Feature	Major Competitors											
	A	**B**	**C**	**D**	**E**	**F**	**G**	**H**	**I**	**J**	**K**	**L**
Category 1												
Feature 1	Y	Y	Y	Y	Y	Y	Y	Y	Y	Y	Y	Y
Feature 2	N	N	Y	N	N	N	?	N	Y	N	Y	N
Feature 3	N	N	N	N	N	N	Y	N	N	N	N	N
Category 2												
Feature 4 (# supported)	Y(15)	Y(15)	Y	Y (10+)	Y (10+)	Y	Y	Y (10)	Y (30)	Y (5)	Y (unl)	Y
Feature 5	N	N	N	N	N	Y	N	N	N	N	Y	N
Category 3												
Feature 6	Y	Y	Y	Y	Y	Y	Y	Y	Y	Y	Y	Y
Feature 7	N	N	Y	N	N	N	Y	?	N	?	?	N
Feature 8	N	N	N	N	N	N	N	N	N	N	Y	Y
Feature 9	Y	Y	?	Y	Y	N	?	N	N	Y	Y	Y
Feature 10	Y	Y	Y	Y	Y	Y	Y	Y	Y	Y	Y	Y
Feature 11	Y	Y	Y	Y	Y	Y	Y	Y	Y	Y	Y	Y

Fig. 11.9 Feature audit by category and competitor.

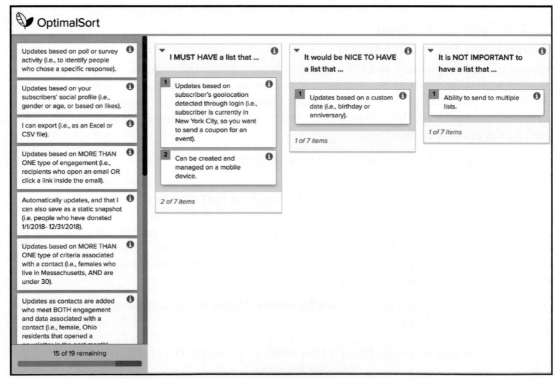

Fig. 11.10 Feature prioritization card sort. (Taken from OptimalSort tool.)

Fig. 11.11 Feature importance score = (3 × MustHave) + (2 × Nice2Have) − (1 × NotImportant)

This weighs the frequencies of placement in the "Must Have" and "Nice to Have" buckets more heavily than that for the "Not Important" bucket. We then use the most important features as the tasks in our summative usability testing.

CHOOSING A COMPETITIVE PRODUCT

After identifying the desirable features and calculating the Feature Importance Score, the product team and UX Research team work together to collaboratively identify one main competitor to use for feature testing. Once a top competitor is selected, a head-to-head comparison can be made.

CALCULATING A FEATURE AVAILABILITY/VALUE SCORE

Next, we calculate a "Feature availability score" by adding the importance scores of the most important features that we identified through the feature prioritization step (e.g., for Constant Contact.

$$\text{Feature availability score} = \text{Feature 2 importance} + \text{Feature 3 importance} + \text{Feature 4 importance} + \text{Feature 5 importance})$$

This gives us an idea of how close the competitors are in terms of the feature set they offer. This kind of calculation allows for a product with a smaller set of high-value features to get a higher feature availability/value score than one with a larger set of lower-value features. This calculation shows us how our feature set stacks up to those of our competitors (See Figure 11.12).

11.2.4 "PCW" (Summative) Usability Testing

As discussed above, the feature prioritization study helps to identify which features are of greatest value to users. From this list, we then create relevant tasks for the summative test where participants are asked to use the most valued/important features. In the summative tests, we measure both Task Success rates, and collect customer Ease of Use ratings (see Figure 11.13). In addition, we collect qualitative feedback that helps inform the project teams about any UX improvements identified as a result of usability

Must Have Features (in user priority order)	Feature Importance	⊙ Constant Contact	*Competitor*
Feature 1	76	✖	✔
Feature 2	64	✔	✖
Feature 3	63	✔	✔
Feature 4	63	✔	✔
Features 5	60	✔	✖
Feature Availability / Value Score		**250**	**202**

Fig. 11.12 Calculating a feature availability score.

Feature/Task	⊙ Constant Contact		*Competitor*	
	Prototype Task Success	**Ease of Use Rating**	**Live Site Success Rate**	**Ease of Use Rating**
Task 1	--		65%	4.0
Task 2	59%	3.4	--	
Task 3	30%	4.1	48%	3.7
Task 4	67%	3.3	57%	2.9
Task 5	64%	4.1	--	
Overall Task Success (average)	55%	3.7	57%	3.5

Fig. 11.13 Comparing task success and ease of use ratings.

testing. Note that in some cases, not all tasks are tested on both products, as we only test the features that are available in each product. By including high-value features that we do not have in our product, we are able to learn from the implementation of our competitors. In our case, we tested a high-fidelity prototype against our competitor's live site in order to get feedback early.

OVERALL VERSUS WORKFLOW SUCCESS RATE

In the case of a workflow, where each step depends on the success of the previous step, the workflow success rate can only be as high as the success rate on the least successful step.

In real life, users would not be able to get beyond any task/step in the flow that they fail. So, in addition to reporting an average Task Success, we also report a "Workflow" Task Success rate (See Figure 11.14).

Workflow Tasks	Constant Contact Prototype Success Rate	Competitor Success Rate
Task/Step 1	76%	70%
Task/Step 2	59%	52%
Task/Step 3	47%	30%
Task/Step 4	57%	67%
Task/Step 5	64%	47%
Workflow Task Success	**47%**	**30%**

Fig. 11.14 Comparing workflow success.

PROTOTYPE VERSUS LIVE SITE TESTING

Until our product is released, we have been comparing our prototype to a competitor's live site. To understand any artifact effects of testing using a prototype versus a live site, we conducted a follow-up live site study testing the same tasks used on the prototype once our feature was released. Design improvements made as a result of our original prototype testing and the live site test validated that task success rates were higher than when we tested the prototype. This is evidence that our prototype testing is at least directionally predictive of success rates upon release.

OVERALL PROGRAM SUCCESS

In 2018, we ran 17 "PCW" tests (only a small fraction of all the UX research the team did during the year). Several initiatives met their stated PCW goals in the first round of testing. Some initiatives failed to meet their PCW goals, mostly projects where we were integrating our workflows with third party tools over which we did not have control. Several projects also improved their task success rates over iterations of design and testing. Early rounds of PCW testing provided the team with qualitative feedback that helped inform design improvements, resulting in better task success rates in later iterations (a UXR dream come true).

The PCW framework was successful in spurring conversations among senior leaders about the level of robustness each initiative was aiming to achieve. By outlining consistent measurable objective criteria and providing summative usability testing, we allowed product management and senior leadership an early idea and accountability on whether they were getting close to achieving their PCW goals. The PCW process was also complementary to our existing UX research and did not interfere with the work we were already doing to provide early feedback and usability improvements. Additionally, it helped increase accountability, improve our product development process, and motivate teams. By performing the initial feature analysis and prioritization we identified high value product features to help drive product design.

BIOGRAPHIES

Sandra Teare, Linda Borghesani, and Stuart Martinez worked together as UX Researchers at Constant Contact, a digital marketing company. The products are aimed at helping small businesses work smarter for their customers throughout their business lifecycle.

Sandra manages the UX Research group whose primary goal is to understand small business users' needs and provide data and insights to help product teams move forward quickly and confidently. She brings many years of experience from several industries, including telecom, finance, job search, and healthcare.

Linda is a Senior UX Researcher and strategist who also teaches at Tufts University. She strongly believes that if you know your audience, you can use purposeful design to ensure products are both usable and enjoyable to use.

Stuart is a passionate UX Researcher and design thinking facilitator whose aim is to learn about users and advocate for them at every step of the design process. He is currently working as a UX Researcher at Chewy.

11.3 ENTERPRISE UX CASE STUDY: UNCOVERING THE "UX REVENUE CHAIN"

By JD Buckley, *JD Usability*

11.3.1 Introduction

A few years ago, a large established enterprise Human Capital Management followed the trend set by several other large companies and made the decision to build their internal user experience design expertise. While executives had identified human-centered design as essential to the company's future success, many were unfamiliar with the design process. They were even less familiar with how best to quantify the return on investing in design and the efforts of design teams. This case study details the efforts of a Fortune 500 UX design and research team tasked with not only proving the team's value but also making a quantifiable connection between the human-centered design process and the company's bottom line.

A significant redesign initiative provided a significant opportunity for our small enterprise UX team, whose primary focus was on human capital management compliance products, meaning, for example, making sure companies pay the appropriate taxes on their employees' wages or can deduct garnished wages for employees' paychecks accurately. Our intention was to develop a UX measurement plan. Our team's ultimate goal was to make the quantitative connection between the quality of user experience and company performance metrics. In order to achieve this goal, we laid out the following objectives:

- Identify the most informative metrics to effectively measure user attitudes and behaviors on an ongoing basis
- Identify end-users' key activities
- Establish a baseline by collecting quantitative and statistically valid measures of attitudes and behaviors
- Determine key drivers of usability, efficiency, effectiveness, and satisfaction
- Identify a set of innovative metrics to measure the value and impact of our enterprise UX team

Our iterative approach to developing our UX Measurement plan included several key phases:

1. Metric identification and selection
2. Top task identification
3. Top task force ranking survey
4. Qualitative and quantitative task-based benchmark study pre-redesign #1
5. Qualitative and quantitative task-based benchmark studies post-redesign (#2, #3, #4)

11.3.1 Metric Identification and Selection

The process for selecting the most informative UX metrics for our measurement initiative required us to address three key questions:

1. Which UX metrics would best capture the influence our team could make on the product?
2. Which UX metrics would best reflect the changes we hoped to make in the product over time?
3. Which UX metrics would make the most sense to executives?

We decided to use the International Organization for Standardization (Technical Committee ISO/TC 159 *Ergonomics*, ISO 9241-11:2018) metrics for usability. These metrics include efficiency, effectiveness, and self-reported satisfaction. For our purposes, we translated these metrics at the task level into measurements such as time on task, task success or failure, and self-reported task satisfaction.

We combined these ISO standards along with other task-level metrics to measure our users' perceptions of time and difficulty. We specifically identified our users' "perceptions" of time as an important metric to include. We rationalized that in isolation, fluctuations in only task time might be hard to understand. However, by comparing actual task time and task completion with users' perceptions of time and difficulty it might help us to decipher whether enhancements meant to improve our users experience were actually discernable to them.

In addition, we included metrics to measure usability and learnability as well as trust, credibility, and site performance. With some reservations we also included the Net Promoter Score (NPS) in our UX measurement plan. NPS metrics can have some inherent drawbacks (volatility, for example, since this calculation emphasizes only the extremes in user attitudes). However, we knew our executives were increasingly identifying NPS as a key company metric connected to revenue and profits. We also knew that our Customer Experience team collected NPS data on our users' service experience. We reasoned this would allow us a solid foundation to better compare and contrast differences in a service NPS versus the NPS results we were gathering in our more user experience–focused studies.

We posited that we could use these UX metrics as a numeric proxy to reflect the quality of our users' experience. We hoped that by comparing shifts in these metrics between our benchmark and subsequent redesign releases it would be possible to determine which changes in certain aspects of our users' attitudes, behaviors, and satisfaction could have the strongest impact on specific company KPIs, therefore allowing us to make the connection to the company's return on investing in our UX team's efforts.

PARTICIPANTS

For our top task survey to achieve a 90% confidence level, we recruited 543 respondents (a statistically representative sample of our target audience) using a between-subjects design.

For our unmoderated remote benchmark studies, we decided on a 90% to 95% confidence level. To achieve this confidence level, we used a between-subjects design collecting a minimum of 25 respondents for each of three products for a total of 75 participants. Reaching this enterprise customer response rate was a challenge each time we ran the study. Therefore, this number fluctuated over the course of our four studies. We were sometimes fortunate to over-recruit. Other times, we were just able to achieve our 75 participant minimum. (Research Design reflected in Fig. 11.15.)

We also carefully monitored completion rates for each benchmark study ensuring relatively equal distributions of participants across important recruiting criteria such as company size, type of compliance module, and whether they used a combination of our compliance products plus other payroll products or solely used our payroll and compliance products.

11.3.2 Methods

TOP TASK IDENTIFICATION

We began our initiative by first identifying our end-users, most important "Top Tasks."

SURVEY TYPE	SAMPLE SIZE	CONFIDENCE LEVEL	STUDY DESIGN	# OF PRODUCTS
Top Task	543 participants	90%	Between Subjects	Three (3) Different Compliance Products
Unmoderated Remote Benchmark (Study# 1-4)	75-130 participants	90-95%	Between Subjects	Three (3) Different Compliance Products
Moderated Remote Benchmark (Study #1-4)	9-12 participants	n/a	Between Subjects	Three (3) Different Compliance Modules

Fig. 11.15 Research design (survey type, sample size, confidence level, study design across products).

A Top Task Management method (McGovern, 2015) provides the opportunity to identify and focus in on users' highest-priority tasks while reducing attention on smaller tasks that matter less. Since it was the foundation for all subsequent steps, identifying our top tasks was an essential phase in our UX Measurement Plan. Without clearly identifying our users' top tasks it would be difficult to make the connection to the contributions design made to improving the most impactful aspects for our users, experience and then to company performance indicators.

As a first step to collecting our "top task" data from our end-users, we surveyed 20 of our internal subject-matter experts and stakeholders using a "free-listing" method. Free listing is a simple qualitative research technique that requires asking an individual or a group to "list as many items on [topic X] as you can." Using this method, we gathered a preliminary list of our users' most important, or high-priority, end-to-end tasks. (Fig. 11.16 shows an example of our free-list survey.)

This survey should take no more than five minutes. As quickly as you can, in order of importance, list the top-five tasks clients perform most frequently related to [Product 1].

1. _____
2. _____
3. _____
4. _____
5. _____

Fig. 11.16 Free-list survey to develop a list of top tasks.

We then cross-checked and augmented this list with analytics and observational research insights as well as stakeholder interviews and even sales and business data. As a check of the final list, we conducted moderated remote pilots with a small number of end-users for feedback prior to launching the actual survey.

TOP TASK FORCE RANKING SURVEY

Top Tasks respondents were first screened to identify factors such as payroll system type, primary product usage, usage frequency and intensity, as well as demographic data that included questions related to gender, age, job title, industry, years of work experience, and position level.

Using a drag-and-drop survey design, participants were first required to rank the steps in their process, placing the most important steps at the top of their list and the least important at the bottom. Participants were then instructed to rank those process steps on a 5-point Likert-type scale in terms of importance and satisfaction. Then, using a "forced ranking" survey method, participants were instructed to identify the individual tasks that made up each process step and prioritize them. "Force Ranking" surveys limit users' options with the intent of requiring users to pick the most important tasks from a total selection set. When presented with our complete list of possible tasks for each of three products (this could mean up to 51 tasks), participants were allowed to pick a limited number (3 to 5 tasks) from the total selection of tasks.

For our post-test questionnaire, we collected several quantitative metrics. Using a 5-point Likert-type scale we sought to assess our respondent's level of overall satisfaction with our product. An adaptation of the Standardized User Experience Percentile Rank Questionnaire (SUPR-Q) (Sauro, 2018) was included using two separate questions to assess our users' level of trust and credibility about our products and the information presented in our products. Finally, we included both the System Usability Scale (SUS) to help us understand our users' perceptions about the usability and learnability of our products as well as the 11-point NPS. Additionally, we required participants to provide a brief explanation of their NPS score.

The most important outcome of our top-task survey was a ranked, prioritized list of process steps and tasks (Fig. 11.17). The results of our research allowed us not only to see the top-ranked tasks across different products but also to identify the lower-ranked tasks. Plus, we were able to see how each task ranked in relation to other tasks.

TASK-BASED BENCHMARK STUDY PRE-REDESIGN #1

Using a subset of the top tasks that received between 20% to 75% of the participant ranking vote identified through our survey (Figs. 11.18 and 11.19), we conducted a qualitative and quantitative task-based benchmark survey using both remote moderated and unmoderated methods.

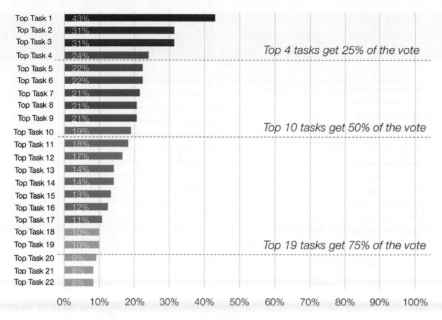

Fig. 11.17 Top-task survey with top task by respondent vote.

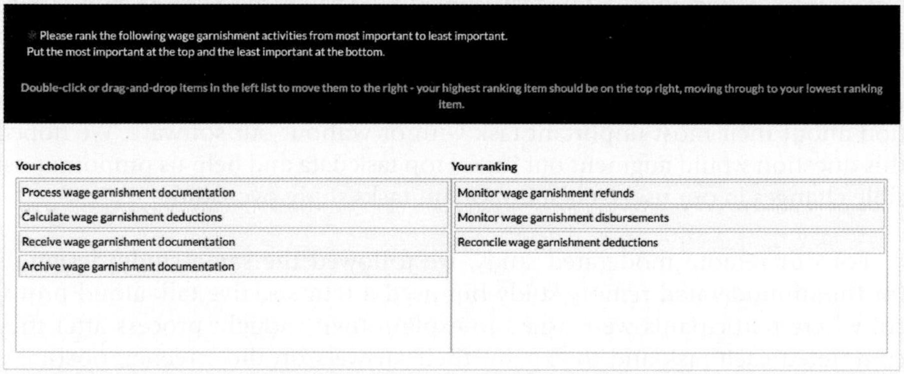

Fig. 11.18 Top-task survey with forced ranking to identify process steps.

For both our moderated and unmoderated benchmark study we collected pre-test, post-task, and post-test metrics. We again first screened our participants for demographic data using the same categories as in our top-task survey to allow the potential to run future statistical comparisons between the top tasks survey and benchmark data.

Our study design then required each participant to complete a series of randomized core tasks. Task measures included task success and failure as well as time on task. A questionnaire after each task assessed participant's perceived time

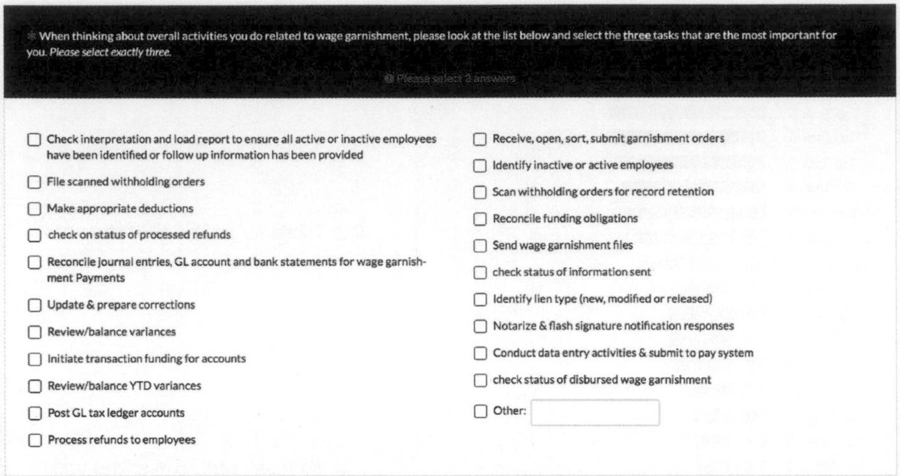

Fig. 11.19 Top-task survey with forced ranking to prioritize user's tasks.

on task, perceived difficulty (e.g., Single Ease Question/SEQ), as well as requiring participants to provide a brief explanation for their task difficulty rating.

For our benchmark post-test questionnaire, we expanded upon the post-test data collected in our top task survey by adding the U-MUX-Lite (Lewis et al., 2013). The U-MUX-Lite is a two-item questionnaire that we hoped might provide additional insights about our users' perceptions of overall site performance. We also added a free response question asking users to provide information about their most important task with or without our software. We hoped this question would augment our initial top task data and help us pinpoint possible changes in our users, most important tasks study-over-study.

For our remote moderated study, we followed the same study design as for the unmoderated remote study but used a retrospective talk-aloud protocol where participants were asked to explain their thought process after they completed each task and to explain their answers on the screener, post-task, and post-test questionnaires. We limited our respondents to between 9 and 12 participants and allowed enough time to gather richer insights into each participant's processes flows as well as on any questions with free responses. This task-based benchmark study conducted prior to the release of the redesign helped us establish a baseline to compare against the initial as well as future iterative releases.

11.3.3 Analysis

When attempting to connect the impact of design to key company performance metrics, an inevitable question was: "Compared to all the other contributing factors external and internal to a company, to what extent does design contribute to the organization's bottom line?" In an effort to better respond to questions regarding measurable design impact, we began to investigate a multi-dimensional model.

Built upon the foundation of the "Service Profit Chain" (Heskett et al., 1997; Fig. 11.20), this model helped us consider the influence of various metrics across the organization, including our UX metrics, and look for correlations with company KPI's such as revenue growth and profitability.

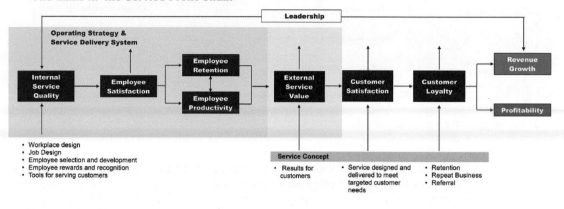

Fig. 11.20 The "Service Profit Chain" model.

11.3.4 Results

After conducting our initial benchmark study pre redesign, we executed the same study three additional times as iterative design releases were made to our platform over a 1.5-year period. We also were careful to collect the same metrics at the same time of year to compensate for any seasonal impact.

Collecting several measurable metrics—pre-test screener, post-task, and post-test for every benchmark study—yielded informative insights over the course of our endeavor. Fig. 11.21 depicts a sample of the metrics we employed in this multi-metric approach, which has allowed us to examine both task-level and overall metrics and gauge the impact of subsequent design iterations and releases on the user experience.

Initially, we had hypothesized that measurable connections between the UX teams' efforts and the company's key performance indicators (KPIs) would reflect correlations in related UX metrics. For example, we assumed that improvements in ISO metrics such as task time and satisfaction would have the greatest influence on customer KPIs such as NPS, as well as on customer-support contacts. However, while improvements in the users' experience do seem to impact

UX METRICS: ATTITUDE & TASK METRICS	ASSUMPTIONS: BENCHMARK VS. REDESIGN	COMPANY METRICS
Efficiency	Efficiency will increase resulting in improved time on task	• Increase in Sales Growth
Effectiveness	Completion rate will increase resulting in increased effectiveness	• Decrease in Contact Volumes
Perceived Difficulty	Perceived difficulty will decrease resulting in improved ease of use	• Decrease in Contact Volumes
Perceived Time	Perceived time will improve resulting in improved ease of use	• Decrease in Contact Volumes
Satisfaction	Usability will improve resulting in increased user satisfaction	• Increase in Customer Experience NPS
Net Promoter	NPS score will increase	• Increase in Customer Experience NPS
SUS	System Usability Score (SUS) will increase	• Increase in Customer Experience NPS
Trust/Reliability About the Product	Trust/Reliability will increase	• Increase in Client Retention
Trust/Reliability about Product Information	Trust/Reliability about Product Information will increase	• Decrease in Contact Volumes

Fig. 11.21 Our UX team's multi-metric approach.

a company's performance metrics, we discovered that the connection is more complex than we had originally anticipated.

As we gathered data study-over-study, we ran comparisons looking to uncover statistically significant correlations between task behavioral, post-task attitudinal, and perception metrics, as well as our post-test metrics SUS, NPS, UX-MUX-Lite, Satisfaction, Trust and Credibility, and Information Trust and Credibility.

Additionally, for our qualitative analysis we continually looked for differences in themes for our three free-response questions (SEQ or post-task difficulty, NPS, and the most important activity to get your job done) and across NPS verbatims (comparing detractors, passives, and promoters).

We found that this qualitative data provided rich insights that often enriched our understanding of our participant's quantitative responses.

It was while running a series of statistical analyses—including linear regression, logistic regression, and analysis of variance—that a surprising model emerged. The revelation? There is a measurable correlation between a high-quality user experience and customer referrals. The team was excited to discover that task-level metrics such as task success and task ease had the strongest correlation to UX metrics such as SUS and overall satisfaction as well as to the product's NPS.

As the team continued to search the data for statistically significant connections between task-level and overall UX metrics and company KPIs, across several comparison studies, they started to think of these connections in terms of the model shown in Fig. 11.22.

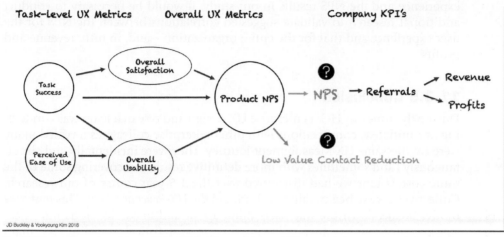

Fig. 11.22 A proposed model correlating UX metrics to company KPI's.

To summarize, new releases of the user experience first had to better support users' ability to complete their top tasks successfully, end to end. Second, if those top tasks felt easier to complete, users were more likely to rate the experience as more satisfying and learnable (Fig. 11.23). Finally, if an experience met these first two conditions, users were more likely to give the product a higher NPS rating.

Satisfaction

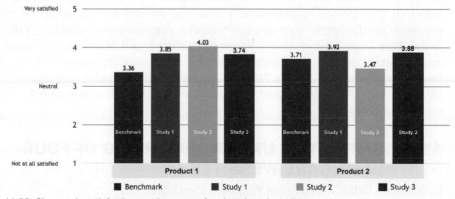

Fig. 11.23 Changes in satisfaction metrics across four benchmark studies.

Research (Derfuss et al., 2017) suggests a strong relationship between NPS, revenue, and profits. However, service quality can dramatically impact NPS scores—especially at enterprise organizations where the quality of customer service can play a significant role in the end-to-end user experience. While the UX team has discovered a statistically significant correlation between the task user experience and the NPS results in our study, it would be necessary to conduct additional research to validate suggested correlations between the NPS for the user experience and that for the entire organization—and, in turn, revenue and profits.

11.3.5 Conclusion

During the time our HCM enterprise UX design and research team was conducting our initiative, conversations with other enterprise colleagues revealed many were on the same UX Measurement journey. They were incidentally and simultaneously (and sometimes with more definitive results) uncovering some of the same correlations we had discovered over the 1.5-year course of our research. Collectively, we've begun calling this model the *UX-Revenue Chain*. This tentative model breaks down the way users think about and make decisions into measurements of four key areas, allowing the use of statistical modeling to explain how user experience impacts business metrics (Buckley and Powers, 2019).

For many of us, this evolving model has inspired discussions across organizational silos regarding the importance of establishing who a product's primary users are—as well as their top tasks and workflows—as an essential design and business-strategy approach.

BIOGRAPHY

JonDelina "JD" Buckley

For more than 15 years, JD has successfully led the introduction of human-centered, holistic, and data-driven user experiences. JD is a passionate UX Research and Design Strategy leader who has worked with a variety of companies from disruptive start-ups to enterprise organizations including Yahoo!, Kelley Blue Book, Disney, Daqri, Kaiser Permanente, and ADP. Her work informs and inspires companies to pursue creating innovative experiences. JD is currently the Director of Service Design at ServiceTitan, provides consultancy services through JD Usability, and is an Adjunct Assistant Professor at Art Center College of Design.

11.4 COMPETITIVE UX BENCHMARKING OF FOUR HEALTHCARE WEBSITES

By Kuldeep Kelkar, SVP Global Research, UserZoom

Executives and business stakeholders believe that what cannot be measured cannot be managed. User experience (UX) is no different. Routinely in business settings, comparing companies versus their competitors on key tasks and key customer journeys is common.

At UserZoom, we benchmarked and compared four healthcare websites across multiple US states. Insurance healthcare providers are regulated at a state level in the US, which results in a fragmented digital presence. As part of this competitive UX benchmarking, we compared Blue Cross Blue Shield (BCBS) sites across Texas, New Jersey, California, and Massachusetts (Fig. 11.24).

Fig. 11.24 Screenshots of the four Blue Cross Blue Shield (BCBS) sites for Texas, New Jersey, California, and Massachusetts.

11.4.1 Methodology

We conducted two studies—one quantitative, one qualitative. Our quantitative study had a sample size of 200 participants and the qualitative study a sample size of 20 participants. All participants had to meet the following criteria:

- Age 26+
- Reside in the specific state (Texas, California, New Jersey, and Massachusetts)
- Be responsible for making healthcare decisions

In order to score these four websites, we combined various measurements, collecting both behavioral data such as Task Success %, task times and page views and attitudinal data (SUPR-Q) to create a single score (qxScore) for each website.

DATA COLLECTION THROUGH USERZOOM FOR BOTH STUDIES

Invited participants go through a screener first. Screened-in participants follow the study instructions and task instructions and navigate the site. Screen recording, clicks, pages navigated, number of clicks, time on task, and behavioral data are collected. Pre-task and post-task attitudinal data are collected as well (Single Use Question, Brand Perceptions, and SUPR-Q Questionnaire).

The second study ($n = 20$) was similar in setup to the above study with one difference: Participants are asked to think out loud (verbalize) their thoughts while navigating the site and the screen and voice are recorded. Thinking out loud provides richer insights behind the "why" there was an issue along with the screen recording for direction observation.

EXPERIMENTAL DESIGN FOR THE QUANTITATIVE *N* = 200 STUDY

At UserZoom, we usually recommend a within-subjects experimental design (one participant going through all of the websites). That's only possible if the number of tasks is limited and the total study time for unmoderated is under 20 minutes. In this case the study had to be between-subjects (each participant going through three tasks on only one of the state-specific websites) because health insurance products are state specific and largely apply to residences of a particular state. So, 50 participants in Texas would perform three tasks on BCBS Texas site and the same for three other states. Fig. 11.25 represents the flow for both the quantitative and qualitative studies.

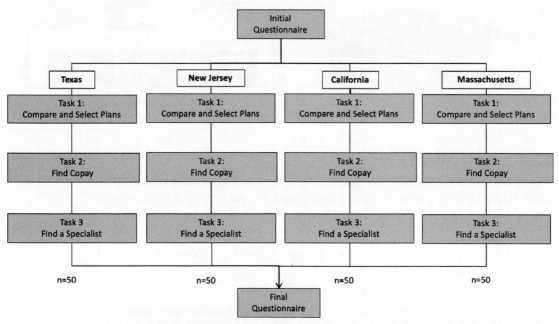

Fig. 11.25 Experimental design and task flows for the quantitative study, as well as the qualitative think out loud study.

METRICS AND KEY PERFORMANCE INDICATORS

Several metrics are collected pre-task, during tasks, post-task, and at system-level KPIs (typically at the end of the study). These are behavioral and attitudinal metrics. A list of KPIs collected are shown in Table 11.1.

	Behavioral Metrics	**Attitudinal Metrics**
Task level metrics	• Task Success % • Average time on task • Average # of page views	• Did not encounter problems or frustrations • Provided just the right amount of information
System level metrics		• Brand perception (pre tasks) • Brand perception (post tasks) • SURP-Q • Appearance • Ease of Use • NPS and Loyalty • Trust

Table 11.1 Task level and system level by metrics from the lens of bevavioral and attitudinal metrics.

11.4.2 Results

QXSCORE

Executives often want to know "who won" before knowing the details and the "why" behind the details. At UserZoom, we have been using a single metric called qxScore (Fig. 11.26). This is an experience score that combines various measurements, collecting both **behavioral data** (such as task success) and **attitudinal data** (such as ease of use, trust, and appearance). Fifty percent

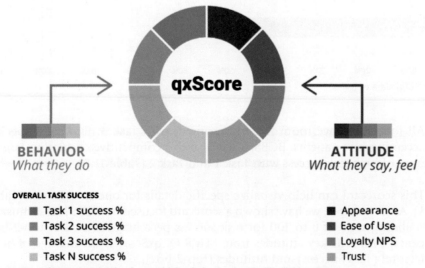

BEHAVIOR
What they do

ATTITUDE
What they say, feel

OVERALL TASK SUCCESS
- Task 1 success %
- Task 2 success %
- Task 3 success %
- Task N success %

- Appearance
- Ease of Use
- Loyalty NPS
- Trust

Fig. 11.26 qxScore visualization for combining behavioral and attitudinal metrics.

weightage is given to system level attitudinal measures (eight questions from SUPR-Q) and 50% weightage is given to Task Success (behavioral metrics). Details can be found here: https://www.userzoom.com/blog/one-ux-metric-to-measure-the-world-introducing-userzooms-single-score-for-experience-benchmarking/.

OVERALL RESULTS

Blue Cross Blue Shield (BCBS) Texas was the overall winner, scoring 76 (qxScore). It offered the best overall experience based on our benchmark score, beating California (63), New Jersey (56), and Massachusetts (48) (Fig. 11.27)

Blue Cross Blue Shield (BCBS) Texas was the overall winner!

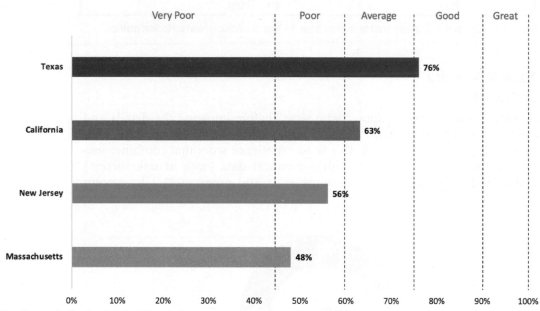

Fig. 11.27 qxScores for the four BCBS state websites.

All four sites have room for improvement with Task 3: Finding a specialist accepting new patients. BCBS Texas won this competitive evaluation largely because of high task success with Task 1 and Task 2 (Table 11.2).

This scorecard can help visualize specific details for one specific site (Table 11.3). As an example, we have shown a scorecard focused on BCBS Massachusetts on a sliding scale of 0 to 100 for task success percentage as well as top-2-box percentage for four key attitudes from SUPR-Q. qxScore is the average of both behavioral (Task Success) and Attitudes (top-2-box).

	BCBS Texas	BCBS New Jersey	BCBS California	BCBS Massachusetts
Task 1: Compare and select health insurance plans	94	88	56	64
Task 2: Finding co-pay amount for the selected plan	94	82	64	60
Task 3: Finding specialist accepting new patients	70	52	58	40
Usability (ease of use)	65	49	52	33
Trust	85	68	72	69
Appearance	62	56	53	45
Loyalty NPS	49	38	31	20
qxScore	**76**	**56**	**63**	**48**

Table 11.2 qxScorecard Across all Three Tasks (Success Rate) and Attitudes (Top 2 Box)

	Very Poor (≥45)	Poor (45–60)	Average (61–75)	Good (76–90)	Great (91–100)
Task 1: Compare and select health insurance plans			64		
Task 2: Finding copay amount for the selected plan			60		
Task 3: Finding specialist accepting new patients	40				
Usability (ease of use)	33				
Trust			69		
Appearance		45			
Loyalty NPS	20				
qxScore		**48**			

Table 11.3 qxScorecard for BCBS Massachusetts

TASK DETAILS

This study used the same three tasks across all four competitor websites. Task selection is critical for any usability study. For competitive benchmarks, it is imperative to select the most representative tasks.

Out of the four Blue Cross Blue Shield (BCBS) websites, participants on the BCBS Texas site were most successful (task success) and most efficient (average time on task) (Table 11.4).

KPIs	TX $n=50$	NJ $n=50$	CA $n=50$	MA $n=50$
Task success (%)	94	56	88	64
Average time on task (min)	3.3	3.8	5.8	4.2
Average # of page views	4.9	6.7	9.0	9.0
Did not encounter problems or frustrations (%)	38	24	22	20
Provided just the right amount of information (%)	58	46	48	44

Table 11.4 KPIS for the four states.

For Texas (TX) site, 38% said they did not encounter problems, which means 62% encountered problems. So, it's reasonable to say that even the best performer of this pack still had lots of room for improvement. For BCBS Massachusetts (MA) site, nearly 80% of participants encountered problems and frustrations while trying to find and compare health insurance plans. A list of problems encountered are shown in Fig. 11.28.

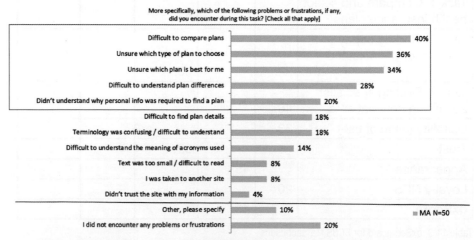

Fig. 11.28 List of problems encountered on BCBS Massachusetts website for Task 1.

Out of the four Blue Cross Blue Shield (BCBS) websites, Texas had the highest Task Success at 94% (above average) and was the fastest for finding copay amounts. Better interaction design, layout, visual design, and clearly understood copy helped (Table 11.5).

KPIs	TX *n* = 50	NJ *n* = 50	CA *n* = 50	MA *n* = 50
Task success (%)	94	64	82	60
Average time on task (min)	0.7	0.9	1.4	0.8
Average # of page views	1.5	2.3	2.1	2.8
Ease of finding copay information (%)	66 Mean 5.7	44 Mean 4.3	48 Mean 4.7	50 Mean 4.5
Did not encounter problems or frustrations (%)	64	48	42	

Table 11.5 Overall KPI's for the four states.

For New Jersey, 48% did not encounter problems, but that means 52% of all participants encountered problems or frustrations, and they are listed in priority order below (Fig. 11.29). The biggest obstacle for New Jersey (NJ) participants was not being clear where to go to find copay information.

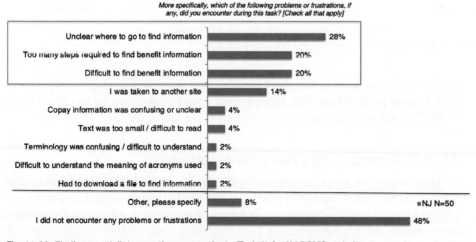

Fig. 11.29 Finding specialist accepting new patients (Task 3) for NJ BCMS website.

PRE-VERSUS POST-SITE PERCEPTION

We recommend including a perception question, "What is your perception of [site]?" before participants perform any tasks, and including the same question after all tasks are completed. It's usually a 7-point scale but can be 5-point scale as well. The intent of this question is to see if participants had a positive, neutral, or negative impression of the site or brand <u>before</u> they take the study and compare it with perceptions post tasks. If there is significant increase in Top-2-box (6 and 7 on 7-point scale) or Top-3-box (5, 6, and 7 on 7-point scale).

Fig. 11.30 shows the pre versus post perceptions, top 2 box on 7-point scale. At 90% confidence level, Blue Cross Blue Shield (BCBS) Massachusetts (MA)

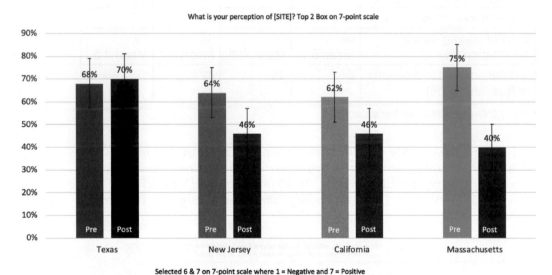

Fig. 11.30 Pre versus post website perception top 2 box on 7-point scale.

saw a significant drop in the top 2 box, leading us to believe that the site experience caused participants who initially had positive impressions to drop significantly (significance testing using Adjusted Wald Method).

11.4.3 Summary and Recommendations

At UserZoom, we help Fortune 500 companies drive better user experiences through continuous customer feedback. We see benchmarking data across several industries: retail/e-commerce, banking, airlines, insurance, healthcare, and many more. As an example, our benchmarking data within e-commerce vertical tends to be higher than healthcare industry in general. There are some time-tested design principles and key recommendations that would benefit all companies within the healthcare industry.

Key recommendations for digital teams that are focused on improving user experience are as follows:

1. **Conduct Benchmarking**: Conduct quarterly, twice a year, or at least an annual competitive benchmarking for your digital experiences. All executives believe that you cannot manage what you cannot measure. The same is true for user experience. This book outlines several metrics. Measure them, present findings, speak the business language.

2. **Look for Best Practices From Other Industries**: It's not enough to only look at what your direct competitors are doing. Consumer expectations are driven by what they experience across all industry websites and applications. Based on the feedback from the four sites we tested for this benchmark, it's clear that there are lots of lower-hanging fruits that can be addressed to dramatically improve website designs and the overall user experience.

3. **Use Qualitative and Quantitative**: For any UX benchmarking, it is imperative to provide qualitative (what happened and why) along with quantitative (how much).

4. **Simplify Health Plan Comparison Design and Content**: Laying out various health insurance options on a long webpage is not enough. Be attentive to key content elements and provide consumers the ability to easily compare multiple plans in a simple, easy-to-read table. As this report shows, several BCBS sites failed to let participants understand all options, and comparing options was certainly a challenge. If customers cannot find the right option, they are unlikely to buy.

5. **Finding a Doctor "Search and Filter"**: Finding the right doctor or knowing if their doctor accepts a particular plan or accepting new patients is critical. But sites usually failed to deliver on search and filtering expectations. It's not an either-or question, and customers expect that search and filtering should work in tandem.

11.4.4 Acknowledgment and Contributions

Ann Rochanayon, Principal UX Researcher at UserZoom, built, conducted, and analyzed this study. This article would not have been possible without key contributions, data analysis, and visualization from Dana Bishop, Sr. Director, UX Research at UserZoom.

Both Ann and Dana have conducted several UX benchmarks in their professional careers, over the decades, across several industry verticals. They routinely speak at UX summits, customer workshops, and webinars on UX research best practices in general and UX benchmarking specifically. Thank you, Ann and Dana.

11.4.5 Biography

Kuldeep Kelkar, SVP Global Research Services at UserZoom, is a UX leader with a proven track record of translating business strategy and user needs into solutions for 20+ years. He has worked as a researcher and designer at small and large organization, including leading UX teams at PayPal for 10 years. He is design leader and mentor with proven ability to manage geographically distributed UX teams to deliver product vision across platforms and devices. Passionate about hiring, retaining, and developing UX talent, Kuldeep is a metrics-driven leader with executive presence (C level), and a great collaborator with product, marketing, engineering, quality, and experience professionals.

11.5 CLOSING THE SNAP GAP

By Eric Benoit, Sharon Lee, and Juhan Sonin, GoInvo

Food insecurity takes a significant toll on public health across the country. Tragically, one out of ten households in Massachusetts are "food insecure" (Project Bread, 2019). The Massachusetts Department of Transitional Assistance (MA DTA) is hard at work to provide support for MA residents through the Supplemental Nutrition Assistance Program (SNAP), which is a monthly benefit to buy nutritious foods.

The previous release of the digital SNAP experience made it difficult for MA residents to apply online to receive benefits. The online application assumed you had access to a desktop computer with internet, could understand questions written for a high-school or college graduate, and had enough patience to answer 90+ questions through a convoluted form (Fig. 11.31). Because of this, most people choose to visit a DTA office to apply in person. In some cases, this means missing work and critical income.

Fig. 11.31 The previous online application was difficult to complete—with only 7.5% of people making it through the entire application.

In collaboration with the MA Department of Transitional Assistance, MA Executive Office of Health and Human Services (EOHHS) IT, GoInvo, and our development partner, we launched a new digital experience for SNAP. The teams focused on a mobile-first, non-intimidating, accessible, and quick service with multiple language options. Although the application is just one part of the whole, it serves as a key entry point for those in need. The ultimate goal was to increase food security for MA residents by making the SNAP application process accessible and approachable for all.

11.5.1 Field Research

We spent time at a local MA DTA office to understand the SNAP process from staff and residents. Our goal was to study and observe the interactions people had trying to apply or manage their SNAP benefits. We conducted this direct observation through four walk-in applications and three phone interviews (Fig. 11.32).

Fig. 11.32 MA DTA staff taking phone calls from residents looking to apply for SNAP.

It was easy to see the stress, language barriers, and confusion that many applicants had throughout this process, which drove us to design the application to be as friendly and streamlined as possible.

One particular area of confusion we consistently heard through the conversations was around the verification documents. For residents, it was unclear what their status was, whether they were just waiting or still needed to send documents in. Therefore, residents would call or visit the MA DTA office to ask for assistance. Not providing the correct documentation will delay access to benefits, so it is important to make sure people understand what they need to provide to expedite their benefits.

We redesigned two sections to better guide residents into submitting the correct documentation and getting their benefits as quickly as possible.

The first redesign was within the application process. We designed logic that would only request for verification documents based on the applicant's answers. Residents now had a clear list of the documents they needed to provide.

The second redesign was within the account management where they could check on their status anywhere and anytime. The documents section would list what documents they need to provide and the status (missing, processing, approved, denied) so they wouldn't need to contact the local MA DTA office to check.

11.5.2 Weekly Reviews

In our collaborative process, we hold weekly design reviews with all stakeholders (Fig. 11.33). During these sessions, we'll review the latest design concepts and research to iteratively evolve the design.

11.5.3 Application Questions

When we first began the project, we did not intend to rewrite the application questions. However, after several feedback sessions with industry experts and our own assessment, it was obvious that these questions were not written in a user-friendly way, causing a lot of confusion and, worse, deterring people from applying (Fig. 11.34).

To put a number on this, of the online applications that were started, only 7.5% ever got submitted online. We'll never know how many people re-attempted applying through other means (fax, mail, office visit) versus quitting altogether, but what's evident is that the online application process was broken and not meeting the needs of the MA residents.

We had to create our own metrics, since the current online experience tracked a limited set of metrics for informing the design. We organized a workshop with industry experts to identify the most difficult application questions based on their experience. The seven participants were given a printout of the entire application and instructed to highlight difficult questions and also suggest better question phrasing.

Fig. 11.33 Reviewing a draft of the rewritten SNAP application questions with MA DTA and SNAP policy experts.

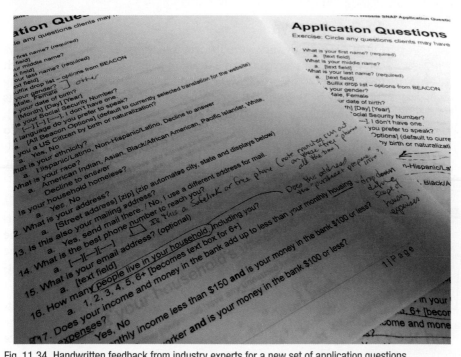

Fig. 11.34 Handwritten feedback from industry experts for a new set of application questions.

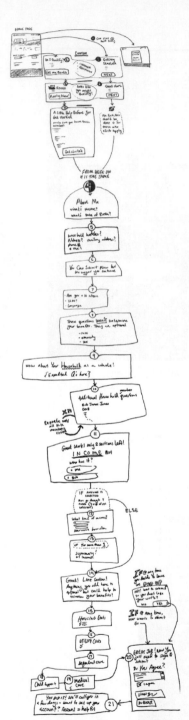

Fig. 11.35 Sketch outlining a revised application workflow.

From this, we had a heatmap of which questions to focus our attention on and potential solutions. What we found were five key areas that consistently caused confusion.

- Using language that people are not familiar with
- Asking irrelevant questions (e.g., Asking about child-care expenses when no child has been declared within the household)
- Asking multiple questions within a single question
- No definition of a "household" led to incorrect amount of people in need of benefits
- Adding the income for people in the household was cumbersome—leading to incomplete applications

Based on the results of the workshop, we drafted a new version of the application questions (Fig. 11.35). This draft went through ~10 iterations to get to what we have today—with some recommendations not permitted due to their ingrained connection with policies that we couldn't change within the confines of the project.

While there is still room for improvement, the feedback received made a significant impact on the design of the application. The application went from ~90 questions to ~40 for a household of two, which meant the time spent applying dropped considerably.

11.5.4 Surveys

Often, we employ surveys to inform the design of a product. Surveys can be useful at any stage of a design project, from a napkin sketch to a live product. For SNAP, we conducted a survey before designing the online benefits portal for people to manage their SNAP benefits (which would occur after submitting an application) (Fig. 11.36). We had a good idea of what the core actions a person would do within the portal, but since we didn't have any analytics data available, we weren't quite sure how often they were being used. The survey was a useful tool for providing us with a foundational understanding of where people would spend their time in the portal.

When we conducted the survey, each person was given a printout that listed the core actions a person would take within the online benefits portal. The instructions were simple; rank order the list in order of their importance to the person using the online portal (Fig. 11.37).

With everyone's survey results, we coalesced them into a spreadsheet to see the general consensus. We began designing the online benefits portal to support the results of the survey. For example, since

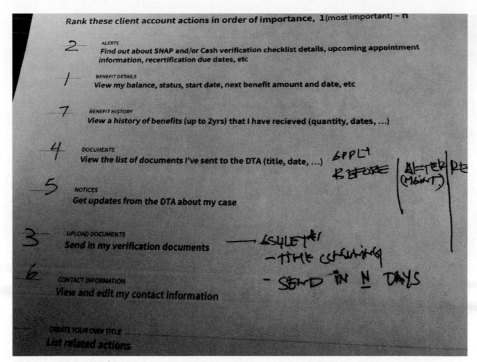

Fig. 11.36 An individual's survey results for rank ordering the importance of core actions within the online portal.

	Brandon	Ashley	Sarah	Crystal	M. Joyce	unknown	unknown	unknown	unknown	Average	FINAL RANK
benefit details	1	4	2	1	1	1	1	1	1	1.44	1
alerts	4	3	1	2	5	4	2	2	3	2.89	2
upload document	2	1	3	4	7	3	3	3	5	3.44	3
notices	5	2	5	3	3	5	4	5	2	3.78	4
documents	3	6	7	5	2	2	6	6	4	4.56	5
contact info	6	5	4	6	4	7	5	4	6	5.22	6
benefit history	7	7	6	7	6	6	7	7	7	6.67	7

Fig. 11.37 Results of the survey identified the top action is for people to see their current benefits.

the "benefit details" were of top importance, we made sure those were the first pieces of information we would display (Fig. 11.38).

11.5.5 Testing Prototypes

For us to truly understand how our design will work—and to get the best feedback—we need to have our designs live in the format we intend for them to exist. This meant putting design into code, viewable in a browser and accessible via a desktop or mobile phone (Fig. 11.39).

Hi, Sharon

You have 3 new messages!

Cash Benefits	View More
$30.03	
EBT Balance	

Active

12.Sep.18, Re-evaluation Date
10.Oct.17, Next TAFDC Benefit

SNAP Benefits	View More
$217.38	
EBT Balance	

Active

12.Dec.17, Re-evaluation Date
10.Oct.17, Next SNAP Benefit

Fig. 11.38 Survey results directly informing the design—the first item shown are the benefit details.

With a prototype that could mimic the real experience, we could begin to measure how the new design would perform prior to launch. During the user testing of the prototype, a few areas measured were:

- Time to complete the application
- Alternative approaches for inputting household income
- Flow of topics and questions is logical
- Accessibility issues

11.5.6 Success Metric

At the start of the project, we identified a metric with which to measure the project's success—closing the SNAP gap. The SNAP gap references the fact that nationally, only 75% of eligible people apply—meaning there are 25% of the eligible population not getting the proper nutrition. Our mission was to reduce that 25%, which would get food in the hands of more eligible MA residents through a redesigned online experience.

Since launch, we've seen a 76% increase year-over-year in online applications and a decrease in the other channels (fax ↓32%, mail-in ↓40%, walk-in ↓13%, drop-off ↓40%). From the looks of it, the new online process seems to be absorbing all other channels of applying.

In regards to the SNAP gap, it appears that the redesigned experience is making a dent with overall applications up 10% year-over-year.

11.5.7 Organizations

GOINVO

GoInvo's design practice is dedicated to innovation in healthcare. Over the past decade, we've created beautiful software for patients, clinicians, researchers, and administrators, working with organizations as far-reaching as AstraZeneca, Becton Dickinson, Johnson and Johnson, 3M Health Information Services, the U.S. Department of Health and Human Services, and Walgreens. Software designed by GoInvo is relied on every day by over 150 million people. Founded

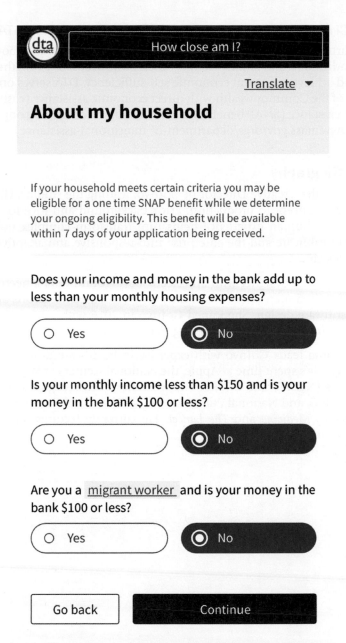

Fig. 11.39 The SNAP application designed for mobile phones. Now MA residents can apply from the palm of their hands, anywhere, anytime.

in 2004, we are a mission-driven organization made up of expert designers, engineers, and researchers with deep expertise in Health IT, Genomics, and Open Source health, dedicated to making tangible and positive change in the world (https://www.goinvo.com).

MASSACHUSETTS DEPARTMENT OF TRANSITIONAL ASSISTANCE

The Department of Transitional Assistance (DTA) assists and empowers low-income individuals and families to meet their basic needs, improve their quality of life, and achieve long term economic self-sufficiency. DTA serves one in eight residents of the Commonwealth with direct economic assistance (cash benefits) and food assistance (SNAP benefits), as well as workforce training opportunities (https://www.mass.gov/orgs/department-of-transitional-assistance).

11.5.8 Biography

Eric Benoit is the Creative Director of GoInvo, leading the studio's UX creation process from concept to production. Eric's background and love for design in the context of human experience helps him transform complex information systems in healthcare and the enterprise into responsive and adaptive human-centered designs.

Sharon Lee is a designer with an eclectic background in engineering, medicine, and art. Passionate about healthcare, she has focused her efforts on human-centered software design. She joined GoInvo in 2016 with a BS in Biomedical Engineering from the University of Virginia.

Juhan Sonin leads GoInvo with expertise in healthcare design and system engineering. He's spent time at Apple, the National Center for Supercomputing Applications (NCSA), and MITRE. His work has been recognized by the *New York Times*, BBC, and National Public Radio (NPR) and published in *The Journal of Participatory Medicine* and *The Lancet*. He currently lectures on design and engineering at MIT.

CHAPTER 12
Ten Keys to Success

CONTENTS

Some of the concepts and approaches we've described may be new to some readers and maybe even a bit overwhelming at first, so we wanted to highlight ten key elements that will help you succeed. These are lessons we've learned—sometimes the hard way—over the years.

12.1 MAKE THE DATA COME ALIVE

An important factor that will determine how much impact you have with your research is the extent to which you can make the data come alive for your stakeholders. It's easy for eyes to start glazing over when looking at a bunch of numbers. However, it is very different when you bring the data to life by showing the actual experiences users are having with a product or service. Even though this is anecdotal, it can have a tremendous impact on getting your point across. Essentially, you are putting a real face to your data. It is much harder to ignore your metrics when someone has a deeper level of understanding or even emotional attachment to the data. Tomer Sharon, in his book *It's Our Research: Getting Buy-in for User Experience Research Projects* (2012), does an excellent job of explaining how critical it is for UX professionals to make their data come alive.

Several techniques can be very helpful in making this happen. First, we recommend that when you are conducting user research you have a way for key decision makers to data collection firsthand. This might be in the form of observing usability testing in a lab setting or through a screen sharing application or coming along on some home visits as part of a field research study. Nothing speaks louder than observing the user experience firsthand.

Once key decision-makers start to see a consistent pattern of results, you won't need to spend much effort convincing them of the need for a design change. But be careful when someone only observes a single interview or usability session. Watching one participant struggle can easily be dismissed as an edge case (e.g., "Our users will be much smarter than that person!"). Conversely, seeing someone easily fly through the tasks can lead to a false sense of security that there are no usability issues with the design. The power of observation is in consistent patterns of results. When key decision-makers attend a session, invite them to "come to at least one more session" to get a fuller picture of the results. In fact, we might even argue that no sessions might be better than just one user session.

Another excellent way to sell UX research is with short video clips. Embedding short video clips into a presentation can make a big difference. The most effective way to illustrate a user experience issue is by showing short clips of two or three different participants encountering the same problem or voicing a similar level of frustration. Showing reliable patterns is essential. In our experience, participants who are more animated usually make for better clips. But avoid the temptation to show a dramatic or humorous clip that is not backed by solid data. Make sure each clip is short—ideally less than a minute and perhaps just 30 seconds. The last thing you want is to lose the power of a clip by dragging it out too long. Before showing a clip, provide appropriate context about the participant (without revealing any private information) and what he or she is trying to do.

If direct observation or video clips don't work, try presenting a few key UX metrics. Basic metrics around task success, efficiency, and satisfaction generally work well. Ideally, you'll be able to tie these metrics to return on investment (ROI). For example, if you can show how a redesign will increase ROI or how abandonment rates are higher on your product compared to your competition, you'll get the attention of senior management.

MEASURING TEAM INVOLVEMENT

Bill Albert and Josh Rosenberg (2017) introduced a new metric to measure team engagement during usability testing—the Team Engagement Score (TES). TES is based on the important role of observation during a usability test by team members including product managers, designers, developers, and senior management.

Three components are used in the calculation of TES: a team's commitment, prioritization, and involvement in the observation of usability sessions. Team commitment is the ratio of how many usability sessions are actually observed relative to the total possible sessions that could be observed. Team prioritization is the ratio of the number of usability sessions that are observed in-person relative to the total possible sessions that could be observed in-person. Team involvement includes a rating by the usability lead or moderator on how involved the product team is during and post observation with respect to questions and feedback.

These three components make up a TES, which ranges from 0 to 1.0. A TES of 0 would indicate the lowest level of team engagement, whereas a TES of 1.0 would indicate the highest possible team engagement during the usability testing observation. While there are certainly other variables that indicate a team's engagement, the Team Engagement Score might be useful for some teams to measure and track how engaged their stakeholders are during usability testing.

12.2 DON'T WAIT TO BE ASKED TO MEASURE

Many years ago, one of the best things we ever did was to collect UX data without directly being asked for it. At that time, we started to sense a certain level of hesitancy or even skepticism about purely qualitative findings. Also, the project teams started to ask more questions, specifically around design preferences and the competitive landscape that we know could only be answered with quantitative data. As a result, we took it upon ourselves to start collecting UX metrics that were central to the success of the design we were working on.

What is the best way to do this? We recommend starting off with something small and manageable. It's critical that you be successful in your first uses of metrics. If you're trying to incorporate metrics in routine formative user research, start with categorizing types of issues and issue severity. By logging all the issues, you'll have plenty of data to work with. For example, it's easy to collect System Usability Scale (SUS) data at the conclusion of each usability session or NPS as part of an online survey. It only takes a few minutes to administer the survey, and it can provide valuable data in the long run. That way you will have a quantitative measure across all of your tests, and you can show trends over time. As you get comfortable with some of the more basic metrics, you can work your way up the metrics ladder.

A second phase might include some efficiency metrics such as completion times and lostness. Consider some other types of self-reported metrics such as usefulness-awareness gaps or expectations. Also, explore different ways to represent task success, such as through levels of completion. Finally, start to combine multiple metrics into an overall UX metric, or even build your own UX scorecard.

Over time, you'll build up a repertoire of different metrics. By starting off small, you'll learn which metrics work for your situation and which don't. You'll learn the advantages and disadvantages of each metric and start to reduce the noise in the data collection process. In our work, it has taken us many years to expand our metrics toolkit to where it is today. So don't worry if you're not collecting all the metrics you want at first; you'll get there eventually. Also, be aware that your audience will have an adjustment period. If your audience is only used to seeing qualitative findings, it may take them a while to get adjusted to seeing UX metrics. If you throw too much at them too quickly, they may become resistant or think you just got back from math camp.

12.3 MEASUREMENT IS LESS EXPENSIVE THAN YOU THINK

Metrics do not take too long to collect or are not too expensive. That might have been true 10 years ago, but no longer. There are many new tools available to UX researchers that make data collection and analysis quick and easy and won't break your budget. In fact, in many cases, running a quantitative-based UX study costs less than a traditional qualitative user research study.

Online tools such as UserZoom (www.userzoom.com) and Loop11 (www.loop11.com) are excellent ways to collect quantitative data about how users are interacting with a website or prototype. Studies can be set up in a matter of minutes or hours, and the cost is fairly low, particularly when you compare it to the time setting up a traditional usability evaluation. These tools also provide ways to analyze click paths, abandonment rates, self-reported measures, and many other metrics. In our book *Beyond the Usability Lab* (Albert, Tullis, & Tedesco, 2010) we highlight many of these tools and provide a step-by-step guide to using online usability testing tools.

Sometimes you are less concerned about actual interaction and more about reaction to different designs. In this situation, we recommend taking advantage the many online survey tools that now allow you to embed images into the survey and ask questions about those images. Online tools such as Qualtrics (www.qualtrics.com), Survey Gizmo (www.surveygizmo.com), and Survey Monkey (www.surveymonkey.com) all provide the ability to embed images. In addition, there are some interactive capabilities such as allowing the participant to click on various elements within the image based on questions you provide. The cost of these survey tools is very reasonable, particularly if you sign up for a yearly license.

There are many other tools that also are very reasonable in price and do an excellent job of collecting data about the user experience. For example, Optimal Workshop (www.optimalworkshop.com) provides a robust suite of tools to build and test any information architecture. In lieu of traditional usability testing, we suggest you look at Usertesting.com (www.usertesting.com) as a way to get quick feedback about your product in a matter of hours. This tool also has a way of embedding questions into the script, as well as analyzing the videos by demographics. While there is certainly some work on the researcher's end, the price can't be beat.

12.4 PLAN EARLY

One of the key messages of this book has been the importance of planning ahead when collecting any UX metrics. The reason we stress this is because it is so tempting to skip, and skipping it usually has a negative outcome. If you go into a UX study not sure which metrics you want to collect and why, you're almost certainly going to be less effective.

Try to think through as many details as you can before the study. The more specific you can be, the better the outcome. For example, if you're collecting task success metrics and completion times, make sure that you define your success criteria and when exactly you'll turn off the clock. Also, think about how you're going to record and analyze the data. Unfortunately, we can't provide a single, comprehensive checklist to plan out every detail well in advance. Every metric and evaluation method requires its own unique set of plans. The best way to build your checklist is through experience.

One technique that has worked well for us has been "reverse engineering" the data. This means sketching out what the data will look like before conducting the study. We usually think of it as the key slides in a presentation. Then we work back from there to figure out what format the data must be in to create the charts. Next, we start designing the study to yield data in the desired format. This isn't faking the results but rather visualizing what the data might look like. Another simple strategy is to take a fake dataset and analyze it to make sure that you can perform the desired analysis. This might take a little extra time, but it could help save more time when you actually have the real dataset in front of you.

Of course, running pilot studies is also very useful. By running one or two pilot participants through the study, you'll be able to identify some of the outstanding issues that you have yet to address in the larger study. It's important to keep the pilot as realistic as possible and to allow enough time to address any issues that arise. Keep in mind that a pilot study is not a substitute for planning ahead. A pilot study is best used to identify the smaller issues that can be addressed fairly quickly before data collection begins.

12.5 BENCHMARK YOUR PRODUCTS

User experience metrics are relative. There's no absolute standard for what is considered a "good user experience" or "bad user experience." Because of this, it's essential to benchmark, or compare the user experience of your product against the competition. This is constantly done in market research. Marketers are always talking about "moving the needle." Unfortunately, the same is not always true in user experience. But we would argue that user experience benchmarking is just as important as market research benchmarking.

Establishing a set of benchmarks isn't as difficult as it may sound. First, you need to determine which metrics you'll be collecting over time. It's a good practice to collect data around three aspects of user experience: effectiveness (i.e., task success), efficiency (i.e., time), and satisfaction (i.e., ease of use ratings). Next, you need to determine your strategy for collecting these metrics. This would include how often the data are going to be collected and how the metrics are going to be analyzed and presented. Finally, you need to identify the type of participants to include in your benchmarks (broken up into distinct groups, how many you need, and how they're going to be recruited). Perhaps the most important thing to remember is to be consistent from one benchmark to another. This makes it all the more important to get things right the first time you lay out your benchmarking plans.

Benchmarking doesn't always have to be a special event. You can collect benchmark data (anything that will allow you to compare across more than one study) on a much smaller scale. For example, you could routinely collect SUS data after each usability session, allowing you to easily compare SUS scores across projects and designs. It isn't directly actionable, but at least it gives an indication of whether improvements are being made from one design iteration to the next and how different projects stack up against each other.

Running a competitive user experience study will put your data into perspective. What might seem like a high satisfaction score for your product might not be quite as impressive when compared to the competition. Competitive metrics around key business goals always speak volumes. For example, if your abandonment rates are much higher than your competition, this can be leveraged to acquire budget for future design and user experience work.

12.6 EXPLORE YOUR DATA

One of the most valuable things you can do is to explore your data. Roll up your shirt sleeves and dive into the raw data. Run exploratory statistics on your dataset. Look for patterns or trends that are not so obvious. Try slicing and dicing your data in different ways. The keys to exploring your data are to give yourself enough time and not to be afraid to try something new.

When we explore data, especially large datasets, the first thing we do is to make sure we're working with a clean dataset. We check for inconsistent responses and remove outliers. We make sure all the variables are well labeled and organized. After cleaning up the data, the fun begins. We start to create some new variables based on the original data. For example, we might calculate top-2-box and bottom-2-box scores for each self-reported question. We often calculate averages across multiple tasks, such as total number of task successes. We might calculate a ratio to expert performance or categorize time data according to different levels of acceptable completion times. Many new variables could be created. In fact, many of our most valuable metrics have come through data exploration.

You don't always have to be creative. One thing we often do is to run basic descriptive and exploratory statistics (explained in Chapter 2). This is easy to do in statistical packages such as SPSS, R, and even in Excel. By running some of the basic statistics, you'll see the big patterns pretty quickly.

Also, try to visualize your data in different ways. For example, create different types of scatterplots and plot regression lines, and even play with different types of bar charts. Even though you might never be presenting these figures, it helps give you a sense of what's going on.

Go beyond your data. Try to pull in data from other sources that confirm or even conflict with your assertions. More data from several other sources lend credibility to the data you share with your stakeholders. It's much easier to commit a multimillion-dollar redesign effort when multiple datasets tell the same story. Think of UX data as just one piece of the puzzle—and the more pieces of the puzzle, the easier it is to fit it all together and get the big (reliable) picture.

We can't stress enough the value in going through your data firsthand. If you're working with a vendor or business sponsor who "owns the data," ask for the raw data. Canned charts and statistics rarely tell the whole story. They're often fraught with issues. We don't take any summary data at face value; we need to see for ourselves what's going on.

12.7 SPEAK THE LANGUAGE OF BUSINESS

User Experience professionals must speak the language of business to truly make an impact. This means not only using the terms and jargon that management understands and identifies with but, more importantly, adopting their perspective. This usually centers on how to decrease costs and/or increase revenue. So, if you're asked to present your findings to senior management, you should tailor your presentation to focus on how the design effort will result in lower costs or increased revenue. You need to approach UX research as an effective means to an end. Convey the perspective that UX is a highly effective way to achieve business goals. If you keep your dialogue too academic or overly detailed, what you say probably won't have the desired impact.

Do whatever you can to tie your metrics to decreased costs or increased sales. This might not apply to every organization but certainly to the vast majority. Take the metrics you collect and calculate how costs and/or revenue are going to change as a result of your design efforts. Sometimes it takes a few assumptions to calculate an ROI, but it's still an important exercise to go through. If you're worried about your assumptions, calculate both a conservative and an aggressive set of assumptions to cover a wider range of possibilities.

Also, make sure the metrics relate to the larger business goals within your organization. If the goal of your project is to reduce phone calls to a call center, then measure task completion rates and task abandonment likelihood. If your product is all about e-commerce sales, then measure abandonment rates during checkout or likelihood to return. By carefully choosing your metrics, you'll have greater impact.

12.8 SHOW YOUR CONFIDENCE

Showing the amount of confidence you have in your results will lead to smarter decisions and help enhance your credibility. Ideally, your confidence in the data should be very high, allowing you to make the right decisions. Unfortunately, this is not always the case. Sometimes you may not have a lot of confidence in your results because of a low sample size or a relatively large amount of variance in the data. By calculating and presenting the confidence intervals, you'll have a much better idea of how much faith or confidence to place in the data. Without confidence intervals, deciding whether some differences are real is pretty much a wild guess, even what may appear to be big differences.

No matter what your data shows, provide confidence intervals whenever possible. This is especially important for relatively small samples (e.g., less than 20). The mechanics of calculating and presenting confidence intervals is pretty simple. The only thing you need to pay attention to is the type of data you are presenting. Calculating a confidence interval is different if the data are continuous (such as completion time) or binary (such as binary task success). By showing the confidence intervals, you can (hopefully) explain how the results generalize to a larger population.

Showing your confidence goes beyond calculating confidence intervals. We recommend that you calculate p-values to help you decide whether to accept or reject your hypothesis. For example, when comparing average task completion times between two different designs, it's important to determine whether there's a significant difference using a *t-test* or ANOVA. Without running the appropriate statistics, you just can't really know.

Of course, you shouldn't misrepresent your data or present it in a misleading way. For example, if you're showing task success rates based on a small sample size, it might be better to show the numbers as a frequency (e.g., six out of eight) as compared to a percentage. Also, use the appropriate level of precision for your data. For example, if you're presenting task completion times, and the tasks are taking several minutes, there's no need to present the data to the third decimal position. Even though you can, you shouldn't because it implies a level of precision that is not there.

12.9 DON'T MISUSE METRICS

UX metrics have a time and a place. Misusing metrics has the potential of undermining your entire UX program. Misuse might take the form of using metrics where none are needed, presenting too much data at once, measuring too much at once, or over-relying on a single metric.

In some situations, it's probably better not to include UX metrics. If you're just looking for some qualitative feedback at the start of a project, metrics might not be appropriate. Or perhaps the project is going through a series of rapid design iterations. Metrics in these situations might only be a distraction and not add enough value. It's important to be clear about when and where UX metrics serve a purpose. If metrics aren't adding value, don't include them.

It's also possible to present too much UX data at once. Just like packing for a vacation, it's probably wise to include all the data you want to present and then chop it in half. Not all data are equal. Some metrics are much more compelling than others. Resist the urge to show everything. That's why appendices were invented. We try to focus on a few key metrics in any presentation or report. By showing too much data, the most important message is lost.

Don't try to measure everything at once. There are only so many aspects of the user experience that you can quantify at any one time. If a product or business sponsor wants you to capture 100 different metrics, make them justify why each and every metric is essential. It's important to choose a few key metrics for any one study. The additional time to run the study and perform the analyses may make you think twice about including too many metrics at once.

Don't over-rely on a single metric. If you try to get a single metric to represent the entire experience, you're likely to miss something big. For example, if you only collect data on satisfaction, you'll miss everything about the actual interaction. Sometimes satisfaction data might take aspects of the interaction into account, but it often misses a lot as well. We recommend that you try to capture a few different metrics, each tapping into a different aspect of the user experience.

12.10 SIMPLIFY YOUR PRESENTATION

All your hard work comes down to the point where you must present results. How you choose to communicate your results can make or break a study. There are a few key things you should pay special attention to. First and foremost, your goals need to match those of your audience.

Often, you need to present findings to several different types of audiences. For example, you may need to present findings to the project team, consisting of an information architect, design lead, project manager, content manager, developer, business sponsor, and product manager. The project team is most concerned with detailed UX issues and specific design recommendations. Bottom line, they want to know the weaknesses with the design and how to fix them.

TIPS FOR AN EFFECTIVE PRESENTATION OF USABILITY RESULTS

- *Set the stage appropriately.* Depending on your audience, you might need to explain or demo the product, describe the research methods, or provide other background information. It all comes down to knowing your audience.

- *Don't belabor procedural details, but make them available.* At a minimum, your audience will usually want to know something about the participants in the study and the tasks they were asked to perform.

- *Lead with positive findings.* Some positive results come out of almost every study. Most people like to hear about features of the design that worked well.

- *Use screenshots.* Pictures really do work better than words in most cases. A screenshot that you've annotated with notes about usability issues can be very compelling.

- *Use short video clips.* The days of an elaborate production process to create a highlights videotape are, thankfully, mostly gone. With computer-based video, it's much easier and more compelling to embed short clips directly in the appropriate context of your presentation.

- *Present summary metrics.* Try to come up with one slide that clearly shows the key usability data at a glance. This might be a high-level view of the task completion data, comparisons to objectives, a derived metric representing overall user experience, or a UX scorecard.

You also may need to present to the business sponsors or product team. They're concerned about meeting their business goals, participants' reactions to the new design, and how the recommended design changes are going to impact the project timeline and budget. You may present to senior management, too. They want to ensure that the design changes will have the desired impact in terms of overall business goals and user experience. When presenting to senior managers, generally limit the metrics and focus instead on the big picture of the user experience by using stories and video clips. Too much detail usually doesn't work.

Most user research studies produce a long list of issues. Many of those issues do not have a substantial impact on the user experience. For example, minor violations of a company standard or one term on a screen that you might consider jargon. Your goal for a test presentation should be to get the major issues—as you see them—addressed, not to "win" by getting all of the issues fixed. If you present a long list of issues in a presentation, you may be seen as picky and unrealistic. Consider presenting a top 5 or at most a top 10 list and leave the minor issue for an offline discussion.

When presenting results, it's important to keep the message as simple as possible. Avoid jargon, focus on the key message, and keep the data simple and straightforward. Whatever you do, don't just describe the data. It's a surefire way to put your audience to sleep. Develop a story for each main point. Every chart or figure you show in a presentation has a story to it. Sometimes the story is that the task was difficult. Explain why it was difficult, using metrics, verbatims, and video clips to show why it was difficult and possibly even highlight design solutions. Paint a high-level picture for your audience. They will want perhaps two or three findings to latch onto. By putting all the pieces of the puzzle together, you can help them move forward in the decision making.

Albert, W., & Dixon, E. (2003). Is this what you expected? The use of expectation measures in usability testing. In *Proceedings of Usability Professionals Association 2003 conference*, Scottsdale, AZ.

Albert, W., Gribbons, W., & Almadas, J. (2009). Pre-conscious assessment of trust: A case study of financial and healthcare websites. In *Human Factors and Ergonomics Society Annual Meeting Proceedings*, *53*, 449–453. Also <http://www.measuringux.com/Albert_Gribbons_Preconsciousness.pdf>.

Albert, B., & Rosenberg, J. (2017). *Introducing a New UX maturity metric: Team Engagement Score (TES) during usability testing*. Toronto, Canada: International Conference of the User Experience Professionals Association. June 2017.

Albert, B. (2016). How sure are we? The predictive power of early UX evaluation methods on live site performance. *World IA Day Boston* 2016. Presentation found at: https://d2f5upgbvkx8pz.cloudfront.net/sites/default/files/inline-files/WorldIADay_2016_Albert_final.pdf.

Albert, B. & Marriott, J. (2019). Is that really me? A case study in measuring emotional engagement of customers using a virtual dressing room in an e-commerce website. In *ReCon Conference*, 2019, New York, NY. Presentation found at: https://d2f5upgbvkx8pz.cloudfront.net/sites/default/files/inline-files/Virtual_Dressing_Room_Presentation_final%20.pdf

Albert, W., & Tedesco, D. (2010). Reliability of self-reported awareness measures based on eye tracking. *Journal of Usability Studies*, *5*(2), 50–64.

Albert, B., Tullis, T., & Tedesco, D. (2010). *Beyond the usability lab: Conducting large-scale online user experience studies*. Boston, MA: Morgan Kaufmann.

Aldenderfer, M., & Blashfield, R. (1984). *Cluster analysis (quantitative applications in the social sciences)*. Beverly Hills, CA: Sage Publications, Inc.

American Institutes for Research. (2001). *Windows XP home edition vs. windows Millennium Edition (ME) public report*. Concord, MA: New England Research Center. Available at <http://download.microsoft.com/download/d/8/1/d810ce49-d481-4a55-ae63-3fe2800cbabd/ME_Public.doc>.

American Customer Satisfaction Index. (2019a). ACSI Federal Government Report 2018. https://www.theacsi.org/news-and-resources/customer-satisfaction-reports/report-archive/acsi-federal-government-report-2018

American Customer Satisfaction Index. (2019b). ACSI Retail and Consumer Shipping Report 2018–2019. https://www.theacsi.org/news-and-resources/customer-satisfaction-reports/reports-2019/acsi-retail-and-consumer-shipping-report-2018-2019

Andre, A. (2003). When every minute counts, all automatic external defibrillators are not created equal. Published in June, 2003 by Interface Analysis Associates <http://www.FsinFusernomics.com/iaa_aed_2003.pdf>.

Babich, N. (2018). The Designer's Guide to Lean and Agile UX. Adobe XD Ideas, June 28, 2018. https://xd.adobe.com/ideas/perspectives/leadership-insights/designers-guide-lean-agile-ux/

Bangor, A., Kortum, P., & Miller, J. A. (2009). Determining what individual SUS scores mean: Adding an adjective rating scale. *Journal of Usability Studies*, *4*, 3.

Measuring the User Experience. DOI: http://dx.doi.org/10.1016/B978-0-12-818080-8.00022-4

Bargas-Avila, J. A., & Hornbæk, K. (2011). Old wine in new bottles or novel challenges? A critical analysis of empirical studies of user experience. *CHI '11 Proceedings of the 2011 annual conference on human factors in computing systems*, 2689–2698.

Barnum, C., Bevan, N., Cockton, G., Nielsen, J., Spool, J., & Wixon, D. (2003). *The "magic number 5": Is it enough for web testing? 2003, April 5–10, Ft.* Lauderdale, FL: *CHI*.

Beasley, M. (2013). *Practical web analytics for user experience: How analytics can help you understand your users* (1st ed.). San Francisco, CA: Morgan Kaufmann Publishers Inc.

Benedek, J., & Miner, T. (2002). Measuring desirability: New methods for evaluating desirability in a usability lab setting. In *Usability professionals association 2002 conference*, Orlando, FL, July 8–12. Also available at <http://www.microsoft.com/usability/UEPostings/ DesirabilityToolkit.doc>. Also see the appendix listing the Product Reaction Cards at <http://www.microsoft.com/usability/UEPostings/ProductReactionCards.doc>.

Bias, R., & Mayhew, D. (2005). *Cost-justifying usability, Second edition: An update for the Internet age*. San Francisco, CA: Morgan Kaufmann.

Birns, J., Joffre, K., Leclerc, J., & Paulsen, C. A. (2002). Getting the whole picture: Collecting usability data using two methods – Concurrent think aloud and retrospective probing. In *Proceedings of the 2002 Usability Professionals' Association conference*, Orlando, FL. Available from <http://concordevaluation.com/papers/paulsen_thinkaloud_2002.pdf>.

Boletsis, C., & Cedergren, J. (2019). VR locomotion in the new era of virtual reality: An empirical comparison of prevalent techniques. *Advances in Human-Computer Interaction*, *2019*, 1–15. https://doi.org/10.1155/2019/7420781.

Bradley, M. M., & Lang, P. J. (1994). Measuring emotion: The self-assessment manikin and the semantic differential. *Journal of Behavior Therapy and Experimental Psychiatry*, *25*, 49–59.

Breyfogle, F. (1999). *Implementing six sigma: Smarter solutions using statistical methods*. New York, NY: John Wiley and Sons.

Broekens, J., & Brinkman, W. P. (2013). AffectButton: A method for reliable and valid affective self-report. *International Journal of Human-Computer Studies.*, *71*, 641–667.

Brooke, J. (1996). SUS: A quick and dirty usability scale. In P. W. Jordan, B. Thomas, B. A. Weerdmeester, & I. L. McClelland (Eds.), *Usability evaluation in industry*. London: Taylor & Francis.

Buckley, J. D., & Powers, A. (2019). *Measuring the ROI of UX in an Enterprise Organization, Part 2*, UXMatters, January 7, 2019. https://www.uxmatters.com/mt/archives/2019/01/measuring-the-roi-of-ux-in-an-enterprise-organization-part-2.php

Burton, L., Albert, W., & Flynn, M. (2014). A comparison of the performance of webcam vs. infrared eye tracking technology. Published in the *Proceedings of the human factors and ergonomics society annual meeting*, Chicago, IL, 2014.

Catani, M., & Biers, D. (1998). Usability evaluation and prototype fidelity. In *Proceedings of the human factors and ergonomic society*.

Chadwick-Dias, A., McNulty, M., & Tullis, T. (2003). Web usability and age: How design changes can improve performance. In *Proceedings of the 2003 ACM conference on universal usability*, Vancouver, BC, Canada.

Chandrashekar, A. (2016). Selecting the best artwork for videos through A/B testing. *Netflix Technology Blog*. https://netflixtechblog.com/selecting-the-best-artwork-for-videos-through-a-b-testing-f6155c4595f6.

Chandrashekar, A., Amat, F., Basilico, J., & Jebara, T. (2017). Artwork personalization at Netflix. *Netflix Technology Blog*. December 7, 2017. https://netflixtechblog.com/artwork-personalization-c589f074ad76.

Chin, J. P., Diehl, V. A., & Norman, K. L. (1988). Development of an instrument measuring user satisfaction of the human-computer interface. *ACM CHI'88 proceedings*, 213–218.

Clifton, B. (2012). *Advanced web metrics with Google analytics*. Indianapolis, IN: Sybex.

Cockton, G., & Woolrych, A. (2001). Understanding inspection methods: Lessons from an assessment of heuristic evaluation. *Joint Proceedings of HCI and IHM: people and computers, XV*.

Cox, E. P. (1980). The optimal number of response alternatives for a scale: A review. *Journal of Marketing Research, 17*(4), 407–422.

Cunningham, K. (2012). *The accessibility handbook*. Sebastopol, CA: O'Reilly Media.

Cyr, D., Head, M., & Ivanov, A. (2006). Design aesthetics leading to m-loyalty in mobile commerce. *Information & Management, 43*, 950–963. https://doi.org/10.1016/j.im.2006.08.009.

Davis, F. (1989). Perceived usefulness, perceived ease of use, and user acceptance of information technology. *MIS Quarterly, 13*(3), 319–340. https://doi.org/10.2307/249008.

Derfuss, K., Hogreve, J., Iseke, A., & Eller, T. (2017). The service-profit chain: A meta-analytic test of a comprehensive theoretical framework. *Journal of Marketing* May 2017.

Desmet, P. M. A., Hekkert, P. & Jacobs, J. J. (2000). When a car makes you smile: Development and application of an instrument to measure product emotions. In: Hoch S.J. and Meyer R.J., (Eds.), *Advances in Consumer Research* Vol. 27, 2000, 111–117.

Desmet, P. M. A., & Roeser, S. (2019). Emotions in design for values. In M. J. van den Hoven, P. E. Vermaas, & I. R. van de Poel (Eds.), *Handbook of ethics, values, and technological design* (p. 203). Dordrecht: Springer.

Dillman, D. A., Phelps, G., Tortora, R., Swift, K., Kohrell, J., Berck, J., et al. (2008). Response rate and measurement differences in mixed mode surveys using mail, telephone, interactive voice response, and the internet. Available at <http://www.sesrc.wsu.edu/dillman/papers/2008/ResponseRateandMeasurement.pdf>.

Ekman, P., & Friesen, W. (1975). *Unmasking the face*. Englewood Cliffs, NJ: Prentice-Hall.

Everett, S. P., Byrne, M. D., & Greene, K. K. (2006). Measuring the usability of paper ballots: Efficiency, effectiveness, and satisfaction. In *Proceedings of the human factors and ergonomics society 50th annual meeting*. Santa Monica, CA: Human Factors and Ergonomics Society.

Farnsworth, B. (2019). UX Research – What Is It and Where Is It Going? iMotions Blog, March 12, 2019. https://imotions.com/blog/ux-research/

Feldman, B. L., & Russell, J. A. (1999). The structure of current affect: Controversies and emerging consensus. *Current Directions in Psychological Science, 8*, 10–14.

Few, S. (2006). *Information dashboard design: The effective visual communication of data*. Sebastopol, CA: O'Reilly Media, Inc.

Few, S. (2009). *Now you see it: Simple visualization techniques for quantitative analysis*. Oakland, CA: Analytics Press.

Few, S. (2012). *Show me the numbers: Designing tables and graphs to enlighten* (2nd ed.). Oakland, CA: Analytics Press.

Filko, D., & Martinović, G. (2013). Emotion recognition system by a neural network based facial expression analysis. *Automatika, 54*(2), 263–272.

Finstad, K. (2010). Response interpolation and scale sensitivity: Evidence against 5-point scales. *Journal of Usability Studies, 5*(3), 104–110.

Fogg, B. J., Marshall, J., Laraki, O., Osipovich, A., Varma, C., Fang, N., et al. (2001). What makes web sites credible? A report on a large quantitative study. *Proceedings of CHI'01, human factors in computing systems*, 61–68.

Foraker. (2010). Usability ROI case study: breastcancer.org discussion forums. Retrieved on 4/18/2013 from <http://www.usabilityfirst.com/documents/U1st_BCO_CaseStudy.pdf>.

Foresee. (2012). ACSI e-government satisfaction index (Q4 2012). <http://www.foresee-eresults.com/research-white-papers/_downloads/acsi-egov-q4-2012-foresee.pdf>.

Friedman, H. H., & Friedman, L. W. (1986). On the danger of using too few points in a rating scale: A test of validity. *Journal of Data Collection*, *26*(2), 60–63.

Galley, N., Betz, D., & Biniossek, C. (2015). Fixation durations: Why are they so highly variable? *Advances Visual Perception Research*, *2015*, 83–106.

Garcia, S. & Hammond, L. (2016). Capturing & measuring emotions in UX. CHI conference extended abstracts on human factors in computing systems, May 2016 pp. 777–785).

Garland, R. (1991). The mid-point on a rating scale: Is it desirable? *Marketing Bulletin*(2), 66–70. Research Note 3.

Green, P. E., & Rao, V. R. (1971). Conjoint measurement for quantifying judgmental data. *Journal of Marketing Research*, *8*(3), 355–363. https://doi.org/10.2307/3149575.

Green, P. E., & Srinivasan, V. (1978). Conjoint analysis in consumer research: Issues and outlook. *Journal of Consumer Research*, *5*(2), 103–123.

Guan, Z., Lee, S., Cuddihy, E., & Ramey, J. (2006). The validity of the stimulated retrospective think-aloud method as measured by eye tracking. In *Proceedings of the ACM SIGCHI conference on human factors in computing systems, 2006* (pp. 1253–1262). New York, NY: ACM Press. Available from <http://dub.washington.edu:2007/pubs/chi2006/paper285-guan.pdf>.

Harrison, M. D. & Monk, A. F. (Eds.), *People and computers: Designing for usability* (pp. 196–214). Cambridge, MD: Cambridge University Press.

Hart, T. (2004). Designing "senior friendly" websites: Do guidelines help? *Usability News, 6.1* <http://psychology.wichita.edu/surl/usabilitynews/61/older_adults-withexp.htm>.

Hart, S. G., & Staveland, L. E. (1988). Development of NASA-TLX (Task Load Index): Results of empirical and theoretical research. In P. A. Hancock & N. Meshkati (Eds.), *Advances in psychology, 52. Human mental workload* (pp. 139–183). North-Holland. https://doi.org/10.1016/S0166-4115(08)62386-9

Hassenzahl, M., Burmester, M., & Koller, F. (2003). AttrakDiff: Ein Fragebogen zur Messung wahrgenommener hedonischer und pragmatischer Qualität. In G. Szwillus & J. Ziegler (Eds.), *Mensch & Computer 2003: Interaktion in Bewegung* (pp. 187–196). Berlin: Vieweg+Teubner Verlag. https://doi.org/10.1007/978-3-322-80058-9_19.

Henry, S. L. (2007). *Just ask: Integrating accessibility throughout design*. Raleigh, NC: Lulu.com.

Hertzum, M., Jacobsen, N., & Molich, R. (2002). *Usability inspections by groups of specialists: Perceived agreement in spite of disparate observations*. Minneapolis, MN: CHI.

Heskett, J., Sasser, W. E., Jr., & Schlesinger, L. (1997). *The Service Profit Chain: How leading companies link profit and growth to loyalty, satisfaction, and value*. New York, NY: Free Press. 1997.

Hewett, T. T. (1986). The role of iterative evaluation in designing systems for usability. In *People and Computers II: Designing for Usability* (pp. 196–214). Cambridge, MD: Cambridge University Press.

Holland, A. (2012). *Ecommerce button copy test: Did 'Personalize Now' or 'Customize It' get 48% more revenue per visitor?* Retrieved on 4/18/2013 from <http://whichtestwon.com/archives/14511>.

Hollander, M., Wolfe, D. A., & Chicken, E. (2013). *Nonparametric statistical methods* (3rd ed.). New York, NY: Wiley Press.

Huey, E. B. (1908). *The psychology and pedagogy of reading*. New York, NY: Macmillan.

Human Factors International. (2002). *HFI helps staples.com boost repeat customers by 67%*. Retrieved on 4/18/2013 from <http://www.humanfactors.com/downloads/documents/staples.pdf>.

Ignatow, G. (2016). Theoretical foundations for digital text analysis: Theoretical foundations for digital text analysis. *Journal for the Theory of Social Behaviour, 46*(1), 104–120. https://doi.org/10.1111/jtsb.12086.

Ignatow, G., & Mihalcea, R. (2017). *An introduction to text mining: Research design, data collection, and analysis*. London: SAGE Publications.

ISO/IEC 25062. (2006). Software engineering – Software product Quality Requirements and Evaluation (SQuaRE) – Common Industry Format (CIF) for usability test reports.

Jacobsen, N., Hertzum, M., & John, B. (1998). The evaluator effect in usability studies: Problem detection and severity judgments. In *Proceedings of the human factors and ergonomics society*.

Jarvenpaa, S. L., Tractinsky, N., & Vitale, M. (2000). Consumer trust in an Internet store. *Information Technology and Management, 1*(1), 45–71. https://doi.org/10.1023/A:1019104520776.

Jokinen, J. (2015). Emotional user experience: Traits, events, and states. *International Journal of Human-Computer Studies, 76*, 67–77.

Kano, N., Seraku, N., Takahashi, F., & Tsuji, S. (1984). Attractive quality and must-be quality. *Journal of the Japanese Society for Quality Control, 41*, 39–48.

Kahneman, D. (2011). *Thinking, fast and slow*. New York: Farrar, Straus and Giroux.

Kaushik, A. (2009). *Web analytics 2.0: the art of online accountability and science of customer centricity*. Indianapolis, IN: Sybex.

Kaya, A., Ozturk, R., & Altin Gumussoy, C. (2019). Usability measurement of mobile applications with system usability scale (SUS). In F. Calisir, E. Cevikcan, & H. Camgoz Akdag (Eds.), *Industrial engineering in the big data era* (pp. 389–400). New York, NY: Springer International Publishing. https://doi.org/10.1007/978-3-030-03317-0_32.

Kirakowski, J., & Cierlik, B. (1998). *Usability from the top and from the bottom*. TU Gdansk, Poland: Transferring Usability Engineering to Industry.

Kirakowski, J., Claridge, N., & Whitehand, R. (1998, June). Human centered measures of success in web site design. In *Proceedings of the fourth conference on human factors & the web*.

Kirakowski, J., & Corbett, M. (1993). SUMI: The software usability measurement inventory. *British Journal of Educational Technology, 24*(3), 210–212. https://doi.org/10.1111/j.1467-8535.1993.tb00076.x.

Kirkpatrick, A., Rutter, R., Heilmann, C., Thatcher, J., & Waddell, C. (2006). *Web accessibility: Web standards and regulatory compliance*. New York, NY: Apress Media.

Kohavi, R., Crook, T., & Longbotham, R. (2009). *Online experimentation at Microsoft*. Third workshop on Data Mining Case Studies and Practice. Retrieved on 4/18/2013 from <http://robotics.stanford.edu/~ronnyk/ExP_DMCaseStudies.pdf>.

Kohavi, R., Deng, A., Frasca, B., Longbotham, R., Walker, T., & Xu, Y. (2012). Trustworthy online controlled experiments: Five puzzling outcomes explained. In *Proceedings of the 18th ACM SIGKDD international conference on knowledge discovery and data mining (KDD '12)* (pp. 786–794). New York, NY: ACM.

Kohavi, R., & Round, M. (2004). *Front line internet analytics at Amazon.com*. Presentation at Emetrics Summit 2004. Retrieved on 4/18/2013 from <http://ai.stanford.edu/~ronnyk/emetricsAmazon.pdf>.

Kohn, L. T., Corrigan, J. M., & Donaldson, M. S. (Eds.), (2000). *Committee on quality of health care in America, institute of medicine. "To err is human: building a safer health system"*. Washington, DC: National Academies Press.

Kortum, P., & Sorber, M. (2015). Measuring the usability of mobile applications for phones and tablets. *International Journal of Human-Computer Interaction, 31*, 518–529. https://doi.org/10.1080/10447318.2015.1064658.

Kruskal, J., & Wish, M. (2006). *Multidimensional scaling (quantitative applications in the social sciences)*. Beverly Hills, CA: Sage Publications, Inc.

Kujala, S., Roto, V., & Väänänen, K. (2011). UX curve: A method for evaluating long-term user experience. *Interacting with Computers, 23*(5), 473–483.

Kuniavsky, M. (2003). *Observing the user experience: A practitioner's guide to user research.* San Francisco, CA: Morgan Kaufmann.

Laurans, G. F. G., & Desmet, P. M. A. (2012). Introduction PrEmo2: Progress in the non-verbal measurement of emotion in design. In J. Brassett, P. Hekkert, G. Ludden, M. Malpass, & J. McDonnell (Eds.), *Proceedings of the 8th international design and emotion conference, 2012* (pp. 11–14). London: Central Saint Martin College of Art & Design. September 2012.

Laurans, G. F. G., & Desmet, P. M. A. (2008). Speaking in tongues—Assessing user experience in a global economy. In *Proceedings of the 6th international conference on design and emotion, 2008*. Hong Kong: Hong Kong Polytechnic University Press.

Laurans, G. F. G., & Desmet, P. M. A. (2017). Developing 14 animated characters for non-verbal self-report of categorical emotions. *Journal of Design Research, 15*(3/4), 214–233.

LeDoux, L., Connor, E., & Tullis, T. (2005). Extreme makeover: UI edition. Presentation at Usability Professionals Association (UPA) 2005 Annual Conference, Montreal, QUE, Canada. Available from <http://www.upassoc.org/usability_resources/conference/2005/ledoux-UPA2005-Extreme.pdf>.

Lewis, J. R. (1991). Psychometric evaluation of an after-scenario questionnaire for computer usability studies: The ASQ. *SIGCHI Bulletin, 23*(1), 78–81. Also see <http://www.acm.org/~perlman/question.cgi?form=ASQ>.

Lewis, J. (1994). Sample sizes for usability studies: Additional considerations. *Human Factors, 36*, 368–378.

Lewis, J. R. (1995). IBM computer usability satisfaction questionnaires: Psychometric evaluation and instructions for use. *International Journal of Human-Computer Interaction, 7*(1), 57–78. Also see http://www.acm.org/~perlman/question.cgi?form=CSUQ.

Lewis, J. R., & Sauro, J. (2009). The factor structure of the system usability scale. *Proceedings of the human computer interaction international conference (HCII 2009)*, San Diego CA, USA.

Lewis, J. R., Brian, S. U. & Deborah, E. M. (2013). UMUX-LITE: When there's no time for the SUS. In *Conference on human factors in computing systems – proceedings*. (pp. 2099–2102). 10.1145/2470654.2481287.

Lewis, J. R., & Mayes, D. K. (2014). Development and Psychometric Evaluation of the Emotional Metric Outcomes (EMO) Questionnaire. *International Journal of Human-Computer Interaction, 30*(9), 685–702.

Lewis, J. R., & Sauro, J. (2017). Revisiting the factor structure of the system usability scale. *Journal of Usability Studies, 12*(4), 183–192.

Lewis, J. R. (2018). Comparison of item formats: Agreement vs. item-specific endpoints. *Journal of Usability Studies, 14*(1), 48–60.

Likert, R. (1932). A technique for the measurement of attitudes. *Archives of Psychology, 140*, 55.

Lin, T., Hu, W., Omata, M., & Imamiya, A. (2005). Do physiological data relate to traditional usability indexes? In *Proceedings of OZCHI2005*, November 23–25, Canberra, Australia.

Lindgaard, G., & Chattratichart, J. (2007). Usability testing: What have we overlooked? In *Proceedings of ACM CHI conference on human factors in computing systems*.

Lindgaard, G., Fernandes, G., Dudek, C., & Brown, J. (2006). Attention web designers: You have 50 milliseconds to make a good first impression!. *Behaviour & Information Technology*, *25*, 115–126.

Liu, B. (2015). *Sentiment Analysis: Mining sentiments, opinions, and emotions*. Cambridge University Press.

Louviere, J. J., & Woodworth, G. (1983). Design and analysis of simulated consumer choice or allocation experiments: An approach based on aggregate data. *Journal of Marketing Research*, *20*(4), 350–367. https://doi.org/10.2307/3151440.

Lund, A. (2001). Measuring usability with the USE questionnaire. *Usability and user experience newsletter* of the STC Usability SIG. See <http://www.stcsig.org/usability/newsletter/0110_measuring_with_use.html>.

Mascias, J. (2021). Enhancing card sorting dendrograms through the holistic analysis of distance methods and linkage criteria. *Journal of Usability Studies*, *16*(2), 73–90.

Martin, P., & Bateson, P. (1993). *Measuring behaviour* (2nd ed.). Cambridge, UK, and New York, NY: Cambridge University Press.

Maurer, D., & Warfel, T. (2004). Card sorting: A definitive guide. *Boxes and Arrows*, April 2004. Retrieved on 4/18/2013 from <http://boxesandarrows.com/ card-sorting-a-definitive-guide/>.

Mayfield, A. (2015). Optional Workshop Blog, April 14, 2015. https://blog.optimalworkshop.com/does-the-first-click-really-matter-treejack-says-yes/

Mayhew, D., & Bias, R. (1994). *Cost-justifying usability*. San Francisco, CA: Morgan Kaufmann.

McGee, M. (2003). Usability magnitude estimation. *Proceedings of human factors and ergonomics society annual meeting*, Denver, CO.

McGovern, G. (2015). What really matters: Focusing on top tasks. *A List Apart*, April 21, 2015. https://alistapart.com/article/what-really-matters-focusing-on-top-tasks/.

McGovern, G. (2016). Measuring the Customer Experience Using Top Tasks. *UIE's All You Can Learn Library*, https://aycl.uie.com/virtual seminars/top_tasks

Harrison McKnight, D., & Chervany, N. L. (2001). Trust and distrust definitions. One bite at a time. In R. Falcone, M. Singh, & Y.-H. Tan (Eds.), *Trust in cyber-societies* (pp. 27–54). New York, NY: Springer. https://doi.org/10.1007/3-540-45547-7_3.

McLellan, S., Muddimer, A., & Peres, S. C. (2012). The effect of experience on system usability scale ratings. *Journal of Usability Studies*, *7*(2), 56–67. <http://www.upassoc.org/upa_publications/jus/2012february/JUS_McLellan_February_2012.pdf>.

Miner, G., Elder, J., Hill, T., Nisbet, R., Delen, D., & Fast, A. (2012). *Practical text mining and statistical analysis for non-structured text data applications*. New York, NY: Elsevier Academic Press. ISBN 978-0-12-386979-1.

Molich, R. (2010). CUE-8 – Task measurement. Retrieved on 3/11/2019 from http://www.dialogdesign.dk/CUE-8.htm.

Molich, R. (2018). Are usability evaluations reproducible? *Interactions*, *25*(6), 82–86.

Molich, R., Bevan, N., Butler, S., Curson, I., Kindlund, E., Kirakowski, J., et al. (1998). *Comparative evaluation of usability tests. Usability professionals association 1998 Conference, 22–26 June 1998* (pp. 189–200). Washington, DC: Usability Professionals Association.

Molich, R., & Dumas, J. (2008). Comparative usability evaluation (CUE-4). *Behaviour & Information Technology*, *27*, 263–281.

Molich, R., Ede, M. R., Kaasgaard, K., & Karyukin, B. (2004). Comparative usability evaluation. *Behaviour & Information Technology, 23*(1), 65–74.

Molich, R., Jeffries, R., & Dumas, J. (2007). Making usability recommendations useful and usable. *Journal of Usability Studies, 2*(4), 162–179. Available at <http://www.upassoc.org/upa_publications/jus/2007august/useful-usable.pdf>..

Mueller, J. (2003). *Accessibility for everybody: Understanding the Section 508 accessibility requirements*. New York, NY: Apress Media.

Nancarrow, C., & Brace, I. (2000). Saying the "right thing": Coping with social desirability bias in marketing research. *Bristol Business School Teaching and Research Review*(Summer), 3.

Nawaz, A. (2012). APCHI '12, August 28–31, 2012, Matsue-city, Shimane, Japan.

Nelson, N. (2016). The power of a picture. Netflix Technology Blog. May 3, 2016. https://about.netflix.com/en/news/the-power-of-a-picture

Nielsen, J. (1993). *Usability engineering*. San Francisco, CA: Morgan Kaufmann.

Nielsen, J. (2000). Why you only need to test with 5 users. *AlertBox*, March 19. Available at <http://www.useit.com/alertbox/20000319.html>.

Nielsen, J. (2001). Beyond accessibility: treating users with disabilities as people. *AlertBox*, November 11, 2001. Retrieved on 4/18/2013, from <http://www.nngroup.com/articles/beyond-accessibility-treating-users-with-disabilities-as-people/>.

Nielsen, J. (2003). Return on Investment for Usability. *Nielsen Norman Group* January 7, 2003. https://www.nngroup.com/articles/usability-metrics/.

Nielsen, J. (2005). Medical usability: How to kill patients through bad design, *Alertbox*, April 11, 2005 <http://www.nngroup.com/articles/medical-usability/>.

Nielsen, J., Berger, J., Gilutz, S., & Whitenton, K. (2008). *Return on Investment (ROI) for usability* (4th ed). Freemont, CA: Nielsen Norman Group.

Nielsen, J., & Landauer, T. (1993). A mathematical model of the finding of usability problems. In *ACM proceedings, Interchi 93*, Amsterdam.

Norgaard, M., & Hornbaek, K. (2006). What do usability evaluators do in practice? An explorative study of think-aloud testing. In *Proceedings of designing interactive systems* (pp. 209–218). University Park, PA.

Ortony, A., Clore, G. L., & Collins, A. (1990). *The cognitive structure of emotions*. Cambridge, MA: Cambridge University Press.

Osgood, C. E., Suci, G., & Tannenbaum, P. (1957). *The measurement of meaning*. Urbana, IL: University of Illinois Press.

Pengnate, S. (Fone), & Sarathy, R. (2017). An experimental investigation of the influence of website emotional design features on trust in unfamiliar online vendors. *Computers in Human Behavior, 67*, 49–60. https://doi.org/10.1016/j.chb.2016.10.018.

Petrie, H., & Precious, J. (2010). Measuring user experience of websites: Think aloud protocols and an emotion word prompt list. In *Proceedings of ACM CHI 2010 Conference on human factors in computing systems, 2010* (pp. 3673–3678).

Peute, L. W. P., Keizer, N. F. de, & Jaspers, M. W. M. (2015). The value of Retrospective and Concurrent Think Aloud in formative usability testing of a physician data query tool. *Journal of Biomedical Informatics, 55*, 1–10. https://doi.org/10.1016/j.jbi.2015.02.006.

Porter, M. E. (1985). *Competitive advantage: Creating and sustaining: Superior performance* (pp. 11–15). New York, NY: The Free Press.

Project Bread (2019). 2019 Annual Report. https://www.projectbread.org/uploads/attachments/ckewxpt4v02b51c4lae8kvnxd-2019-annual-report.pdf

Reichheld, F. F. (2003). One number you need to grow. *Harvard Business Review.* December 2003.

Rodden, K., Hutchinson, H., & Fu, X. (2010). Measuring the user experience on a large scale: User-centered metrics for web applications. In *Proceedings of the SIGCHI conference on human factors in computing systems* (pp. 2395–2398). Association for Computing Machinery. https://doi.org/10.1145/1753326.1753687.

Sangster, R. L., Willits, F. K., Saltiel, J., Lorenz, F. O., & Rockwood, T. H. (2001). *The effects of Numerical Labels on Response Scales*. Retrieved on 3/30/2013 from <http://www.bls.gov/osmr/pdf/st010120.pdf>.

Sauro, J., & Kindlund, E. (2005). A method to standardize usability metrics into a single score. In *Proceedings of the conference on human factors in computing systems (CHI 2005)*, Portland, OR.

Sauro, J., & Lewis, J. (2005). Estimating completion rates from small samples using binomial confidence intervals: Comparisons and recommendations. In *Proceedings of the human factors and ergonomics society annual meeting*, Orlando, FL.

Sauro, J. & Dumas J. (2009). Comparison of three one-question, post-task usability questionnaires. In *Proceedings of the conference on human factors in computing systems (CHI 2009)*, Boston, MA.

Sauro, J. (2010). Does better usability increase customer loyalty? MeasuringU Blog, January 7, 2010. <http://www.measuringusability.com/usability-loyalty.php>.

Sauro, J. (2010). "Why You Only Need to Test with Five Users (Explained)." MeasuringU Blog, March 8, 2010, https://measuringu.com/five-users/#.

Sauro, J., & Lewis, J. R. (2011). When designing usability questionnaires, does it hurt to be positive. In *Proceedings of the conference on human factors in computing systems (CHI 2011)*, Vancouver, BC, Canada.

Sauro, J. (2011). "What Is A Good Task-Completion Rate?." MeasuringU, 21 Mar. 2011, https://measuringu.com/task-completion/.

Sauro, J. (2012). 10 things to know about the Single Usability Metric (SUM). *MeasuringU*, May 30, 2012, https://measuringu.com/sum/

Sauro, J. (2012). 10 things to know about the Single Ease Question (SEQ). *MeasuringU*, October 30, 2012, https://measuringu.com/seq10/

Sauro, J. (2014). "How to Conduct a Top Task Analysis." *MeasuringU.com*, September 10, 2014. https://measuringu.com/top tasks/

Sauro, J. (2015). "10 Metrics to Track the ROI of UX Efforts." *MeasuringU*, September 1, 2015. https://measuringu.com/ux-roi/

Sauro, J. (2015). "How To Find The Sample Size For 8 Common Research Designs." *MeasuringU*, 6 May. 2015, https://measuringu.com/sample-size-designs/.

Sauro, J. (2015). SUPR-Q: A comprehensive measure of the quality of the website user experience. *Journal of Usability Studies*, 10(2).

Sauro, J. (2016). "A Checklist for Planning a UX Benchmark Study." MeasuringU.com, April 19, 2016. https://measuringu.com/benchmark-checklist/

Sauro, J. (2016). "Creating a UX Measurement Plan." MeasuringU Blog, April 26, 2016. https://measuringu.com/ux-measurement/

Sauro, J. (2017). Measuring usability: From the SUS to the UMUX-Lite. MeasuringU Blog, October 10, 2017. https://measuringu.com/umux-lite/

Sauro, J. (2018). 10 Things to Know About the SUPR-Q, MeasuringU Blog, June 12, 2018, https://measuringu.com/10-things-suprq/

Sauro, J. (2018). "The One Number You Need to Grow (A Replication)." MeasuringU Blog, December 2018. https://measuringu.com/nps-replication/

Sauro, J. (2019a). 10 things to know about the NASA TLX. MeasuringU Blog, August 27, 2019. https://measuringu.com/nasa-tlx/

Sauro, J. (2019b). 10 things to know about the Technology Acceptance Model (TAM). MeasuringU Blog, May 7, 2019. https://measuringu.com/tam/

Sauro, J. (2019c). SUM: Single Usability Metric. MeasuringU Blog, October 21, 2019, https://measuringu.com/sum-2/

Schall, A. (2015). The Future of UX Research: Uncovering the True Emotions of Our Users, UXPA Magazine, April, 2015. https://uxpamagazine.org/the-future-of-ux-research/

Schrepp, M., Hinderks, A., & Thomaschewski, J. (2017). Design and evaluation of a short version of the User Experience Questionnaire (UEQ-S). *International Journal of Interactive Multimedia and Artificial Intelligence*, 4, 103. https://doi.org/10.9781/ijimai.2017.09.001.

Schwarz, N., Knäuper, B., Hippler, H. J., Noelle-Neumann, E., & Clark, F. (1991). Rating scales: Numeric values may change the meaning of scale labels. *Public Opinion Quarterly*, 55, 570–582.

Section 508. (1998). Workforce Investment Act of 1998, Pub. L. No. 105–220, 112 Stat. 936 (August 7). Codified at 29 U.S.C. § 794d.

Shaikh, A., Baker, J., & Russell, M. (2004). What's the skinny on weight loss websites? Usability News, 6.1, 2004. Available at <http://psychology.wichita.edu/surl/usabilitynews/ 61/diet_domain.htm>.

Sharon. T. (2012). *It's our research: Getting stakeholder buy-in for user experience research projects*. Boston, MA: Morgan Kaufmann.

Sinclair, R., Mark, M., Moore, S., Lavis, C., & Soldat, A. (2000). An electoral butterfly effect. *Nature*, 408, 665–666. https://doi.org/10.1038/35047160.

Smith. P. A. (1996). Towards a practical measure of hypertext usability. *Interacting with Computers*, 8(4), 365–381.

Snyder, C. (2006). Bias in usability testing. In *Boston Mini-UPA Conference*, March 3, Natick, MA.

Sostre, P., & LeClaire, J. (2007). *Web analytics for dummies*. Hoboken, NJ: Wiley.

Spencer, D. (2009). *Card sorting: Designing usable categories*. Brooklyn, NY: Rosenfeld Media.

Spool, J., & Schroeder, W. (2001). Testing web sites: Five users is nowhere near enough. *CHI* 2001, Seattle.

Stover, A., Coyne, K., & Nielsen, J. (2002). Designing usable site maps for Websites. Available from <http://www.nngroup.com/reports/sitemaps/>.

Stuchbery (2010). Tracking KPI's with confidence. Natureresearch.com website, September 1, 2010. https://www.natureresearch.com.au/2010/09/tracking-kpis-with-confidence/

Tang, D., Agarwal, A., O'Brien, D., & Meyer, M. (2010). Overlapping experiment infrastructure: More, better, faster experimentation. In *Proceedings of the 16th ACM SIGKDD international conference on Knowledge Discovery and Data mining (KDD '10)* (pp. 17–26). New York, NY: ACM.

Teague, R., De Jesus, K., & Nunes-Ueno, M. (2001). Concurrent vs post-task usability test ratings. *CHI 2001 extended abstracts on human factors in computing systems* (pp. 289–290).

Technical Committee ISO/TC 159. *Ergonomics*, Subcommittee SC 4, *Ergonomics of human-system interaction*. ISO 9241-11:2018(en) Ergonomics of human-system interaction. Part 11: Usability: Definitions and concepts. https://www.iso.org/standard/63500.html

Tedesco, D., & Tullis, T. (2006). A comparison of methods for eliciting post-task subjective ratings in usability testing. In *Usability Professionals Association (UPA) 2006 annual conference*, Broomfield, CO, June 12–16.

Tufte, E. R. (1990). *Envisioning information*. Chesire, CT: Graphics Press.

Tufte, E. R. (1997). *Visual explanations: Images and quantities, evidence and narrative.* Chesire, CT: Graphics Press.

Tufte, E. R. (2001). *The visual display of quantitative information* (2nd ed). Chesire, CT: Graphics Press.

Tufte, E. R. (2006). *Beautiful evidence.* Chesire, CT: Graphics Press.

Tullis, T. S. (1985). Designing a menu-based interface to an operating system. In *Proceedings of the CHI '85 conference on human factors in computing systems,* San Francisco, CA.

Tullis, T. S. (1998). A method for evaluating Web page design concepts. In *Proceedings of CHI '98 conference on computer-human interaction,* Los Angeles, CA.

Tullis, T. S. (2007). Using closed card-sorting to evaluate information architectures. In *Usability Professionals Association (UPA) 2007 Conference,* Austin, TX. Retrieved on 4/18/2013 from <http://www.eastonmass.net/tullis/presentations/ClosedCardSorting.pdf>.

Tullis, T. S. (2008a). *SUS scores from 129 conditions in 50 studies.* Retrieved on 3/30/2013 from <http://www.measuringux.com/SUS-scores.xls>.

Tullis, T. S. (2008b). *Results of online usability study of Apollo program websites.* <http://www.measuringux.com/apollo/>.

Tullis, T. S. (2008c). Results of an online study comparing the Obama and McCain websites. MeasuringUX website. November 9, 2008. https://www.measuringux.com/Obama-McCain/index.htm

Tullis, T. S., Connor, E. C., & Rosenbaum, R. (2007). An empirical comparison of on-screen keyboards. In *Human factors and ergonomics society 51st annual meeting,* October 1–5, Baltimore, MD. Available from <http://www.measuringux.com/OnScreenKeyboards/index.htm>

Tullis, T. S., & Stetson, J.. (2004). A comparison of questionnaires for assessing Website usability. In *Usability Professionals Association (UPA) 2004 conference,* June 7–11, Minneapolis, MN. Paper available from <http://www.upassoc.org/usability_resources/conference/2004/UPA-2004-TullisStetson.pdf>.

Tullis, T. S., & Tullis, C. (2007). Statistical analyses of e-commerce websites: Can a site be usable and beautiful? In *Proceedings of HCI international 2007 conference,* Beijing, China.

Tullis, T. S., & Wood, L. (2004). How many users are enough for a card-sorting study? *Proceedings of Usability Professionals Association Conference,* June 7–11, Minneapolis, MN. Available from http://home.comcast.net/~tomtullis/publications/UPA2004CardSorting.pdf.

Van Den Haak, M., De Jong, M., & Schellens, P. J. (2003). Retrospective vs. concurrent think-aloud protocols: Testing the usability of an online library catalogue. *Behaviour & Information Technology, 22*(5), 339–351.

Van den Haak, M. J., de Jong, M. D. T., & Schellens, P. J. (2004). Employing think-aloud protocols and constructive interaction to test the usability of online library catalogues: a methodological comparison. *Interacting with Computers, 16,* 1153–1170.

Virzi, R. (1992). Refining the test phase of the usability evaluation: How many subjects is enough? *Human Factors, 34*(4), 457–468.

Vividence Corp. (2001). Moving on up: move.com improves customer experience. Retrieved on October 15, 2001, from <http://www.vividence.com/public/solutions/our+clients/success+stories/movecom.htm>

Waardhuizen, M., McLean-Oliver, J., Perry, N., & Munko, J. (2019). Explorations on single usability metrics. In CHI EA '19: Extended abstracts of the 2019 CHI conference on human factors in computing systems (p. 8). https://doi.org/10.1145/3290607.3299062

Wilson, C., & Coyne, K. P. (2001). Tracking usability issues: To bug or not to bug? *Interactions, 8*(3). May, 2001.

Wilson, C. (2011). "Method 3 of 100: Freelisting." *Designing the User Experience at Autodesk*, January 13, 2011. https://dux.typepad.com/dux/2011/01/this-is-the-third-in-a-series-of-100-short-articles-about-ux-design-and-evaluation-methods-todays-method-is-called-freeli.html

Withrow, J., Brinck, T., & Speredelozzi, A. (2000). *Comparative usability evaluation for an e-government portal*. Diamond Bullet Design Report, #U1-00-2, Ann Arbor, MI, December. Available at <http://www.simplytom.com/research/U1-00-2-egovportal.pdf>

Wixon, D., & Jones, S. (1992). *Usability for fun and profit: A case study of the design of DEC RALLY, Version 2*. Digital Equipment Corporation.

Wong, D. (2010). *The Wall Street Journal guide to information graphics: The do's and don'ts of presenting data, facts, and figures*. New York, NY: W. W. Norton & Company.

Woolrych, A., & Cockton, G. (2001). Why and when five test users aren't enough. In *Proceedings of IHM-HCI2001* (Vol. 2, pp. 105–108). Toulouse, France: Ce´padue`s-E´ditions.

Note: Page numbers followed by "*b*," "*f*," and "*t*" refer to boxes, figures, and tables, respectively.